Divine Omniscience and the Future

Analyzing Theology Series

Divine Omniscience and the Future

Anselmian Reflections on Open Theism

Benjamin H. Arbour

FOREWORD BY
Elijah Hess

AFTERWORD BY
James S. Spiegel

EDITED BY
S. Mark Hamilton AND
Gregory E. Trickett

CASCADE *Books* • Eugene, Oregon

DIVINE OMNISCIENCE AND THE FUTURE
Anselmian Reflections on Open Theism

Analyzing Theology

Cascade Books
An Imprint of Wipf and Stock Publishers
199 W. 8th Ave., Suite 3
Eugene, OR 97401

www.wipfandstock.com

PAPERBACK ISBN: 979-8-3852-0015-3
HARDCOVER ISBN: 979-8-3852-0016-0
EBOOK ISBN: 979-8-3852-0017-7

Cataloguing-in-Publication data:

Names: Arbour, Benjamin H. [author]. | Hess, Elijah [foreword writer]. | Spiegel, James S. [afterword writer]. | Hamilton, S. Mark [editor]. | Trickett, Gregory E. [editor].

Title: Divine omniscience and the future : Anselmian reflections on open theism / by Benjamin H. Arbour ; foreword by Elijah Hess ; afterword by James S. Spiegel ; edited by S. Mark Hamilton and Gregory E. Trickett.

Description: Eugene, OR: Cascade Books, 2026 | Series: Analyzing Theology | Includes bibliographical references.

Identifiers: ISBN 979-8-3852-0015-3 (paperback) | ISBN 979-8-3852-0016-0 (hardcover) | ISBN 979-8-3852-0017-7 (ebook)

Subjects: LCSH: God (Christianity)—Attributes. | Philosophical theology. | Open theism. | God—Omniscience. | God—Omnipotence.

Classification: BT130 A73 2026 (paperback) | BT130 (ebook)

VERSION NUMBER 03/02/26

For the family and friends of Ben and Meg Arbour

To the God of Abraham, Isaac, and Jacob—the God of Israel, the God of David, the God and Father of the Lord, Jesus Christ, and the God of Anselm: to whom all first fruits rightly belong. All praise and honor and glory are due to the Father, and to the Son, and the Holy Spirit, forever and ever. *Soli Deo Gloria*.

Contents

Analyzing Theology

The 1980s witnessed a sea change in the academic, philosophical study of Christian doctrines on the heels of a renewal in philosophy of religion initiated by such prominent figures as Alvin Plantinga, Marilyn McCord Adams, William P. Alston, Eleonore Stump, and Nicholas Wolterstorff. At the turn of the second millennium, interest in the analysis of Christian doctrine only grew more profound as analytic philosophers and systematic theologians began to interact in more substantive ways. These interactions eventuated in the rise of analytic theology, an explicitly constructive theological program equipped with the tools and methods of analytic philosophy.

Despite its significant promise for driving theology forward in both the academy and the church, much of analytic theology remains outside the grasp of nonspecialists. One of the fundamental goals of this series is to broaden analytic theology's audience and influence.

Analyzing Theology is a series of books in Christian theology that showcases cutting-edge work in analytic and systematic theology. Monographs in the series are aimed at: (i) introducing cutting-edge analytic and systematic theology, (ii) providing a platform for original contributions in analytic and systematic theology, and (iii) connecting questions of theoretical significance to theology with the practices of actual theological communities.

Analytic theology is an emerging methodology that draws from the tools and methods of contemporary analytic philosophy to serve the ends of constructive systematic theology. Those methods make use of contemporary logical and conceptual analysis, emphasize the virtues of clarity and concision (as employed within the analytic philosophical tradition), and typically include a commitment to the objectivity of truth, goodness, justice, and rationality.

The monographs in the series span a range of Christian traditions and encompass a range of subject matter. This includes discussions of the method of analytic theology, exploring its engagements with other theological disciplines (such as biblical studies), as well as exemplifying this method by addressing underexplored theological topics from an analytic perspective.

Foreword

A. W. Tozer once said, "What comes into our minds when we think about God is the most important thing about us."[1] Whenever I read my friend Benjamin Arbour's work, I sense this sentiment on nearly every page. And this essay is no exception.

In *Divine Omniscience and the Future: Anselmian Reflections on Open Theism*, Arbour has delivered a remarkable study in analytic theology. Writing as a deeply Christian scholar, he sets out to explore whether various expressions of the view known as "open theism" should be thought consistent with an Anselmian perfect being conception of God. If, as open theists claim, the future is not fully settled or determinate in the divine mind, then how can God be thought of as maximally perfect in knowledge, power, and goodness? Like many others who Arbour knew and discussed these issues with, he and I had fantastic conversations. As an open theist myself, there were many occasions for disagreement to arise. I'm often amazed, though, at how much I agree with in this essay—the first four out of six chapters to be exact!

Arbour and I often dreamed of compiling our exchanges one day in a manner similar to what Christopher Hall and John Sanders produced in their stimulating book.[2] Sadly, it was not to be. In the spirit of our numerous dialogues, then, I don't think my old friend would mind me pushing back on a couple points in his stellar essay.

First, a philosophical dispute. In chapter 5, Arbour presents an interesting argument against all forms of open theism. He wants to demonstrate that the various notions of necessity open theists often appeal to when arguing for the incompatibility of human freedom and divine

1. Tozer, *Knowledge*, 1.

2. See Hall and Sanders, *Does God?*

foreknowledge would also apply to God's knowledge of present reality, since the present is just as necessary (in a relevant sense) as the past. So, if God's foreknowledge that Sally *will* do X rules out Sally's ability to do otherwise, God's knowledge that Sally is *now* doing X likewise rules out her ability to do otherwise. The result, Arbour claims, is that open theists must deny that God knows the present if they wish to maintain Sally's power of contrary choice. The best God can do is come to know what Sally has done as soon as this information is logically knowable. Of course, the idea that God doesn't even know the present is something open theists of all stripes want to avoid, and so Arbour concludes that openness proponents ought to give up one of their main motivations for denying God's foreknowledge of future contingents.

When assessing various responses open theists might give to this argument, Arbour mentions that one potential way out is to claim that God immediately comes to know what Sally chooses the moment she chooses to do it. After all, it is *because* Sally does what she does that God knows what he knows. However, Arbour believes that such a move on the part of openness advocates would involve affirming the reality of simultaneous causation—a highly contentious view of causation that many doubt is even possible. But here I must confess something. I've never understood why Arbour thought that God's knowledge of what Sally is currently doing would be an instance of simultaneous causation. In fact, I'm quite convinced that it wouldn't be, for the simple reason that it arguably isn't an instance of causation at all. For note: The true proposition God knows, i.e., "Sally is doing X," depends on Sally doing X. But this is arguably the sort of dependence relation contemporary philosophers have dubbed *metaphysical dependence*. One reason for this is that propositions—if such entities exist—are abstract and therefore do not stand in causal relations (e.g., compare: "Ted died *because* Ted was stabbed in the heart" describes a causal dependence whereas "the set [Socrates] exists *because* Socrates exists" describes a non-causal, metaphysical dependence). Unlike causal relations, such metaphysical dependence relations obtain simultaneously. Thus, open theists can plausibly maintain that God exhaustively knows whatever obtains in the present immediately when it comes to be. Divine omniscience doesn't rob Sally of her ability to do otherwise in the present, therefore, because the propositions that describe what Sally is doing from moment to moment depend on her and are comprehended by God as soon as they become true.

Still, as *Christian* philosophers we weren't always engaged in what some might think of as mere "logic games." Biblical arguments also played a role in discussions between us. One argument that gave me particular pause is included in chapter 6 of the present study. Arbour points out that, in the Olivet discourse, Jesus claims that only God the Father knows the time of Christ's return (Matt 24:36; Mark 13:32). But since Christ's return is conditioned on the fulfillment of the Great Commission—a fulfillment that arguably involves many contingent actions—it would seem to follow that God knows future contingents. My response, now formulated over much thought, is this. If one wishes to maintain a trinitarian Christian theism (as Arbour certainly did), then a dilemma arises for critics who want to use this argument against the openness position. For suppose that the knowledge Jesus credits God the Father with having is propositional in nature. Then God the Father will know *that* at such and such time, Christ shall return. But the Spirit of God, according to this passage, will not have this propositional knowledge, for *only* the Father knows it. So, the Trinitarian conception of Father, Son, and Spirit being coequal in knowledge is refuted. To get out of this, it seems to me that Trinitarians need to adopt an approach to this passage that views the relevant knowledge as something other than propositional. The knowledge in question, I say, is better thought of as a relational sort of knowledge. For example, it is God the Father who alone determines or decides what conditions are going to be the grounds for ushering in the second coming. Unlike the Son or Spirit, it is the Father who has set by his own authority what these conditions will be (see, e.g., Acts 1:7). But while this move arguably rescues Trinitarianism, it's an interpretation that is equally available to the open theist.

Such is a taste of the disagreements we had. For Arbour's part anyway, they were always held with charity and humility. I have no doubt that as you read the pages of this important work, you'll glimpse the man I once knew. A man whose heart was as big as his intellect.

Requiescet in pace, Ben.

—Elijah Hess

Preface

The last time I (Mark) spoke with Ben, we were going round and round about systematic metaphysics and the doctrine of atonement. He had been reading a draft of a chapter of a book I am writing on atonement and was—as was his custom—kindly poking holes in my argument(s). I say kindly because Ben was ever helping to improve my work. I say that it was his custom because he was always up for a rich theological discussion, particularly one where he could help others think with more clarity and rigor.

Ben was often calling people to discuss this or that intellectual curiosity, whether it was his idea or yours. Many will undoubtedly recall how, more often than not, he would skip the pleasantries of a greeting, grab you by your mental hand, as it were, and plunge headlong into that place he spent so much of his time called "the limits of human reason." Ben was among the brightest intellectual lights that I ever had the privilege to know; a true mind on fire. He showed me (and countless others, I'm sure) what loving God with all my mind looked like (Luke 10:27). It is my great honor to have seen this—one of my friend's final literary contributions—through to publication. I am grateful to the Arbour family for entrusting me and Greg with curating this project. So, too, am I grateful to Cascade for their interest and support in publishing it.

The first time I (Greg) met Ben, we discussed philosophy. Shortly after, we took a road trip with other friends to Baylor University to listen to a lecture on justice by Nicholas Wolterstorff. On that trip, Ben's intellect, acuity, wit, and boldness were on full display. For me, it was a foreshadow of the man I would come to know and admire and the time we would spend in other (longer) road trips, conferences, lectures, and discussions. Not a little of that time was spent discussing the topic and writing of this book. It was something about which Ben was as passionate as he was knowledgeable. Many write passable dissertations when completing their PhDs; Ben became a veritable authority on omniscience, philosophy of time, and open theism. In these pages the reader will find a well-crafted, fair, and studied case against open theism. The volume begins with a foreword by one of Ben's friends and dialectical opponents (at least with respect to open theism), Elijah Hess, in which Elijah offers a preliminary look at Ben's arguments from an open theist's perspective. It ends with an afterword by another of Ben's close friends, Jim Spiegel, who will reflect on Ben's thesis from the perspective of an advocate of the arguments against open theism. Our hope is that framing Ben's work in this way exemplifies the way in which Ben engaged these topics with those he respected and considered friends. Ben loved philosophy, but he loved people more. I heard him claim more than once that he loved attending and holding conferences because he saw it as a good excuse to get together with all of his friends. In this way, Ben was a singular individual—focused and driven to do philosophy and do it well but motivated by his love for God and his desire to cultivate the life of the mind in Christ's church. He took to heart Christ's instruction to love God and neighbor with everything you are. For this reason, while Ben was a great philosopher, teacher, and student, he was an even better friend.

I reiterate Mark's thanks to the Arbour family, especially Jimmy and Candy (Ben's parents), Drew (Ben's brother), and Wesley, Abby, Micah, and Noah (Ben and Meg's amazing kids). Their trust in us to care for the work Ben left behind is an honor and a privilege that we do not take lightly. I'm equally appreciative of Cascade's help in finding a home for this work. Additionally, Bradley Palmer helped with reworking Ben's figures so they looked better and were the correct resolution. I'd also like to thank all of those who turned out at the memorial dinners during the 2021 annual meeting of the ETS/EPS in Fort Worth and each year since. I can think of no better way to honor Ben's memory than by continuing to meet together in Christian fellowship to discuss things that were important to him. I would also like to thank Bradley Palmer, David Williams, and John (Jay) Howell (together, with Ben, the GPS—Grey Pilgrim Society) for their support for this project and their collective love for Ben and Meg and their family. Ben's and Meg's passing has deeply affected all who knew them, and in its wake (even two years later), we continue to grieve deeply but not as those with no hope. *Maranatha.*

Soli Deo Gloria
SMH and GET
Fort Worth, Texas
Summer 2023

Acknowledgments

I would be remiss if I did not thank numerous persons who have helped me along the way. Oliver Crisp has been a wonderful supervisor; without his help, this project would be significantly poorer than it is. David Alexander and Greg Welty not only helped motivate me to pursue doctoral work, but also helped by reading drafts of chapter 1. Doug Blount, Jonathan Chan, Scott Cleveland, Bob Hartman, and Dan Johnson all helped me improve chapter 2. Daniel Hill, Jordan Wessling, and Linda Zagzebski each helped me think more clearly about analytic notions of divine omniscience. Bob Hartman, Brian Leftow, Patrick Todd, and Greg Trickett each made helpful suggestions that helped me improve the way I discuss the modal reformulations of divine omniscience defended by advocates of limited foreknowledge open theism. William Lane Craig, J. R. Gilhooly, Elijah Hess, Chad Meeks, and numerous anonymous referees all suggested ways of improving the arguments against limited foreknowledge open theism in chapter 4. William Hasker, Daniel Hill, Paul Helm, Joshua Farris, Robin Le Poidevin, Richard Swinburne, and Peter van Inwagen each played an important part in helping me clarify the arguments contained in chapter 5. Finally, Lindsey Cleveland, Elijah Hess, Jay Howell, Josh Rassmussen, Alan Rhoda, Greg Trickett, and Jerry Walls played a significant role in offering criticisms of early drafts of chapter 6. Of course, any remaining errors in the manuscript are entirely my own. Most of all, I am thankful to the Lord for creating me such that I am able to reflect upon the divine nature at all. I am grateful for the opportunities I have had to study, and that I've been exposed to so many fascinating subjects along the way. I am humbled to know so many wonderful, brilliant people whom I am privileged to call friends. But most of all, I am thankful for the love of the Father, who sent his Son, Jesus Christ, who now calls me "friend" because of what he accomplished on my behalf on the cross of Calvary. My prayer is that God receives this attempt at defending the Anselmian thesis—that God is a maximally great being, and all that it entails for divine omniscience—as an act of worship. *Soli Deo Gloria.*

BHA

Fort Worth, Texas, 2017

Introduction

Abby is a bright student who is getting ready to begin the spring semester of her third year of undergraduate studies at a prestigious university. She is very excited that her schedule is finally allowing her to take a course in philosophy of religion. After taking an introduction to philosophy course during her first semester and two survey courses during the spring of her freshman year—one in metaphysics, the other in epistemology—Abby felt she was ready to pursue some more advanced topics in philosophy. So, during her sophomore year, in the fall she took an introduction to ethics course as well as a course in ancient philosophy; in the spring, she took a class on philosophy of language and a course in medieval philosophy.

In the fall of her third year, Abby felt prepared to take an advanced elective, so she took a course covering the philosophy of action while also taking a course in modern philosophy. She learned about how different thinkers understand free will and the nature of causation. Her professor covered topics as far ranging as determinism, chaos theory, and even a few lectures on moral responsibility and free will.

In the spring, Abby was ready to put her religious beliefs to the test by examining whether what she believes can stand up to the scrutiny of rigorous philosophical analysis. Naturally, she decided to take a course in the philosophy of religion, taught by one of the world's leading philosophers of religion who also happens to be very well-published in numerous areas of metaphysics, including time, causation, and modality.

Having already been exposed to the basic ideas in metaphysics and epistemology and related issues in her introductory courses, Abby found the majority of the material in the class enjoyable, and she didn't have any difficulty squaring her conservative Christian beliefs with reasonable positions in analytic philosophy. However, one puzzle in analytic philosophy of religion causes Abby much trouble, namely, the dilemma of freedom and foreknowledge.

Abby's religious commitments include the belief that God knows the future exhaustively, such that God knows what is going to happen in the future, even though much of what is to take place is not determined. She is also deeply committed to the idea that human beings have free will. But after being exposed to various constructions of the dilemma of freedom and foreknowledge, Abby finds herself genuinely wondering how God could know whether or not Abby herself will drink orange juice with her breakfast tomorrow if it is genuinely up to her to make the decision. Imagine the conversation Abby has with herself in her head.

"If God is infallible," she thinks, "then God cannot be wrong. So if God believes that I will drink orange juice tomorrow, then it must be the case that I drink orange juice tomorrow. But," she reasons to herself, "if God believes that I will drink the orange juice tomorrow, and if God cannot be wrong, then how can I be free to not drink the orange juice? Now, if I know anything to be true, it's that I have control over whether or not I'll drink orange juice tomorrow."

Abby's friends and family are concerned about her. In the face of such an argument, Abby finds herself flirting with the idea that God doesn't know whether or not Abby will drink orange juice tomorrow. Her pastor and some folks from her religious community are also concerned. Some have encouraged her to give up on philosophy, arguing that philosophy is at fault for corrupting her faith. Others have said that she simply needs to read the Bible more but without giving up on her philosophical quest for wisdom and understanding.

In an effort to answer the vexing question of whether or not God knows which future contingents will obtain, Abby begins to research the dilemma of freedom and foreknowledge. She is overwhelmed by the volume of the literature on the subject until she realizes that she's not trying to read up on Molinism, divine timelessness, or compatibilistic articulations of human freedom. In fact, she isn't interested in most of what has been written about the dilemma of freedom and foreknowledge. Rather, she is interested in a particular take on the dilemma known as open theism. So, she begins her investigation by looking for defenses of classical theism against open theism, which means that she is looking for ways to preserve traditional articulations of divine omniscience against the claims of open theism. However, she is disappointed at what she finds.

These days, Abby's story is far from uncommon. Since open theism began to attract attention nearly fifty years ago, scholars have written about the subject from the stance of either theology or philosophy, with very little attention being given to the overlap of these two disciplines. Theologians tend to interact principally with special revelation, whereas philosophers who have written on open theology have, to date, ignored the questions about Scripture and exegesis. From a theological perspective, those who defend open theism include Terrence Fretheim, Clark Pinnock, Richard Rice, and John Sanders.[1] Philosophically motivated open theists include David Basinger, William Hasker, Alan Rhoda, Richard Swinburne, Dale Tuggy, Peter van Inwagen, and Dean Zimmerman.[2] Greg Boyd is one of the few who is as interested in the theology as he is the philosophy.[3]

Interestingly, throughout the entire history of Christianity, faithful Christians across both East and West, Roman Catholic and Protestant have maintained that God enjoys exhaustive knowledge of the future, including which of various future contingents will obtain. However, although many have thought that Anselmian perfect being theology requires as much, open theists have been insisting that alternatives to this classical conception of divine knowledge need not impugn Anselmian conceptions of the divine. When one surveys responses to open theism, sadly, very little of what has been offered by way of rejoinder to openness advocates involves substantial philosophical reflection.

This is by no means to suggest that the work put forward by conservative theologians isn't valuable. Accordingly, Christians like Abby will do well to read the work of Millard Erickson, John Frame, Norman Geisler, John Piper, Steven Roy, James Spiegel, Bruce Ware, and others, even if most Christians disagree with the Calvinistic and/or Thomistic

1. Fretheim, *Suffering of God*; Pinnock, *Most Moved Mover*; Rice, *God's Foreknowledge*; Sanders, *God Who Risks*.

2. Basinger, *Freewill Theism*; Hasker, *God, Time, and Knowledge*; Rhoda, "Fivefold Openness"; Rhoda, "Generic Open Theism"; Rhoda, "Case for Open Theism"; Swinburne, *Christian God*; Swinburne, *Coherence of Theism*; Tuggy, "Three Roads"; Van Inwagen, "Omniscient Being"; Zimmerman, "A-Theory of Time, Presentism."

3. Consider Boyd, *God of the Possible*. There are certainly other open theists who are just as deeply concerned about Scripture as they are about the metaphysical and philosophical issues involved in these debates, but few publications demonstrate this concern in the content of what has been written. One significant exception stands out: Basinger et al., *Openness of God*.

theologies of divine providence that they advocate.[4] That is, if anyone wants to understand theological critiques of open theism, one needn't look too far to find them.

However, philosophical critiques of open theism are far more difficult to find.[5] This is especially tragic since the advances made on behalf of open theism have taken place more on the philosophical side of things than in theology.[6] That is, the majority of those who are advancing openness theology do so by appealing to philosophical and metaphysical motivations for their relatively novel conception of divine omniscience.

Hence, there is need for a project in this area. Because opponents of open theism have yet to offer comprehensive philosophical critiques of open theism, I am seeking to fill that lacuna. However, although I will make use of many areas of contemporary analytic philosophy in arguing against openness theology, I also employ Scripture along the way. Accordingly, it seems to me that analytic theology as a methodology has the best potential to adjudicate in the debates over the extent of divine knowledge. In order to avoid arguments about whose exegesis is superior, I appeal to a long held traditional articulation of theology proper, namely, Anselmian perfect being theology. I maintain that numerous versions of open theism are incompatible with the idea that God is a maximally great being, and while two versions of open theism are likely compatible with Anselmianism, the metaphysical costs associated with adopting either of those versions of open theism are so high that they should not be defended.

A robust analytic theology of divine omniscience that is consistent with Christian orthodoxy and also accounts for what omniscience entails for the debates about the extent of God's knowledge of the future

4. Erickson, *What Does God Know*; Frame, *No Other God*; Geisler, *Creating God*; Helseth et al., *Beyond the Bounds*; Roy, *How Much Does God*; Spiegel, *Benefits of Providence*; Ware, *God's Lesser Glory*. Consider also two anthologies on the subject of open theism: Huffman and Johnson, *God Under Fire*; Wilson, *Bound Only Once*.

5. Three articles constitute the bulk of academic philosophical work that has been put forward against openness theology: Craig and Hunt, "Perils"; Rogers, "Necessity of the Present"; and Rota, "Problem for Hasker." Consider also two volumes that contain point-counterpoint exchanges between defenders of differing perspectives: Beilby and Eddy, *Divine Foreknowledge*; Basinger and Basinger, *Predestination and Freewill*.

6. Some debates over the extent of divine foreknowledge take shape principally by way of appeal to Scripture, but these debates often reduce to something like "My exegesis is superior to other interpretations" and fail to account for the role that various philosophical presuppositions have in shaping the way different people interpret Scripture. See Arbour and Blount, "Camel's Nose."

(including future contingents) requires an understanding of numerous areas in both philosophy and theology. Accordingly, as I seek to critique openness theology in all of its contemporary expressions, I appeal to contemporary analytic work in various areas of metaphysics, including causation, modality, ontology, and time, as well as issues in philosophy of language, studies concerning the nature of truth, and action theory (especially free will and moral responsibility), not to mention aspects of the history of philosophy and theology that pertain to the Christian tradition and classical expressions of theology proper and divine omniscience. In fact, it seems to me that this project would have been strengthened if space and time had allowed for an even more in depth accounting of all of these issues, especially constructive accounts of systematic metaphysics (which is the combination of properties, causation, laws of nature, and modality). Below I outline the project as it stands.

I begin by motivating my project with Anselmian perfect being theology and its entailment of divine omniperfection. This conception of the divine nature is rooted historically in the Christian tradition, and is considered a staple of orthodoxy. Furthermore, it comports well with contemporary analytic metaphysical claims in philosophy of religion and philosophical theology. I defend divine omniperfection against a novel interpretation of Anselmian perfect being theology offered by Yujin Nagasawa. He suggests that God need not be omniperfect (which is the property of being omnipotent, omniscient, and omnibenevolent all at once) in order to count as a maximally great being. Nagasawa employs thought experiments and epistemically possible scenarios to motivate the idea that Anselmians needn't defend the idea that omniperfection entails Anselmian polytheism, but I argue that if Nagasawa is right about these epistemically possible scenarios, polytheism follows. Because polytheism is incompatible with orthodox Christianity, I maintain that Anselmian perfect being theology guarantees monotheism if and only if maximal greatness entails omniperfection.

Having established a basis for perfect being theology and argued against the idea that maximal greatness could be anything less than omniperfection, I turn my attention to divine omniscience. After surveying the literature on the subject, I offer my own definition of omniscience. I also suggest that utilizing Linda Zagzebski's doctrine of omnisubjectivity helps to preserve important features of divine knowledge relevant to omniscience.

I begin critiquing open theism in chapter 3. Some open theists such as William Hasker, Richard Swinburne, and Peter van Inwagen (whom I call limited foreknowledge open theists) claim that there exist truths about future contingents that are unknown by God. They do not, however, deny that God is omniscient. Rather, these thinkers offer modal reformulations of omniscience such that God knows all truths that are logically knowable. I argue that this fails to preserve the kind of omniscience required by Anselmian omniperfection. I also argue that there are relevant differences between omnipotence and omniscience that won't allow for the kenotic move that is required for any modally reformulated account of omniscience to be properly motivated in the first place. I conclude that limited foreknowledge open theism is incompatible with Anselmian perfect being theology.

In chapter 4, I continue critiquing limited foreknowledge open theism. The very existence of truths about future contingents, together with the omnitemporality of truth, entails a logical problem of fatalism that obtains regardless of whether or not God enjoys exhaustive definite foreknowledge of future contingents. I maintain that efforts on the part of Hasker to avoid this conundrum by appealing to a distinction between hard facts and soft facts allows Ockhamism to avoid motivation for open theism. Furthermore, I suggest that the way Hasker uses divine names raises significant problems in the area of philosophy of language. Accordingly, limited foreknowledge open theism should be rejected.

Chapter 5 contains an argument that cuts not only against limited foreknowledge open theism, but also against other versions of openness theology known as open futurism. The chapter begins by discussing the relevant features of necessity involved in various constructions of the dilemma of freedom and foreknowledge that are employed by open theists. I note that these versions of necessity either allow for alternative responses to the dilemma or entail far more than advocates of open theism realize. I argue that if open theism is the proper response to the dilemma of freedom and foreknowledge, it isn't merely knowledge of which future contingents will obtain that God lacks; rather, it is also divine knowledge of all present realities involving free will. Taking this as an obviously undesirable conclusion, all versions of open theism should be rejected since they are incompatible with Anselmian perfect being theology.

In chapter 6, I argue against two forms of open future open theism. I begin by describing how these two versions differ from one another and go on to critique each of them. I argue that the rejection of the principle of bivalence required by Zimmerman's account is too high a cost, so it needs to be rejected. I also argue that the Peircean semantics Alan Rhoda employs to explain how his version of open futurism preserves the principle of bivalence renders his version of open theism self-contradictory. In the second part of the chapter, I argue that the metaphysics that would be necessary to motivate open futurism cannot be squared with any of the contemporary articulations of systematic metaphysics. I also argue that the nature of time that open futurists use to motivate their position, if true, is only contingently true. Therefore, if such a theory of time entails any kenotic move on the part of God, then such a theory should be rejected since it cannot be squared with Anselmian perfect being theology. Finally, I conclude by offering a theological counterexample to open future open theism. Therefore, even if open futurists could offer a coherent systematic metaphysics to provide a foundation for their view, this account wouldn't correspond to the actual world, at least not if biblical orthodoxy is true.

1

Perfect Being Theology and Monotheism

A Reply to Nagasawa

Since Anselm first suggested that God is the being than which none greater can be conceived in the second half of the eleventh century, perfect being theology has been an important methodology for philosophers and theologians reflecting on the divine nature and especially important for Christians. For centuries now, the movements of logic reflected in ontological arguments have fascinated atheists, agnostics, and theists when considering the Divine Being. Axiological judgments about what constitutes the greatest possible being continue to play an important role in ongoing discussions among philosophers and theologians alike. However, there is widespread agreement that, if God does exist, God possesses whatever attributes together comprise maximal greatness.

In what follows, I won't take time to argue for the existence of God, although there are numerous arguments for the existence of a divine being that I find persuasive. Rather, because this is a project in Christian analytic theology, I presuppose that God does, indeed, exist. Furthermore, I will also presuppose that God is a maximally great being, which is just the sort of being one would expect of the Christian God, at least if modal articulations of the ontological argument accurately describe the sort of God that Christians believe to be revealed in the Bible.[1] Additionally, I presuppose that the "God of the philosophers" and the "God of Abraham, Isaac, and Jacob" are one and the same Being, and I think that

1. I agree with the thoughts expressed in Morris, "God of Abraham," reprinted in his *Anselmian Explorations*, 10–25.

it is important for readers to recognize this when seeking to understand the various appeals to Scripture in what follows.

However, one needn't be a Christian, or even a theist, to comprehend what I offer throughout this project. Those who deny the existence of God can approach this treatise on divine omniscience as a thought experiment about what God would be like if, in fact, God were to exist. But before we focus our attention on divine omniscience, which is one aspect of the divine nature, we will be well served to pay close attention to key claims about maximal greatness insofar as these are related to Anselmian perfect being theology more generally.

Dogmatic theologians agree that there are distinctively Christian approaches to the doctrine of God (e.g., Triunity), yet different approaches to issues surrounding the divine nature have led theologians to different understandings of the divine nature. I maintain that the Anselmian approach to the doctrine of God is not only helpful heuristically, but also that it yields true results about who God is. Accordingly, as a Christian philosopher reasoning in the style of St. Anselm, I take it that God—who is a maximally great being—is whatever it is better to be than to not be. Historically, Anselmians seem to have presupposed that the uniqueness of God stems in part from maximal greatness such that there is one and only one God. One recent reformulation of Anselmian theism seems to preclude the idea that Anselmianism alone can preserve monotheism. For reasons that will become apparent in future chapters, getting this portion of Anselmianism right is important to how one understands the nature of divine omniscience, and therefore to how one might respond to the dilemma of freedom and foreknowledge.

In this first chapter, I respond to Yujin Nagasawa's reformulation of Anselmian theism.[2] Traditionally, Anselmians have defended divine omniperfection—the idea that God is omnipotent, omniscient, and omnibenevolent—and have thought that omniperfection preserves the uniqueness of God (e.g., monotheism). Nagasawa denies that omniperfection is necessary for the success of Anselmian monotheism, arguing that maximal greatness does not necessarily entail omniperfection.[3] I argue, *pace* Nagasawa, that the success of Anselmianism requires

2. Nagasawa, "New Defence." All parenthetical citations in the body of this chapter refer to Nagasawa's article.

3. Rea and Murray also endorse a version of the same idea when discussing the ontological argument, although they don't develop it to the extent that Nagasawa does. See Murray and Rea, *Introduction to the Philosophy*, 132.

omniperfection, at least so long as Anselmianism precludes polytheism. The concept of divine omniperfection, and the idea that it necessarily follows from Anselmian perfect being theology, will prove especially valuable in responding to certain articulations of open theism, as I show in chapters 4 and 5.

Nagasawa's Anselmian Theism

Nagasawa's central thesis is rather simple: The success of Anselmian theism does not hinge on the omniGod thesis. The core of Anselmian theism is:

> *The Anselmian Thesis*: God is the being than which no greater can be thought.[4]

Traditionally, philosophers and theologians have understood Anselmian theism to entail:

> *The OmniGod Thesis*: God is an omniscient, omnipotent, and omnibenevolent being.

Nagasawa explains that he is defending monotheism based on Anselm's core theological commitment—that God is the being than which no greater can be thought—and that this commitment makes sense even if God is not "omniperfect."

Following Nagasawa, I use the term "omniperfect" to denote the conjunction of omniscience, omnipotence, and omnibenevolence.[5] In light of numerous types of arguments against Anselmian theism, any denial that the coherence of Anselmianism hinges on omniperfection

4. I am aware of the debate concerning fidelity to Anselm's original intentions with regard to his discussion of God as "being" with relation to *aliquid quo nihil maius cogitari possit*, but I won't concern myself with those issues here. I also make no apology for focusing on possibility rather than conceivability, following contemporary articulations of modal ontological arguments, which are certainly different than what Anselm likely intended. What has come to be known as Anselmian theism obviously owes much to him for historical reasons, regardless of how Anselm intended his writings to be so interpreted. For recent discussions of these matters, as well as many others concerning Anselm, see Visser and Williams, *Anselm*; Hogg, *Anselm of Canterbury*.

5. That Nagasawa does not incorporate other attributes, such as omnipresence, into his understanding of omniperfection is irrelevant to his thesis. Therefore, since it is unwise to complicate things further than necessary, like Nagasawa, I will focus on a minimal set of attributes when discussing omniperfection so as to argue against Nagasawa's reformulation.

is significant. Nagasawa suggests that arguments against the Anselmian conception of God fit into one of three categories. A-type arguments attempt to demonstrate the incoherence of one of the attributes comprising omniperfection (580–81). The paradox of the stone, which suggests that omnipotence is incoherent, is a paradigmatic example of an A-type argument. B-type arguments purport to show some internal inconsistency in the coinstantiation of two or more attributes that comprise omniperfection (581–82). For example, consider the argument that omnipotence and moral perfection are not compossible, because an omnipotent being can do all things, whereas a morally perfect being cannot sin. Finally, C-type arguments point to inconsistencies between omniperfection and a contingent fact (582–83), such as the existence of evil. Nagasawa notes that debates over Anselmian theism have produced "an endless exchange of arguments and counter-arguments between opponents and proponents of the position" (584). If the Anselmian thesis entails divine omniperfection, then Anselmians must shoulder the burden of responding to any and all objections against the coherence of omniperfection, be they A-type, B-type, or C-type arguments. Believing that responding to each and every argument against Anselmian theism is not economical, Nagasawa suggests a reformulation of Anselmian theism, arguing not only that a defense against each and every argument against omniperfection is not economical, but also that such is unnecessary for successfully defending the core of Anselmian theism.

Nagasawa also explains why he thinks traditional conceptions of Anselmian theism defend omniperfection. According to him, Anselmians have believed the following argument to be valid:

1. If Anselmian theism is true, then the Anselmian thesis is true.
2. If the Anselmian thesis is true, then the omniGod thesis is true.
3. If the omniGod thesis is true, then God is an omniperfect being.
4. There cannot be an omniperfect being.
5. Therefore the omniGod thesis is false.
6. Therefore the Anselmian thesis is false.
7. Therefore Anselmian theism is false.

Nagasawa rejects Proposition 2, believing instead that the Anselmian thesis only requires a weaker thesis:

> *The MaximalGod Thesis*: God is the being that has the maximal consistent set of knowledge, power, and benevolence.

Nagasawa goes to great lengths in defending the idea that a less than omniperfect being can still be defined as that than which nothing greater can be thought.[6]

Traditionally, Anselmian theism has been used to defend the idea that God is (i) omniperfect, and as such, God is "(ii) greater than the second greatest possible being, X, with respect to at least one of knowledge, power and benevolence; (iii) at least as great as X with respect to the remaining attributes; (iv) greater than X overall" (588). Such a being is represented by my Figure 1, which is identical to Nagasawa's Figure 1 (588).

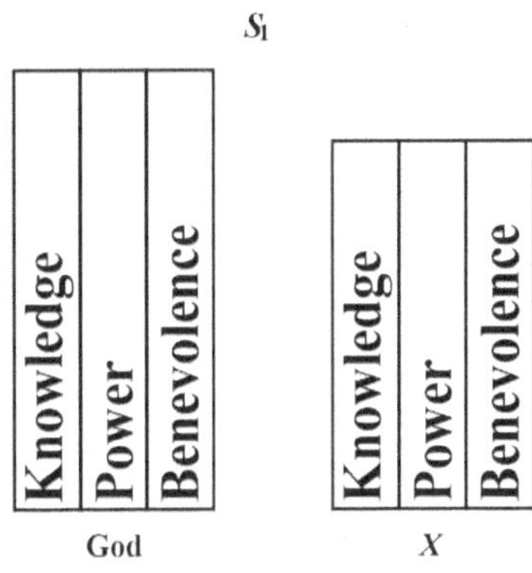

Figure 1

I should note that the Anselmian tradition affirms divine simplicity, which has very serious consequences against Nagasawa's reformulation.[7] Even though simplicity has fallen very much out of favor among contemporary philosophical theologians, it is worth mentioning that the Anselmian affirmation of simplicity requires that our understanding of the divine "attributes" turns out to be heuristic in nature. We can conceive of divine power in abstraction from, say, divine knowledge, but, by taking

6. Timpe also discusses this concept and related concepts in his "Introduction to Neo-Classical Theism."

7. That is, Anselm affirmed simplicity. "Life and wisdom and the other [attributes], then, are not parts of You, but all are one and each one of them is wholly what You are and what all the others are." Anselm of Canterbury, *Proslogion* 18. Cf. Nash-Marshall, "Properties, Conflation, and Attribution."

the Anselmian affirmation of simplicity into account, when speaking of the technical ontology involved, divine knowledge and divine power aren't separable from one another. So, if we are to speak of divine attributes at all, Anselmians ought to speak of a single divine attribute—perhaps "divinity" (or "perfection," or "maximal perfection," or "omniperfection")—with which God himself is numerically identical, at least when trying to be ontologically precise.[8] In the interest of focusing on the main thrust of Nagasawa's reformulation, and for the sake of those less inclined to affirm divine simplicity, I'll set these concerns aside.[9]

Suppose that one (or more) of the many arguments against omniperfection succeed. Even though God wouldn't be accurately described as omniperfect, Nagasawa contends that Anselmians would still rightly be defining God as a maximally perfect being by way of the Maximal-God Thesis. Nagasawa offers various "epistemically possible scenarios" in which he argues that God is rightly defined as that than which nothing greater can be thought even if God is not omniperfect. He contends against critics who maintain that it is analytically true that the Anselmian thesis entails the omniGod thesis, arguing that such an assertion is far from obvious.[10]

Consider the following examples. In the first scenario, "God is (i) slightly less than omniperfect; (ii) greater than X with respect to at least one of knowledge, power and benevolence; (iii) at least as great as X with respect to the remaining attributes; (iv) greater than X overall" (588). According to Nagasawa, the Anselmian key is simply that, in some way, God is greater than any other being.[11]

8. I recognize this isn't perfectly consistent with simplicity, but we can go at least this far down the road towards simplicity: I will set to one side the problems associated with predicating any attribute to God, given divine simplicity. I recognize the difficulty involved in finding a semantics to accurately describe the metaphysics of a perfect being, but I leave those puzzles to philosophers of language. As best I am able to tell, the path one takes in navigating through those mazes does not affect my arguments.

9. As I show later, it is difficult, and perhaps impossible, to defend Anselmian theism without appealing to divine simplicity, or affirming something very close to it.

10. That the Anselmian thesis doesn't obviously entail omniperfection is a point I'm happy to concede to Nagasawa. My contention is that if Anselmianism is thought to preclude polytheism, then the Anselmian thesis does entail omniperfection, as I show below.

11. This point itself is debatable. The fundamental Anselmian commitment isn't that God simply happens to be greater than any other being. Rather, Anselmians claim that God is necessarily greater than any other being. This brings the modality of attributes into play. Clearly a divine being who possesses great-making attributes essentially is superior to the being whose omniscience is contingent or accidental. So, the nature

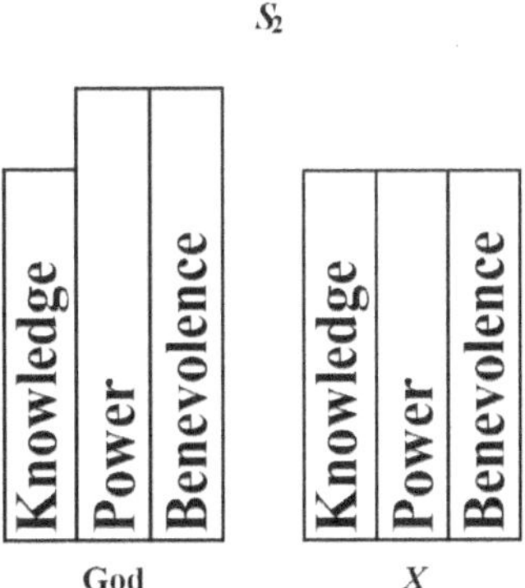

Figure 2

In a second scenario, God remains maximally perfect even if not omniperfect, because it is possible that "God is (i) slightly less than omniperfect; (ii) less great than X with respect to at least one of knowledge, power and benevolence; (iii) at least as great as X with respect to the remaining attributes; (iv) greater than X overall" (589).

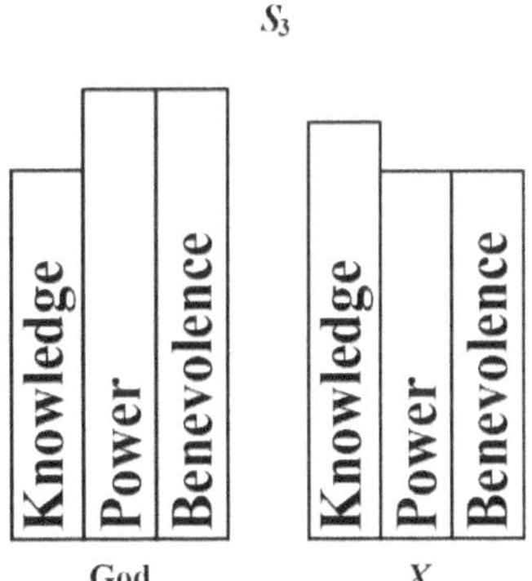

Figure 3

My objection against Nagasawa's reformulation of Anselmian theism does not hinge upon the failure of these scenarios. The scenarios he offers do show that a less than omniperfect being might still be maximally

---

of maximal greatness is attenuated if we limit the discussion so as to involve only the quantity of power, knowledge, and benevolence, rather than also including the mode of possession of these same attributes.

great, especially if one (or more) of the numerous arguments against the omniGod thesis succeeds. My concern is that Nagasawa's concession that an Anselmian God need not be omniperfect fails to preserve monotheism, which is central to any Abrahamic understanding of Anselmian theism. Nagasawa maintains that, if arguments against Anselmian theism are to succeed, then the epistemically possible scenarios mentioned above need to be eliminated. While I don't identify with those who proffer arguments against the Anselmian thesis, I do see problems for monotheism for those who champion Nagasawa's reformulation. My efforts to clarify these problems should not be understood as an attempt to provide arguments against Anselmianism.

Rather, I argue against Nagasawa because his claim that a less than omniperfect being still qualifies as God via Anselmian perfect being theology entails not only the possibility of polytheism but the necessity of such. In what follows, I develop my concerns and explain why anticipated objections to my arguments fail. If I am correct, it follows that Nagasawa's reformulation of Anselmian theism needs be rejected, at least so long as anyone maintains that Anselmianism preserves monotheism by precluding multiple maximally great beings.

Epistemic Possibility

Nagasawa's careful use of the phrase "epistemically possible scenarios" requires further attention.

> By the phrase "epistemically possible scenarios" I mean scenarios such that it is not immediately obvious that they are metaphysically impossible, even though they might in fact be contingently or even necessarily metaphysically impossible. I use the phrase "epistemically possible" instead of "conceivable" here because some philosophers claim that conceivability entails metaphysical possibility. I also use the word "scenario" instead of "world," because claims about a specific scenario could have implications which bear on more than one world. (587)

Nagasawa's use of epistemic possibility accords with the following definition of epistemic possibility:

> For any agent S, some *p* is epistemically possible for *S* if *p* is consistent with all the relevant background knowledge that is uncontroversially held by S.

Nagasawa suggests that a scenario could be epistemically possible for some agent S so long as S isn't aware that the scenario is metaphysically impossible. This account of epistemic possibility allows for a person to maintain that no square circles exist, but that square circles could exist, at least until that person comes to recognize the logical and metaphysical impossibility of square circles. What Nagasawa fails to recognize is that Anselmian theism, because of its strict commitment to monotheism, which operates as an uncontroversial aspect of the relevant background knowledge amongst Anselmians, precludes the epistemically possible scenarios he proposes, at least if the concept of maximal greatness serves to exclude multiple maximally great beings.[12]

Suppose that the following account of epistemic possibility is true. If a proposition *p* is logically and/or metaphysically impossible and S knows, not only that ~*p* but also that *p* is logically and/or metaphysically impossible, then *p* is not epistemically possible for S. However, if S does not know that *p* is logically and/or metaphysically impossible, then *p* may or may not be epistemically possible for S. Thus, even if *p* is metaphysically impossible, *p* may be epistemically possible for S so long as S is not aware of either the logical and/or the metaphysical impossibility of *p*. Consider Goldbach's conjecture that every even number is the sum of two prime numbers. This thesis is either necessarily true, or necessarily false. If true, the falsity of Goldbach's conjecture is metaphysically impossible, and vice versa. Yet both the truth and falsity of Goldbach's conjecture remain epistemically possible precisely because the status of the truth or falsity of Goldbach's conjecture remains undetermined.

In order to understand the problems that Nagasawa's epistemically possible scenarios raise, we need to complicate our account of epistemic possibility. It seems that belief is not closed under entailment, but rather is closed under *known* entailment. If S knows *q*, and (unknown to S) *q* implies that *p* is necessarily false, it might be that S still thinks that *p* is epistemically possible, because S does not know that *q* implies that *p* is necessarily false. But, if S knows *q*, and S also knows that *q* implies that *p* is necessarily false, S cannot rationally, coherently, and consistently affirm the epistemic possibility of *p*, because the logical and/or metaphysical impossibility of *p* is known to S because of S's knowledge of *q* and S's

12. Nagasawa's account of epistemic possibility appears to be a bit idiosyncratic, but I won't critique it here because my argument succeeds even if his account holds. For those interested in what I take to be a better account, see Littlejohn, "Concessive Knowledge Attributions," which I discuss below.

knowledge that *q* implies the necessarily falsehood of *p*. Furthermore, *p* is not epistemically possible for S, regardless of whether or not S knows that *p* is logically impossible. S's knowledge that *q* implies that *p* is false, together with S's knowledge of *q*, is enough to rule out the epistemic possibility of *p* for S. But, S may or may not know any such *q* that implies the falsity of *p*; and, it might be the case that S does know some such *q*, but does not know that *q* implies the falsity of *p*. In any case, *p* remains epistemically possible for S even if *p* is metaphysically impossible so long as S is not aware of the metaphysical impossibility of *p*. So, I maintain that

> (EPc) *p* is epistemically possible for S iff ~*p* isn't obviously entailed by something S knows with certainty.

This account of epistemic possibility best accounts for why belief is not closed under entailment but is closed under known entailment.

What does any of this have to do with debates over Anselmian monotheism? My claim is that an Anselmian monotheist can know with certainty that if God exists, then God is a maximally great being. I also maintain that only one maximally great being can exist. Call this Anselmian monotheism. It is obvious to me, as I show below, that Anselmian polytheism is entailed by the various epistemically possible scenarios put forward by Nagasawa. Therefore, Nagasawa's reformulation of Anselmian theism is improperly motivated, and divine omniperfection should be defended by all Anselmian monotheists.

As the remarks above hint, epistemic possibility is, at least to some degree, relative to an individual. However, since epistemic possibility is a function of knowledge and not of mere belief, epistemic possibility is likely less relative than meets the eye, especially if knowledge is taken to be factive.[13] For example, if God exists, no one possesses knowledge that God does not exist, and there cannot be any *q* such that S knows *q* and *q* entails the non-existence of God. However, God's non-existence may be epistemically possible for S, if S does not know some *q* that entails God's existence or S does know some *q* that entails God's existence, but S does not know that *q* entails God's existence.

Given this account of epistemic possibility, let us suppose that the same rules apply to epistemic possibility that apply to any other modal

13. Special thanks to David Alexander for many conversations and emails in which we discussed epistemic possibility. A helpful collection of essays on the subject can be found in Egan and Weatherson, *Epistemic Modality*. See especially Stalnaker, "Conditional Propositions," 227–47.

properties. I use (EP) to denote epistemic possibility, and will use (EP) in a way that is consistent with (EPc). Neither knowledge nor belief is closed under entailment. Knowledge and belief are, it seems to me, closed only under *known* entailment. Thus, the following is invalid:

> $p \rightarrow q$
>
> S knows that p
>
> Hence, S knows that q

However, the following argument is valid:

> S knows that ($p \rightarrow q$)
>
> S knows that p
>
> Hence, S knows that q
>
> The same holds true when we replace "S knows that . . . " with "It is (EP) for S that . . ."[14]

With this understanding of epistemic possibility in view, I will now show why Nagasawa's reformulation of Anselmian theism (p), apart from some additional extra-Anselmian argument to the contrary, entails the epistemic possibility of polytheism (q). According to the understanding of epistemic possibility outlined above, polytheism will be rendered epistemically possible for anyone made aware of the entailment relation between Nagasawa's reformulation of Anselmian theism and a multiplicity of equally maximally great beings. But, for anyone who holds that Anselmian theism entails the metaphysical impossibility of polytheism, then Nagasawa's reformulation will cease to be epistemically possible for that person.[15]

14. I am aware that this account of closure is contested. Here I am thinking especially of Kvanvig's work. Suppose, for instance, that S believes p, q, and r, and S has equal warrant and/or justification for each of p, q, and r. To complicate things, suppose that S knows that p, q, and r form an inconsistent set. Which of these should S reject? If this isn't compelling, imagine expanding the inconsistent set to contain ten members. Some have suggested that such puzzles show that belief and knowledge are not closed, even under known entailment. I maintain that such inconsistencies are enough to generate serious problems for Nagasawa even for those who reject my position on closure. Cf. Kvanvig: "Closure and Alternative Possibilities"; "Closure Principles"; "Coherentism and Justified Inconsistent Beliefs"; "Contrastivism and Closure."

15. This depends on my contention that if S knows that p is metaphysically impossible, then p cannot be epistemically possible for S. I recognize that there are at least a few philosophers who maintain that the whole point of epistemic possibility is to give us

Nagasawa's Reformulation and Anselmian Polytheism

Monotheism is one of the central claims of Anselmian theism. Throughout his essay, Nagasawa maintains that his reformulation of Anselmian theism preserves monotheism (577, 578, and 595). Polytheism, then, is known to be metaphysically impossible, for those who know (or claim to know) that Anselmian theism is true. Therefore, polytheism should not be epistemically possible for the Anselmian because holding to both Anselmian theism and the epistemic possibility of polytheism produces an inconsistent set of beliefs. Because belief is not closed under entailment, but rather under known entailment, I acknowledge that there may be persons, such as Nagasawa, who rationally defend both monotheism and his reformulated MaximalGod Thesis. However, in what follows, I show why such reformulations give rise to the possibility of multiple maximally great beings (polytheism), which ought not be possible on Anselmianism. I take it that pointing out this problem helps people see and therefore know the entailment, thereby satisfying the conditions necessary for belief to be closed.

In this light, I will argue that any conception of God that allows for even the epistemic possibility of polytheism is, by definition, not Anselmian. Nagasawa's reformulation—based on various epistemically possible scenarios—ought not to allow for the possible existence, or even the epistemic possibility of the existence, of more than one maximally great being. If such scenarios do render the existence of multiple maximally great beings epistemically possible, then Nagasawa's scenarios do not successfully establish his thesis because these scenarios, while attractive on the surface, yield the possibility of polytheism and thereby undermine Anselmian presuppositions.

Consider the following case, which is epistemically possible, given Nagasawa's scenarios. Suppose some argument succeeds in showing that a maximally great being must be less than omniperfect. So, with respect to at least one of the three traditional great-making attributes, God enjoys a less than omni-conception of knowledge, power, or benevolence. Whether this concession hinges on the success of a B-type or C-type

a way to think about what is metaphysically necessary or impossible in alternative ways. As one who defends metaphysical realism about Anselmianism, and about analytic theology in general, I contend that this way of thinking is deeply mistaken. To clarify, I maintain that Nagasawa's reformulation must be rejected by anyone who desires to defend Anselmian monotheism. Of course, for anyone who rejects the idea that Anselmian theism precludes polytheism, Nagasawa's reformulation remains a live option.

argument is irrelevant.[16] If this is epistemically possible, then it is possible that (at least) one of the following three beings exists (see Figure 4).

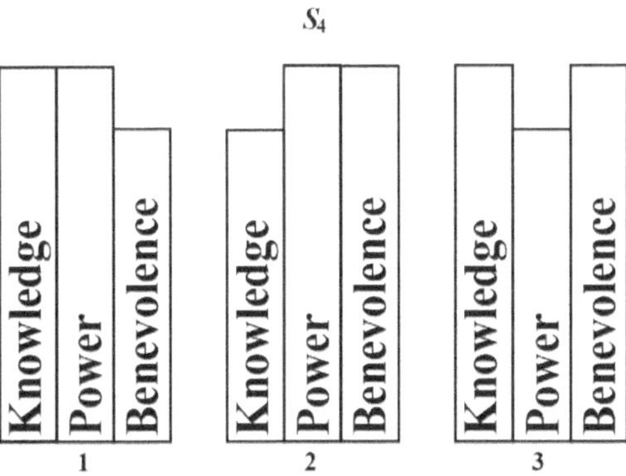

Figure 4

Furthermore, each of these beings could exist simultaneously.[17] Following the most obvious interpretations of Nagasawa's graphs, it seems that each of these three beings is equally maximally great.

Let us name an omniscient, omnipotent, but less than omnibenevolent (1)-type being Puck. And let us name an omnipotent, omnibenevolent, but less than omniscient (2)-type being Wilterchard. And let us name an omniscient, omnibenevolent, but less than omnipotent (3)-type being Bono. To make things easier, in what follows I focus primarily on Puck- and Bono-like beings, because I have argued elsewhere against the possibility of Wilterchard-like beings.[18] Nagasawa might contend that the possibility of multiple equally maximally great beings doesn't present a problem for his reformulation of Anselmian theism. Rather, only the actual existence of multiple equally maximally great

16. A-type arguments, however, avoid the dilemma I raise for Nagasawa because if omnipotence turns out to be logically impossible, then certain types of beings that I discuss turn out to be metaphysically impossible. Furthermore, such would obviously generalize to include omniscience and omnibenevolence, should some A-type argument succeed in showing those attributes to be logically impossible.

17. Any protest insisting against the possible existence of multiple beings that are equally maximally great that comes without an argument demonstrating exactly why such is impossible would be exceedingly *ad hoc*.

18. I offer arguments against the logical possibility of Wilterchard-like divine beings in chapter 4 because they don't possess knowledge of all truths and therefore cannot count as maximally great beings. Additionally, see my "Future Freedom."

beings presents a problem, for so long as only one of the multiple equally maximally great beings exists, monotheism obtains.[19] However, the actual existence of a maximally great being follows from the mere logical possibility of the existence of such a maximally great being, and we have no reason to believe something is epistemically possible unless we also believe it to be logically possible.[20] Therefore, if Anselmianism alone is thought to preserve monotheism without the aid of any other argument, then Anselmianism somehow entails that only one being can be maximally great; otherwise, it would be possible for Anselmianism to allow for polytheism. Therefore, even the epistemic possibility of more than one equally maximally great being poses problems for Anselmianism. Given the fact that any maximally great being exists necessarily, if any of Nagasawa's scenarios entails the possibility of multiple equally maximally great beings but somehow precludes their actual existence, we should note a distinction between Nagasawa's conception of Anselmian theism and that of Anselm himself. We would also need an argument as to how such beings can be (EP) if they are known to be metaphysically impossible. Nagasawa could respond by saying that the point is that we don't know whether God is Puck, Bono, or Wilterchard but insist that only one of these beings exists. Interestingly, this rejoinder is only reasonable in light of a prior commitment to Anselmian monotheism. However, Nagasawa's reformulation opens the door to the simultaneous coexistence of multiple beings who are equally maximally great. Merely insisting that such isn't possible on the grounds of prior commitments to Anselmian monotheism at this juncture appears exceedingly *ad hoc*, for we need some argument as to why it is that Bono and Puck (and Wilterchard) cannot simultaneously coexist.

Accordingly, in light of Nagasawa's various scenarios, if it is (EP) that a maximally great being such as Puck exists, then it is also (EP) that Bono exists. But, given Anselmian monotheism, it ought not be (EP) that more than one maximally great being exists. But recall that any being that is genuinely maximally great exists of necessity. Furthermore, recall that Puck and Bono have different natures, and are therefore different beings. However, since both Puck and Bono are each maximally great, they each exist of necessity. Without some argument to the contrary, there is no

19. Again, I take up issues related to the Tripersonal nature of God at the end of the chapter.

20. The inference rests upon Plantinga's now famous modal ontological argument. See Plantinga, *Nature of Necessity*, 196–221.

good reason to deny that it is (EP) for both Puck and Bono to exist at the same time; therefore, on Nagasawa's reformulation of Anselmian theism, it is (EP) that Anselmian polytheism obtains.[21]

But are there any good reasons for thinking that Puck and Bono are equally maximally great? I answer this question with another: Without an objective, all-encompassing value scale upon which all beings can be judged, why shouldn't we think so? Furthermore, I wonder what, if any, argument could be given for why Puck and Bono cannot be equally maximally great apart from the existence of some objective, all-encompassing value scale which determines the objective value of all beings. Interestingly, rather than develop such an account, Nagasawa denies that any such objective, all-encompassing value scale is necessary in order for his reformulation of Anselmian theism to succeed (592–93). Thus, for the sake of simplicity, following the most obvious interpretation of the bar graphs Nagasawa provides, I suppose that power, knowledge, and benevolence are all equally valuable in contributing to the overall greatness of a being. On this model, let us suppose that an omnipotent being gets ten great-making points, whereas an extremely powerful but less than completely omnipotent being can have a maximum of nine great-making points from the "power" category. Suppose also that the same holds for omniscience and omnibenevolence. On such a model, both Puck and Bono have a total of twenty-nine great-making points and should therefore be considered equally maximally great.

We must examine more carefully the relationship between Puck and Bono, in light of some of Nagasawa's responses to anticipated objections. I agree with Nagasawa that it is perfectly reasonable to compare various beings to one another when seeking to determine which is greater (592). I also agree with Nagasawa that God is value commensurable with every being (593). But, even if omniperfection turns out to be impossible, we still need a way to determine which of Puck and Bono is divine, unless both are. Of course, this requires some objective, all-encompassing value scale upon which all beings can be judged. But, again, Nagasawa denies that such is necessary.

More precisely, it isn't just an objective, all-encompassing value scale upon which all *beings* can be judged that is necessary; we also need some way to adjudicate between the value and significance of individual

21. I should note that Nagasawa's interest in only the "big three" attributes forestalls a solution. Assuming divine aseity, the notion of more than one maximally great being likely becomes vacuous, unless it is possible for more than one being to enjoy aseity.

attributes. That is, we need some way of determining whether power or knowledge or benevolence contributes more or less towards a being's overall greatness in comparison to the other attributes in question; only this will allow us to determine whether Puck or Bono is maximally great.[22] After all, on Anselmian monotheism, only one God exists, and since the oneness of God means that there is exactly one maximally great divine nature, it follows that there exists exactly one maximally great being. Therefore, Anselmian approaches to the thought experiment require that either Puck or Bono is superior to the other.[23] It cannot be the case that Puck and Bono are the same being with different properties in different worlds because the Anselmian is committed to the idea that God enjoys all of the divine great-making attributes essentially, and not merely contingently. Therefore, the only way to preserve the idea that one of these beings is superior to the other is to insist that some given attribute contributes more heavily towards the greatness of a being than the other attributes in question. But such a claim appears unmotivated without an objective, universal value scale, or some other reason for thinking it true.

If we grant Nagasawa's claims that an objective, all-encompassing value scale is unnecessary, such that we are not able to adjudicate whether knowledge or power or benevolence is more valuable than the other competing great-making properties, we run into yet another problem as well. Apart from such a scale, Puck and Bono are either equally valuable (thus, two maximally great beings exist, so polytheism is true) or Puck and Bono are incommensurable, and there really is no way to determine which of Puck or Bono is maximally great or which is the God that one should worship. If there is no way to determine which attribute is more valuable than the other, then there is no way to determine the overall value of Puck in comparison to Bono, and vice versa. To restate this in a different

22. Morris has argued that knowledge, power, and goodness are value incommensurate, so mustering an argument that could save Nagasawa's reformulation would need to overcome Morris's concerns. See "God of Abraham" reprinted in his *Anselmian Explorations*, 10–25, especially 15–20.

23. One might be tempted to suggest that these two beings are equally maximally great, but this yields polytheism, which is precisely what we are trying to avoid. Additionally, suggesting that these beings are merely conceptual, that is, epistemically possible although metaphysically impossible is not a view that any Christian will entertain since that position would yield ontological atheism for Anselmians with respect to the actual divine nature. To explain this, consider the idea that some maximally great divine nature is epistemically possible but metaphysically impossible. This means that we can conceive of the idea of God in our minds, but that metaphysical laws preclude the existence of such a being.

way, unless we have some objective way of determining the significance of the contribution each individual attribute makes towards a being's overall greatness, then there is no way to determine whether Puck or Bono is superior to the other, or whether they are equally maximally great. The mere assertion that they cannot be equally maximally great beings, then, would be either *ad hoc*, improperly motivated, or an argument from ignorance. Therefore, given Nagasawa's arguments for reformulation and the epistemically possible scenarios he uses to motivate his arguments, both Puck and Bono could be equally maximally great.

Nagasawa faces an even more precarious situation than I have suggested. It has been argued that only one being can be genuinely omnipotent.[24] But the existence of multiple beings that are equally powerful, yet less than omnipotent, is clearly possible. Recall that Nagasawa specifically denies that the success of Anselmian theism depends on refutations of A-type arguments, which seek to show that some omni-attribute is logically incoherent (including arguments against omnipotence, such as the paradox of the stone). Furthermore, nothing precludes the coupling of the property "nearly omnipotent" with the properties of omniscience (or near omniscience) and omnibenevolence (or near omnibenevolence) in multiple beings.[25] So, nothing is incoherent about multiple less than omnipotent beings; and we have no good reason to deny the possible existence of multiple beings whose nature consists of the properties "nearly omnipotent," omniscient, and omnibenevolent. Therefore, we see that conceding arguments such as the paradox of the stone requires that we admit that Anselmian polytheism is (EP). So, in yet another manner, Nagasawa's reformulation of Anselmian theism entails the epistemic possibility of polytheism.

24. So goes the argument in Wainwright, "Monotheism." Wainwright maintains that his conclusion follows from the intuitive notion that an omnipotent being could frustrate the will of any other being. Of course, if there were two omnipotent beings whose wills could conflict, that would bring about a situation in which an omnipotent being could not frustrate the will of some other being, thereby limiting his own power. I am not persuaded by this type of argument, which is reminiscent of Duns Scotus, especially in light of articles such as Mele and Smith, "New Paradox"; Wielenberg, "Stone Revisited." However, I won't pursue this discussion further at this juncture because the possibility of multiple omnipotent beings is enough for my argument against Nagasawa's reformulation of Anselmian theism.

25. I add this clarification in order to make the reader aware that my concern with Nagasawa's reformulation of Anselmian theism does not rely on the logical possibility of omniscience and/or omnibenevolence. However, my concern remains even if omnipotence proves impossible while other omni-attributes remain unscathed by A-type arguments.

Responses to Anticipated Objections

Some might object that my argument is too strong. After all, isn't it epistemically possible that there be more than one maximally great being even if the traditional conception of Anselmian theism holds? What prevents the existence of multiple omniperfect Gods? In response, I appeal to the principle of the identity of indiscernibles, which together precludes the possibility of more than one omniperfect being. Perhaps some "thisness" could apply to multiple *physical* entities that share the exact same natures.[26] But, apart from additional properties that are not essential to the nature of *immaterial* beings, there would be no way to individuate, much less distinguish between, a plurality of such immaterial beings who, lacking physicality, all share exactly the same nature.[27] All omniperfect beings would share the same will, for it doesn't seem possible for two rational omniperfect beings to disagree with respect to any issue.

Take what seems to be an innocuous issue, such as whether I drink orange juice or apple juice with my breakfast. Given divine knowledge of all modalities, God would know all the possibilities that would follow given my decision one way or the other.[28] But surely some future scenario hinges on my decision such that an omnibenevolent God has some regard for how I might choose. Perhaps God knows that I need vitamin C in order to prevent some besetting illness from getting worse, so God desires that I drink orange juice. Or perhaps God knows that if I drink apple juice I am more likely to buy more apple juice the next time I go to the store, which is exactly what is needed to benefit the economy in some precise way such that a revolution among apple farmers and migrant workers is prevented, which would have led to civil war and eventually

26. Cf. Black, "Identity of Indiscernibles," 156. See also Swinburne, *Christian God*, 33–50.

27. Swinburne believes in the thisness of souls, but, given the law of indiscernibility of identicals, thisness must serve as a property that helps to individuate each particular immaterial soul. Shortly, I take up the issue of whether or not such differentiating properties might be present in multiple equally maximally great beings.

28. This is true even if God doesn't know which one I will choose. Thus, even if the dilemma of freedom and foreknowledge logically entails open theism, my argument still holds. One might argue that God, being omnipotent, could make the world just as it would have been had I chosen differently, but this seems to undercut the idea that decisions can affect the natural world, leading to moral implications. Assuming that humans enjoy free will, standard defenses against the problem of evil note that divine intervention of the sort described here are generally thought to be incompatible with stability in the created order.

nuclear apocalypse. Either way, if God is a rational being, God must have some will with respect to my drinking orange juice or apple juice. Presumably, this generalizes such that God's perfect will is inclined in one way or another concerning any and all possible decisions.[29]

The only way that one might seek to individuate multiple equally maximally great beings is by appealing to some property that these beings do not share. But because these beings would share the exact same nature, one couldn't rightly predicate any such property to these beings, for such would amount to the charge that they do not, in fact, share the exact same nature.[30] If it were the case that some haecceity attaches to each of the multiple equally maximally great beings so as to allow for someone to differentiate between them, then it is clearly possible that Anselmian polytheism obtains, given that maximally great beings exist of necessity. But this is exactly what we are trying to avoid. What to say, then?

Perhaps the different wills of multiple beings could serve to individuate them one from another, but I have argued against this possibility. Moreover, I doubt that there is any good reason to think that some "thisness" could be instantiated by more than one omniperfect being. Therefore, given the principle of the identity of indiscernibles as it applies to immaterial beings, it is impossible that more than one omniperfect being exists. At least, Aquinas seems to have argued as much. "God himself is his own nature. . . . It is therefore in virtue of one and the same fact that he is God and this God."[31]

Furthermore, supposing with Anselm that simplicity is a property enjoyed by God, it seems to follow that there are entailment relations between the various great-making attributes such that being omnipotent entails, say, being omniscient. In such a case, Nagasawa's argument wouldn't get going because the notion of three distinct beings with twenty-nine great-making points distributed differently across the individual attributes doesn't make sense in the first place.[32]

29. Some might find this point difficult to accept. After all, why couldn't a rational (and omniscient) being be indifferent with respect to certain decisions which humans face? Perhaps nothing significant follows from someone's decision between apple and orange juice. If this is true, however, it seems that a rational being would necessarily be indifferent, and this is enough to secure my point.

30. I take up issues related to distinctly Trinitarianism concerns that arise from the properties of "begetting" and "begotten" towards the end of this chapter.

31. *Ipse Deus est sua natura. . . . Secundum igitur idem est Deus, et hic Deus*." Aquinas, *Summa Theologiae* 1a.11.3.

32. Thanks to Doug Blount for first bringing this to my attention.

Can Nagasawa defuse the dilemma I raise against him by appealing to this same line of defense? After all, one might object that there is no way to distinguish between a plurality of beings if they all share exactly the same nature and exactly the same will, and, given the principle of the identity of indiscernibles, this is enough to conclude that more than one divine being cannot exist.[33] But Puck and Bono do not share the exact same nature, so this defense won't work, even if Puck and Bono shared the same will. Additionally, nothing precludes the existence of multiple beings such as Wilterchard. Even if multiple Wilterchard-like beings have the same nature, they might differ in their wills on some matter, which is obviously possible for multiple beings who are not omniscient. Perhaps there is some issue upon which they disagree, even though each of multiple Wilterchard-like beings are equally maximally great.[34] Therefore, polytheism would be possible, given that each of these beings would be valued at twenty-nine great-making points.[35]

Nagasawa anticipates an objection based on the idea that the value of two beings could be jointly greater than God. I share his intuitions that "it is peculiar to compare the greatness of one being against the greatness of two beings combined" (595). But his intuitions do nothing to overcome my chief concern, which he has overlooked. That is, Nagasawa has failed to recognize the possibility that two (or more!) beings

33 I return to this subject towards the end of this chapter, and then I will discuss the differences in application of the identity of indiscernibles to divine *Individuals* as opposed to the uniqueness of divine being.

34. As an example, consider a case in which multiple omnipotent, omnibenevolent, equally knowledgeable yet less than completely omniscient beings disagree on some matter. This could apply to the same example I used earlier concerning what type of juice I drink with my breakfast. But it seems plausible to suppose that beings that lack omniscience might be unable to determine whether my drinking orange juice or apple juice is morally better than the alternative. Thus, perhaps multiple Wilterchard-like beings disagree as to whether it is more benevolent to will that I drink orange juice than apple juice, or vice versa, even if one of these decisions might be the key to staving off nuclear holocaust. Of course, for reasons I've already discussed, the possible existence of more than one Wilterchard-like God entails polytheism.

35. Perhaps differences such as these account for the value in a plurality of divine beings in religions such as Hinduism. I raise this only because someone will likely object against my intuition that monotheism is to be preferred over polytheism. That is, my monotheistic intuitions are far from universal. Moreover, such an intuition rests upon value judgments that cannot be adequately defended in a sufficiently analytic fashion so as to persuade opponents. Nonetheless, I am principally concerned here with those religious traditions that most frequently make use of the Anselmian conception of God, namely Abrahamic faiths, so I won't pursue discussions concerning Hinduism further. Special thanks to Jonathan Chan for helpful discussions on this point.

could be equally maximally great. Anyone can insist that either Puck or Bono is greater than the other and/or maintain that Puck and Bono are incommensurable, but we need some way to determine which of these is greater, or why they are incommensurable, at least if Anselmian theism is thought to serve as a means of identifying which being we ought to worship and simultaneously preserve monotheism. But, as we shall see, the mere epistemic possibility of multiple equally maximally great beings who do not share the same nature makes Anselmian polytheism epistemically possible. However, on traditional Anselmianism, for any Anselmian that knows that it is logically impossible for more than one maximally great being to exist, it should not be epistemically possible that more than one maximally great being exists. However, such is seemingly entailed by the epistemically possible scenarios Nagasawa relies on to establish his reformulation of Anselmian theism, and that is enough to refute Nagasawa's reformulation of Anselmian theism, at least so long as Nagasawa's reformulation is thought to preserve the monotheistic nature of the Anselmian theism on the basis of Anselmianism.

A Way Out for Nagasawa?

If we make one modification, there may be a way to save Nagasawa's argument, so long as monotheism is superior to polytheism.[36] If omnipotence is possible, and if it can be successfully shown that only one being can be omnipotent, then it might follow that any omnipotent being is superior to all others.[37] This is so because only one omnipotent

36. Of course, this is merely assertion and an argument would be necessary to persuade anyone who does not share the intuition that monotheism is superior to polytheism. One might attempt to construct such an argument on the basis that there exists an inverse correlation between the value of an object and its commonality, upon which an object's rarity contributes towards its value. So, the uniqueness of a divine being might lend support to its being more valuable (thereby greater) *ceteris paribus*, than a plurality of divine beings. But because Anselmian theism is supposed to entail monotheism, and because I am principally concerned only with the impact of Nagasawa's reformulation on Abrahamic faiths (all of which are monotheistic traditions), I set aside the need for such an argument.

37. Again, for reasons that go far beyond the scope of this chapter, I disagree with the suggestion that one and only one being can be genuinely omnipotent, because I am persuaded by arguments offered by Wielenberg, "New Paradox." But, given the possibility that such arguments fail in regards to the possibility of more than one omnipotent being, it does seem possible for Nagasawa's reformulation to succeed in the way I detail below.

being could exist, which obviously precludes any type of polytheism in which multiple divine beings with the same nature exist. Additionally, an omnipotent being has the power to eliminate the existence of any being with any degree of power less than omnipotence. Of course, this means that, given omnipotence, any being such as Bono is contingent and exists only so long as a being such as Puck wills the continued existence of Bono. This, it seems, diminishes the greatness of Bono, and provides the data necessary for us to adjudicate whether Puck or Bono is greater, which, in turn, eliminates my concern.

Of course, this only holds true if omnipotence turns out to be metaphysically possible, and if it can be shown that only one being can be omnipotent. Both of these possibilities involve substantial revision to Nagasawa's original thesis. Recall that Nagasawa believes that defending the logical coherence of any attribute, including omnipotence, is superfluous to the success of Anselmian theism. But, even given this concession (which remains rather dubious), the success of Nagasawa's reformulation turns on, at minimum, giving up his idea that Anselmian theists can ignore all A-type arguments. Setting that aside for a moment, if this attempt to save Nagasawa's reformulation holds, we now have an argument as to why power should be valued more than either knowledge or benevolence, which is the first step towards developing some sort of objective, all-encompassing value scale of individual attributes, which (again) Nagasawa maintains is unnecessary. Furthermore, it seems that we have now incorporated divine aseity into the mix of what constitutes maximal greatness. This, of course, lends support to the idea that we cannot discuss the individual merits of any single divine attribute without also investigating how it might bear on other divine attributes. But this lends at least partial support to the doctrine of divine simplicity, which I have pointed out seems to preclude any conception of maximal greatness other than omniperfection. However, in an effort to be as fair and charitable as possible, it does seem that given significant modifications, Nagasawa's thesis could plausibly show that Anselmian monotheism need not entail omniperfection.

What About the Christian Doctrine of the Holy Trinity?

I have argued that in order for the Anselmian understanding of God to preserve monotheism on the basis of Anselmianism and without further argument, the Anselmian thesis ought not give rise to the possibility of there being multiple beings that are seemingly equally maximally great. But if there can be only one maximally great being, questions immediately arise as to how Christians ought to understand the doctrine of the Trinity. These questions are very important, and how one responds to such questions hinges on how one understands the metaphysics of substance, quantity, and individuation.[38] Furthermore, there are important issues that come into play from philosophy of language.

When using language to describe the relation between the three Persons of the Trinity to the singularity of God, we must almost certainly use the word "Being." If we employ the word "Being" as often used in ordinary language, then we take "Being" to be among the most basic count-nouns in the English language.[39] On this analysis, it might make sense to say that the Christian doctrine of the Holy Trinity entails that there are three divine Beings. Taking "Being" in this way, one might suggest that since the doctrine of the Trinity entails that there are exactly three distinct divine Persons (and therefore there are three divine Individuals), it is the case that three equally maximally great Beings exist, and that these three Beings together compose God. Perhaps some contemporary defenders of social Trinitarianism would utilize this conception of Being to motivate their view as an alternative to Latin Trinitarianism.[40] For those who prefer this conception of God's Triunity, I admit that it must be the case that either my analysis of Anselmianism is incorrect, or, alternatively, God is not maximally great as understood by Anselmianism.

38. Van Inwagen notes that, when discussing the issues that arise in discussions concerning the Trinity, many difficulties present because "these questions are, after all, questions about number, identity, discernibility, personhood, and being. That is to say, they are logical and metaphysical questions." Van Inwagen, "And Yet They Are," 226.

39. "The word 'God' in English is sometimes a common noun ('There is one God') and sometimes a proper noun ('In the beginning, God created the heavens and the earth'). When 'God' is a common noun in English, it is a count-noun." Van Inwagen, "And Yet They Are," 251.

40. See, for example, several of the essays in McCall and Rea, *Philosophical and Theological Essays*, especially Craig, "Tenable Social Trinitarianism," 89–99. Leftow has criticized social Trinitarianism and has offered an alternative view. See his "Latin Trinity."

Nonetheless, I maintain that on such an analysis (which I take to be mistaken), one might be able to modify Anselmianism so as to accommodate for there being three divine Beings.

Given that perfect love is among the perfections that are the divine nature, Richard of St. Victor argued in the twelfth century that there must be three divine Individuals, otherwise God's love is imperfect. Swinburne summarizes,

> In *De Trinitate* he [Richard of St. Victor] developed the points both that perfect love involves there being someone else to whom to be generous; and also that perfect loving involves a third individual, the loving of whom could be shared with the second. The Father needs *socium et condilectum* (an ally and one fellow-loved) in his loving. Richard also gives what are in effect two further arguments for the necessary bringing about of a third divine individual—that anyone who really loves will seek the good of the beloved both by finding someone else for him to love and (by the same act) finding someone else for him to be loved by. That demand too will be fully satisfied by three persons.[41]

In the light of Richard of St. Victor's arguments, we have reason to think that maximal greatness requires three divine Persons. But nothing seems to be further perfected by the addition of any additional individuals. Therefore, if one takes "Being" as a fundamental count-noun such that God's Triunity requires us to say that there are three divine Beings, we can modify Anselmianism by abandoning the need for a singular maximally great Being by suggesting instead that there are three maximally great Beings who somehow share one divine nature. If we further suppose that rarity contributes to a Being's value, we can suggest that modified Anselmian maximal greatness would require there to be exactly three Beings who are equally maximally great. Of course, if this modification makes way for Nagasawa's reformulation to go through, Christian theologians will stand in great need of help from divine revelation to understand who God is and what the nature of the divine is because, as I have shown, multiple different natures might be considered equally maximally great apart from some scale of universal value commensurability.

Having said all this, one ought not overlook the fact that affirming a multiplicity of divine beings raises yet another problem for Nagasawa's

41. Swinburne, *Christian God*, 190–91. Swinburne cites Richard of St. Victor, *De Trinitate*, 3.14 and 3.15; Swinburne also notes that Alexander of Hales agrees with Richard of St. Victor in *Summa theologiae* 1.304, as does St. Bonaventure in *Itinerarium* 6.

reformulation of Anselmianism. Recall that Nagasawa argues that a maximally great being, in order to qualify as being genuinely maximally great, must satisfy the criteria of existing with a nature that is somehow greater than all other beings overall. Of course, on Nagasawa's definition of maximal greatness, if multiple divine Beings are equally great, it follows that none of them are *maximally* great, for they each lack the property of being greater than all other beings overall, and therefore don't qualify as divine.[42] Supposing that this is the only property of maximal greatness that these beings lack, we can see that the possibility of multiple beings that are equally almost-maximally great yields the possibility of God's non-existence. This is a far cry from the God of Anselm, who is thought to exist of necessity.

However, I don't think this is the right way to appropriate the language of "Being" when discussing the Christian doctrine of God. Rather than saying that there are three divine Beings, it seems prudent to say that there is exactly one divine Being who exists as three distinct Persons. In fact, many English translations of the Nicene Creed use the phrase "of one being with the Father" when speaking of how God the Son is *homoousios* with God the Father. I would be remiss if I did not point out that orthodox Christians have repeatedly repudiated the idea that there are three divine beings.[43]

Van Inwagen, who is especially well known for being extremely precise with technical terminology, repeatedly affirms "that God is (somehow) three Persons in one Being." When introducing an extended discussion about the logic of relative identity, he suggests that it is possible to articulate "the doctrine of the Trinity (or part of it: the part that raises all those pointed logical and metaphysical questions) in such a way that it is demonstrable that no formal contradiction can be derived from

42. I stipulate "on Nagasawa's definition" because "maximally" usually means "cannot be exceeded." But this account of maximal greatness allows for multiple maximally great beings, so long as the greatness of each maximally great being cannot be exceeded. Thanks to Daniel Hill for bringing this to my attention.

43. Also, Christian theologians have (and should) flatly deny that there are three divine Beings. See Gregory of Nyssa, "On 'Not Three Gods'" (*NPNF*^{2} 5:331–36); Basil the Great, *On the Holy Spirit* (*NPNF*^{2} 8:1–51); Gregory of Nazianzus, "Theological Orations 3 and 4" (*NPNF*^{2} 7:403–38); Boethius, *De Trinitate*, ch. 3; Gregory Thaumaturgus, *On the Trinity* (*ANF* 6:7–10); John of Damascus, *De Fide Orthodoxa* (*NPNF*^{2} 9:1–105). For the definitive statement on this matter, see Augustine, *Trinity*, especially 1.4. Thanks are due to J. R. Gilhooly for bringing this material to my attention.

the thesis that God is three persons and, comma, at the same time, one being."[44] Elsewhere, he writes,

> Suppose we have the two relations of relative identity:
>
> is the same being (substance, *ousia*) as
>
> is the same person as.
>
> I shall not attempt to explain what either of these phrases mean in any philosophically satisfactory way, but I shall make two remarks. First, I use "being" for whatever it is that "there is one of" in the Trinity, and I use "person" for what it is that "there are three of" in the Trinity.[45]

This requires that we understand the word "Being" to pick something out in a way that makes sense of it not being used as a basic count-noun. But this is neither problematic, nor is it uncommon. Furthermore, Van Inwagen argues that if "absolute identity exists but is not subdominant—if, in particular, it is not dominated by 'same being'—then it may be true that there is one divine Being counting by beings and, at the same time, true that there are three divine Beings counting absolutely."[46] This understanding of the language surrounding and including the word "Being" allows us to individuate the three Persons of the Trinity, and even ascribe maximal greatness to each of them, without having to say that there are three maximally great Beings in any way that would violate the maxims of Anselmian monotheism. In light of this, I agree with Van Inwagen that "the singular term 'God' should obviously be thought of as an abbreviation for 'the divine Being' or (like the Arabic 'Allah') 'the God.'"[47]

Another citation from Van Inwagen illustrates not only how philosophers and theologians can navigate around some of the tricky issues involved in predicating divinity of the three divine Persons, but also why the alternative view proves problematic:

> We have, to start with, two undefined RI [relative identity]-predicates:
>
> is the same being as
>
> is the same person as.

44. Van Inwagen, "And Yet They Are," 225 and 227, respectively.
45. Van Inwagen, "Three Persons," 94.
46. Van Inwagen, "And Yet They Are," 250.
47. Van Inwagen, "And Yet They Are," 251.

> We shall not assume that either of these predicates dominates the other. And, of course, we shall not assume that either of them is eliminable in favor of RI-predicates and ordinary predicates. It is of particular importance that we not assume that "same being" dominates "same person," for that would entail that if *x* is the same being as *y* and *x* is a person, then *x* is the same person as *y*. (In at least one other context—the theology of the Incarnation—it would be important not to assume that "same person" dominates "same being.")

It is clear that problems would arise if "same being" dominates "same person," for such would eliminate the possibility of three distinct divine Persons. However, one could suggest that by affirming three distinct divine Beings, one can avoid this difficulty. However, not only would such fail to be in keeping with Van Inwagen's central point, it is difficult to see how one could then argue from the position of three divine Beings to a single divinity.

Once this analysis of "Being" is brought into play, we can further analyze Swinburne's remarks concerning the divine nature. Recall that Swinburne argues that "any individual who had the essential divine properties of omnipotence, omniscience, etc. would be the same individual; in other words, there could not be a possible universe in which different individuals were God."[48] In light of the clarifications Swinburne makes about exactly how one should take this,[49] we can see that Swinburne is talking about how one might employ Leibniz's Law and the principle of the identity of indiscernibles with respect to *individuals*. That is, he isn't concerned with "Being" qua *being* in the way that we are presently concerned with in regards to Anselmianism. To clarify, Christians agree that there are three divine Individuals who share exactly the same nature. These three divine Persons have all the same essential divine properties

48. Swinburne, *Christian God*, 36. For a recent defense of the idea that God is identical to his essence, see Robinson, "Can We Make Sense"; as well as Dolezal, *God Without Parts*.

Of course, this is just the problem of haecceities, and, supposing that there were some "thisness" which allowed multiple omniperfect beings to be individuated, the rebuttal against my claims stands. But there seem to be good reasons for rejecting such a possibility, for doing so necessitates Anselmian polytheism since omniperfect beings exist of necessity; and this is true regardless of whether my claims against Nagasawa hold. Hence, I won't pursue this further here because if some "thisness" does allow for the individuation of beings with the same nature, this presents as much a problem for traditional Anselmian theism as it does for Nagasawa's reformulation.

49. Cf. Swinburne's chapter on the divine nature in *Christian God*, 150–69.

of omnipotence, omniscience, etc. Yet, although these three Persons are not the same Individual, they are the same Being, for there is only one God. There is only one divine nature, and these three Persons share all the properties that are essential to that divine nature. How, then, are we to differentiate the divine Persons? We differentiate the divine Persons by predicating properties that each Person has that are not possessed by other members of the Godhead.[50] Of course, these properties which serve to aid in the differentiation of the various members of the Trinity are not essential to the divine nature, so such properties pose no threat to Anselmian monotheism. Furthermore, recall that if some haecceity allowed for the differentiation of multiple equally maximally great beings, then we have a strong case for the possibility of Anselmian polytheism, because maximally great beings exist of necessity. Of course, Anselmian polytheism is exactly what we are trying to avoid, so we do well to eschew Nagasawa's reformulation.

Conclusion

As I conclude, I wish to briefly restate my argument. Nagasawa argues that Anselmianism has to shoulder the burden of responding to the numerous objections to divine omniperfection only if the Anselmian thesis entails omniperfection. But Nagasawa insists that Anselmianism does not entail divine omniperfection. Therefore, Nagasawa maintains that Anselmians do not have to deal with a tremendous apologetic task. I argue, *pace* Nagasawa, that if the Anselmian thesis does not entail divine omniperfection, then Anselmianism does not entail monotheism. Obviously, if Anselmianism does not entail monotheism, then polytheism is (EP), even for those who defend the Anselmian thesis. But, because Nagasawa intends for his reformulation of Anselmian theism to be compatible with traditional understandings of Anselmianism, Anselmian polytheism ought not be (EP) for him, at least not on (EPc). This is because traditional Anselmians maintain that God is logically necessary, and that monotheism is logically necessary. Therefore, polytheism is logically impossible, and for anyone who knows that polytheism is logically impossible, polytheism should not be (EP).

I have shown that the sorts of (EP) scenarios Nagasawa uses to motivate his reformulation are exactly the sort of scenarios that Anselmian monotheism renders metaphysically impossible. Taking belief to be closed

50. For example, the Son is begotten of the Father, but the Father is not begotten of the Son (or the Spirit).

under known entailment, for anyone who realizes that Anselmianism entails the thesis that monotheism is logically/metaphysically necessary, such a person cannot coherently maintain that any scenario that allows for Anselmian polytheism is (EP). It seems to me, then, that these scenarios (p) are problematic, for $\sim(p)$ is obviously entailed by Anselmian monotheism. Therefore, I contend that since Anselmianism does not allow for even the epistemic possibility of polytheism, it must be the case that Anselmianism entails monotheism, and if Anselmianism entails monotheism, then the Anselmian thesis entails divine omniperfection.

Either Nagasawa is wrong to deny that Anselmianism precludes the epistemic possibility of polytheism, or he is wrong to hold that the Anselmian thesis does not entail divine omniperfection. Nagasawa's reformulation of Anselmian theism suggests that God, a maximally great being, might turn out to be less than omniperfect. I have shown that the various (EP) scenarios that Nagasawa uses to motivate his reformulation of Anselmian theism entail that it is (EP) for an Anselmian that multiple beings could be equally maximally great beings. I have also shown that apart from a modification of his thesis so as to necessitate an Anselmian defense against certain A-type arguments attempting to show the logical incoherence of omnipotence, Nagasawa's thesis entails not just that polytheism is (EP), but that Anselmian polytheism follows in actuality from his reformulations. Additionally, I have shown that if Anselmian theism does preclude polytheism, Nagasawa is wrong to contend both that God could turn out to be less than omniperfect and that we don't need an objective, all-encompassing value scale upon which the merits of individual attributes are taken into account. Because Anselmian theism, by definition, is supposed to preserve the absolute uniqueness of God, Nagasawa owes us an argument as to why either Puck is superior to Bono (or vice versa) or why it is impossible that they both exist simultaneously as equally maximally great beings. Therefore, I contend that Nagasawa's reformulation of Anselmian theism, as it stands, should be rejected by all Abrahamic adherents of Anselmianism, even if such a rejection entails that the logical coherence of Anselmian theism hinges on the hard work of successfully responding to each and every argument against the possibility of omniperfection.[51]

51. I am grateful for many friends who have offered helpful critiques of these arguments in discussion and in reading earlier versions of this chapter. In particular, I am indebted to Oliver Crisp, David Alexander, Jonathan Chan, Joshua Farris, Jordan Wessling, Jay Howell, Greg Trickett, Doug Blount, Scott Cleveland, and Dan Johnson.

2

Defining Omnipotence and Omniscience in the Light of Maximal Greatness

Having established in chapter 1 the fact that if God exists, God is a maximally great being, and that Anselmian perfect being theology entails divine omniperfection, I now turn to the application of the concept of maximal greatness to other puzzles in philosophical theology.[1] This chapter proceeds in four parts. The first concerns biblical interpretation and how philosophy necessarily shapes the way Christians read Scripture. In light of this necessity, in the second part I briefly defend the idea of using philosophy for doing Christian theology along the lines of what has come to be called perfect being theology.[2] In the third part I offer a brief analysis of omnipotence, and in the fourth I offer a longer analysis of omniscience. I offer each of these as pieces of analytic perfect being theology, both of which I take to be perfectly consistent with historic Christian orthodoxy.[3] I offer a new definition of divine omniscience that I believe is superior to alternatives.

1. For the remainder of the thesis, I will speak of "maximal greatness" rather than "maximal excellence." Although I mean to speak of the divine nature as God exists in the actual world (which would make maximal excellence a more precise term), I use maximal greatness for two reasons. First, as we have seen, maximal greatness, because it speaks of maximal excellence in all possible worlds, logically entails maximal excellence in the actual world. Second, whereas maximal excellence might be a contingent property, maximal greatness is a necessary property. Thus, by speaking of God's maximal greatness, I do not only suggest the way that God is in this world, but the way that God is necessarily in all worlds. In the end, if I am right, the project yields necessary truths, not merely accidental truths about the nature of God.

2. In light of the arguments in chapter 2, a maximally great being is perfect. Hence, I use these terms interchangeably.

3. In the next chapter, I build on the material in this chapter by discussing how

Great-Making Attributes and Philosophical Interpretation of Scripture

Some strains of open theism, as well as process theology, challenge the great-making status of certain attributes that Christians traditionally assign to God (e.g., omnipotence, impassibility, immutability, etc.). Open theists such as Greg Boyd, John Sanders, and Clark Pinnock argue that where the tradition finds value in such attributes, such owes more to Greek philosophy than to Scripture, especially in favoring stability over change as in divine immutability, or in favoring "strength" over emotional interaction as in divine impassability.[4] These issues become particularly important when considering biblical interpretation. On the open view, it seems that any interpretive approach which fails to yield an open theology is to be dismissed because, as open theists see it, disagreement with their interpretations of Scripture demonstrates subservience to Greek philosophy in general and to Plato in particular.[5] But can the claim that historic Christian orthodoxy has been significantly influenced by Greek philosophy be substantiated? Moreover, even if such a claim could be substantiated, would that undermine the validity and/or veracity of the tradition's reading of Scripture? As far as I can see, a reading's being informed by Greek philosophy should no more disqualify it than its being informed by metaphysical libertarianism or theological incompatibilism.[6]

Anselmian perfect being theology is immensely valuable for those seeking to do analytic theology, especially in ruling out certain conceptions of the divine nature offered by open theists. This involves the application of God's maximal greatness to the paradox of the stone, and by parallel argument, against one particular form of open theism held by Hasker, Van Inwagen, and Swinburne.

4. Boyd, *God of the Possible*; Pinnock, *Most Moved Mover*; Sanders, *God Who Risks*.

5. Sanders, "Historical Considerations," 59–60. Cf. Boyd, *God of the Possible*, 86, 115, 130. Sanders is especially concerned about the influence of Middle Platonism on Christian philosophy. See *God Who Risks*, 74, 141–42, 147, 162, 186–87. Sanders accuses Philo and Augustine of committing the same error in "Historical Considerations," 69 and 82, respectively.

6. Metaphysical libertarianism, as I use the term, is the view that in order to possess significant freedom (which is necessary to be morally accountable for our actions), we must have the ability to choose between alternative possibilities that are genuinely available. This libertarian account of free will is said to require the principle of alternative possibilities, or PAP for short. The term "theological incompatibilism" is used in two very different ways. Historically, "incompatibilism" refers to the view that determinism and freedom cannot be co-instantiated—that they are incompatible. But, when speaking of *theological* incompatibilism, I follow the contemporary literature in which the term denotes the idea that metaphysical libertarianism about free will is incompatible with exhaustive definite divine foreknowledge.

And what is the alternative to a philosophically informed reading of the sacred text? *Is* there an alternative to such a reading?[7]

Even if the tradition's theology were significantly influenced by Greek philosophy, this would be problematic only insofar as the specific tenets of that philosophy that undergird the tradition are false.[8] If those tenets were true, their influence would be benign.[9] Moreover, however deserving of scrutiny such tenets might be, the assumptions underlying open theism deserve no less attention.[10]

Adolf von Harnack and Wolfhart Pannenberg not withstanding,[11] I doubt that the tradition's interpretive approach has been as heavily influenced by Greek philosophy as open theists suggest, at least not to the point of early Christian theology being *dependent* upon Greek philosophy more than Scripture, which is what open theists suggest.[12] Sadly, I cannot entertain open theists' arguments to the contrary for the simple

7. See Blount, "Togas," which argues that the question is not *whether* one brings philosophical assumptions to one's reading of Scripture but rather *which* assumptions one brings to that reading.

8. Insofar as this suggests that ancient Greece enjoyed a single, distinct philosophy, it misleads. For ancient Greek philosophy comprises a plethora of differing—even incompatible—perspectives. And this point raises an ironic difficulty for open theists: If the church fathers had read the text as open theists do, *they would nonetheless be open to precisely the same charge that open theists now raise against them*. Open theists themselves thus risk being impaled by their own swords; by emphasizing change rather than stability in the Godhead and thus giving "becoming" priority over "being," they can *by their own lights* be rightly accused of falling under the sway of Heraclitus of Ephesus, according to whom one cannot step in the same river twice. Here our point is not that *we* charge open theists with being unduly Heraclitean—and thus unduly influenced by Greek philosophy—but rather that *the argument they themselves make* leads inexorably to their being so charged.

9. Cf. Roy, *How Much?*, 204–6.

10. So, despite their claims to the contrary, open theists present us, not with a choice of *whether* to read Scripture in light of extrabiblical assumptions but rather with a choice of *which* extrabiblical assumptions to bring to our reading of it.

11. Harnack provides perhaps the most influential statement of the Hellenization thesis. Cf. Harnack, *History of Dogma*. More recently, Pannenberg has advanced Harnack's thesis, especially in "Appropriation of the Philosophical" in *Basic Questions in Theology*, 2:119–83. See also Hatch, *Influence of Greek Ideas*. It should be noted that many evangelicals fail to recognize that the roots of the Hellenization thesis lie in neither Pannenberg nor Harnack, but rather in the early, inchoate higher critical arguments of Spinoza. I can't help wonder why it is better to be informed by Spinoza than by Aristotle. What has Berlin to do with Jerusalem? Surely neither more nor less than Athens! Cf. Spinoza, *Theologico-Political Treatise*.

12. Cf. Blount, "Togas," 181–85.

reason that they have put forward no such arguments.[13] That traditional Christian readings of Scripture have been unduly influenced by Greek philosophy is not a conclusion *for* which open theists argue but rather an assumption *from* which they argue.[14] So, for instance, Sanders—who proclaims the point persistently and pointedly—does nothing to show that the tradition has been so influenced; he also does nothing to show *which* Greek philosophical doctrines are problematic for Christian theology, not to mention *why* they are so. Apparently, he takes the point to be beyond dispute; it is not.[15]

In any case, a causal connection between Greek philosophy and the Christian tradition's understanding of God has yet to be demonstrated.[16] Sanders argues that the tradition's theologians arrive at conclusions regarding God similar to those held by certain Greek philosophers, but nowhere does he demonstrate that patristic theologians use—much less depend on—such philosophers to arrive at their conclusions.[17] And in the absence of such a demonstration, the charge that the early church's understanding of God owes more to Greek philosophy than to Scripture is uncharitable and unwarranted.[18]

13. Curiously, this point applies also to both Harnack and Pannenberg. The alleged influence of Hellenistic philosophy on early Christian doctrine strikes me as much ado about nothing. And so it will seem until those pressing the allegation against the tradition refrain from trumpeting it as though it were obvious and instead provide evidence for it.

14. Cf. Pinnock, "God Limits His Knowledge," 150, 154.

15. Of course, I do not dispute that Augustine draws from Plato, and that Aquinas highly esteemed Aristotle. That Anselm claimed passibility to be beneath divine perfection is not the point in dispute. Rather, it is the nature of the connection between Greek philosophy and early Christian theology that has yet to be sufficiently established. Until it can be proven that Greek philosophy was the starting point for patristic theology, rather than Scripture, the causal relationship cannot be established, and those who affirm the Hellenization thesis appear to be committed to the *cum hoc ergo propter hoc* fallacy in their argumentation against the tradition's interpretation of Scripture.

16. Despite its obvious Eurocentrism, such a connection is simply assumed. Cf. Oden, *How Africa Shaped*.

17. This is not to say that there is no good evidence of use. In point of fact, there is. Regardless, Sanders offers no evidence in his argumentation, so his argument seems little more than unsubstantiated assertion. But use of philosophy is not the issue; dependence is. It seems to me that Christians have always made use of philosophy in doing theology (at least when theology has been done in any systematic fashion). Pulling apart philosophy from theology is no easy task, and might even be impossible. Additionally, I see no reason to think doing so would even be desirable. Thanks to Oliver Crisp for helping me think through this issue.

18. See Sanders, "Historical Considerations." Roy, in opposition to open theism,

Moreover, some open theists' charge that the tradition's doctrine of God has been unduly influenced by Greek thought suggests that they themselves read the Bible *without* philosophical assumptions.[19] In short, the charge suggests that they see themselves as reading Scripture more objectively and with less philosophical bias than the tradition. However, the quest for objectivity is itself driven by philosophical assumptions concerning interpretation and epistemology. Moreover, as Paul Helm correctly points out, when someone disagrees with a philosophical conception of God and puts forward an alternative one, that alternative—whatever it happens to be—is just as much a philosophical conception of God as the one with which he or she disagrees.[20] Hence, in rejecting the philosophical conception of God put forward by the tradition's reading of Scripture, open theists put forward their own philosophical conception of God; and the claim that they take a less philosophical path than the tradition turns out to be mistaken. So, despite claims to the contrary, open theists also bring philosophical assumptions to their reading of Scripture.[21]

One rather obvious assumption drawn from Greek philosophy that open theists bring to their reading of Scripture is the law of non-contradiction. If, as open theists suggest, the influence of Greek philosophy on theology is to be eschewed, should we not do away with appropriating the laws of logic when interpreting the Bible, especially since they were first articulated by Aristotle? Of course, if we give up the laws of logic when reading Scripture, then *any* interpretation will turn out to be as good—or bad—as any other. In short, if we abandon the laws of logic—laws put forward by Greek philosophers—we abandon all hope of making sense of the biblical text and consign ourselves to an interpretive inferno; if we choose to avoid such untenable consequences by embracing those laws, we implicitly acknowledge—*pace* open theists—that philosophy, even

---

argues similarly in *How Much?*, 202–4; in discussing Platonism, Erickson also agrees with the tradition and opposes open readings of Scripture in *What Does God Know?*, 144.

19. Sanders thus states, "We believe the biblical portrayal of God [as lacking comprehensive knowledge of the future] is paramount and should not be trampled underfoot by philosophical speculation." Sanders, *God Who Risks*, 16, 141. Boyd also displays a similar interpretive naïveté in claiming that "exegesis should always drive our philosophy instead of the other way around." Boyd, "Open-Theism View," 14. Cf. Blount, "Togas," 180.

20. Helm, "Augustinian-Calvinist Response," 124–33, especially 129.

21. Roy, *How Much?*, 211–17.

Greek philosophical assumptions, *does* have a legitimate role to play in our reading of Scripture.[22]

Open theists seeking to avoid such naïve positions regarding biblical interpretation are likely to retort (correctly, it seems to me) that certain principles of logic such as the law of non-contradiction are not in dispute; instead, it is the controversial metaphysical claims of middle Platonism that shape classical theology to which they object. Thus, so long as certain philosophical claims are beyond dispute (such as the laws of logic), then these don't count as the disputed and controversial claims to which they object. Hence, utilization of the laws of logic to guide biblical interpretation is not necessarily "Greek" in the way that middle Platonism is. The laws of logic, someone might argue, are no more "Greek" in nature than our understanding of gravity is European. Aristotle's discovery of the law of non-contradiction (at least in being the first to articulate it in writing) does not mean that he invented it, and therefore the laws of logic aren't "Greek" in the relevant sense any more than Newton's discovery of gravity makes it a uniquely European notion.[23]

Two replies to this objection are in order. First, it should be noted that open theists such as Boyd and Sanders have framed the debate concerning biblical interpretation as if they do not utilize *any* philosophical presuppositions to guide their interpretation of Scripture, but rather let Scripture alone determine their theology. Nonetheless, it seems eminently reasonable to suppose that an open theist could retort in the ways outlined above. However, since the law of non-contradiction is not taught explicitly in the Bible, the issue isn't so much whether Aristotelian logic is relevantly "Greek" or not, but rather whether or not openness claims of non-philosophically influenced interpretations of Scripture can be defended. Were openness advocates to concede that they may have overstated their case, "in shifting the field of debate, I should count that worth while."[24]

22. In all fairness, it strikes me as obvious that some of the more philosophically inclined open theists would take issue with Boyd's assertions. I cannot imagine Hasker or Van Inwagen agreeing with Boyd's naïve approach to biblical interpretation.

23. Thanks to Oliver Crisp for bringing this objection to mind. Such a claim would be similar to Robert Jenson's concern that the influence of Greek philosophy on the concept of God is not adequately Christian, not because it includes "reason" per se but because a secularized theology prevents Christian revelation from having an adequate pride of place in theological method, much less the actual construction of Christian theology. See Jenson, *Systematic Theology*.

24. I owe this phrase to Peter Geach, who uses the saying in discussing the

Second, once certain indisputable laws of logic are allowed to shape the way we do theology, the burden of proof is back on the open theist to refute the principles of perfect being theology established by Anselmian monotheism.[25] Until such an argument is mustered, I see no reason to abandon the type of perfect being theology that has been dominant for the vast majority of Christian history.

On Perfect Being Theology[26]

It is intuitive that certain properties are valuable. Among those that we intuitively know to be valuable are the properties of being knowledgeable and being powerful. In discerning that such properties are valuable, our intuitions do not lead us astray. I am not aware of any theologically relevant arguments which establish anything other than the value of both knowledge and power, at least when co-instantiated with the property of moral perfection, and especially when oriented towards God.[27] Additionally, similarly to the way that conceivability is thought to be reliable until

---

relationship of omnipotence to the problem of evil. Geach, *Providence and Evil*, 38–39. My point here is that were open theists to admit that they had overstated their claims about the role that philosophy plays in biblical interpretation, such an admission would advance the discussion beyond its present state even if it didn't resolve the questions as to whether the tradition's reading of Scripture is more veridical than that proposed by open theists.

25. The concept of maximal greatness is sufficient to pursue perfect being theology, at least as I understand it. Hence, open theists need to show where Anselmian intuitions fail before discrediting perfect being theology as an appropriate philosophical hermeneutic to guide biblical interpretation.

26. I comment only briefly on perfect being theology here. However, this approach to philosophical theology seems eminently reasonable to me and very defensible. For a more detailed account of the approach that I only sketch out here, see Hill, *Divinity and Maximal Greatness*, 1–26. See also Rogers, *Perfect Being Theology*. For more recent defenses of perfect being theology, see Leftow, "Why Perfect Being Theology?"; Wierenga, "Augustinian Perfect Being Theology."

27. Some suggest that power isn't a great-making property by quipping the cliché, "Power corrupts, and absolute power corrupts absolutely." Of course, this isn't an argument, but rather mere assertion. Nonetheless, Anselmians maintain that moral perfection is co-instantiated alongside omnipotence, which suffices as a rejoinder. Also, this serves to stave off objections related to the extent of divine knowledge. If knowledge is power, as is frequently stated (and as might be defended if omniscience is logically entailed as the perfection of cognitive power), then moral perfection must be co-instantiated alongside omniscience. Hence, if the Christian understanding of God is to be defended philosophically, the triad of attributes common to traditional perfect being theology must be held together: omniscience, omnipotence, and moral perfection.

shown otherwise,[28] so, too, should our intuitions about what is valuable be thought reliable until shown otherwise. Thus, Thomas Morris notes that "most practitioners of perfect being theology take our intuitions about matters of value, as they do most other intuitions, to be innocent until proven guilty, or reliable until proven deceptive. The alternative is a form of skepticism with few attractions."[29]

These properties are not merely instrumentally valuable; rather, they are intrinsically valuable. That is, to possess knowledge is a good in and of itself, not merely because one can use such knowledge for some other purpose, and the same holds for power. Not all good properties are intrinsically valuable. Consider the property of being wealthy. Although few would disagree that money is valuable, having money is not valuable in and of itself; instead, having money is valuable because one can spend money to buy things or contribute to a cause. But why is being wealthy good? Presumably, having money is good because the purchasing of some object, such as food, makes one happy, and happiness is intrinsically good. Consider someone who has the extrinsically valuable property of being wealthy and uses her wealth to donate funds to feed the hungry. Perhaps she does so because doing so makes her feel good, and that euphoria brings about happiness, which is intrinsically good. Also, starvation is bad. Thus, by using her wealth to save lives, she proves that there are intrinsic goods, because life is intrinsically valuable.[30]

Among those attributes that the Christian tradition has predicated of God are omnipotence, omniscience, and moral perfection. Other than process theology, which I take to be beyond the bounds of Christian orthodoxy, little debate exists concerning the great-making status of these three attributes.[31] Again, it is obvious that certain properties

28. Here I am referencing the comments I made in chapter one regarding the reliability of conceivability as it pertains to modal metaphysics. Recall that I disagree with certain segments of an important article by R. Adams, "Presumption."

29. Morris, *Our Idea of God*, 39.

30. Cf. Morris, *Our Idea of God*, 35–39.

31. Process theologians deny divine omnipotence, which I take to be necessary for preserving orthodox Christianity. Additionally, process theology is incompatible with the Christian tradition precisely because it entails the denial of a Creator-creation distinction. Even Geach, who is sometimes wrongly supposed to be the founder of open theism, denies that process theology is a live option. See his *Providence and Evil*, 42. Cf. Basinger, *Divine Power in Process Theism*; Cobb and Pinnock, *Searching for an Adequate God*. For another philosophical assessment as to why process theology is heterodox, see Morris, "God and the World."

Interestingly, the fact that life is intrinsically valuable lends support to the ontological

such as knowledge, power, and moral goodness contribute to the excellence of a being's nature, and a perfect being would have those properties maximally. Hence, it is clear that omniscience, omnipotence, and moral perfection count among great-making attributes, and it can be logically deduced that God, if he exists as the greatest possible being—a claim I defended in chapter one—must possess these properties, unless it can be demonstrated that these three attributes are not compossible. However, efforts to show that omniscience, omnipotence, and moral perfection cannot be co-instantiated have repeatedly been shown unsuccessful, most recently by Richard Swinburne.[32] I do not mean to suggest that there are only three great-making attributes, but these three have received the most attention by recent analytic philosophers of religion and analytic theologians concerned with theology proper. For this reason, I now turn to explore the first two of these: omnipotence and omniscience.[33]

Maximal Greatness and Divine Power[34]

Graham Oppy has written extensively on ontological arguments, which clearly depend on the type of perfect being theology defended above;

argument, for the property of being alive is possessed by only that which exists. Thus, existence is a property and a great-making property at that. Accordingly, a maximally great being must possess the property of existence. From this, the steps of the ontological argument flow to prove the existence of God.

32. See Swinburne, *Coherence of Theism*.

33. I choose not to discuss moral perfection for three reasons. First, the whole of this project focuses on divine omniscience and metaphysical and theological reasons for affirming that God enjoys exhaustive definite knowledge of future contingents, *contra* the claims of open theists. Thus, an examination of moral perfection is outside the scope of not only this chapter but the entire project as well. Second, the vast amount of literature on moral perfection, the problem of evil, and ethics in general renders discussing God's moral perfection almost impossible apart from an entire separate thesis; that is, it would be too difficult and ultimately unnecessary. Third, the specific point that I make in this chapter with regards to perfect being theology and the usefulness of Anselmian intuitions for refuting one type of open theism does not require a discussion of moral perfection, but discussing divine omnipotence proves quite helpful in elucidating my point.

34. In this section, I give a cursory overview of omnipotence. I will not go into as much detail in discussing omnipotence as I will with respect to omniscience. The reason for this is that the entire project of this thesis focuses on what I believe are incorrect articulations of divine omniscience, namely open theism. The point that I want to make regarding the utilization of modal ontological arguments for perfect being theology's being able to solve puzzles in philosophical theology does not require a detailed investigation of omnipotence. However, in order to lay a foundation that is

he does not believe that any type of ontological argument is of any real value, whether for proving God's existence, or even for establishing the rationality of theistic belief.[35] Robert Kane has argued similarly, stating, "The OA [ontological argument] seems to prove that God necessarily exists, say these critics, but all it does prove is that if God exists, God necessarily exists."[36] But the necessary existence of a God who is maximally great (and therefore possesses great-making attributes essentially) proves rather powerful for solving other puzzles in philosophical theology.[37] Thus, *contra* Oppy, even if modal ontological arguments prove to be unsuccessful as pieces of natural theology, this does not by any means render them worthless, for Oppy fails to take into account how the logic of modal ontological arguments can be used as a foundation for abstract perfect being theology.[38] As Plantinga notes, these arguments "cannot, perhaps, be said to *prove* or *establish* their conclusion. But since it is rational to accept their central premises, they do show that it is rational to *accept* that conclusion. And perhaps that is all that can be expected of any such argument."[39] Modal ontological arguments might not *prove* that God exists, but they can show the rationality of faith, especially when someone takes the key premise—possibly, a maximally great being exists—as true on the basis of other evidence.

If such amended versions of modal ontological arguments are later rejected even for establishing the rationality of theistic belief, there are

necessary for a later argument concerning omnipotence and omniscience, I show that certain conceptions of omnipotence are relevant for defeating certain conceptions of divine knowledge. However, I will give a much more detailed account of the discussions concerning divine omniscience in another section.

35. See Oppy, *Ontological Arguments and Belief*, 186–97.

36. Kane, "Modal Ontological Arguments," 338.

37. This is the second of four uses of theistic arguments noted by Plantinga. "Second, [theistic arguments, including the modal ontological argument] reveal interesting and important connections between various elements of a theist's set of beliefs. For example, a good theistic argument reveals connection between premises and conclusions, connections that in some cases can also contribute to the broader project of Christian philosophy by showing good ways to think about a certain topic or area from a theistic perspective." Plantinga, "Two Dozen," 209.

38. I use the term "abstract" to denote the idea of theology being done as a thought experiment. Thus, even if modal ontological arguments of any kind fail to succeed in proving God's existence, they could be employed by someone willing to grant that God exists for the sake of argument, and then proceed in analyzing what God must be like according to perfect being theology as dictated by any ontological argument which rests on the concept of maximal greatness.

39. Plantinga, *Nature of Necessity*, 221.

still relevant applications of the logic from the valid argument, despite the fact that its soundness remains uncertain.[40] In the same way that mathematicians can utilize Goldbach's Conjecture to determine other potential mathematical truths without having established its certainty, so, too, can modal ontological arguments be utilized to solve puzzles presented by other areas of philosophical theology. As an example, let us turn to see how the concept of maximal greatness applies to divine omnipotence and the varieties of arguments used in arguing against it.

Philosophers and theologians have motivated the doctrine of divine omnipotence by appealing to numerous biblical texts such as:

> The Lord . . . can do all things. (Job 42:2)
>
> Our God is in heaven; He does whatever pleases Him. (Pss 115:3; 135:6)
>
> Lord . . . nothing is too hard for you. (Jer 32:17)
>
> With God all things are possible. (Matt 19:26)[41]

Christians have defended the idea that Yahweh is an omnipotent being throughout the history of the church, and the revival of interest in philosophical theology during the second half of the twentieth century resulted in a proliferation of literature on divine omnipotence. Contributions to the discussion about the extent of divine power have come from proponents of the traditional understanding of God, open theists, process theologians, as well as skeptics and atheists.[42] The best of these

40. These relevant applications can be made not by ignoring the soundness of the modal ontological argument *qua* ontological argument to prove God's existence, but rather because we can suspend judgment on the veracity of the key possibility premise and suppose it true for the sake of argument. Doing so thereby allows the logical steps of argumentation in modal ontological arguments to be utilized for the sake of philosophical theology. After all, Christians presuppose that Yahweh is the greatest of all possible beings.

41. See Leftow, "Omnipotence," 167. Leftow also includes Luke 1:37 as a proof text, which many translations render as something like "nothing is impossible with God." However, this translation rests on a historical error dating to the Latin Vulgate. A more accurate translation, and one which brings out the inter-textual connection to Gen 18, would be "every word of God will not be impossible."

42. For some of the best defenses of omnipotence, see Flint and Freddoso, "Maximal Power"; Leftow, "Omnipotence"; Mavrodes, "Defining Omnipotence"; Savage, "Paradox of the Stone"; Swinburne, "Omnipotence"; Wainwright, "Omnipotence, Omniscience, and Omnipresence"; Wierenga, *Nature of God*, 12–35; Wierenga "Omnipotence Defined." For skeptical and atheistic arguments against omnipotence, see Grim, "Impossibility Arguments"; La Croix, "Failing to Define Omnipotence"; La Croix, "Impossibility of Defining 'Omniscience'"; Oppy, "Omnipotence."

accounts have taken the historical development of the doctrine into account, noting how Augustine, Anselm, Aquinas, and William of Ockham all offer variant, nuanced definitions of omnipotence throughout the Middle Ages.[43] Of all the definitions on offer, Leftow's account appears to be the strongest, for it takes not only range but also strength into account. If two agents are each able to bring about all possibilities, but it is rather difficult for one and quite easy for the other, it seems that the latter is "more omnipotent" than the first. But of course it is absurd to suggest that there can be degrees of omnipotence, for the very definition of the word does not allow for this.[44] Leftow offers the following definition:

> *x* is omnipotent at *t* if and only if (i) it is not the case at *t* that there is some state of affairs *x* is unable to bring about at least partially due to lack of power, (ii) all truthmakers of modal truths are either *x*, *x*'s being in some intrinsic state or items *x* brings to be, (iii) at *t*, (*P*) (◊ (something(s) at some time(s) or timelessly cause(s) it to be the case that *P* and *P* is not the doing of an action with incompatibilist freedom by someone distinct from *x*) ⊃ (*x* is intrinsically such as to strongly actualize it that *P*)).[45]

Even with this sophisticated and nuanced account of omnipotence, some philosophers have sought to undermine if not outright attack the faith of defenders of divine omnipotence, especially Christians who take a realist approach to theology and the content of the Nicene-Constantinopolitan Creed, believing God to be the Almighty Creator of heaven and earth.[46]

43. Leftow provides an excellent recapitulation of the discussion in "Omnipotence," 168–70. See also his "Aquinas on Omnipotence."

44. Cf. Leftow, "Omnipotence," 183–85; Wielenberg, "Omnipotence Again," 26–47, especially 42.

45. Leftow, "Omnipotence," 190–91.

46. I take these words directly from the first line of the Nicene-Constantinopolitan Creed (affirmed in AD 381) for an important reason. It might appear that Christians could avoid these attacks by jettisoning omnipotence, and of course certain groups have done so while continuing to call themselves Christians. But such a move is certainly not in keeping with historic Christian orthodoxy, per the creed, which declares God to be almighty. This is another reason, then, why process theology cannot rightly be maintained simultaneously with Christian beliefs. See Hartshorne, *Omnipotence*.

However, Geach (who is not a process theologian) thinks he can jettison omnipotence in favor of God's being almighty. See Geach, *Providence and Evil*, 3–28. Given the developments in contemporary literature concerning omnipotence, I do not find any distinction between omnipotence and almighty-ness helpful; I believe the terms are interchangeable.

For example, consider the well-known paradox of the stone, an argument put forward by some as if to show that God cannot be omnipotent. Given the law of the excluded middle, either God can or cannot create a stone so heavy that he cannot lift it. Accordingly, it appears that no matter how one responds to the paradox, we have an example that demonstrates the incoherence of an omnipotent being. This follows logically on two grounds. On the one hand, if God can create such a stone, then he cannot do something, namely, lift the created stone. On the other hand, if God is unable to create such a stone, then right from the go we find God unable to do something; therefore, God is not omnipotent.[47]

Philosophers of religion have provided various explanations of this paradox in defense of the coherence of omnipotence. Many rest on the Thomistic idea that a nuanced definition of omnipotence does not demand that an omnipotent agent have the power to bring about logical impossibilities such as square circles.[48] Wielenberg offers an account of this principle:

> Thomistic Principle (TP): If A is an impossible task, then the fact that a given being cannot perform A does not imply that that being is not omnipotent.[49]

On Thomism, God's ability to do any "thing" means that if something is possible (in the broadly logical sense), God can do it. Because square circles aren't "things," per se, we need not understand omnipotence to demand that God has the ability to do a non-"thing," for logical impossibilities don't count as genuine "things" that could be done.

Another proposed solution to this paradox involves the suggestion that affirming God's inability to create such a stone does not entail the predication of any weakness of God. If God is so strong that God cannot fail to lift any stone, then the divine inability to create a stone so heavy that God cannot lift it only proves how strong God really is. One might consider this solution to be tantamount to saying, "God is so strong that

47. Many variants of this puzzle exist, and are quite well-known. I take this particular argument from Savage, "Paradox of the Stone," 9.

48. Not surprisingly, opponents have argued that if God is truly all-powerful, then he must be able to accomplish even the impossible. For this reason, Leftow's definition includes (ii), which entails that God is the Lord of all metaphysics. That is, the reason that square circles are not possible rests somehow on God, perhaps the divine nature itself.

49. Wielenberg, "Stone Revisited," 262. This principle seems to be derived, at least in part, from Aquinas, *Summa Contra Gentiles*, 2.25.

God cannot create a stone so heavy that God cannot lift it." In much the same way that it is no insult to say of a warrior, "He is so strong that he cannot be defeated in battle," it turns out that denying God the "ability" to create a stone so heavy that it cannot be lifted attributes power, not weakness, to God. As Savage points out, "'God can create stones of any poundage, and God can lift stones of any poundage' entails 'God cannot create a stone which He cannot lift.'"[50] But, so long as God can both create stones of any poundage and lift stones of any poundage, God's inability to create a stone that God cannot lift does not impugn divine omnipotence. Thus, God remains omnipotent even if unable to create a stone so heavy God cannot lift it.

One other proposed solution is especially interesting to defenders of perfect being theology. Although proffered by notables such as Swinburne, and also Rosenkrantz and Hoffman, this solution proves unsuccessful in light of the validity of Anselmian perfect being theology.[51] In an attempt to resolve the paradox of the stone, Swinburne suggests that it might be possible for God to create a stone so heavy that God cannot lift it, but God does not will to create such a stone and therefore remains omnipotent.[52] Were God to create such a stone, God would cease to be omnipotent from the moment of the stone's beginning to exist. Rosenkrantz and Hoffman seem to be content to affirm that an omnipotent agent has the power to cease to be omnipotent.[53] On the contrary, neither Anselmian nor Thomistic understandings of omnipotence allow for this solution. Aquinas notes that "since a deprivation is a certain loss of being, it follows that God can lack nothing."[54] Hence, it is impossible for anyone, including God, to deprive the divine of any great-making attribute, including omnipotence.

Additionally, such a solution requires that God's omnipotence be understood as contingent, rather than an essential part of his necessary being. But, according to Anselmian perfect being theology, God

50. Savage, "Paradox of the Stone," 12.

51. Swinburne articulates a view, but does not defend it because he later argues (in part 3 of his book) that God has his attributes essentially and not contingently. He writes such in order "to avoid the misunderstanding that I might be committed to the view that God was able to abandon his powers." Swinburne, *Coherence of Theism*, 162–63. In contrast, Rosenkrantz and Hoffman defend the view articulated below in their article "What an Omnipotent Agent Can Do."

52. Swinburne, *Coherence of Theism*, 153–66; see especially 157–63.

53. Rosenkrantz and Hoffman, "What an Omnipotent Agent."

54. Aquinas, *Summa Contra Gentiles*, 2:25; translation mine.

is not accidentally omnipotent; rather God is essentially so, at least as long as power, and therefore omnipotence is considered a great-making property. Recall that if God is a maximally great being, then God possesses maximal excellence necessarily. And because maximal excellence entails omnipotence, God's necessary maximal greatness entails his essential omnipotence. Therefore, God is omnipotent in every possible world. But, were God to create a stone so heavy that God could not lift it, in ceasing to be omnipotent, God would have the ability to instantiate a world in which God is not omnipotent. Wainwright articulates this point extremely well:

> Nor can a maximally perfect being have powers the possession or exercise of which entails a limitation or weakness. Thus, God can't destroy himself or divest himself of his knowledge or power. Why not? A maximally perfect being would be eternally wise and powerful. It would also seem to possess these attributes essentially—that is, have them in every possible world in which it exists. Now if a maximally perfect being *could* destroy itself or divest itself of its knowledge or power, there would be possible worlds in which it does so and, in those worlds, it wouldn't be *eternally* wise and powerful. But given that eternal wisdom and power are *essential* properties of any maximally perfect being that has them, a maximally perfect being would possess those properties in *every* world in which it exists. If so, it can neither destroy itself nor make itself ignorant or weak.[55]

Of course, this means that God could bring it about that God is not maximally great, which, by definition of "God," is impossible. Although this is not explicit per the definition of God, such a notion is definitely implied by Anselmianism. That God cannot cease to be omnipotent is derived from divine maximal greatness in that a maximally great being is maximally great necessarily. To deny this is to simultaneously affirm that a maximally great being could change from being omnipotent to being not-omnipotent while remaining the same maximally great being. Of course, this is absurd, because an omnipotent being is clearly greater than a semi-potent being. Therefore, any maximally great being must be omnipotent, and immutably so.[56] To restate the obvious, maximal greatness

55. Wainwright, "Omnipotence, Omniscience, and Omnipresence," 47; emphasis added.

56. For more on this point, see Morris, "Properties, Modalities, and God," reprinted in his *Anselmian Explorations*, 76–97.

entails at least some conception of immutability. If God is immutable, then nothing has the ability to deprive a divine being of omnipotence, as that would be contradictory ("the immutable being is mutable").

The scope of this chapter precludes a more detailed investigation of either divine omnipotence (or divine immutability), but this brief discussion of omnipotence and the paradox of the stone demonstrates that if (36) is true,[57] then the coherence of theism allows us to understand that certain properties/attributes of God are essential to the divine nature. Such realizations are the by-product of natural Anselmian theism, and such applications are extremely useful in philosophical theology, regardless of whether modal ontological arguments are sound. Therefore, in utilizing such versions of the ontological argument, theologians and philosophers of religion can exclude certain proposed solutions to the paradox of the stone based on the mere validity of the logical steps of the argument. Although many other applications of modal ontological arguments will undoubtedly prove useful in solving many other theological dilemmas, I will focus on but one—the dilemma of this solution will not satisfy anyone who insists that an omniscient being must know the very same proposition I know and that the proposition expressed by (1) differs from that expressed by (3), but I think that this account succeeds in preserving cognitive perfection even if it does not succeed in preserving one traditional account of omniscience and foreknowledge and the suggestion that God lacks exhaustive definite foreknowledge.

Defining Omniscience in Light of Maximal Greatness

Philosophers generally agree that omniscience, however it might be defined, is a great-making attribute. It follows, then, that if God is the greatest of all possible beings, God is omniscient, and essentially so. Therefore, God is necessarily omniscient because God is essentially omniscient, and God exists of necessity. In all worlds in which God obtains, God is omniscient; there are no worlds in which God exists and is not omniscient; also, since God exists in all possible worlds, God is omniscient in all possible worlds. But these facts don't help us in answering

57. Recall that (36)—"*Maximal greatness* is possibly exemplified"—is the key premise upon which Plantinga's modal ontological argument hinges. I remind readers also that a maximally great being is necessarily maximally excellent, and that a maximally excellent being is essentially omnipotent, omniscient, and morally perfect. See Plantinga, *Nature of Necessity*, 214–16.

another important question: How are we to define omniscience? No small amount of ink has been spilt on the subject. It will prove quite helpful to later discussions concerning open theism if we take time to discuss some of the definitions of omniscience and issues surrounding those definitions. After briefly surveying the philosophical/theological literature concerning omniscience, I will put forward my own definition of omniscience, which I call maximal omniscience in order to bring into account the modal character of this property.

Perfect being theologians maintain that omniscience is one of the divine attributes. Although numerous definitions have been offered throughout history, all theologians and philosophers who have defended omniscience have done so at least partially because they believe omniscience is a great-making property. Most simply, omniscience is thought to be "the divine attribute of possessing complete or unlimited knowledge."[58] Additionally, cognition seems to be a species of strength, so an omnipotent being has the ability to cognize perfectly. Because we take God to be perfectly rational, we see that omnipotence (together with perfect rationality) implies omniscience since perfect cognition seems to entail omniscience, and it's obviously true that a perfectly intelligent being cognizes perfectly. Therefore, regardless of which definition of omniscience is in view, "the relevant *root* notion in discussions of God's omniscience is that of the most perfect possible knowledge."[59] Those operating within the tradition of perfect being theology must develop a definition of omniscience that is consistent with maximal greatness. Christian theologians usually motivate doctrines of divine omniscience that are perfectly commensurate with perfect being theology by appealing to numerous passages of Scripture, but two verses stand out as the best proofs of divine omniscience. First John 3:20 asserts that God knows everything, and Job 37:16 asserts that God is perfect in knowledge. These two assertions combine to form a proper definition of divine omniscience.

58. Wierenga, "Omniscience," 129.

59. Wainwright, "Omnipotence, Omniscience, and Omnipresence," 51. He continues, "But if that is correct [most perfect possible knowledge, that is], and the knowledge of all truths is logically impossible, the knowledge of all truths isn't included in the concept of the most perfect *possible* knowledge. Its impossibility therefore doesn't pose a significant threat [to omniscience]." Wainwright, "Omnipotence, Omniscience, and Omnipresence," 51. Cf. Plantinga and Grim, "Truth." However, in order for such Anselmian strategies to prove successful with respect to omniscience (or any other attribute), one must demonstrate why such a maneuver doesn't entail the possibility of multiple, equally maximally great beings, for reasons discussed in chapter 1.

Wierenga lists four of the most promising definitions of omniscience that philosophical theologians have defended. First, consider the following:

> (D1)—S is *omniscient* $=_{df}$ for every proposition P, if P is true, then S knows P.[60]

Initially, this seems to satisfy anyone seeking to defend the idea that omniscience is cognitive perfection. However, in order to avoid certain naysayer objections, Plantinga offers a modified version of this same definition. Wierenga interprets Plantinga (correctly it seems to me) as suggesting,

> (D2)—S is *omniscient* $=_{df}$ for every proposition P, if P is true, then S knows P, and if P is false, then S does not believe P.[61]

Such a modification may be unnecessary, however. I cannot improve on Wierenga's commentary, so I quote him: "Unless it is possible to know all truths and yet believe some falsehood, (D2) is equivalent to (D1). But it seems highly implausible that someone could have knowledge of all truths and nevertheless believe the denial of one of the propositions he or she knows to be true."[62] In order to avoid this highly implausible possibility, Linda Zagzebski offers an alternative definition that acutely captures the nature of the principle of bivalence. According to that principle, every proposition is either true or false. When coupled with the law of noncontradiction, every proposition is either true or false, and no proposition is simultaneously both true and false. Zagzebski suggests,

> (D3)—S is *omniscient* $=_{df}$ for every proposition P, either S knows that P is true, or S knows that P is false.[63]

60. Wierenga, "Omniscience," 130. Cf. Wierenga, *Nature of God*, 36. An almost identical definition is discussed, but not defended, by Hill in his *Divinity and Maximal Greatness*, 29.

61. Wierenga, "Omniscience," 130. Originally synthesized from Plantinga, *God, Freedom, and Evil*, 68. Both Stephen Davis and Joseph Runzo explicitly endorse this definition. See Davis, *Logic and the Nature*, 26; Runzo, "Omniscience and Freedom," 132. Cf. Wierenga, *Nature of God*, 38–39, where he identifies this definition as a modification of (D1), naming it (D1').

62. Wierenga, "Omniscience," 130.

63. Wierenga, "Omniscience," 130. This definition was originally suggested by Zagzebski in "Omniscience," 262. Technically, as stated, this definition doesn't rule out the possibility of S's believing the negation of something that S knows. However, assuming that knowledge entails belief, if S knows that *p*, then S believes that *p*. If S believes that *p*, one can reasonably infer that S does not also believe that ~*p*, especially if we take S to be God.

Peter van Inwagen suggests that we take seriously the possibility that someone can believe what they know to be false (what he deems inconsistency).

> One might define "classical" omniscience like this:
>
> An omniscient being is a being who, for every proposition, either knows that that proposition is true or knows that that proposition is false (and whose beliefs are consistent).

Or one might define it like this:

> An omniscient being is a being who, for every proposition believes either that proposition or its denial, and whose beliefs cannot (this is the "cannot" of metaphysical impossibility) be mistaken.[64]

Of course, this is very similar to a more detailed definition Van Inwagen articulates elsewhere. Wierenga summarizes that definition:

> (D4)—S is *omniscient* $=_{df}$ for every proposition P, S either believes P or the denial of P and it is metaphysically impossible that there is a proposition Q such that S believes Q and Q is false.[65]

Some of these qualifications seem unnecessary. Specifically, the fact that Van Inwagen's definitions trade on what an omniscient being *believes* makes his qualifications important. But, omniscience, as I understand it, as an expression of cognitive perfection, deals with what an omniscient being *knows*.[66] A detailed investigation of all things epistemological is well beyond the scope of this chapter, and even this thesis, but suffice it to say that if definitions of omniscience focus on knowledge rather than belief, some of the problems that Van Inwagen is concerned with turn out to be impossible. That Van Inwagen's concerns disappear when we deal with divine knowledge rather than merely what God believes is owing partially to the idea that knowledge is factive.

64. Van Inwagen, "Omniscient Being," 221.

65. Wierenga, "Omniscience," 131. Originally taken from Van Inwagen, *Problem of Evil*, 26.

66. To be fair, omniscience is frequently taken to deal also with what an omniscient being does not believe, but this is still relevantly different from what an omniscient being *does* believe. Additionally, whether or not God has beliefs is a contested matter. See Alston, "Does God Have Beliefs?" (reprinted in *Divine Nature*, 178–93); Hasker, "Yes, God Has Beliefs!" 385–94. If Alston's arguments against God having beliefs hold, then a being can be omniscient without actually having beliefs.

More importantly, his point is that a proper definition of omniscience includes a clause that precludes an omniscient being from having false beliefs. That is, what a knower *knows* must be true; what a knower *knows* cannot be false; and this knower must not believe anything that is false. Thus, it is impossible for an omniscient being to know that 2 + 2 = 5, regardless of whether God has beliefs.

On any of the definitions discussed so far, if a proposition has a truth-value, God knows whether that proposition is true or false. That might not seem to be the case for (D1), which says that God knows only true propositions, but further reflection will show otherwise. Consider the proposition "2 + 2 = 5." Of course, since this proposition isn't true, according to (D1), it seems that (D2), (D3), and (D4) account for an omniscient being's knowledge of certain facts not available to a being with (D1) omniscience. However, (D1) would allow an omniscient being to know the truth of the proposition "It is false that 2 + 2 = 5." Thus, it appears that (D1) offers as much knowledge to an omniscient being as any of the other definitions discussed thus far. However, the other definitions offer analytic clarity that proves helpful in eliminating the need to discuss certain issues such as false propositions.

But what are we to make of propositions that include indexicals, which come in quite a variety? When someone utters the locution (a) "I am painting a house," the pronoun "I" seems to convey more than personal identity, at least epistemically. That is, when someone says, "I am painting a house," this proposition reflects knowledge beyond what can be known *de re* by a similar proposition (b) "Jones is painting a house"—namely, the fact that (a) expresses *de se* knowledge by virtue of the fact that the "I" in (a) refers to the same object that "Jones" refers to in (b). Amnesia cases help to clarify why (a) and (b) express different propositions. Consider the following thought experiment, in which I suffer from partial amnesia. If a doctor asks me, "Do you believe that Ben Arbour is Ben Arbour?" I might respond, remembering some basic philosophy: "Of course! That's a tautology." But, suppose the doctor follows up by asking a simple question: "Are you Ben Arbour?" Perhaps I am unable to answer because either I don't know or I cannot remember. We can deduce from this thought experiment that the proposition (a) asserted by the sentence, "Ben Arbour is Ben Arbour" is not the same proposition (b) asserted by the sentence "I am Ben Arbour." Therefore, proposition (a) differs, at least in some way, from proposition (b). It seems, then, that only the person represented by the indexical can know propositions of the variety expressed by (a). Does this mean that God lacks knowledge of certain groups of propositions possessing truth-values? If so, does this count against divine omniscience, and perhaps even the possibility of such?[67]

Linda Zagzebski argues compellingly that God possesses an attribute she calls omnisubjectivity.[68] Utilizing a model of human empathy, she argues that God knows nearly all of the truths expressed by (b) because God is capable of perfect empathy, which is more complex than one might initially realize. Zagzebski suggests that there are five distinguishing traits of empathy:

i. Empathy is a way of acquiring an emotion like that of another person.
ii. A thinks that the fact that B has a given emotion is a reason for her to have the same emotion.
iii. When A empathizes with B, A takes on the perspective of B.
iv. When A empathizes with B, A is motivated from A's own perspective to assume the perspective of B.
v. An empathetic emotion is consciously representational. The empathizer does not adopt the intentional object of the emotion she represents as her own intentional object.[69]

According to this model, God could know all of the content in propositions such as (b). If omniscience is defined in any of the four ways mentioned above, then God must know all knowable propositions, including personally indexed propositions such as (b).[70] Thus, as Wieringa suggests, we need to expand the definition of omniscience such that

67. Thanks are due to Daniel Hill, who helped me think more deeply about omniscience, the problem of indexicals, and related issues. Many believe that indexicals prove that God cannot be omniscient. For the strongest of these arguments, see Grim, "Against Omniscience." Cf. Kretzmann, "Omniscience and Immutability." Castañeda offers the best attempt at showing that personally indexed propositions reduce to, and can be expressed by, propositions without any personal indexes. See Castañeda, "Omniscience and Indexical Reference." However, I remain unconvinced by these arguments, as does Hill, who provides numerous counter examples which show why Castañeda's arguments fail. Cf. Hill, *Divinity and Maximal Greatness*, 41–44.

68. Zagzebski, "Omnisubjectivity."

69. Zagzebski supports each of these points with commentary in her article. The individual points are taken from Zagzebski, "Omnisubjectivity," 238, 238, 239, 239, 240, respectively.

70. I do not mean to suggest something trivial by defining omniscience such that God must know all knowable propositions, such that a lack of knowledge of what is logically unknowable wouldn't count against omniscience. I elaborate on this below, and at length in the next chapter.

> (D5)—S is *omniscient* $=_{df}$ for any proposition P and perspective < *x* >, (i) if P is true at < *x* > then S knows that P is true at < *x* >, and (ii) if S is at < *x* > and P is true at < *x* >, then at < *x* > S knows that P.[71]

On this point, Zagzebski offers an important comment, which I quote at length:

> Suppose instead that Patrick Grim is right and the proposition expressed by (1) [I made a mess in the market and everybody is staring at me] differs from the proposition expressed by (3) [She (e.g., that woman in the mirror) is making a mess and people are staring at her], and only I can know (1). This is a problem for omniscience if omniscience entails knowing the truth-value of all propositions. But if the only difference between knowing (3) and knowing (1) is the point of view, it is reasonable to think that a being who knows (3) and who also perfectly empathizes with me when I know (1) knows everything I know when I know (1). This solution will not satisfy anyone who insists that an omniscient being must know the very same proposition I know and that the proposition expressed by (1) differs from that expressed by (3), but I think that this account succeeds in preserving cognitive perfection even if it does not succeed in preserving one traditional account of omniscience. On the view of this paper God knows exactly what is going on at every moment, and in addition, God knows what each conscious state directed at what is going on is like, including first-person states. It seems to me that this account makes God's knowledge more perfect that it is on the standard account of omniscience even if Grim is right that God doesn't know propositions like (1).[72]

71. This definition includes only personal perspective, a slight modification of what Wierenga offers in "Omniscience," 137. His modification of (D1) (which is typographically errant in being labeled (D4), because Wierenga has already attributed the label (D4) to Van Inwagen's definition on page 131) includes temporal indexicals in addition to personal indexicals, but I have excluded temporal indexicals at this point in order to reserve comment on that subject later in the chapter. I include Wierenga's exact modified definition later. Although Wierenga takes indexicals into account in this definition, the problem hasn't been solved. If there are personally indexed propositions, and if God is necessarily unable to be at personal indexes other than God's own, then it follows that God isn't omniscient because there exist truths unknown to God. My thanks to Daniel Hill for helping me realize this.

72. Zagzebski, "Omnisubjectivity," 244.

So far as I can see (and I think Zagzebski would concur),[73] there is no reason to deny the metaphysical possibility of an omnisubjective being—especially if God is omnipresent.[74] She supports her view with Scripture, citing Ps 139 as evidence for divine omnisubjectivity.

> Oh Lord, you have searched me and you know!
> You know my sitting and my standing;
> You understand my thoughts from afar.
> My journey and my lying down, you observe,
> And you are familiar with all my ways.
>
> Because not even a word is on my tongue
> Behold, oh Lord, you know it altogether.
> Behind and before, you hem me in;
> Your hand is ever set upon me.[75]

Zagzebski continues, "Some lines in this poem might suggest the image of God following me around like a shadow, marking my movements, his hand ever upon me. But when the psalmist says, 'All my ways lie open to you,' 'Before ever a word is on my tongue, you know it,' that suggests that God is much more intimately bound to me than a shadow."[76] The fact that God not only knows but also "understands" our thoughts from afar lends credit to Zagzebski's thesis. Of course, this comes as no surprise to Christians, who maintain that humans are made in the image of God. Furthermore, believers (such as David, who is thought to have

73. Zagzebski, "Omnisubjectivity," 242.

74. Although I think defenses of omnisubjectivity can succeed (especially those based on omnipresence), I believe Zagzebski's own account of omnisubjectivity fails. To have empathy presupposes that someone already knows what it is like to feel *x*; so Zagzebski can't use empathy as an explanation for why God know what it is like to feel *x*. Wessling points this out in chapter 5 of his dissertation, "The Christian God of Love," at the University of Bristol. Thus, I motivate a doctrine of divine omnisubjectivity with divine omnipresence. For cogent and lucid defenses of accounts of the kinds of divine omnipresence that enable alternative accounts of omnisubjectivity, see both Hudson, "Omnipresence"; Wainwright, "Omnipotence, Omniscience, and Omnipresence," 52–64.

75. Psalm 139:1–5, my translation. Interestingly, Kvanvig motivates his understanding of divine omniscience from this same passage of Scripture. See Kvanvig, *Possibility*, ix. Regardless, Kvanvig does not think that the existence of indexed propositions presents a problem to the traditional understanding of omniscience. See Kvanvig, *Possibility*, 46.

76. Zagzebski, "Omnisubjectivity," 244–45.

authored Ps 139) are united to God by faith. The apostle Peter writes that we have become partakers of the Holy Spirit (2 Pet 1:4). Perhaps these theological notions help to account for divine omnisubjectivity, but I leave further pursuit of, and application of, these themes to biblical theologians rather than analytic philosophers.

Presumably, omnisubjectivity supports certain cognitive perfections associated with omniscience, and we know that omniscience is a great-making property. Therefore, appealing to the same type of argumentation that establishes our understanding of God as a maximally great being, I suggest that God is omnisubjective. Apart from any evidence against the possibility of omnisubjectivity, we do well to think that the conceivability of omnisubjectivity entails its metaphysical possibility. Furthermore, it seems that no being can enjoy the cognitive perfections necessary for omniscience without omnisubjectivity. If this is true, omniscience logically entails omnisubjectivity. Because God is the greatest of all possible beings, God must possess omnisubjectivity. I now want to show how this attribute helps to alleviate some (but not all) of the tensions raised against omniscience based on personally indexed propositions, and also how omnisubjectivity also disarms similar objections based on temporally indexed propositions.

Throughout history, the vast majority of Christian philosophical theologians have believed that existing timelessly is superior to existing temporally. However, in relatively recent times, understanding timelessness as one of the divine perfections has fallen out of favor. Some philosophers have even attempted to use the concept of divine timelessness to show that God, if timeless, cannot be omniscient. William Wainwright offers a very basic form of such an argument. Despite the fact that Christians have traditionally included omniscience among the divine attributes, Wainwright contends that this need not mean that God knows all truths, for, on his account, there are certain truths that God cannot know. He asks,

> Yet *can* God know all truths? There are reasons for thinking that he can't. In the first place, if God is timeless it seems that he can't know some things I know. For example, God can timelessly know that at 7 P.M. on July 2, 2010, I assert the true sentence 'It is now 7 P.M.' God can also timelessly know that a thunderstorm occurs at my location at 7 P.M. on July 2, 2010. But it seems that he can't know that it is NOW 7 P.M. or that the thunderstorm is *now* starting, for knowing what time it now is or that an event

> is now starting (or has started or will start) presupposes that the knower is in time and, by hypothesis, God isn't. But of course I *do* know things like these. It thus appears that I know things that God can't know. If I do, God doesn't know everything and so isn't omniscient.[77]

Consider a variation of Wainwright's position. Take a proposition such as (c) "Today is a sunny day." If we presuppose for the sake of argument that God is timeless, could God know such a proposition?[78] Some philosophers (including many B-theorists about the philosophy of time) believe that proposition (c) is identical to proposition (d) "May 31, 2016 is a sunny day."[79] However, other philosophers object to this idea because they think that the way that a personal pronoun indexes a person in proposition (a) "I am Ben Arbour," is similar to the way that "today" indexes a particular time that doesn't reduce to a date stamp such as May 31, 2016. If God is timeless such that the divine essence does not experience temporal progression in the same way that we do, it seems that God cannot know propositions such as (c). But, many do not believe this poses any problem for divine omniscience. Wainwright articulates why: "The *mode* in which God knows temporal happenings differs from that in which we know them, for we are in time and God is not. But *what* we know (substances, events, and their relations) is the same."[80]

Suppose that B-theorists are incorrect regarding the identity of (c) and (d).[81] On the A-theory of time, the present is dynamic such that the present moment is always changing. Given divine maximal greatness, and therefore divine omniscience, God must always know the present, so it follows that God's knowledge of the present is always changing. Many believe this change is sufficient for being temporal, so God must

77. Wainwright, "Omnipotence, Omniscience, and Omnipresence," 48–49.

78. For an excellent synopsis of various competing positions regarding God's relation to time, see Craig, "Divine Eternity."

79. Helm, "Eternal Creation"; Helm, *Eternal God*, 25–27, 44, 47, 52–79. Again, I withhold detailed commentary on the difference between A-series and B-series understandings of time until the next chapter, in which I will explain these concepts in much greater detail. The information regarding the B-theorist's position on temporally indexed propositions relevant to the point I make here is sufficiently explained in the main text. Philosophers who defend this idea as it relates to divine omniscience include: Kvanvig, *Possibility*, 150–65; Kvanvig, "Omniscience and Eternity"; Wierenga, *Nature of God*, 179–85; Wierenga, "Omniscience and Time"; Leftow, *Time and Eternity*, 312–27.

80. Wainwright, "Omnipotence, Omniscience, and Omnipresence," 49.

81. To clarify, not all B-theorists defend this position regarding temporal indexicals in tensed propositions.

be temporal if his knowledge of the present is ever changing. One way to avoid this conundrum is by defending the B-theory of time, such that there is no present that changes (as "the present" is merely indexed from a perspective), together with divine omnipresence.[82] Thus,

> (D6)—S is *omniscient* $=_{df}$ for any proposition P and perspective < *t* >, (i) if P is true at < *t* > then S knows that P is true at < *t* >, and (ii) if S is at < *t* > and P is true at < *t* >, then at < *t* > S knows that P.[83]

This definition is thought to stave off problems raised by temporal indexicals. However, as is the case with Wieringa's modification of omniscience to account for personal indexicals, so, too, does the same problem present with respect to temporal indexicals. Supposing with the tradition that God is timeless, clause (ii) proves useless because God is never at any time. If God is timeless, and if there are temporally indexed propositions, it seems that God must be ignorant of these truths. Alternatively, if there are no temporally indexed propositions, then this clause is unnecessary.

As I hinted above, divine omniscience has interesting applications for the issue of God's relation to time. William Lane Craig defends an argument for divine temporality on the basis of divine omniscience. His argument, although simple and straightforward, proves unsuccessful in definitively establishing divine temporality. Craig writes,

26. A temporal world exists.
27. God is omniscient.
28. If a temporal world exists, then if God is omniscient, God knows tensed facts.
29. If God is timeless, he does not know tensed facts.
30. Therefore, God is not timeless.[84]

82. Special thanks to Jordan Wessling for bringing this to my attention. He suggests that given divine omnipresence and a four-dimensional understanding of B-theoretic approaches to time as spacio-temporal, God may be properly understood to be omnitemporal (although he does not defend this view). Wessling also notes that this view need not rely on omnisubjectivity, which seems correct to me. However, because of the impact of omnisubjectivity on how maximal omniscience is related to God's relationship to time, which I discuss immediately below, it seems best to defend omnisubjectivity.

83. Again, this definition includes only temporal perspective, a slight modification of what Wierenga offers in "Omniscience," 137. Recall that his modification of (D1) includes not only temporal indexicals but also personal indexicals.

84. Craig, "Divine Eternity," 160, numeration in original. See also Craig, "Omniscience."

The argument is valid, but one man's *modus ponens* is another man's *modus tollens*. One could just as easily argue as follows:

31. God is omniscient.
32. God is timeless.
33. If God is timeless, God does not know tensed facts.
34. If a temporal world exists in such a way so as to give rise to tensed facts, then if God is omniscient, God knows tensed facts.
35. But it is impossible for it to be true both that God does not know tensed facts and that God knows tensed facts.
36. Therefore, the world is not temporal in such a way so as to give rise to tensed facts.

The fact that one's indexically conditioned experience of the present is constantly changing (from the phenomenological perspective of a perceiver) does not mean that God's knowledge is always changing, for God's knowing that I know what time it is seems insufficient to establish God as a temporal being. Thus, if Craig maintains that one can successfully argue for divine temporality on the basis of omniscience *alone*, he fails to establish what he thinks his argument does. Rather, it must be the case that the world includes tensed facts that cannot reduce to date and time stamps, and it must be the case that in order for God to count as omniscient, God must know all truths.[85] However, a refutation of Craig's argument does not necessitate that God is timeless. Rather, it means only that how one reasons concerning divine omniscience and whether or not God enjoys knowledge of temporally indexed propositions does not definitively establish divine temporality. In light of this, it seems that whatever God's relation to time is should be settled by appealing to other arguments.

If omniscience requires that God knows, for each proposition, whether that proposition is true or false, and that for all true propositions God knows those truths, including personally indexed, temporally indexed, and personally/temporally indexed propositions, then we need to account for how God can know "I am Ben Arbour" or how a

85. Notice that Craig's argument, given the way he reasons concerning an implied definition of omniscience, seems to presuppose some solution to the equally vexing problem of personal indexicals. After all, if one assumes God can still count as omniscient without knowledge of all truths (perhaps because some truths are logically unknowable), then what harm is there in denying that God enjoys knowledge of tensed facts, especially if one thinks it logically impossible for a timeless being to know tensed facts?

timeless being can know "It is now 5:00." It seems to me that the claim that only Ben Arbour can know "I am Ben Arbour" relies on the presupposition that the content of the proposition "I am Ben Arbour" cannot be comprehended apart from anyone's existential experience of being Ben Arbour. By parallel reasoning, a similar presupposition leads one to think that knowing the content of "It is now 5:00" requires existential experience of time. It very well might be that the content of "I am Ben Arbour" does not reduce to "Ben Arbour is Ben Arbour," as Grim and others have argued. Moreover, it might be that God cannot know "I am Ben Arbour" apart from existentially *being* Ben Arbour. Additionally, although Zagebski's doctrine of omnisubjectivity helps preserve some of the cognitive perfections associated with omniscience, not even omnisubjectivity allows God to know exactly what I know when I know "I am Ben Arbour." Recall that she states,

> This solution will not satisfy anyone who insists that an omniscient being must know the very same proposition I know and that the proposition expressed by (1) differs from that expressed by (3), but I think that this account succeeds in preserving cognitive perfection even if it does not succeed in preserving one traditional account of omniscience.[86]

Nonetheless, Grim and others who argue in this manner move too quickly in concluding that God cannot be omniscient.

Daniel Hill offers a comprehensive survey of the literature on divine omniscience that includes a solution proposed by the late David Lewis.[87] Lewis "suggests that we construe the objects of belief, and, hence, knowledge, as properties rather than propositions."[88] Given several other aspects of Lewisian philosophy, including the idea that properties are sets of possibilia and the idea that propositions are sets of possible worlds, whereupon a distinct property corresponds to every proposition, we get the following definition of omniscience:

> (D7)—For every being, *x*, *x* is omniscient if and only if, for every property, *F*, *x* warrantedly self-ascribes *F* if and only if *x* possesses *F*.[89]

86. Zagzebski, "Omnisubjectivity," 244.

87. Hill, *Divinity and Maximal Greatness*, 54–59. Cf. David Lewis, "Attitudes *De Dicto*."

88. Hill, *Divinity and Maximal Greatness*, 54.

89. Hill, *Divinity and Maximal Greatness*, 55. Hill identifies this definition with the marker (D2.1) in the original text.

On this definition, it is no problem for omniscience that God doesn't know "I am Ben Arbour" because

> the definition accommodates our intuition that in some sense no one else can truly believe what I believe when I believe that I'm Daniel Hill, yet this does not count against omniscience. It introduces relativity, but relativity concerning the possession of properties, rather than truth. In other words, Lewis does not allow any relativity among propositions, since they are sets of possible worlds, among which the actual world is either absolutely a member or absolutely not a member. Clearly, however, there is relativity concerning the possession of properties: it makes no sense to ask whether a property is absolutely possessed or not; one needs to ask, "possessed by what?"[90]

After explaining how the complexities involving indexicals impact this definition, Hill proposes a modification to the Lewisian definition of omniscience:

> (D8)—For every being, *x*, *x* is omniscient if and only if for every being, *y*, and for every property, *F*, and for every description, *Z*, if *Z* captures the essence of *y* or *Z* is a relation of acquaintance that *x* bears to *y*, then *X* ascribes *F* to *y* under *Z* if and only if *y* has *F*.[91]

The type of relativity that this definition uses isn't relativity of truth. Rather, "the relativity of the definition is safely contained: what is relative is that different individuals will bear different relations of acquaintance to an object, which is harmless."[92] Despite the fact that the Lewisian definition of omniscience avoids several vexing problems, it turns on the counterintuitive idea that propositions are not the objects of belief.

So we must continue to find a definition of omniscience that avoids problems concerning indexicals without giving up the idea that propositions are the objects of beliefs. Let us suppose that it is logically impossible for anyone other than Ben Arbour to know what I know when I know "I am Ben Arbour." Initially, this admission seems to entail that God lacks a tremendous amount of knowledge, and one wonders what other types of knowledge God lacks. Opponents of divine omniscience

90. Hill, *Divinity and Maximal Greatness*, 55.

91. Hill, *Divinity and Maximal Greatness*, 58. In the original text, Hill identifies this definition with the marker (D2.3).

92. Hill, *Divinity and Maximal Greatness*, 58.

might suggest that any and all types of phenomena that yield some existential experience cannot be known apart from some experience of the phenomena in question, but this would be much too quick.

If omnisubjectivity is possible, then perhaps God's inability to know "I am Ben Arbour" does not eliminate the possibility of his knowing everything about what it is like to be Ben Arbour. This does not solve the problem of indexicals, but it does solve the problem of *qualia*.[93] Given God's vast knowledge of all the relevant data, perhaps God knows everything about me, and even what it is like for me to be me. It is uncontroversial that God can know *that* I know that "I am Ben Arbour." Even if God cannot know *what* I know when I know "I am Ben Arbour," God can still know what it is like to be Ben Arbour. If knowledge of the relevant facts about me is enough for God to obtain knowledge of what it is like to be Ben Arbour, then we must acknowledge that at least some of God's knowledge is discursive knowledge, rather than direct knowledge. What may be the case, then, is that an omnisubjective being other than Ben Arbour can know everything about what it is like to be Ben Arbour in an indirect (discursive) way apart from existential experience of being Ben Arbour.

Some will retort that God still lacks the knowledge, then, of what it is (like) to *be* Ben Arbour. But the reply misses the point of the argument. Omnisubjectivity addresses the presupposition that certain knowledge requires existential experience. My claim is that an omnisubjective being need not experience *being* Ben Arbour in order to know, via synthetically adding all the relevant data together, what it is for Ben Arbour to be Ben Arbour, even though God is certainly a different being than Ben Arbour, and vice versa. Hence, although God lacks the experience of *being* Ben Arbour, God does not lack the knowledge of what it is like to be Ben Arbour, albeit through synthetic and discursive means.

Some will be concerned about affirmations that divine knowledge is anything other than direct. That is, discursive or synthetic knowledge doesn't seem befitting of God.[94] I am sympathetic to this concern. How-

93. For a detailed analysis of the possibility of God's knowledge of *qualia*, see Hill, *Divinity and Maximal Greatness*, 66–68.

94. So, Rogers, *Perfect Being Theology*, 70–76. Cf. Aquinas, *Summa Theologica* I, Q. 85; Aquinas, *Summa Contra Gentiles* 1.66.7. The issues involved in the mode of divine knowledge, and the subject of divine epistemology generally considered, are fascinating and deserve much more attention than I can possibly afford them here. As will become clear, I want to defend that God enjoys knowledge in whatever turns out to be the most perfect, logically possible way. After all, "It would be fatuously

ever, I am unaware of any way of preserving knowledge of certain truths, which seems to be important to divine omniscience, apart from appealing to indirect divine knowledge. Were there some way to preserve direct, non-discursive knowledge of all that can be known, I would gladly endorse as much. Nonetheless, if there is no such way of preserving direct knowledge of all truths, it seems better to me to advocate for divine knowledge of *de re* propositions even if doing so entails giving up a preferable mode of knowledge. The alternative of denying genuine omniscience is surely less palatable for those who favor Anselmian approaches to perfect being theology. Of course, all of this assumes that it is possible to preserve divine knowledge of all truth in the first place, but this may turn out to be a logical impossibility.

Still others will object that omnisubjectivity doesn't achieve what is needed to preserve genuine omniscience. After all, issues in philosophy of mind require that in order to have genuine *de se* knowledge of a given proposition such as "I am Ben Arbour," the knower must be Ben Arbour.[95] Objections of this nature seem to miss the forest for the trees because they fail to take into account the details of what adding "perspective < x >" and "perspective < *t* >" in (D5) through (D8) accomplishes. To state the obvious, since Ben Arbour is not God, it isn't true from God's perspective that "*I* am Ben Arbour" in the *de se* sense, or that "It *is* 5:00" if God is a timeless being. And surely God knows that Ben Arbour is not God, so God cannot know "I am Ben Arbour" in the *de se* sense, for such is false, and nothing that is false can be known since knowledge is factive. Omnisubjectivity, however, by way of perfect empathy, gets God all the relevant information so that it makes sense to say that God knows what it is like to be Ben Arbour, even though God isn't Ben Arbour and Ben Arbour isn't God. That God lacks the *de se* knowledge doesn't impugn omniscience, not only because such knowledge isn't possible (although that is also the case), but more importantly because it isn't true for God. From the divine perspective, the proposition "I am Ben Arbour" is false.[96] So, even if God doesn't know in the *de*

unjustified at best, and blasphemous at worst to attribute to [God] some second-rate mode of knowledge." Alston, "Does God Have Beliefs?," 298. However, my primary focus throughout this project is the *scope* of divine knowledge rather than the *mode* in which God knows what God knows.

95. As this pertains to the current discussion, here I have in mind Jackson, "Epiphenomenal Qualia"; Jackson, "What Mary Didn't Know"; and some of the essays in Ludlow et al., *There's Something About Mary.*

96. I explain why defenses of omniscience that hinge on modal claims about impossible knowledge fail to preserve genuine omniscience in chapter 3.

se sense that "I am Ben Arbour," God still knows all that can be known, and the mode of knowledge at issue with *de se* propositions is precisely why God *doesn't* know "I am Ben Arbour" in the *de se* sense.[97]

With all of this in place for personally indexed propositions, by parallel reasoning we can see rather easily how a timeless being can know what it is like to be in time despite a lack of knowledge of tensed facts and lacking the existential experience of being in time. If God is timeless, then perhaps God lacks the ability to know tensed facts, but the fact that God lacks knowledge of tensed facts (if they exist) doesn't impugn omniscience. Again, that divine omniscience is preserved is owing to the fact that tensed facts aren't true from the divine perspective. From the vantage point of divine timeless eternity, the proposition "Today is May 31, 2016" is false. A timeless God can, however, via omnisubjectivity, know what it is like to know tensed facts and experience temporal progression by adding all the relevant data together (thus making God's knowledge of tensed facts synthetic). God has indirect (discursive) knowledge of all the relevant data by perfectly knowing his creation, which does experience time. Hence, God can discursively know what it is like to experience time, *pace* Wainwright, even if God lacks the existential experience of time. Any rebuttal that God still lacks knowledge of what it is like to experience time commits the same error as noted above when discussing personally indexed propositions.

Interestingly, this defense of omniscience only works if God is timeless.[98] On the supposition that the key to knowing tensed facts is the *de se* character of such knowledge, it seems that if God were temporal, then God would lack *de se* knowledge of timelessly indexed propositions. Thus, omnisubjectivity preserves classical omniscience only if God is timeless, for otherwise it seems that God would lack the ability to know personally indexed timeless truths, even discursive or synthetic knowledge of such, for omnisubjectivity only allows for such knowledge given the existence of some other timeless being who knows timelessly indexed propositions (and all of them, at that).[99] The combination of personally

97. Nagasawa suggests a similarly styled argument in his "Divine Omniscience and Knowledge."

98. Presumably, if God (who is the ground of all being) were temporal, then there would be no timeless propositions.

99. Cf. Helm, "Divine Timeless Eternity," 40–42. I reserve further comment on the nature of God's relation to time for chapter 5. In chapters 4 and 5, I focus on those open theists who acknowledge that propositions concerning future contingents are either true or false, whom I call limited foreknowledge open theists. The discussion

indexed and temporally indexed omniscience, which can be defended by way of Zagzebski's doctrine of omnisubjectivity, can be articulated as Wierenga's robust definition of omniscience:

> (D9)—S is *omniscient* $=_{df}$ for any proposition P and perspective $< x, t >$, (i) if P is true at $< x, t >$ then S knows that P is true at $< x, t >$, and (ii) if S is at $< x, t >$ and P is true at $< x, t >$, then at $< x, t >$ S knows that P.[100]

In a recent article, Daniel Diederich Farmer goes beyond Zagzebski's omnisubjectivity in arguing that feminist approaches to epistemology offer a more comprehensive account of what omniscience entails. Building on the work of Lorraine Code,[101] Vrinda Dalmiya,[102] and Alison Jaggar,[103] Farmer believes that certain types of knowledge are best captured by way of knowledge of other persons rather than knowledge of propositions. Thus, rather than construe omniscience along lines such as "S knows that *p*," we should instead involve knowledge "of" others, not merely knowledge "about" others.[104] As a result, Farmer believes "S knows S" epistemologies offer more to defenders of divine omniscience than do articulations of such that depend on traditional propositional approaches.

For this reason, rather than defining omniscience along propositional lines (which Farmer suggests are based on the model of the "ruling male"), Farmer suggests an alternative understanding of omniscience based on divine omnipresence. "Better resources for 'naming towards God,' then, are provided when we imaginatively reconnect God's knowledge and presence. God *knows* all, on this model, because she is present *in* all."[105] This seems to account for God's knowledge of that which cannot

---

of God's relation to time will prove vital to proving unsuccessful attempts to preserve omniscience offered by another strand of open theism, which I call open future open theism, whose advocates deny that any propositions concerning future contingents are presently true.

100. Wierenga, "Omniscience," 137. Given divine omnipresence, this definition also accounts for special indexicals such as "here" and demonstratives such as "this" or "that."

101. Code, "Taking Subjectivity into Account."

102. Dalmiya, "Why Should a Knower Care?"; Dalmiya and Alcoff, "'Old Wives' Tales' Justified?"

103. Jaggar, "Love and Knowledge."

104. Farmer, "Defining Omniscience," 312–13.

105. Farmer, "Defining Omniscience," 316. Farmer incorporates the phrase "naming towards God" from feminist theologian Johnson, *She Who Is*, 62. One need not rely

be rendered propositionally, such as what an instrument sounds like, or what a color looks like.[106]

All that stated, there do seem to be two rather serious problems with Farmer's account of divine omniscience. First, because Farmer is so reluctant to give a place to any propositional accounts of omniscience, God's knowledge must be based on omnipresence and omnisubjectivity, so divine knowledge appears to be mediated by other agents. Therefore, none of God's knowledge is direct, but rather is discursive. As a result, God's knowledge of that which cannot be rendered propositionally appears to be part of his free knowledge rather than his natural knowledge. That is, God knows what a clarinet sounds like only because he is aware of what a person hears when she hears a clarinet (or what a dog hears when it hears a clarinet). But it is certainly a cognitive ideal to know as much as can be known directly, so some modification of Farmer's thesis is in order.[107] Perhaps even God cannot know certain facts such as personally indexed propositions, or temporally indexed propositions (if God is timeless) apart from some mediating agent(s). But I see no reason to attribute God's knowledge of necessary truths such as the laws of logic or mathematical truths (which ought to be categorized as part of God's natural knowledge) to God's perfect knowledge of contingent beings (which obviously situates knowledge of necessary truths as part

on overly feminist renderings of omniscience here, especially since divine omnipresence, as classically construed, or even as defended by Hudson, accomplishes the same thing. Cf. Hudson, "Omnipresence."

106. Cf. Wittgenstein, *Philosophical Investigations*, §116, where he writes, "Compare *knowing* and *saying* how many feet high Mont Blanc is; how the word 'game' is used; how a clarinet sounds. If you are surprised that one can know something and not be able to say it, you are perhaps thinking of a case like the first. Certainly not one like the third." As a musician, I think elements of sound can be expressed propositionally, at least for those with a trained ear. So, when someone describes my guitar, when played well, as producing a "warm" yet "crisp" sound, I understand their meaning, especially when compared against another guitar that sounds "tinny." But any further investigation into the philosophy of language as it relates to propositions concerning music or aesthetics in general is well beyond the scope of this project. I interject these comments only to show that possible defenses of propositional accounts of omniscience might be mustered, even against Wittgensteinean objections, were someone motivated to do so.

Farmer relies on an interesting and somewhat analogous puzzle concerning color he takes from Jackson, "Epiphenomenal Qualia." Zagzebski takes a similar example from Jackson, "What Mary Didn't Know."

107. Cf. Alston, "Does God Have Beliefs?," 297. Most theists deny that God's knowledge is discursive. Instead of knowing by inference, perfect being theologians have traditionally understood God to grasp truth directly, perhaps by intuition. Also, cf. Nagasawa, "Divine Omniscience and Experience," 94–99.

of God's free knowledge). Thus, while I partially agree with Farmer that some knowledge is knowledge *of* and not always merely knowledge *that*, I want to preserve the cognitive ideals for perfect being theology demanded by maximal greatness. It's best to say that God knows all that can be known—all that there is *to* be known—as perfectly as such can be known. Accordingly, we should acknowledge that some truths are known directly by God, whereas those truths which either cannot be known directly are still known by God, but are known discursively.

Farmer acknowledges that such a reformulation of omniscience in the way he proposes cannot "ultimately be reconciled with so-called 'meticulous' conceptions of providential control."[108] Moreover, the philosophical defense Farmer offers in making this concession rests on the version of open theism which I call Limited Foreknowledge Open Theism (LFOT) as developed by William Hasker in his seminal work *God, Time, and Knowledge*. But, as I show in the next two chapters, Hasker's account of divine omniscience is quite problematic, especially in the light of Anselmian conceptions of maximal greatness.

A better way forward, then, heeds Taliaferro's suggestion that we follow the tradition in understanding that "the notion of God's omniscience was conceived of as the exercise of God's omnipotent power," which entails that "it is metaphysically impossible for there to be a being with greater cognitive power."[109] Alston articulates a similar view in arguing that direct awareness of all facts "represents the fullest and most perfect realization of the cognitive ideal."[110] Regardless of how specific one gets in offering a nuanced definition of omniscience, it must be the case that if God is omniscient, then God knows all facts that have truth-values.[111] That is, God knows all truths. Furthermore, if omniscience entails the perfection of divine cognitive powers as it pertains to the cognitive

108. Farmer, "Defining Omniscience," 319. He goes on to cite three open theists in defense of this concession: Fretheim, Sanders, and Hasker.

109. Taliaferro, "Divine Cognitive Power," 135 and 133, respectively. This does not, however, require us to say that omniscience is dependent upon omnipotence, and might not even require that omnipotence entails the power to become omniscient (although I am inclined to affirm the latter). I mean only to suggest that there is a connection between divine knowledge and divine power. This clarification is important for reasons I discuss towards the end of this chapter.

110. Alston, "Does God Have Beliefs?," 297.

111. This qualification—that the cognitive ideal entails knowledge of all truths—is extremely important, especially since the connection of omniscience to omnipotence could provide a way out for those who maintain that certain truths are unknowable. I discuss this at length in the next chapter.

ideal, and if the perfect use of divine cognitive powers entails that direct knowledge is a superior mode of knowing than discursive knowledge, then all facts that can be known directly must be known directly by God. True, Farmer does advance the discussion concerning omniscience, and his contributions need to be taken into account. Omniscience (which, we are reminded, literally means "all-knowing") certainly entails that an omniscient agent knows all truths, even truths that cannot be rendered propositionally. But this hardly means that no truths can be rendered propositionally. Thus, in preserving the cognitive ideal, some definition which combines Farmer's contributions with the best of the propositional accounts of omniscience is in order.

Daniel Hill offers the following definition:

> (D10)—For every being, *x*, *x* is omniscient if and only if, for every type of belief state, *B*, if *x* is in a token of *B* then *x*'s token of *B* has as object a true proposition, and if *x* is not in a token of *B* then if *x* were in a token of *B* then *x*'s token of *B* would have as object a false proposition.[112]

This definition avoids the problem of indexicals, and with two minor modifications we can arrive at a definition that avoids problems raised by Farmer.

> (D11)—For every being, *x*, *x* is omniscient if and only if, for every type of belief state, *B*, if *x* is in a token of *B* then *x*'s token of *B* has as object a truth, and if *x* is not in a token of *B* then if *x* were in a token of *B* then *x*'s token of *B* would have as object a falsehood; and, *x* enjoys all cognitive perfections such that everything known by *x* is known perfectly and, therefore, infallibly.

On this definition, if there is anything that God does not know, it must be the case that such knowledge is logically impossible for God, and, were God to be in a token of such a belief state, *per impossible*, that token would have as object a falsehood. Also, by removing any references to propositions, this definition accommodates concerns raised by Farmer and others regarding the nature and extent of divine omniscience. Additionally, the perfection clause in this definition preserves other perfections in an omniscient being's knowledge, which is supported by Scripture (Job 37:16), and should be interpreted as including the exercise of maximal cognitive powers. Consider two people, Suzie and Bobby. If both work

112. Hill, *Divinity and Maximal Greatness*, 64.

on a math exam and earn perfect scores, but Suzie finishes with ease and in half the time it takes Bobby (who finds the exam very challenging), it would seem that Suzie's cognitive powers are superior to those of Bobby. In God's case, because divine omniscience entails the maximally perfect cognitive ideal, it follows that a properly Anselmian description of omniscience requires construing the divine intellect as obtaining all knowledge as efficiently as possible. Such entails that divine deliberation almost never happens, except in those cases where it is metaphysically impossible to obtain knowledge without discursive reasoning.[113]

Next, let us examine the infallibility clause. If we consider the same two people, Suzie and Bobby, and were to give them dozens of math exams, and if Suzie works the exams more quickly than Bobby but Suzie lacks the property of being infallible, despite her better speed, it seems that she lacks the perfect cognitive ideal, despite her quickness and earning the highest scores on her exams. If Bobby is infallible in working math exams, it seems that despite his inability to work the problems as quickly as Suzie, he does possess a cognitive perfection that Suzie lacks. If omniscience is the perfect cognitive ideal, then an omniscient agent's perfect knowledge entails not only a lack of deliberation, but also infallibility in knowledge. But there are two ways of understanding divine infallibility: either God is accidentally infallible (which opens the possibility of God holding incorrect beliefs in other possible worlds) or God is essentially infallible (whereby in all worlds in which God exists it is impossible that God hold incorrect beliefs).

Recall that Anselmian perfect being theology entails that God is a maximally great being. I take it as obvious that essential infallibility is superior to accidental infallibility. A maximally great being would not only be omniscient in the sense that such a being knows everything that can be known and knows directly all that can be known directly, but would also be infallible and essentially so. Thus, the perfection clause of the (D11) definition of omniscience, together with the notion of maximal greatness established by Anselmian perfect being theology requires not only that God know all knowable truths, but that God cannot—it is

113. The issue of speed is also raised by Kvanvig, although in an entirely separate context. Kvanvig addresses this issue when comparing competing epistemologies while preparing to advocate his own account of virtue epistemology. See Kvanvig, *Intellectual Virtues*, 99. Cf. Pendergraft, "Divine Deliberation."

not possible for God—to be wrong about any truth, nor can God fail to know any truth.[114]

With this (D11) definition of omniscience in view, I now begin explaining why Anselmian perfect being theology, and the doctrine of omniscience that it entails, is incompatible with various models of open theism. In the next chapter, I'll show that the (D11) conception of omniscience, together with Anselmian intuitions, precludes the efforts on the part of open theists who attempt to save omniscience on LFOT by appealing to modal reformulations of omniscience. Open theists deny that God enjoys exhaustive definite foreknowledge, and most open theists deny that this impugns divine omniscience.[115] I will now show why arguments offered for holding Anselmian perfect being theology together with LFOT ultimately prove unsuccessful.

114. Thus, my definition of omniscience, together with both an understanding of omniscience as a great-making property as well as the concept of maximal greatness established by Anselmian perfect being theology, preserves the notion of God's essential omniscience and essential divine infallibility. I concur with the way Zagzebski defines these properties: "*A* is *essentially omniscient* ↔ It is impossible that *A* exist and fail to know the truth value of any proposition." And, "*A* is *essentially infallible* ↔ It is impossible that *A* fail to be infallible. For any proposition *p*, if *A* believes *p* at any time in any world, *p* is true in that world." Zagzebski, *Dilemma of Freedom*, 5.

115. The word "definite" may appear redundant and overly nuanced in the phrase "exhaustive definite foreknowledge," especially given a theory of knowledge that requires truth as a condition for knowledge. The phrase comes from Gregory Boyd, whose view is parsed rather technically but entails denying that God knows which future contingents will obtain. See Boyd, *Satan and the Problem*, 86. The "definiteness" also gets around the Geachian idea that the metaphysics of prevention allows for propositions concerning future contingents to change their truth-value both from false to true and from true to false, even multiple times! Cf. Geach, *Providence and Evil*; and Todd, "Geachianism." In light of these difficulties, it seems that Tuggy's suggestion of "temporally complete knowledge" is a better phrase to capture all that is at issue. See Tuggy, "Roads to Open Theism," 46n3.

3

Maximal Greatness, Divine Omniscience, and Limited Foreknowledge Open Theism

In the previous chapter, after discussing perfect being theology, I briefly discussed omnipotence and went on to offer (D11) as a definition of omniscience: for every being, *x*, *x* is omniscient if and only if, for every type of belief state, *B*, if *x* is in a token of *B* then *x*'s token of *B* has as object a truth, and if *x* is not in a token of *B* then if *x* were in a token of *B* then *x*'s token of *B* would have as object a falsehood; and, all that *x* knows is known perfectly and, therefore, infallibly. I maintain that Scripture supports this definition, so Christians should understand omniscience in this way, at least as long as we defend Anselmian understandings of theology proper. Given this definition of omniscience, I will now show how and why it is that modal reformulations of omniscience fail to preserve the proper scope of divine knowledge that is necessary for Anselmian perfect being theology. William Hasker, Peter van Inwagen, and Richard Swinburne each defend a version of open theism that I call limited foreknowledge open theism (hereafter LFOT). These three open theists each deny that God possesses knowledge of the truth-values of at least some propositions concerning future contingents (PCFC), and they each affirm that at least some of these same propositions concerning future contingents are presently true. Nonetheless, all three of these thinkers insist that they affirm divine omniscience. In what follows, I argue that such a position is untenable, and that arguments for modal reformulations of divine omniscience fail for a variety of reasons.

Open Theism, Omniscience, and Maximal Greatness

Open theism comes in a variety of expressions. In fact, a survey of the relevant literature shows that although some commonalities exist among almost all the varieties of open theism, the way that openness advocates arrive at their respective positions varies greatly.[1] The most obvious commonality among open theists is the belief that libertarian accounts of freedom require not only source incompatibilism, but also what is called the Principle of Alternative Possibilities (PAP). According to PAP, an agent can be held morally responsible for an action if and only if either: (a) the agent had it within her power, at minimum, to choose to refrain from performing the action, or perhaps she could have performed some other action altogether; or (b) if the agent lacked the ability to do otherwise in that particular situation, the reason she lacked such an ability is because of other decisions she made previously during which her character and psychological tendencies became sufficiently concretized to form who she is such that she wouldn't choose to do otherwise—and these decisions were made when she genuinely did have the ability to do otherwise. Believing that humans should be held responsible for their actions, open theists maintain that a multiplicity of genuinely available options must be live metaphysical possibilities.[2] Furthermore, open theists believe this type of freedom is incompatible with exhaustive definite foreknowledge. Thus, in an effort to alleviate tensions created by the dilemma of freedom and foreknowledge (DFF), openness advocates deny that God knows which future contingents will obtain.[3]

Philosophers and theologians have offered numerous versions of the DFF; some are more complex than others. For our present purposes, any version that creates a dilemma significant enough to persuade a theist to opt for "theological incompatibilism" (i.e., either eliminating divine

1. For more on this, see Rhoda, "Generic Open Theism."

2. Even apart from the theological implications of this view, various accounts of what constitutes human freedom remains a hotly contested topic of discussion among metaphysicians. For an excellent overview of contemporary discussions, see Kane, "Introduction" (2005), 3–41; as well as Kane, "Introduction" (2011), 3–35.

3. I assume that readers are familiar with the basic outline of the freedom/foreknowledge dilemma. For those unfamiliar with the debate, an excellent overview is provided by Pike in his "Divine Omniscience and Voluntary Action," as well as Van Inwagen, "What Does an Omniscient?," 216–30, especially 216–23; Hasker, *God, Time, and Knowledge*, 64–74. Additionally, more in-depth analyses can be found in Craig, *Divine Foreknowledge*; Robinson, *Eternity and Freedom*, 1–25; Zagzebski, *Dilemma of Freedom*, especially 3–35.

foreknowledge by adopting open theism to preserve significant freedom, or eliminating the ability to do otherwise by adopting some type of determinism to preserve divine foreknowledge) instead of another solution will be sufficient to work with, at least during this chapter.[4] So consider an uncomplicated version of the DFF, which has come to be called the simple incompatibility argument:

> If God knows that I will do A, then surely I must do A.
>
> God knows that tomorrow I will do A (whatever that may be).
>
> Therefore, tomorrow I must do A.[5]

Mavrodes argues, "Since I *must* do A I have no freedom with respect to A."[6] If one *must* do some action, then according to the open theist, that person is not significantly free with respect to A. The alleged incompatibility between freedom and foreknowledge comes into sharper focus when divine foreknowledge of future contingents is juxtaposed with the idea that future choices are not determined, either metaphysically (as maintained by some naturalists) or theologically. That is to say, most people's natural inclination is to think that we are free to choose to do, or choose not to do some action A in the future. If God infallibly knows what choice we will make, how can we possibly do otherwise? Of course, if we lack the freedom to do other than what we end up doing, then there is no problem with God's knowing what we will do. However, if we are free in the relevant sense, then it seems that God cannot know whether or not we will or will not do A—or at least this is what open theists want us to conclude.

It is easy to see why some theologians find open theism appealing—it simply does away with the DFF by denying that God has foreknowledge of future contingents. Philosophers and theologians have offered various articulations of open theism, each of which offers a unique interpretation of why God does not (or cannot) know the truth-value of PCFC. Philosophically interesting versions of open theism are quite detailed and

4. Recall that I, following the conventional open theism literature, use the term "theological incompatibilism" to denote the idea that the significant freedom (i.e., freedom according to libertarian accounts) and divine foreknowledge cannot be co-instantiated. For additional clarification, see footnote 57 in the previous chapter.

5. Mavrodes, "Is the Past Unpreventable?," 131.

6. Mavrodes, "Is the Past Unpreventable?," 131. I discuss the concept of free will as it relates to the ability to make choices that are not metaphysically determined (which is held by all open theists) below.

nuanced, so much so that it seems almost no two open theists share perfectly identical views. It is beyond the scope of this project, and certainly this chapter, to detail all of the positions of every significant contributor in the philosophical/theological discussions pertinent to open theism. However, we should identify those groupings of open theistic doctrine that allow themselves to be analyzed such that we need not break down the specifics of each individual philosopher/theologian. One of the more obvious divisions among openness thinkers is whether or not PCFC presently have truth-values. Some thinkers such as William Hasker, Richard Swinburne, and Peter van Inwagen believe that some PCFC are presently true, while others such as Dean Zimmerman, Alan Rhoda, Dale Tuggy, and Gregory Boyd maintain either that all PCFC are false or that they presently lack truth-values of any kind at all.[7] In this chapter, it is the former grouping, advocates of LFOT, with which I concern myself; I take up alternative open theistic systems (which I call open future open theism, hereafter OFOT) in later chapters.

Just as anything beyond this brief sketch of some of the varieties of open theism is beyond the scope of this chapter, so, too, is an in-depth survey of free will, or even an in-depth survey of one account of free will such as agent-causal libertarianism (indeed, beyond the scope of the project). However, in order to better understand open theistic motivations, I will briefly comment on open theistic conceptions of free will. All open theists believe that humans are significantly free, in the libertarian sense of free will. However, we should be even more specific than merely stating that humans are free in the libertarian sense, especially since philosophers differ over what exactly constitutes libertarian freedom (hereafter LFW).[8]

7. Numerous others hold/have held to the latter of these positions, which Tuggy calls "the wide road." Included among those thinkers are Socinian theologians, process theologians, Charles Hartshorne, A. N. Prior, and Bas van Fraasen. See Tuggy, "Roads to Open Theism," 30–34.

Swinburne is another very important contributor to the discussion, himself an open theist. His view fits best alongside Hasker and Van Inwagen, but his only comment in print (that I am aware of) is that, "in normal usage, propositions about a named future time . . . are true or false—timelessly. We may not *know* them to be true or false, until the occurrence of that of which they speak. That which makes them true or false may also lie in the future. But what I claim may be true, even if I do not know it to be true, and even if what I claim has yet to occur." Swinburne, *Coherence of Theism*, 180. The phrases "in normal usage" and "timelessly," as Swinburne uses them in the first sentence of this quotation, give me pause in definitively identifying him with Hasker and Van Inwagen.

8. Two major strands of LFW include event-causal libertarianism (defended most

All open theists maintain that in order for humans to possess significant freedom—which open theists believe is necessary in order to preserve moral responsibility[9]—humans must have the ability to choose between various possible options that are not metaphysically determined.[10] The options, or possibilities, need not be understood as choosing between more than two options, but rather necessitate only that an agent is free just in case she has the ability to choose between performing or not performing some action. Thus, Hasker (representative of LFOT)

notably by Laura Ekstrom) and agent-causal libertarianism (defended by many, including O'Connor and Timpe). For an overview of the former position, see Ekstrom, "Libertarianism and Frankfurt-Style Cases," 309–22; Clarke "Libertarian Views," 356–85. For an overview of the latter, see O'Connor, "Libertarian Views," 337–55; and his more recent essay "Agent Causal Theories"; as well as O'Connor, *Persons and Causes*.

9. Of course, it isn't only open theists who believe that moral responsibility requires the ability to do otherwise. However, open theists insist that the ability to do otherwise is the essence of freedom. In describing what he calls a strong definition of freedom, Pinnock writes, "The idea of moral responsibility requires us to believe that actions are not determined either internally or externally." Pinnock, "God Limits His Knowledge," 149. Later in the same essay, in describing the relationship between God's will and his knowledge, Pinnock argues that meticulous providence "implies that freedom is not freedom because there are not genuine alternatives." Pinnock, "God Limits His Knowledge," 153–54.

10. Hasker defends this idea in great detail throughout *God, Time, and Knowledge*, but especially on pages 66–69. Additionally, he briefly outlines how PAP fits together with various theories of time, as well as proposed solutions to the DFF in his "Eternity and Providence," 84 and 87. In arguing against the B-series, or four-dimensional view of time, Hasker writes, "If the events of my future timelessly exist in the inalterable four-dimensional continuum, the 'alternative possibilities' needed for free will simply are not there; it is categorically impossible that I should perform any action different than the one that exists timelessly in the space-time continuum." See Hasker, *God, Time, and Knowledge*, 84.

Van Inwagen defends LFW in *An Essay on Free Will*. In all fairness to the complexity of the situation, Van Inwagen does not believe that PAP is always a necessary condition of free will in the libertarian sense. However, that humans make decisions and choices that are not metaphysically determined *is* a necessary condition of significant freedom, at least according to Van Inwagen. Insofar as free will relates to open theism, the possibility of doing or not doing some action is vital to Van Inwagen's argument for theological incompatibilism as a response to the DFF as expressed in "What Does an Omniscient?," 216–20. There, Van Inwagen constructs his version of the freedom/foreknowledge dilemma by raising the question of whether God could know that someone would lie or tell the truth. Of course, this choice is sufficient such that even Hasker's understanding of PAP applies in this case, for a choice between lying and telling the truth is parallel to the decision to lie or not to lie (to perform *A* or refrain from performing *A*). Part of the difficulty in analyzing Van Inwagen's position stems from the fact that Van Inwagen's own position has shifted from a strict libertarian account of freedom towards libertarian mysterianism in response to objections to his previously held position. See Van Inwagen, "Free Will Remains."

offers the following definition of freedom, which I take to be a precise articulation of a libertarian account of free will:

> (FW) N is free at *T* with respect to performing *A* $=_{df}$ It is in N's power at *T* to perform *A*, and it is in N's power at *T* to refrain from performing *A*.[11]

Hasker later clarifies and further nuances his libertarian account of free will in defining it as follows.

> (FW') N is free at *T* with respect to performing *A* $=_{df}$ It is in N's power at *T* to perform *A* and it is possible at *T* for N to exercise that power, and it is in N's power at *T* to refrain from performing *A*, and it is also possible at *T* for N to exercise *that* power.[12]

On the view advocated by all open theists (not just Hasker, Swinburne, and Van Inwagen, but surely including them), the existence of this kind of freedom entails that those portions of the future that are to become actual, which are not metaphysically determined, cannot be known by God because the future is presently undetermined. Instead, the future remains "open" to multiple possibilities. Although all these possibilities and all the possible futures that could result from any choice are known by God in virtue of divine natural knowledge (which includes knowledge of all possible modalities), God does not know which of a potentially infinite number of possible futures will actually obtain. Additionally, all

11. Hasker, *God, Time, and Knowledge*, 66.

12. Hasker, *God, Time, and Knowledge*, 138. To clarify yet further, one need not be committed to the idea that a human has free will for every decision he makes in order to be a libertarian on the matter of free will. Regardless of which account of libertarianism one defends, all that needs be defended is that at least some of our actions are free in the libertarian sense. Thus, just because we find ourselves in certain situations where we make decisions that do not seem truly free given our character and psychological tendencies, this does not preclude a defense of libertarian accounts of freedom. I note character and psychological tendencies because Hasker denies that choices that someone makes which are made on the basis of the overwhelming influence of character and/or psychological tendencies are free in the libertarian sense. Hasker, *God, Time, and Knowledge*, 24, 31.

Furthermore, even those who defend the libertarian account of free will are likely to acknowledge that we might be morally responsible for actions we take even if certain actions are not free in the libertarian sense. This might be because previous actions that we took have concretized our character such that our psychological tendencies prevent us from having PAP in a given decision. However, so long as a person was responsible for the formation of his character in making earlier decisions, then the fact that his character is so concretized is his own doing, and therefore he is still morally responsible for his actions.

open theists deny that any of the proposed solutions to the DFF succeed.[13] Because they see no alternative, and because of their commitment to human LFW, openness advocates reject the view that God enjoys exhaustive definite foreknowledge.[14] With this understanding of openness views of human freedom, let us now more carefully examine LFOT.

All proponents of LFOT share a strong commitment to the idea that the principle of bivalence applies to PCFC. This principle states that for any proposition *p*, it is either the case that *p* is true, or it is the case that *p* is false, and, because of the Aristotelian law of non-contradiction, it is impossible that both *p* and ~*p* be true at once. Restated, assuming the principle of bivalence and the law of non-contradiction, all propositions are either true or false, so either *p* or ~*p*, and it is not the case that both *p* and ~*p*.

Advocates of LFOT maintain that all propositions are either true or false, including not only propositions about aspects of the future that are determined but also PCFC. Some open theist philosophers deny that the principle of bivalence applies to propositions concerning future contingents because truth-values do not exist for future contingents, given a particular take on the metaphysics of time.[15] Unlike these open futurists (among whom are Zimmerman, Rhoda, Boyd, and Tuggy), advocates of LFOT believe that PCFC *do* have truth-values. Thus, when someone declares, "I will read a book sometime next year," according to LFOT, despite the fact that God lacks knowledge of whether this

13. Among the possible solutions currently on offer, defenders of both LFOT and OFOT reject: compatibilistic conceptions of free will (which is an alternative to LFW), divine timelessness as eliminating the problem of "foreknowledge," Molinism, and Ockhamism. Additionally, because they have no desire to punt to antinomy, like other open theists, Hasker and Van Inwagen are happiest in resolving the DFF by denying that God knows which future contingents will obtain.

14. It is worth noting that both Hasker and Van Inwagen (and Swinburne as well) seem to rely on what Craig calls a perceptualist model of divine knowledge, in which God would "foresee" the future and thus "foreknow" what will happen. This, Hasker and Van Inwagen argue, is impossible, for the future does not exist to be "seen." However, a conceptualist model of divine knowledge eliminates this problem, for God's knowledge is not based on perception, but rather "is more like a mind's knowledge of innate ideas. It is therefore inappropriate to speak of God's *acquiring* knowledge at all. Rather, as an omniscient being, God has essentially the property of knowing all truths; there are truths about future events; *ergo*, God knows all truths concerning future events." Craig, "Divine Eternity," 148–49. This is another argument (rather undeveloped, it seems to me) against the openness account of divine omniscience I offer later in this chapter.

15. In chapter 6 I discuss in some detail the metaphysics of God and time as well as what differing views concerning the truth-values of future contingents entail for divine omniscience.

proposition is true, the proposition to which this utterance refers is presently either true or false.

LFOT's affirmation that the principle of bivalence applies even to PFPC ought not be confused with simple affirmation of the obvious. Limited foreknowledge open theists do not mean to suggest that it is true that "either I will or will not read a book sometime next year," for this amounts to nothing more than an affirmation of the law of the excluded middle. Instead, advocates of LFOT mean to affirm that it is either true or false that "I will read a book sometime next year." Furthermore, nothing changes on their view if the personal and temporal indexicals are removed. Thus, "Ben Arbour will read a book sometime in 2017," is either true or false. What makes such a proposition true or false? Van Inwagen answers this question lucidly in a passage that deserves quoting at length:

> Anyone who wishes to embrace the thesis that at least some propositions about events subsequent to *t* are neither true nor false at *t* will have to find some sort of response to the following argument (it can obviously be generalized, for it does not depend on any feature peculiar to propositions about future sea-battles):
>
> The proposition that there will be a sea battle at *t* [where *t* is some moment in the future] is true if and only if there will be a sea battle at *t*
>
> The proposition that there will be a sea battle at *t* is false if and only if it is not the case that there will be a sea battle at *t*
>
> *hence,*
>
> Either the proposition that there will be a sea battle at *t* is true or the proposition that there will be a sea battle at *t* is false.
>
> This argument—it is formally valid—is a rather hard argument to get round. I should not like to have to try to find something wrong with it. (And, in any case, it is hard to see how someone who believes that God exists outside time and is omniscient can coherently suppose that propositions about events subsequent to *t* are neither true nor false at *t*.)[16]

Hasker holds the same view, which he calls the omnitemporality of truth. He defends this view against the idea that PCFC are neither true

16. Van Inwagen, "Omniscient Being," 220. See also Van Inwagen, *Essay on Free Will*, 52–54. Van Inwagen's reference to Aristotle's *De Interpretatione* is obvious.

nor false, noting that those views are quite controversial and that his position "seems not to lend itself to further argument as readily as the considerations that arise if the existence of truths about the contingent future is granted."[17]

Of course, affirming that PCFC have truth-values entails radical consequences for defenders of LFOT. If statements such as "Ben Arbour will read a book in 2017" are either true or false, and it is the case that I am endowed with LFW, then because LFOT is a version of theological incompatibilism,[18] it must be the case that there are some true facts which even God does not know. Hence, advocates of LFOT cannot affirm that God knows all truths. And despite all his protestations to the contrary, Boyd is simply wrong to deny that LFOT entails God's lacking comprehensive foreknowledge; it is a simple fact of the matter that, on LFOT, God is not all-knowing.[19] In fact, on this view, there are a great many truths that God does not know. As Richard Swinburne states, defenders of LFOT, if consistent, acknowledge that God's ignorance is vast:

> To leave God with any freedom at any time, God's omniscience must be understood in a restricted way. The obvious natural restriction that God is ever ignorant of how he will act, except when rational considerations, that is, his perfect goodness,

17. Hasker, "Foreknowledge Conundrum," 112n10. See also Hasker, *God, Time, and Knowledge*, 107–8, 122–25; Tuggy, "Roads to Open Theism," 48n18. In that footnote, Tuggy details an equivocation on the part of Hasker, which can only be cashed out if Hasker abandons the "narrow road" and travels along the "wide road." For one interesting view that denies that PCFC follow the regular bivalent systems of logic (in which propositions have only two values, either true or false), see Purtill, "Fatalism and the Omnitemporality."

18. Hasker's most thorough defense of open theism is his *God, Time, and Knowledge*. However, he has also defended this position in numerous journal articles. Van Inwagen details his account of open theism in "Omniscient Being," especially page 230, where he states, "God does not foreknow the free acts of human beings."

19. Boyd, *God of the Possible*, 124–26. Boyd has since changed his view, for he now defends OFOT. Despite the fact that he rejects "the wide road" version of open theism offered by Hasker, Swinburne, and Van Inwagen, Tuggy nods incorrectly in agreement with Boyd, calling such characterizations of open theism "obnoxiously question-begging." See Tuggy, "Roads to Open Theism," 46n3. Tuggy, himself an open theist, agrees that such views entail too weak a definition of omniscience—"It takes the 'omni' out of 'omniscience,' for according to it, an 'omniscient' being can fail to know an infinity of truths. Such a being may know a lot, we are inclined to say, but doesn't know all, even though he may know more than any other being in existence, or perhaps even more than any other possible being could know. One can see why some of Hasker's critics are given to complaints that he and other open theists 'deny omniscience' or 'deny foreknowledge.'" Tuggy, "Roads to Open Theism," 29.

> require him to act in a certain way, has the consequence that, since in virtue of God's omnipotence the whole future of everything depends on God (including whether there are any free human beings after the present instant), his ignorance of the future must be vast—confined only to what his perfect goodness requires him to bring about.[20]

So in no way can God rightly be called all-knowing if PCFC have truth-values that remain as of now unknown to God.

Anticipating objections, Hasker offers an alternative definition of omniscience. "God is omniscient," for Hasker, means that "it is impossible that God should at any time believe what is false, or fail to know any true proposition such that his knowing that proposition at that time is logically possible."[21] In clarifying that God need not know all truths in order to be omniscient, Hasker states, "God's omniscience entails his knowing, not all true propositions whatsoever, but only those that it is logically possible for him to know."[22] In order to add some element of perfection to divine knowledge, Hasker adds, "(C2) It is impossible that God should at any time believe what is false, or fail to believe any true proposition such that his knowing that proposition at that time is logically possible. (Premise: divine omniscience)."[23] Hasker believes that (C2) is a definition of omniscience that both theological compatibilists (those who believe that solutions to the DFF exist) and theological

20. Swinburne, *Christian God*, 134. He immediately follows this by arguing that such "ignorance does not diminish his greatness, since it arises from the greatness of his power over the future." I will not take up the issue of divine freedom at this juncture, for it is well beyond the scope of this chapter and my project. I use this quote only to show that Swinburne, himself an open theist, is consistent in recognizing what his position entails with respect to divine knowledge whereas other proponents of openness theology are not.

21. Hasker, *God, Time, and Knowledge*, 187. More recently, Hasker states, "Omniscience . . . means that God knows everything that is logically capable of being known." Hasker, "Foreknowledge Conundrum," 111. Basinger agrees with this definition of omniscience. Basinger, *Case for Freewill Theism*, 39; Basinger, "Can an Evangelical Christian," 133. Cf. Tuggy, "Roads to Open Theism," 46n4. Pinnock offers a similar definition: "God is omniscient in the sense that he knows everything which can be known, just as God is omnipotent in the sense that he can do everything that can be done. But free actions are not entities which can be known ahead of time." Pinnock, "God Limits His Knowledge," 157. However, Kvanvig offers yet another argument as to why a definition similar to my (D11) is superior to the modal definition offered by Hasker. See Kvanvig, "Analogy Argument."

22. Hasker, *God, Time, and Knowledge*, 73. Craig also notes that he believes this account of omniscience is unsatisfactory in "Divine Eternity," 164n7.

23. Hasker, *God, Time, and Knowledge*, 73.

incompatibilists (those who deny that solutions to the DFF exist) can agree on.[24] Towards the conclusion of his book, Hasker offers a final definition of divine omniscience:

> (DO) God is omniscient $=_{df}$ It is impossible that God should at any time believe what is false, or fail to know any true proposition such that his knowing that proposition at that time is logically possible.[25]

This definition of omniscience is similar to (D11), but there is a significant disagreement amongst Christian philosophers and theologians as to whether it is logically possible for God to enjoy knowledge of PCFC. Insofar as Christians aren't bothered by God's lacking knowledge of certain indexical truths such as "I am Ben Arbour" because such knowledge is logically impossible, so, too, should Christians not be bothered by God's lacking knowledge of PCFC, or so advocates of LFOT might argue. However, this assumes that open theism is the only legitimate response to the DFF, and that is exceedingly controversial.

Also, Hasker fails to differentiate between the two very different types of theological incompatibilists: (1) those who deny that humans possess the ability to do otherwise, such as the vast majority of Reformed theologians who deny that humans possess LFW; and (2) open theists, who go the other direction by denying that God enjoys exhaustive definite foreknowledge. In fact, Hasker rightly notes that both of his arguments for theological incompatibilism lead to equally valid conclusions for either (1) or (2). He goes on to suggest incorrectly that "relatively few incompatibilists accept this conclusion [(1)—that humans do not possess freedom according to the libertarian account]."[26] But Hasker is simply mistaken about this, for a brief survey of theological history will show that very few theological incompatibilists affirm (2). Instead, it has been far more popular to deny (2) in affirming God's exhaustive definite foreknowledge by either denying that humans have LFW, or affirming some version of theological compatibilism.[27] Regardless of this, I take is-

24. Hasker, *God, Time, and Knowledge*, 74.

25. Hasker, *God, Time, and Knowledge*, 187.

26. Hasker, *God, Time, and Knowledge*, 73.

27. In fact, the only historical examples that open theists could cite include the Socinians and perhaps Jerome. Swinburne relayed the possibility of Jerome's inclusion among open theists to me in a personal conversation which took place at the University of Notre Dame, sometime during a conference celebrating the retirement of Plantinga, May 20–22, 2010.

sue with Hasker on this point because (C2) is an insufficient definition of omniscience, which I demonstrate below.

Richard Swinburne agrees with Hasker's nuanced definition of omniscience. When offering his own account, Swinburne argues that

> it seem to me more satisfactory to . . . define God's omniscience accordingly, not as knowledge at each period of time, of all true propositions, but as knowledge of all propositions that it is logically possible that he entertain then and that, if entertained by God then, are true, and that it is logically possible for God to know then without the possibility of error.[28]

But Swinburne's proposal entails other problems for divine freedom if we maintain that certain future events are known by God. And, for the Christian tradition, abandoning God's knowledge of certain theological truths concerning eschatology is not a viable option. Not enough philosophers or theologians have recognized what Swinburne notes in writing that

> God, if he is necessarily and eternally perfectly free, must be ignorant of his own future actions—except in so far as his perfect goodness . . . constrains him to act in certain ways. And since he is omnipotent, and thus able to make any difference he chooses to the future, he must in general be ignorant of that future.[29]

If certain truths regarding the last days are established, as must be maintained given Christian commitments to the veracity of Scripture, particularly the book of Revelation, then God must know that there will be a universe in the future, which precludes God's deciding not to uphold the universe; and this entails a denial of divine freedom in this regard. But could God know this? Many philosophers think not. Daniel Hill argues,

> So it seems that, if we are to preserve the omnipotence and infallibility of every divine being, then we must admit that every divine being has hardly *any* non-trivial beliefs about the future, since even the belief that there will be something non-divine tomorrow is one that a divine being could make false by annihilating everything else. It seems as if all we are left with as possible beliefs for a divine being are that he will exist tomorrow and that he will not do evil tomorrow, and similar beliefs about his necessary actions, and all the beliefs that the set of these entails.

28. Swinburne, *Christian God*, 133. Cf. Swinburne, *Coherence of Theism*, 172–83.
29. Swinburne, *Christian God*, 134.

> It seems odd to admit that humans have more true beliefs about the future than a divine being does. It also seems odd to admit that no divine being knows, or even has a view about, whether the universe will exist tomorrow. Every divine being could, of course, know the *probability* that there will be a universe tomorrow, and presumably this probability will be high, but no divine being has a view about the simple question of whether or not there will be a universe tomorrow.[30]

However, Swinburne notes that the preservation of such divine knowledge is allowable if the elimination of those freedoms, which would preclude such knowledge, is necessitated by God's perfect goodness. If God knows these truths about the future, then God has always known them, and it must have been the case that God knew he would create this world, and therefore lacked the freedom to not create it.[31] But this lack of freedom requires that God has eternally lacked such freedom, which means that God lacked LFW in deciding what kind of world to create. This might bolster the arguments favoring the creation of the so-called best of all possible worlds, given God's moral perfection, but it also comes at a significant price, namely, abandoning any notion of divine freedom with respect to what type of world to create, or even whether or not to create at all.

Linda Zagzebski appears to be more sympathetic to some of Hasker's concerns regarding definitions of omniscience and knowledge of what is logically possible. She writes,

> It will be objected that it is no violation of omniscience to be unable to do what it is impossible to do. For example, those who deny infallible foreknowledge typically claim that the future is unknowable in an infallible way. Hence, the lack of infallible

30. Hill, *Divinity and Maximal Greatness*, 87. In a paper presented to the Society of Christian Philosophers, Greg Ganssle raised similar concerns. Ganssle, "God's Knowledge." Building on some of Ganssle's work, Robinson published an extensive critique of open theism based on the radical cost to divine knowledge in general that is entailed by denying God's complete and exhaustive foreknowledge. See Robinson, "Why Divine Foreknowledge?"

31. My claim here is not that divine perfect goodness necessitates creation, for Swinburne explicitly denies this, although Swinburne affirms conditionals of the sort such that "if God were to create a world, its inhabitants could not be treated unjustly." Rather, my claim is that if God enjoys knowledge of the future of a world that God created, and if God has always known as much (which is entailed by divine omniscience), then there is a dilemma of divine freedom and divine foreknowledge that, given divine infallibility, necessitates the creation of the world as God knows it.

> foreknowledge is no violation of divine omniscience. Similarly, it can be argued, if the conscious states of other beings are unknowable in the way they know those states themselves, then it is no violation of omniscience if God fails to have such knowledge.
>
> It seems to me perfectly true that it is no violation of omniscience to be unable to do the impossible, but just as defenders of infallible foreknowledge maintain that there is a very strong prima facie case that omniscience (more accurately, essential omniscience) includes infallible foreknowledge, similarly I want to maintain that there is a very strong prima facie case that omniscience entails the ability to perfectly grasp the conscious states of every conscious being and to be able to distinguish among them.[32]

But defenses of divine omniscience resting on the inability to know truths that are logically unknowable fail for many reasons, which I will now detail.

First, according to some advocates of LFOT, it isn't that these truths are unknowable *simpliciter*, but rather that God chooses not to know them.[33] Clearly this is an inadequate view of omniscience, for this view essentially amounts to something along the lines of: "God is not omniscient, technically speaking, since God does not know all truths, but that's only because he chooses not to know them."[34] Obviously, no one can coherently maintain that God chooses not to be omniscient while simultaneously affirming omniscience, much less Anselmian perfect being theology, which entails that God is essentially omniscient. If God is a maximally great being, the road to open theism in which God chooses to limit what God knows is blocked by the metaphysics of perfect

32. She continues, "If the ability I describe in this paper is impossible, then it is not entailed by omniscience and God doesn't have it. But I will argue that it is not impossible, at least, its possibility should not be ruled out." Zagzebski, "Omnisubjectivity," 234. If the impossibility to know things is of no concern to the defender of omniscience, at least part of the motivation for open theism is eliminated in that there seems to be little if any advantage of the A-theory of time over the B-theory, at least with respect to temporally indexed propositions, for it would pose no threat to omniscience if God were unable to know propositions such as "Today is a sunny day," for such knowledge is logically impossible. More on this in the next chapter.

33. Cf. Pinnock, "God Limits His Knowledge." I will comment more on the idea of God's limiting his knowledge later.

34. That some maintain that this lack of knowledge, by choice, still counts as omniscience strikes me as absurd. I do not understand the logic of the argument that "God chooses to limit his knowledge such that he does not know all truths" somehow still amounts to "God is an omniscient, all-knowing being."

being theology. Given Anselmian perfect being theology, all of God's great-making attributes (including omniscience) are not contingent or accidental properties of the divine nature, but rather are essential to the divine nature.[35] Thus, given Anselmian perfect being theology and the modal metaphysics derived from it, there are no worlds in which God chooses to be anything other than omniscient. In fact, worlds in which God voluntarily gives up omniscience are worlds that don't even exist in the realm of possibilia, so it's obvious that this world—the one that has been actualized—isn't one in which God is anything less than omniscient. In fact, since no such world exists even in the realm of possibilia, it follows that such worlds are metaphysically impossible, in the broadly logical sense, given a Plantingian metaphysics of modality.

Other advocates of LFOT take a different approach. Instead of arguing that God willingly limits his knowledge, some maintain that certain truths, given LFW, are simply unknowable even to God. These thinkers maintain that omniscience doesn't demand that God actually know all truths, but rather that God knows all truths that are logically knowable.[36] Although this initially appears to be an attractive defense of LFOT, it also fails. Even if divine knowledge of PCFC were logically impossible, the resulting conception of omniscience is far too weak. Suppose God were to create Simon, a creature whose essence makes knowledge of anything besides "2 + 2 = 4" metaphysically impossible; the only truth that Simon can know is "2 + 2 = 4." Due to Simon's essence, it is logically impossible that he knows anything else. On Hasker's definition, Simon is omniscient, which is patently absurd.[37] Thus, Hasker's definition of omniscience must be rejected.

35. Again, for more on this, see Morris, "Properties, Modalities, and God."

36. Hasker pushes this line of thinking in many places, but one example will suffice. "This [open theistic] line of thinking should not be seen as a denial of omniscience, any more than it is a denial of omnipotence to say that God cannot perform actions that are logically impossible." Hasker, "Analytic Philosophy of Religion," 437.

37. This example is analogous to the infamous Mr. McEar, who is omnipotent on some accounts of omnipotence despite the fact that the only thing McEar can do is scratch his left ear. If omnipotence is defined as the ability to do all that is logically possible, then if all McEar can logically do is scratch his ear, then he qualifies as omnipotent, which is obviously problematic for a genuine account of omnipotence. Unsurprisingly, the same holds for omniscience. The fact that no one has so remarked against Hasker's definition of omniscience is a bit surprising (although I should note that Hill offers a similar, albeit different, argument about McStupid, but he does not bring it to bear against open theism). See Hill, *Divinity and Maximal Greatness*, 44. McEar was first put forward as a counterexample to certain articulations of divine omnipotence in Plantinga, *God and Other Minds*, 168–73, but Flint and Freddoso recognize that a similar case was present in William of Ockham in their essay "Maximal Power," 109–10n4.

Another attempt to defend the openness view comes from Dallas Willard who offers an interpretation of omniscience that he believes is analogous to omnipotence. Just as maximal power does not entail that God actually does all that he has the power to do, so, too, does Willard think that divine omniscience guarantees God's ability to know all truths, not that he actually does.[38] But this account fails for two reasons. First, according to Hasker, Swinburne, and Van Inwagen, it isn't that God chooses not to know; rather, God *cannot* know the truth-values of propositions concerning future contingents; such knowledge is logically impossible.[39]

Second, Willard's account of omniscience isn't analogous to the modal claims involved in Thomistic understandings of omnipotence, at least not in the way that Willard seems to suggest. Potentiality is a virtue when one considers omnipotence, but the potential to know something doesn't guarantee the same virtues when one considers omniscience. When considering power, the ability to perform a given action even if that agent doesn't actually perform the action still counts as a great-making property; but this is only partially so when it comes to knowledge. Suppose two people both have the ability to learn how to perform open-heart surgery, but one lacks the knowledge of how to do so at *t*, while the other has already finished medical school. It seems that the latter is greater than the former, in at least one sense. It doesn't matter which person is more intelligent; if I needed to have open-heart surgery, I would elect that the latter perform the surgery rather than the former, even if by all accounts the former is deemed the smarter of the two. This counterexample shows that it is not merely the ability to know truths that is great-making with respect to omniscience, although it is trivially true that a being with the ability to know is greater than a being without this ability. Moreover, it is the actual possession of the knowledge itself that yields the most robust great-making features of any account of omniscience.[40] Thus, given any two beings, the one who knows more

38. Willard expresses his views in *Divine Conspiracy*, 244–53. Sanders summarizes Willard's position well in an essay entitled "On Heffalumps and Heresies," 7. It is difficult to know where exactly Willard himself stands on the issue of divine foreknowledge. Perhaps he is an open theist, but it is also possible that he merely defends the possibility of alternative conceptions of divine omniscience against those he believes are overly critical of open theism.

39. Van Inwagen elaborates on this in an interview for the Closer to Truth series. See Van Inwagen, "If God Knows," 9:14.

40. That knowledge itself is valuable is demonstrated by the fact that "we want more of it, and consider it the sort of thing that we would like to be possessed by any children

than the other is, *ceteris paribus*, greater than the less knowledgeable being. Therefore, a maximally great being must be actually omniscient, thereby knowing all truths, rather than just potentially so. As a result of this line of argumentation, Willard's proposal fails.

Finally, let us consider how the concept of maximal greatness as established by Anselmian perfect being theology weighs in against LFOT. Suppose for a moment that arguments against the compatibility of exhaustive definite foreknowledge and LFW are correct, as open theists suggest. Supposing further that the principle of bivalence applies to PCFC, and also that at least some PCFC are presently true, then in order for God to rightly qualify as omniscient, God must know which PCFC are true. In light of this fact, it's worth restating that on LFOT, God is not omniscient, because God doesn't know all truths.

One might object that if God creates a world in which conscious agents other than God exist, then God already lacks knowledge of 100 percent of all truths because God lacks knowledge of *de se* propositions involving personal indexicals. According to (D11) standards of omniscience, advocates of LFOT might seek to get out of this conundrum by suggesting that knowledge of PCFC is logically impossible. However, divine ignorance concerning true PCFC remains a problem for defenders of LFOT, and this move cannot be squared with (D11) omniscience. To put it succinctly, *it is* not *the case that if God's token beliefs were of true PCFC that these tokens would have as objects falsehoods*, but this is what would need to be the case for the analogous reasoning concerning *de se* propositions to save LFOT. It may be that God has good reasons for creating agents who enjoy consciousness such that God lacks knowledge of 100 percent of all truths; and God may also have good reasons for endowing creation with LFW. However, given that there are alternative accounts of time that philosophers think it sufficient to preserve LFW and ground PCFC, it doesn't obviously follow that God's

---

we have. In addition, we are, I think, inclined to admire the knowledgeable and pity the ignorant—else why are there so many knowledge contests in the media?" Hill, *Divinity and Maximal Greatness*, 27. Hill goes on to make a case that knowledge is not just instrumentally valuable, but is intrinsically valuable, as evinced by the fact that there are so many who devote entire careers to pursuing knowledge in various disciplines. Hill, *Divinity and Maximal Greatness*, 27. Although sympathetic to his position, I am not as yet convinced that knowledge is intrinsically valuable, as there seem to be cases where knowledge is evil (i.e., a literal reading of the fall of man as described in Genesis). However, the idea that knowledge genuinely counts as great-making seems to be undisputed when considering omnibenevolent beings, and all the more so in the case of a perfect being, especially an omniperfect being.

lack of knowledge of true PCFC is a special problem for Anselmians.[41] After all, once tense is removed from the equation (which can be done via divine timelessness and also with B-theoretic aspects of the moving spotlight theory), we are not left with temporally indexed truths that cannot be known by God. We are left wondering how it can be that some PCFC can be true in a way that preserves LFW, yet God cannot know these truths. Arguments that it is divine foreknowledge of such truths that eliminates LFW rather than the alethic settledness of these PCFC prove problematic, as I demonstrate in the next chapter.

There is more to say than this, especially since advocates of LFOT offer modal reformulations of omniscience to assuage concerns about unknown truths. As it turns out, on LFOT, God's decision to create beings with LFW results in imposing a limit on divine foreknowledge since the actualization of a possible world in which agents enjoy LFW brings about the logical impossibility of God knowing PCFC. But Anselmian perfect being theology establishes that God possesses all great-making properties essentially, not contingently. Therefore, if the elements of LFOT described at the beginning of this paragraph are true, then either God isn't a maximally great being, or it is logically impossible for God to actualize any worlds in which agents enjoy LFW.[42]

Some might argue that, given theological incompatibilism, God's decision to create a world with agents who possess LFW is not impossible because God doesn't give up anything, as would be the case if God gave up omnipotence by creating a stone so heavy that not even God could lift it. But the actualization of a world in which agents enjoy LFW does not bring about a loss of divine foreknowledge; it is not the case that God knew truths about PCFC prior to actualizing a world in which agents enjoy LFW, and upon actualizing such a possible world a state of affairs obtains in which God lacks knowledge that God previously had. Accordingly, some

41. Here I am thinking of moving spotlight theories of time that seem to be compatible with LFW. See Cameron, *Moving Spotlight*; Deasy, "Moving Spotlight Theory"; Skow, *Objective Becoming*. For arguments that this view of time is compatible with LFW, see Hess, "Reconciling Divine Foreknowledge."

42. This is true for the same reasons I discussed in the section on omnipotence in chapter 3. In resolving the paradox of the stone, it is no solution to suggest that God is contingently omnipotent and *could* create a stone so heavy that he cannot lift it, but chooses not to do so. Because of this, Bruce Reichenbach's proposal also proves ineffective as a solution to the freedom/foreknowledge dilemma. See Reichenbach, "God Limits His Power," 101–24. In order to uphold the type of maximal greatness demanded by Anselmian perfect being theology, it must be the case that God is both omnipotent and omniscient—and essentially so.

argue that the modal reformations of omniscience required by LFOT can be squared with Anselmian perfect being theology since almost everyone agrees that God is free to decide what kind of world to create. Also, if God wants to instantiate a world with LFW, then doing so entails the limitation of access to some truths, but denying that this is possible entails denying the very existence of worlds in which agents enjoy LFW, or so defenders of LFOT would argue. Moreover, there is widespread agreement amongst philosophers, even those philosophers who deny that we have LFW, that it is reasonable to talk about worlds in which agents enjoy LFW, and that these worlds are within the domain of possibilia. And again, some are likely to say that nothing was lost, per se, by strongly actualizing a state of affairs in which agents enjoy LFW.

On the contrary, if LFOT is true, the actualization of a possible world in which agents enjoy LFW entails the actualization of a world in which God is not essentially omniscient. But the actualization of a world in which God is not essentially omniscient is logically impossible, given the validity of Anselmian perfect being theology.[43] Furthermore, other commonly held metaphysical principles raise additional concerns. Almost all philosophers who defend realism about truth defend the idea that truth supervenes upon being (TSB).[44] One popular way of teasing this idea out is known as truthmaker theory, according to which no proposition can be true unless there is a corresponding state of affairs that "makes" the proposition true.[45] To be sure, there are several philosophers who reject truthmaker theory but remain committed to TSB, and still others who reject both truthmaker theory and TSB, yet remain committed to realism about truth. Nonetheless, given a minimalist commitment to realism about truth, advocates of LFOT ought to agree that "a proposition is true if and only if what that proposition says to be the case actually is the case."[46]

43. I find it disturbing that Hasker does not recognize his inconsistency in espousing perfect being theology while simultaneously affirming the idea that God limits his knowledge by creating beings with LFW. In affirming maximal perfection he writes, "A perfect being that cannot lose its perfections is superior to an otherwise perfect being that is able to lose its perfection." Hasker, "Eternity and Providence," 83.

44. Trenton Merricks is a notable exception. See his *Truth and Ontology*.

45. I set to one side debates about which of many competing theories of truth is the right one, for my point stands regardless of whether a correspondence theory, axiomatic theory, or minimalist theory of truth obtains. What is important for my point is realism along the lines of Alston, *Realist Conception of Truth*.

46. Rolnick, "Realist Reference to God," 212. Thanks to Daniel Hill for bringing this quote to my attention and for reminding me that certain conceptions of truth maintain realism without requiring the ontology required by truthmakers (e.g., the redundancy/

I have already argued that given Anselmian perfect being theology, if the components of LFOT are true, possible worlds in which agents enjoy LFW do not exist even in the realm of possibilia, so there is no existent thing—no "being" or state of affairs that is actually the case—that truth can supervene upon to make the relevant PCFC true in the first place.[47] But supposing that this were not the case, yet another problem obtains that renders LFOT incompatible with Anselmianism.

Again, for the sake of argument, let's assume LFOT. Prior to creation, God possessed the property of being in possession of knowledge of 100 percent of all truths that pertain to reality. I say "all truths that pertain to reality" so as to distinguish not only between God's natural knowledge and God's free knowledge, but also to distinguish between God's knowledge of all modalities—that is, God's knowledge of everything in the realm of possibilia—and God's knowledge of what is actual. We assume that God's knowledge of all that was actual prior to creation included truths about God, God's existence, and all necessary truths (e.g. laws of logic, mathematics, etc.). What presents a problem for the compatibility of LFOT and Anselmianism is the fact that the creation of a world in which agents enjoy LFW entails that God has actualized a state of affairs which results in a negative change in the overall percentage of truths about reality that are known by God.

On LFOT, God's creation of a world in which agents enjoy LFW means that upon creation God lost the property of knowing 100 percent of all truths concerning reality, since at least some PCFC are presently true, yet unknown by God. This loss, I believe, is incompatible with Anselmian conceptions of divine maximal greatness. Therefore, on LFOT, the creation of worlds in which agents enjoy LFW remains metaphysically impossible, even for God, at least if LFOT is the right articulation of theological incompatibilism.[48] Of course, this objection only holds given the Anselmian conception of maximal greatness and the fact that divine great-making attributes are essential to the divine nature, not

disquotational/minimalist theory of truth). However, since advocates of LFOT advance various grounding objections as arguments against Molinism, these thinkers clearly cannot consistently employ their anti-Molinist arguments while defending minimalist conceptions of truth. I discuss this more in the next chapter.

47. Cf. Todd, "Against Limited Foreknowledge."

48. To clarify, I am not arguing that the creation of a world in which humans possess LFW is metaphysically impossible. I am arguing that, given LFOT open theism, one must choose between Anselmian perfect being theology and worlds in which agents enjoy LFW. It is worth mentioning that OFOT avoids this problem.

accidental or contingent to the divine nature. Open theists might seek to avoid the dilemma I raise against them by denying that reasoning by way of Anselmian perfect being theology is an appropriate theological method. However, it would be incumbent upon them to show exactly where Anselmianism fails if such an objection is to be taken as anything other than *ad hoc*. Furthermore, one should note that any such argument amounts to abandoning perfect being theology. For those who think this is too strong a claim, such a move by open theists, at minimum, entails abandoning the idea that God's great-making attributes are essential properties of the divine nature, which is an intuitive claim that has been defended by the vast majority of Christian philosophical theologians throughout church history.

Open theists might respond by saying that if the creation of a world in which agents enjoy LFW is metaphysically impossible, then it seems that God's knowledge is limited no matter what, so the tension I raise amounts to nothing. Considering this objection, let us imagine what a conversation between God and Joe would be like if LFOT were true. Suppose Joe asks God what a person with LFW (let's call him Bob) would do if Bob were in situation S. According to my argument, it would seem that God would respond by saying "I don't know," even if God never created Bob. This objection, then, means that even *sans* creation of a world in which agents enjoy LFW, God cannot know all truths.

In response, I want to reintroduce the importance of distinguishing between truths that concern the realm of possibilia and truths that concern the realm of actuality. If Anselmian perfect being theology is an accurate guide to understanding the divine nature, then if God exists, God is essentially omniscient, and not merely accidentally or contingently so. Accordingly, as we have seen, if the DFF entails that LFOT is the correct articulation of theological incompatibilism, then LFW is incoherent because worlds in which agents enjoy LFW do not exist even in the realm of possibilia, for they are metaphysically impossible in the broadly logical sense.

If this is correct, God remains omniscient by (D11) standards, despite divine ignorance of the metaphysically impossible situation in which Bob were placed in some indeterminate situation because there are no such truths concerning PCFC to know (whether possible but non-actual, or actual and therefore real). In fact, it might not even be fair to say that God is ignorant of anything at all, for to be ignorant of some*thing* presupposes that such a "thing" exists. Of course, if LFW turns out to be metaphysically impossible, then God's ignorance of what Bob would do in situation S is identical to God's ignorance of what a square circle looks like. Both "things" are metaphysically impossible; therefore knowledge of such "things" is likewise metaphysically impossible in any relevant sense of the term "some*thing*" as used above. Thus, because neither LFW nor a square circle is a "thing" in the relevant sense, there is no "thing" to be known of which God is ignorant. As it turns out, TSB eliminates any motivation for LFOT. On TSB, God know all truths, despite not possessing knowledge of impossibilities.

One might raise concerns related to the idea that it is logically impossible for God to know certain personally indexed truths such as "I know Ben Arbour." Therefore, one might argue, it is either not a problem that God lacks knowledge of 100 percent of all truths, or it must be the case that worlds in which agents enjoy consciousness are also logically impossible. However, we must recall the precise definition of omniscience offered by proponents of (D11). Again, assuming LFOT for the sake of argument, prior to creation God was in a token of 100 percent of all belief states that have as objects truths. Yet, after creation, on LFOT, God is no longer in a token of 100 percent of all belief states that have as object truths, and there are belief states that, were God in a token of them, these belief states would have as objects truths. It is this move away from perfect knowledge on LFOT that constitutes a threat to Anselmian understandings of perfect knowledge.

What about other objections to my arguments? Consider first the relationship between divine power and divine knowledge. If omnipotence entails perfect cognitive power (which entails the power to become omniscient), can the same methods of responding to the paradox of the stone that are thought to preserve omnipotence be employed by open theists in response to the DFF? That is, if God's inability to create a stone so heavy that God cannot lift it does not count against omnipotence because such constitutes a logical impossibility, isn't it also the case that God's inability to know certain things such as PCFC doesn't count against omniscience precisely because such knowledge is logically impossible (according to theological incompatibilists, anyway)?

I want to offer a number of responses to these types of objections, which I believe will show that such objections ultimately prove unsuccessful. First, such arguments fail to recognize that the case of the paradox of the stone is not perfectly analogous to the account of PCFC on LFOT. Whereas stones so heavy that they cannot be lifted even by

God are not "things" in that they do not exist, true PCFC about the actual world do exist if LFOT is true. The reason that the paradox of the stone doesn't raise a problem for omnipotence is the simple fact that no such stone *can* exist. But in order for openness arguments for theological incompatibilism to succeed along this line of defense, advocates of LFOT need to abandon the idea that PCFC are true (that is, they need to become open futurists). But LFOT maintains that some PCFC *are* true, and that such truths cannot be known by God, and all this *despite the fact that if God were in a token of these PCFC, the tokens would have as objects truths and not falsehoods.* In all fairness, LFOT does not simply beg the question, for its advocates have offered arguments as to why such knowledge is impossible, even for God.[49]

Before going on any further, I should clarify my understanding of the relationship between divine power and divine knowledge. It seems to me that divine omnipotence entails the possibility of divine omniscience.[50] There exists a connection between perfect power and knowledge, such that, necessarily, if an agent is omnipotent, then that agent has the ability to be omniscient. However, the connection between omnipotence and omniscience does not allow for the types of rebuttals that defenders of LFOT offer for at least one reason. Omnipotence entails possible omniscience, but omniscience does not entail (possible) omnipotence, for it is certainly possible that an agent can be omniscient even if that same agent lacks the great-making property of omnipotence. Divine omniscience is not dependent on God's being omnipotent, although God's enjoying omniscience is bolstered by divine omnipotence in that omnipotence entails the possibility of omniscience. This does not allow for the kinds of Thomistic paradoxes for omniscience that advocates of LFOT offer as defense of their position. These paradoxes are not perfectly analogous to those paradoxes used to modify definitions of omnipotence by taking modal issues under consideration. Divine omniscience can exist independently of omnipotence.[51] That is, it seems

49. Cf. Hasker, *God, Time, and Knowledge*, 64–74. I am not persuaded that open theism is the only philosophically responsible option for the Christian in the face of the freedom/foreknowledge dilemma.

50. As to the extent of the divine knowledge allowed by omnipotent cognitive powers, some will argue against my account of omniscience, (D11), for reasons that I discuss below. For now, suffice to say that at least the possibility of omniscience is entailed by omnipotence.

51. I can conceive of an instance where God grants someone omniscience without simultaneously also granting that person omnipotence. Perfect power entails perfect

logical to suppose omniscience *could* exist independently of omnipotence until someone offers some new reason to think that omniscience is incoherent, or that omniscience cannot exist apart from being co-instantiated along with omnipotence.

But what about those who aren't convinced by arguments for theological incompatibilism in the first place?[52] I'm not suggesting that all of the arguments for theological incompatibilism are weak or unconvincing. Rather, I mean that such arguments might not be strong enough to unseat a stronger belief that God is omniscient, and therefore knows all truths, including PCFC. Daniel Hill notes, "It is very counter-intuitive to think that one's ability to do otherwise precludes divine foreknowledge, even if this ability to do otherwise is not necessary for freedom."[53] Such a defense is strengthened when we consider the entire history of philosophy and theology, in which an extremely small minority of philosophers and theologians (and an even smaller number who are Christians!) defend open theistic responses to the DFF. Perhaps a person is not aware of any of the alternatives to open theism, but finds himself with a strong inclination to affirm God's knowledge of those PCFC that are presently true.[54] Given an Anselmian conception of perfect being theology proper, any philosophical theologian has a *prima facie* argument, based on God's maximal greatness, that God is maximally omniscient and therefore knows all truths—even truths about PCFC—so long as possession

cognitive power, which in turn enables possible perfect knowledge. However, it does not seem that perfect knowledge entails, or even enables, perfect power.

52. After all, I might find myself believing that God knows the future because I believe God is a maximally great being. Plantingian modal ontological arguments surely establish the rationality of holding such a view, given perfect being theology, which entails God's maximal omniscience.

53. Hill, *Divinity and Maximal Greatness*, 71. I should mention that Hill goes on to clarify in great detail *why* he isn't persuaded by arguments for open theism, especially in Hill, *Divinity and Maximal Greatness*, 99–100. Hill denies that open theists have successfully argued against the possibility of our having counterfactual power over the past, which would be sufficient to overturn arguments for theological incompatibilism.

54. It may be that a person doesn't even need a foundation for this belief. Even if someone is unaware of alternative solutions to the DFF, that person might find himself with a properly basic belief that God knows which of many possible futures will obtain. Of course, this leaves open whether one finds that arguments to the contrary lead to understandings of the ontology of time in either the direction of LFOT or OFOT. I won't trace out exactly *how* this could be true, but I am not aware of any reason why Plantinga's arguments for reformed epistemology would fail to allow someone to have such knowledge, even apart from any foundation for such a belief. See Plantinga, *Warranted Christian Belief*.

of knowledge is great-making. And if God enjoys (D11) omniscience, then indeed God must know even those truths about the truth-values of PCFC. So, based on Anselmian perfect being theology, philosophers and theologians have an undercutting defeater of arguments for theological incompatibilism of any stripe, but especially LFOT.[55]

What, then, of modal reformulations of divine omniscience such as those offered by open theists? To be candid, yes, these novel definitions provide a solution, but not a very good one. The word "omniscience" is made up of two root words: *omni*, meaning all, and *scientia*, meaning knowledge. Redefining omniscience as something other than knowledge of all truths is unfaithful to the general idea that traditional articulations of omniscience are thought to preserve, especially once we take tokens of belief into account and whether these tokens have as objects truths or falsehoods. Therefore, such modal reformulations of "omniscience" are not consistent with the general meaning of omniscience.[56] Not to make too light a thing of this, but redefining omniscience to mean something other than knowledge of all truths is similar to someone redefining the term "cat" and calling oneself a feline to suit whatever interests that person may have. That is, redefining a term cuts against the notion that ideas have meaning, and that words refer to these ideas according to any philosophy of language in which ordinary usage of a term indicates meaning.[57] LFOT's redefining omniscience to mean

55. Note that such an undercutting defeater need not entail that those who employ it identify which solution to the freedom/foreknowledge dilemma they find most successful. Hence, a person who employs such an undercutting defeater need not come out in support of Molinism, divine timelessness, Ockhamism, or any other alternative as a more viable solution to the DFF in opposing open theism. Perhaps the DFF will remain a mystery everlastingly as a true theological antinomy. Or, perhaps some philosophical theologian in the future will offer another solution we have yet to see. Regardless, in my view, the intuition that God *does* know all truths is sufficiently established by way of Anselmian perfect being theology such that one need not feel overly pressured in responding to arguments for theological incompatibilism. To restate this another way, the concept of maximal greatness as generated by Anselmian intuitions makes it perfectly rational for someone to defend (D11) as a proper definition of divine omniscience.

56. I do not here mean to employ the genetic fallacy, wherein one determines the meaning of a word by etymologically adding up the sum of its parts. I am quite aware that a butterfly is not a stick of butter that can fly and that reasoning in this way often creates as many problems (if not more) than it solves. However, in the case of omniscience, it just so happens that the term does mean precisely what the sum of the root words mean.

57. I discuss issues involving reference and philosophy of language as they pertain to open theism in more detail in the next chapter.

something other than knowledge of all truths seem to me as equally unhelpful as redefining the word "cat."

Supposing that all of the proposed solutions to the DFF fail, would it be problematic for open theists to simply acknowledge that omniscience is impossible? Taking this line of reasoning, advocates of LFOT might suggest that, because God has actualized a world in which at least some agents enjoy LFW, God lacks knowledge of the bivalent truth-values of PCFC and therefore isn't omniscient, but rather possesses the maximum amount of knowledge that is consistent with a decision to create a world in which agents enjoy LFW. This response is a real solution; however, it comes with quite a cost to those who defend LFOT, since this solution entails denying that God is omniscient. In the debates concerning the extent of divine knowledge, all Christian philosophers and theologians have sought to defend versions of omniscience that are compatible with Anselmian perfect being theology rather than capitulate to arguments against the coherence of omniscience. Hence, if open theists concede that omniscience is impossible given that agents enjoy LFW, such a concession would radically alter the discussion. But just how radical would these suggestions be? Quite a bit more radical than we might initially realize, especially since philosophers and theologians suppose that omniscience is a great-making property. Many philosophers and theologians have shown that omniscience can be co-instantiated with other great-making attributes such as omnipotence and/or omnibenevolence.[58] Therefore, if someone (including an open theist) were to acknowledge that God is not omniscient, such a concession would entail that the person is abandoning an Anselmian conception of perfect being theology.

It might be that an open theist would not be frightened by such a concession, and perhaps he would claim that open theistic views about God's foreknowledge (or lack thereof) are more consistent with the witness of Christian Scripture than whatever arguments perfect being theology can muster. Given a high view of Scripture and its place in the theological task, open theists might suggest, then, that Christians abandon Anselmian perfect being theology as a *dignum Deo* in favor of a more biblical theology proper.[59] There are two responses to this.

58. See especially Bernstein, "Is God's Existence Possible?"; Bernstein, "Giving the Ontological Argument."

59. To clarify, this is one approach that I suppose open theists might take. Contemporary discussions of openness theological method reveal significant disagreement amongst open theists, as expressed in numerous publications from those primarily

First, I find it quite impious to say of God that there could be another being who is greater. My intuitions concerning perfect being theology stem from concerns about what it would mean to ascribe glory and honor to a being who may, in fact, not be the Supreme Being. I take it that this is sufficient to establish the concept of divine maximal greatness, which serves to properly motivate Anselmian perfect being theology in the first place. Thus, if anyone suggests that Christians should eschew allowing Anselmian perfect being theology to guide one's exegesis, those who desire to abandon such an approach should show how one ought to speak about God as a possibly less-than-supreme being, and they should also suggest some alternative hermeneutic. Perhaps such theologians could commit themselves to a position of fideistic irrationalism concerning the relationship between faith and reason, for it seems that all other options (process theology, attenuated perfect being theology à la Nagasawa's reformulation, or some other theology proper) are incompatible with historic Christian orthodoxy. But this latter move would not seem to gain much traction given the affirmation of Aristotelian laws of logic as necessary and proper tools to be used in biblical interpretation (especially since open theists utilize these laws of logic in motivating their arguments for theological incompatibilism).

Second, in the last chapter I briefly discussed the way that philosophy necessarily shapes one's interpretation of Scripture. Apart from any argument showing where I've gone wrong on those points, it seems wise to interpret Scripture according to a rubric of Anselmian perfect being theology. Not only is this defensible, but failure to do so would be foolish since one finds philosophical tools helpful in the construction of a biblical, philosophically rational doctrine of God. Hence, until open theists (or anyone else, for that matter) put forward arguments showing exactly where such philosophically guided interpretations of the Bible are misinformed, the tradition appears unfettered by calls to reject perfect being theology.[60]

---

interested in theologically motivated open theism. Some reject Anselmianism because they don't think it is biblical; others reject it because they find it unacceptable to read the Bible through a lens of *a priori* reasoning.

60. Open theists have attempted to show that philosophy has misled classical theologians, but the arguments contained in these attempts are rife with problems. Theologians who argue thus either approach the subject of biblical interpretation with a philosophical naïveté on the one hand, or equivocate as to when/how philosophy should be appropriated in the hermeneutical task on the other hand. See Arbour and Blount, "Camel's Nose."

LFOT faces yet another problem when compared against another version of openness theology. Consider OFOT, an alternative approach defended by the majority of open theists. Suppose that open futurists are right in denying that any PCFC are presently true. Note that on both LFOT and OFOT, God possesses exactly the same amount of knowledge; that is, on both LFOT and OFOT God knows the truths (and falsehoods) of the same number of propositions. Even though both approaches to open theism suggest that God possesses the same sum total of knowledge, in OFOT, it is technically correct to predicate omniscience to God, whereas it is not correct at all to call God omniscient on LFOT. This is so because, on OFOT, PCFC aren't presently true, so there is nothing to be known, regardless of whether or not knowledge of such truths would be possible for God if they did exist to be known.[61] Thus, according to OFOT, God knows 100 percent of all truths as concerns PCFC, and is therefore omniscient, even by (D11) standards.

Alternatively, God knows a very small percentage of all non-necessary truths on LFOT, at least if the future contains beings with LFW, for the future is potentially infinite.[62] Hence, God's knowledge by percentage is far superior on OFOT when compared to what would be the case on LFOT. If a higher overall percentage of truths known by God counts as

61. In chapter 6, I discuss these views in much more detail, paying particular attention to issues in philosophy of language and the metaphysics/ontology of time that advocates of OFOT employ in motivating their position.

62. I stipulate "non-necessary truths" because, as Daniel Hill thankfully brought to my attention, God knows all the *a priori* truths of math, etc., and there are infinitely many of them (0=0, 1=1 . . .). Indeed, there are uncountably many of them (for each real number, r, God knows the corresponding truth of the form "r=r"). So God knows most truths, for sure. Nonetheless, with respect to God's potential free knowledge, Swinburne is right to note that God's ignorance is vast.

At least one person has objected that he finds this assertion unfair and massively speculative. However, consider the scope of decisions we make everyday, and the fact that there are more than six billion persons on the planet, each of whom is commonly thought to make free decisions every day, each decision of which opens new possibilities. In light of the sheer magnitude of possible futures that might obtain if only humans (much less other agents!) enjoy LFW, it seems to me that the number of truths God does know pales in comparison to those truths that God does not know. At least this seems intuitive if we presuppose both LFOT and a future in which humans continue to enjoy LFW. In trying to argue against this worry, the only way that I could affirm that God's knowledge of all truths is even more than 50 percent involves suggesting that at some point in the future people would cease to have the ability to do otherwise, and that the duration of total history in which agents did have the ability to do otherwise is less than half of the total amount of time that will exist in the universe (of course, taking into consideration the total quantity of free agents, and also the total number of decisions in which an agent has the ability to do otherwise should be accounted for).

great-making (an intuitively obvious supposition), then God isn't as great in the world as understood by advocates of LFOT than God would be if the world were in reality what OFOT says is true. Suppose that God is free with respect to what metaphysicians of time instantiate,[63] and that the metaphysics of time entails whether or not future contingents lack truth-values. If both of these statements are true, then since we have already demonstrated that LFOT is logically impossible, given Anselmianism, we can see that if theological incompatibilism about freedom and foreknowledge is true, then God must have created a world in which OFOT is true rather than a world in which LFOT obtains.[64] This is true because Anselmian perfect being theology establishes that God's great-making attributes are essential to the divine nature. Therefore, God cannot limit himself by creating a world in which God is anything less than omniscient. It goes without saying that the property of knowing 100 percent of all truths is a great-making property.[65] Were God to create the world as understood by LFOT, such a creation would entail God's self-limitation

63. At least some metaphysicians of time have sometimes argued that certain views of time are necessarily false. See, for example, Sider, "Presentism and Ontological Commitment"; and chapter 2, "Against Presentism," in Sider, *Four Dimensionalism*, 11–52. However, no philosopher has argued that any particular understanding of time is necessary in either the broadly logical or narrowly logical sense. Recall that I defended in chapter 1 the principle that it is best to presume something possible until we have reason to think it impossible. Therefore, it seems to me that since most philosophers believe that the nature of time (in the areas of both tense and ontology) is contingent, God is free with respect to the nature of time to instantiate. Apart from some argument for the necessity of some particular understanding of time, it seems wise to conclude with the extant arguments that favor the idea that the nature of time (whatever it is) is contingent. Although McTaggart argues explicitly that time must be an A-series, his arguments do not establish whether such an A-series should be understood along the lines of presentism, or growing-blockism (or shrinking-blockism). Cf. Arbour "Unqualified Divine Temporality."

64. Tom Crisp offers arguments for the contingency of the nature of time, despite his commitment to presentism, in his essay, "Presentism."

It appears to me quite dubious that God could create a world in which PCFC either lack truth-values or are all false. I offer reasons for my doubts about such possibilities in chapter 6. For now, I mean only to show that given two different accounts of open theism (namely, LFOT and OFOT), God is greater in OFOT's system than in that of LFOT. But, if elements of the LFOT account of openness are less problematic than that of OFOT (as I argue later), then by pitting the two accounts of open theism against each other, we come to see that both have tremendous difficulties, and Christians therefore have adequate reason for rejecting open theism, perhaps in favor of some alternative solution to the DFF or perhaps by remaining agnostic about any solution to the DFF, but denying that open theism is a live option. Again, one need not be committed to any particular solution to the DFF to recognize that open theism is not a valid option.

65. To clarify, a being that only knows 99 percent (or any other value less than 100 percent) of all truths is inferior to a being that knows 100 percent of all truths.

(e.g., not being omniscient) by virtue of actualizing a state of affairs in which humans enjoy LFW, but by my analysis, if LFOT is an accurate picture of theological incompatibilism about divine foreknowledge and human freedom, worlds in which agents enjoy LFW bear a certain affinity to square circles in that they are logical impossibilities.

Here it seems appropriate to bring Scripture back into the discussion again. Theologians have understood the scope of divine omniscience to include knowledge of the future in part because of biblical texts.[66] Consider the following passages in which God speaks through the prophet Isaiah:

> Behold, the former things have come to pass,
> and new things I declare;
> before they spring forth
> I tell you of them. (Isa 42:9)

> Who is like me? Let him shout the name.
> Let him declare it and present it to me,
> since I set an ancient people.
> Let them declare what is to come, and what will happen. (Isa 44:7)

> Remember this and take courage,
> bring it back to heart, you transgressors,
> remember the former things of old;
> for I am God, and there is no other;
> I am God, and there is none like me,
> declaring the end from the beginning
> and from ancient times things not yet done,
> saying, "My counsel shall stand,
> and all my purpose will be accomplished." (Isa 46:8–10)

> I declared to you from of old,
> before coming to pass I announced to you,
> lest you should say, "My idol did *it*,
> my carved image and my metal image commanded."

66. The following verses of Christian Scripture also motivate Hill's defense of omniscience against open theistic denials of God's exhaustive definite foreknowledge. See Hill, *Divinity and Maximal Greatness*, 88–89.

> You have heard; now see all this!
> And will you not declare *it*?
> From now I will cause you to hear new things,
> hidden things previously unrevealed that are unknown to you. (Isa 48:5–6)[67]

Consider another aforementioned passage that speaks directly to God's foreknowledge of human speech:

> Because not even a word is on my tongue
> Behold, oh LORD, you know it altogether. (Ps 139:4)[68]

If anything counts as something done freely, certainly human speech would seem to qualify. Not only does it seem (at least to those who defend LFW) that we are free in regards to whether or not to speak, but it also seems that we are free with respect to *what* we speak. But Ps 139:4 suggests that God not only knows *that* we will speak but also the exact words that we will say.[69]

If God knows the future, as the natural reading of these texts suggests, then philosophers and theologians who are concerned with maintaining coherent accounts of the blending of natural revelation (e.g., philosophical reasoning) and special revelation (e.g., Scripture) should conclude that the knowledge of future contingents must be included in any definition of omniscience.

In all fairness to open theists, a plain reading of these texts does not demand that the future events known by God are free in the libertarian sense. However, neither does a plain reading of Isaiah's prophecies demand that the future events are metaphysically determined. Furthermore, it would be a strained interpretation to think that the speech referred to

67. Translations mine. The italicization of *it* in verses 5 and 6 of Isa 48 is meant to denote the fact that the relative pronoun is not in the Hebrew text. This translation method follows those used in the NASB.

68. Again, my own translation.

69. Open theists might retort that this verse doesn't demand foreknowledge. However, I see no way to reasonably understand the psalmist's meaning apart from foreknowledge. Consider a sampling of translations: "Certainly my tongue does not frame a word, without you, O Lord, being thoroughly aware of it" (NET); "Before a word is on my tongue you, Lord, know it completely" (NIV); "Even before a word is on my tongue, behold, O Lord, you know it altogether" (ESV); "Even before there is a word on my tongue, Behold, Lord, You know it all" (NASB). The idea the psalmist is communicating is not merely the comprehensiveness of what YHWH knows, but also when he knows it in relation to the agent; believers can take comfort in this.

by the psalmist cannot be free in the libertarian sense, but rather must be determined since God knows it. Regardless, the passage from Isaiah as well as the one taken from Psalms ought be read as evidence favoring exhaustive definite foreknowledge, for these texts demand foreknowledge of the events in question. That is, there is no way to responsibly interpret these passages such that God lacks foreknowledge of the content of future human speech, or that God is unsure of how things will end. If such interpretations preclude open theism, so much the worse for it; perhaps some other response to the DFF succeeds. And, if theological incompatibilism between divine foreknowledge and human freedom is the right way to respond to the DFF, verses such as those above require those with commitments to a high view of Scripture to adopt determinism and/or compatibilist understandings of free will since open theism cannot make sense of divine knowledge of future contingents such as the content of human speech. But we should remember that one only needs to go this direction if one defends theological incompatibilism, so defenders of simple foreknowledge, divine eternity, theological antinomy, or Molinism as adequate responses to the DFF need not worry. But are there any other texts of the Bible that further bolster my claims that open theism is inadequate in generating a maximally great vision of God, specifically because of the value of divine knowledge?

Consider 1 John 3:20, which declares that God knows everything. If some PCFC are presently true as understood according to LFOT, then according to Scripture, God knows those truths. Of course, this knowledge is exactly what open theists deny God possesses. Advocates of LFOT are likely to defend their position against my interpretation of 1 John 3:20 by responding that the future doesn't exist. Because of the future's lack of existence, future contingents aren't "things" in the relevant sense, and therefore God doesn't have to know them for 1 John 3:20 to be true.[70] This response seems *ad hoc* at this point, unless defenders of LFOT are also willing to go the way of the open futurist and admit that because the future doesn't exist, PCFC either lack truth-values or are all false, so there is nothing to be known. I cannot see how defenders of LFOT can have their philosophical cake (in affirming that at least some PCFC are presently true) and eat it too (in denying that future contingents are "things" in the relevant sense of 1 John 3:20). This is all the more clear when we apply

70. This defense is similar in nature to remarks Hasker makes in his *God, Time, and Knowledge*, 127, where he takes issue with Mavrodes on the possibility of bringing about the past.

TSB. If some PCFC are true, there must be some kind of "thing" that exists in order to ground the truth of these PCFC. So LFOT is incompatible with John's assertion that God knows everything.

Also, Job 37:16 asserts that God is "perfect in knowledge." If this is true (and the Christian tradition affirms the veracity of Scripture), then God must know 100 percent of all truths whereupon God's possession of a token of some belief state maps onto a truth. For the sake of simplicity, let us call this a "knowable truth." Anything less than knowledge of 100 percent of all "knowable truths" would not constitute perfect knowledge. Finally, I wish to note that all of the scriptural data provides ample warrant for those who maintain that God possesses all cognitive perfections, including knowledge of what might otherwise *seem* impossible. It might be that philosophers offer very strong arguments seeming to show how and why knowledge of true PCFC would be impossible. But Scripture, properly understood, carries more authority than general revelation, which includes logic, reason, and philosophy. Although reason is vital to any theological project, it cannot overturn the authority of the Bible. I confess that I do not know *how* God knows many of the truths that God knows, but such ignorance doesn't move me to affirm divine ignorance of true PCFC or divine ignorance of any other "knowable truths." This position should not be misconstrued as a premature appeal to theological antinomy, or as a theological appeal to fideism, for it is consistent with robust notions of divine mystery, which are perfectly kosher in orthodox Christian doctrine, including analytic philosophical theology. In fact, what I am arguing doesn't necessitate antinomy, though it could if one did not wish to specifically endorse any particular solution to the DFF. What I *am* arguing is that Anselmian conceptions of perfect being theology offer more philosophical support for thinking that divine omniscience includes knowledge of true PCFC than arguments for LFOT in the face of theological incompatibilism as the proper response to the DFF. That is, if there really is a deep incompatibility between divine foreknowledge and free will, LFOT is not a live option since it compromises the metaphysics of perfect beings.

One final objection against my arguments needs to be considered. Advocates of LFOT might seek to eliminate the problems I raise by suggesting that traditional taxonomies of divine knowledge preserve omniscience, even on LFOT. Historically, philosophical theologians have distinguished between God's natural knowledge (divine knowledge of all necessary truths along with knowledge of the entire domain of possibilia) and God's free knowledge (divine knowledge of whichever actual world God chooses to instantiate). An open theist might suggest that God's knowledge of all modalities includes knowledge of the truth-values of PCFC in various possible worlds, which appears sufficient to defend absolute omniscience. However, if God lacks knowledge of PCFC in the actual world, then the actualization of the actual world would be logically impossible, for God is essentially omniscient, and essential omniscience precludes the logical possibility of any world where God lacks knowledge of all there is to know about that world (including PCFC). Furthermore, consider the results of such a concession. If God lacks knowledge of PCFC, then God does not know which world has been created. Since possible worlds are maximally consistent states of affairs, it follows that no two worlds are exactly alike.[71] Distinguishing between worlds, then, would require knowledge of all PCFC, lest God, upon creating, becomes ignorant of which possible world has been actualized. So, if God lacks knowledge of PCFC as part of divine free knowledge, then God is not omniscient, and the problems I raise remain. It goes without saying, then, that in order to qualify as genuinely omniscient, God would know which possible world, if any, has been actualized. Therefore, objections based on a distinction between God's natural knowledge and God's free knowledge fail to alleviate the problems for LFOT created by the existence of true PCFC that are unknown by God.

Conclusion

Advocates of LFOT are likely to object that my proposal limits divine power, for, in my view, God does not have the ability to create beings with LFW. However, given the Thomistic principle I defended in chapter 2 when discussing divine omnipotence, I see no reason to agree that the inability to create beings with LFW amounts to a limitation of divine power (if such creation proves to be a genuine impossibility) any more than the inability to bring about any logical impossibility (such as square circles) results in a limitation of divine power. However, I need not concede that the creation of beings with LFW is a logical impossibility.[72] On

71. For an extended account of possible worlds as maximally consistent states of affairs, see Armstrong, *World of States*. For an alternative view, see Jacobs, "Powers Theory of Modality." I will elaborate on these matters in chapter 6.

72. At this juncture, one's perspective as to the extent of human freedom is irrelevant. Nonetheless, it seems to me that a variety of solutions to this conundrum are available for anyone wishing to defend LFW.

my view, God's inability to create beings with LFW results *if and only if* LFOT-type arguments for theological incompatibilism are sound. In the face of Anselmian perfect being theology, it seems to me that LFOT is false. My point in this chapter is not to say that LFW is incoherent, given God's maximal greatness.[73] Instead, I argue that the co-instantiation of two premises is untenable. These premises are: (1) LFOT is the correct account of theological incompatibilism; and (2) that at least some PCFC are presently true. Therefore, in order to avoid inconsistency, defenders of theological incompatibilism about divine foreknowledge and free will can respond in four ways. They can: (1) abandon open theism (perhaps in favor of one of the other proposed solutions to the DFF, or perhaps acknowledge the mysterious antinomy of freedom and foreknowledge); (2) abandon constructions of the DFF which demand that the ability to do otherwise is a requirement for genuine free will; (3) abandon the idea that PCFC are presently true (i.e., adopt OFOT); or (4) abandon Anselmian perfect being theology.[74]

To date, contemporary open theism has sought to differentiate itself from process theology by defending perfect being theology, so I doubt that any openness advocates would respond with (4). Because advocates of LFOT are deeply committed to the sort of LFW that requires the ability to do otherwise, I seriously doubt that either will opt for (2).[75] They have argued against both of the alternative proposed solutions to the DFF, which leads me to think that rather than opting for (1), they are most likely to abandon the idea that any PCFC are presently true, and find another way to deal with the way that the principle of bivalence applies to those propositions. This path, labeled the "wide road" by Dale Tuggy, is

73. That is, I do not mean to defend here the idea that LFW is incoherent in the same way that square circles or four-sided triangles are incoherent. Rather, I argue only that such is incoherent given the co-instantiation of: (1) God's maximal greatness; (2) theological incompatibilism (or, if you prefer, open theism); and (3) that some PCFC are presently true. That is, if (1), (2), and (3) in the previous sentence are co-instantiated, then worlds in which agents possess LFW are not metaphysically available to be created by a maximally great being. But, if any alternative solutions to the DFF prove successful in defeating open theism (appeals to compatibilism as the accurate conception of freedom and moral responsibility excluded), I believe that LFW is *not* incoherent, and therefore God certainly has the ability to create such beings if God so chooses.

74. A change with regard to the truth-values of PCFC would entail abandoning what Tuggy calls "the narrow road" and joining those open theists who favor "the wide road." I take up that perspective and argue against it in the next chapter.

75. We are reminded of Hasker's comments that "relatively few incompatibilists accept this conclusion [that humans do not possess libertarian freedom]." Hasker, *God, Time, and Knowledge*, 73.

defended by many open theists on the basis of various understandings of the philosophical nature of time.[76] In chapter 6, I examine those defenses of open theism and show why they, too, fail to adequately account for divine omniscience in light of God's maximal greatness. For those who are not convinced by my arguments thus far that LFOT poses a threat to Anselmian conceptions of divine omniscience, in the next chapter, I examine another problem LFOT faces, and this problem is also related to PCFC and the omnitemporality of truth.

76. Tuggy, "Roads to Open Theism," 30–34.

4

Future Freedom and the Fixity of Truth

Closing the Limited Foreknowledge Road to Open Theism[1]

Recall that philosophically driven open theism divides neatly into two categories: limited foreknowledge open theism (LFOT), which affirms that at least some PCFC are true (a position defended by William Hasker, Peter van Inwagen, and Richard Swinburne), and open future open theism (OFOT), which denies this (e.g., Richard Purtill, Alan Rhoda, Dale Tuggy, and Dean Zimmerman). In this chapter, I focus on those who travel the road to open theism by affirming that at least some propositions concerning future contingents (PCFC) are presently true, yet God does not know this, a view that I will continue to refer to as LFOT.[2] I interact principally with William Hasker's articulation of this position, taking his writing to be representative of LFOT. In addition to the reasons given in the previous chapter, I further maintain that LFOT is untenable because it requires the defense of four positions that together

1. A slightly shorter version of this chapter has been published as Arbour, "Future Freedom."

2. To clarify, I do not include Arthur Prior or Rhoda among those who defend LFOT even though they believe that propositions concerning future contingents have truth-values, for they think that all such propositions are false. Furthermore, the argument of this chapter in no way impugns what I label OFOT, although I define that view in much more detail and explain the difficulties faced by OFOT in chapter 6. My argument in this chapter hinges on the affirmation of LFOT that propositions concerning future contingents presently possess truth-values. The idea of different paths, or "roads," which all arrive at open theism was first suggested by Tuggy, "Roads to Open Theism."

form an inconsistent set. These are: (1) the omnitemporality of truth;[3] (2) the fixity of the past;[4] (3) that a distinction between hard facts and soft facts does not allow for Ockhamism to alleviate the tensions raised by the dilemma of freedom and foreknowledge (DFF); and (4) that humans possess significant freedom, as understood by the libertarian (LFW).[5]

Limited Foreknowledge Open Theism

In his seminal work *God, Time, and Knowledge*, William Hasker defends theological incompatibilism—the idea that divine foreknowledge of future contingents is incompatible with our possession of LFW.[6] Hasker defends his view in part by denying divine timelessness, thereby precluding attempts to eliminate any tensions raised by the DFF based on divine atemporality.[7] As a theological incompatibilist who defends LFW,

3. "By the omnitemporality of truth I mean the doctrine that any statement which is true at any time is true at all times previous to and all times subsequent to that time." Purtill, "Fatalism and the Omnitemporality," 185.

4. Purtill calls this the unchangeability of the past. "By the unchangeability of the past I mean the doctrine that there is nothing which we can do now which will make any statement about the past either true or false, the past is beyond our control." Purtill, "Fatalism and the Omnitemporality," 185.

5. Hasker offers a precise definition of free will: "(FW) N is free at T with respect to $A =_{df}$. It is in N's power at T to perform A, and it is in N's power at T to refrain from performing A." Hasker, *God, Time, and Knowledge*, 66.

6. So as to ensure that I do not misrepresent his positions, I will quote from Hasker frequently, and often at length. I ask forgiveness in advance from those readers who find this cumbersome.

With respect to free will, there is no such thing as libertarian free will *and* compatibilist free will as such; rather, either libertarianism or compatibilism is true about freedom and determinism, one or the other, and whichever is correct rightly defines what is meant by "free will." Additionally, either compatibilism or libertarianism, one or the other, is true about determinism and moral responsibility. Nonetheless, following the conventional use of terms in the relevant contemporary literature, I will make use of the phrase "libertarian freedom/free will" or LFW for short, to refer to the idea that free will is incompatible with determinism, and freedom is necessary for moral responsibility.

7. I expect that readers already have a general familiarity with the DFF. For those unfamiliar with this ancient philosophical puzzle, no better introduction exists than the first chapter of Zagzebski, *Dilemma of Freedom*, 3–35. For the precise formulations of the DFF that concern Hasker, see chapter 4, "Two Arguments for Incompatibilism," of his *God, Time, and Knowledge*, 64–74.

I should also note that at the time of writing *God, Time, and Knowledge*, Hasker believed that divine timelessness, were it true, would offer a genuine solution to the DFF. He has since changed his mind, and he currently denies that divine timelessness

Hasker goes further by concluding in favor of open theism—a view that denies that God possesses foreknowledge of future contingents. Rather, according to open theists, God knows the future only insofar as it is presently determined. The version of openness theology defended by Hasker, LFOT, entails the affirmation that God does not know the truth-values of any PCFC—despite the fact that such truths about the future exist—because divine foreknowledge of such would eliminate the contingent nature of the future, thereby eliminating LFW.[8]

Along with Swinburne and Van Inwagen, Hasker affirms (*pace* Aristotle) that the principle of bivalence applies even to PCFC;[9] that is, all propositions about the future presently possess truth-values; they are either true or false.[10] If all propositions about the future presently possess bivalent truth-values, then PCFC do as well. That is, according to Hasker, the future is alethically settled, even if it remains presently causally undetermined. Because the ontology of when things exist is an important feature of the debates about divine foreknowledge, we should note that

---

offers such a solution. See Hasker, "Absence." As I will show below, divine timelessness supports the existence of soft facts; so if soft facts offer a potential solution to the DFF, we need not capitulate to theological incompatibilism, much less open theism.

8. Any open theist who defends divine infallibility of knowledge and also maintains that God has beliefs (as does Hasker, contra Alston) must go on to conclude not only that God doesn't "know" the future but also that God does not even have *beliefs* about future contingents, for infallible beliefs constitute knowledge for God, and knowledge is enough to generate the very dilemma to which open theists respond by denying that God possesses exhaustive foreknowledge. See Alston, "Does God Have Beliefs?," reprinted in *Divine Nature*, 178–93; Hasker, "Yes, God Has Beliefs!"

9. Cf. Aristotle, *De Interpretatione*, ch. 9. For a lucid interpretation of Aristotle's understanding of an argument for fatalism, see Anscombe, "Aristotle and the Sea." The principle of bivalence asserts that a proposition is either true or false and not both.

10. Hasker refers to this as the omnitemporality of truth. He defends this view against alternatives, including the idea that PCFC are neither true nor false, noting that those views are quite controversial and that his position "seems not to lend itself to further argument as readily as the considerations that arise if the existence of truths about the contingent future is granted." Hasker, "Foreknowledge Conundrum," 112n10. Cf. Hasker, *God, Time, and Knowledge*, 107–8, 122–25, as well as Tuggy, "Roads to Open Theism," 48n18. In that footnote, Tuggy details an equivocation on the part of Hasker, which can only be cashed out if Hasker abandons the "narrow road" and travels along the "wide road," which I call OFOT.

Swinburne agrees, noting, "All statements have an invariant truth-value; if true, they are always true." Swinburne, *Christian God*, 100. Van Inwagen expresses his agreement in his essay, "Omniscient Being."

For one interesting view that denies that propositions concerning future contingents follow the regular bivalent systems of logic (in which propositions have only two values, either true or false), see Purtill, "Fatalism and the Omnitemporality."

OFOT avoids these issues by denying that the future is presently alethically settled. Some propositions about what "will" happen are true, even presently, on LFOT, whereas this is not the case for OFOT.[11]

I will argue that LFOT, when combined with both its position regarding hard facts and soft facts as well as its denial of the possibility of counterfactual power over the past, entails a logical problem of fatalism—a problem that exists completely independently of divine foreknowledge. That is, if the past is fixed (accidentally necessary), and if it is also the case that PCFC have omnitemporal truth-values, then LFOT logically entails that we do not possess significant freedom, regardless of whether or not God knows the future. Whereas advocates of LFOT maintain that the incompatibility between freedom and foreknowledge lies in divine knowledge, I agree with Richard Purtill that the incompatibility is more precisely located between the omnitemporality of truth and LFW (i.e., Aristotle's articulation of the problem of logical fatalism).[12]

Allow me to summarize Purtill's argument. If omnitemporal truths exist, and if "I am typing now" (just before midnight on Sunday, January 24, 2014) is one such truth, then it was true yesterday that I would be typing just before midnight on the following day. But if I have LFW, then I possess the power to change the past, such that I can presently (by refraining from typing) bring it about that yesterday it was *not* true that I would be typing now. If I lack counterfactual power over the past, then I do not possess LFW with respect to typing presently. Now, intuition confirms that the past is fixed in such a way that, if it was true yesterday that I would type today, then I don't have it within my power to bring

11. I elaborate more on the linguistics of PCFC in chapter 6 when I discuss why advocates of OFOT interpret the word "will" in such propositions to eliminate contingency, for they defend the alethic openness of the future. It's worth mentioning that defenders of OFOT do not affirm that any PCFC are presently true. Geach might have been a notable exception, but this is debatable. Cf. Geach, *Providence and Evil*; Todd, "Geachianism."

12. The central argument of this chapter bears a significant affinity to that of Purtill's article, "Fatalism and the Omnitemporality of Truth." Purtill, himself an open futurist, concludes against LFOT, as do I. Nonetheless, this chapter advances the discussion by showing exactly why it is that Hasker's position fails to address the problems raised by Purtill. This involves a significantly more detailed examination of hard facts and soft facts than Purtill offers in his article precisely because Hasker thinks a distinction between hard facts and soft facts is the key to refuting Purtill. "I therefore do not agree with Purtill that the omnitemporality of truth, together with the unchangeability of the past, entails fatalism. The answer to this contention is found in the distinction between hard and soft facts—a distinction that Purtill considers but rejects for (in my opinion) inadequate reasons." Hasker, *God, Time, and Knowledge*, 125n10.

it about now that what *was* true was *not*, in fact, true. That is to say, the past is now fixed and unchangeable; it's too late to do anything that would alter the truth-values of anything that was true in the past since we do not possess any power over the past.[13] Hence, the omnitemporality of truth eliminates LFW—at least with respect to all truths that are omnitemporal.[14] To clarify, Purtill suggests that fatalism logically follows from the conjunction of the omnitemporality of truth together with the unchangeability of the past. Because he maintains the fixity/unchangeability of the past while also defending LFW, Purtill concludes against the omnitemporality of truth.

Part of the difficulty in understanding Hasker's position is that certain passages of *God, Time, and Knowledge* suggest that he agrees with Purtill's line of argumentation, but other passages suggest that Hasker disagrees with Purtill, which is confusing. For instance, in one place Hasker notes, "If we hold to the omnitemporality of truth, then there seems no alternative to saying that in performing an action today I make it the case that certain propositions were true in the past, that someone who expressed those propositions spoke truly, and the like."[15] But elsewhere Hasker (summarizing a response that entails power over the past) writes,

> It is noteworthy that although persons not familiar with the foreknowledge controversy find the terminology of "changing the past" almost irresistible, most writers on the topic hold that such talk is irremediably confused. No, the response comes back, we cannot change the past. But then, neither can we change the future. It cannot be the case that an event *E* has occurred, and someone subsequently brings it about that *E* has not occurred. But neither can it be the case that it is true that an event *E will occur*, and someone subsequently brings it about that *E* never occurs. If someone *prevents E*'s occurrence, then it was *never* true that *E* would occur. . . . The difference between past and

13. This explication of Purtill's argument is not meant to conflate counterfactual power over the past with actual power over the past, although it may seem to do so. I discuss these issues further later in the chapter when I take up the question of truthmakers.

14. I limit the extent of just how much LFW is eliminated just in case someone wishes to suggest that not all truths are omnitemporal. Suffice it to say that any action which is omnitemporally true cannot involve LFW, at least not unless we possess counterfactual power over the past.

15. Hasker, *God, Time, and Knowledge*, 107. For Hasker, "making it the case" cannot in any sense entail causation or *exerting causal influence*, for he denies any sort of backward causation, counterfactual or otherwise.

> future, then, comes down to the fact that most, if not all, of the causal arrows run from the past to the future rather than from the future to the past.[16]

Of course, because Hasker affirms what he calls temporal asymmetry—that the past is relevantly different from the future in that we can causally affect the future, but we cannot presently causally affect the past—he rejects the type of responses to the DFF offered by Mavrodes because such a response "create[s] and emphasize[s] a *symmetry* between the past and the future, whereas the point of the expression ['You can't change the past'] as it is ordinarily used is precisely to stress the *asymmetry* between the two."[17]

After all this, Hasker goes on to affirm that the omnitemporality of truth entails that propositions are omnitemporally true, such that they cannot change from being false to true, or vice versa.

> It will be noticed that the interpretation given takes the notion of changing the past (or the future) as having to do with *changing the truth-values of propositions* about the past (or the future). Further, these truth-values are taken, as they normally are in logic, to be *omnitemporal*—if "Jones walks at T_1" is true, it is true at all times whatever (and of course, "Jones *will walk* at T_1" is true at all times *prior* to T_1, "Jones *walked* at T_1" at all times *after* T_1). But the notion of *changing* an *omnitemporal* truth value is indeed hopelessly confused; in this context the saying that the past cannot be changed makes very little sense.[18]

Let me be clear: I agree with Hasker that "the notion of *changing* an *omnitemporal* truth value is hopelessly confused." But if this notion is hopelessly confused, then it must be the case that whatever was true yesterday is now fixed. But this seems to undermine LFW, since genuine freedom requires the ability to do otherwise. According to the Principle of Alternative Possibilities (or PAP), in order for an agent *A* to be free

16. Hasker, *God, Time, and Knowledge*, 120. Hasker is careful to clarify in a footnote, "If someone *brings about* E's occurrence, it will no longer be true that *E will* occur—but this is not the sort of 'change in the future' that is in question." Hasker, *God, Time, and Knowledge*, 120n5. Cf. Mavrodes, "Is the Past Unpreventable?"

17. Hasker, *God, Time, and Knowledge*, 121. Hasker offers a more precise definition of what he means by temporal asymmetry: "*It is often in our power to determine which of two* [or more] *ways the future shall be, but it is never in our power to determine which of two* [or more] *ways the past shall be.* The past and the future are in this way fundamentally asymmetrical." Hasker, *God, Time, and Knowledge*, 123.

18. Hasker, *God, Time, and Knowledge*, 121–22.

with respect to some action *S*, at minimum, it must be within *A*'s power to do *S* and it must also be in *A*'s power to refrain from doing *S*. However, assuming the omnitemporality of truth, whatever was true yesterday about whether or not I would type is now fixed. Suppose that it was true yesterday that I would type, and suppose also (with Hasker) that I am free with respect to whether or not I type. If I have the ability to bring it about that I don't type, then it seems that I have the ability to bring it about that what *was* true was *not*, in fact, true. The only way that advocates of LFOT can avoid the charge that this amounts to changing of omnitemporal truth-values of propositions comes from appealing to counterfactual power over the past.

With the idea of counterfactual power over the past in view, we should revisit the idea of freedom. Let us assume that it was true yesterday that I would type today. Let us also assume that I am free with respect to whether or not to type. Advocates of counterfactual power over the past insist that, were I to refrain from typing, it is not the case that I would change the past, such that it *was* true that I would type, but then it *became false* that I would type. Rather, they maintain, were I to refrain from typing, it would have always been the case that I would not have typed today. As a result, omnitemporal truth-values don't change, even if I am free with respect to typing, *even if such freedom entails the ability to do otherwise*. Unfortunately for Hasker, appeals to counterfactual power over the past conflict with what he has written about truthmakers, as we will see below.

In the face of this problem, Hasker offers a different response that completely misses the point. He begins by noting how tenaciously logicians defend the notion of omnitemporal truth-values, but writes,

> It is quite clear that the locution we are examining is *misinterpreted* if placed in the context of such truth-values. It should be noted that such locutions as "You can't change the past" (cf. "There's no use crying over spilt milk") are used by a wide variety of persons, many of whom have never heard of propositions or of truth-values and are quite unaware of all they are missing by such sad deprivations. The dairy boy who has let the milk pail get kicked over isn't crying over any *proposition*—it's the spilt milk that bothers him! And although some philosophers may insist that "You can't change the future," it is worth noticing that it is *only* philosophers who say this—and then, only when they are bent on undermining the force of the parallel expression concerning the past. The context in which the ordinary person

talks about (not) changing the past is one in which the question of changing the future does not arise at all.[19]

Despite Hasker's insistence to the contrary, the metaphysical issues involved in the DFF in no way hinge on how accurately the philosophically unsophisticated communicate. Either it is true or it is false that the omnitemporality of truth entails that "You can't change the future," even if philosophers are the only ones who recognize it. Hasker *does* recognize this potential effect of the omnitemporality of truths, but appeals to counterfactual power over the past in order to avoid the conclusion.

Hasker demonstrates an awareness of another way out, but fails to take that route of escape:

> I have emphasized that the framework of omnitemporal truth-values fundamentally distorts the ordinary meaning of "You can't change the past." Indeed, this framework tends in general to cut across the grain of our natural way of regarding time and temporal processes. The most appropriate framework—the one that most closely parallels our ordinary ways of thinking about such matters—would, I maintain, be one in which it is *not* the case that if Jones walks at T_1, then "Jones will walk at T_1" was true at all previous times. It would be a framework in which propositions about contingent future events are not said to be true or false in the ordinary way.[20]

Hasker discusses a number of ways that such a framework might look.[21] First, he rejects the system developed by Arthur Prior in which all PCFC are false.[22] He also mentions (quite favorably) the non-bivalent system put forward originally by Richard Purtill which involves probability theory wherein PCFC range anywhere between zero and one up until the action/event in question is no longer contingent (either it becomes determined, or, by becoming actual in the present, is accidentally necessary).[23] But Hasker's desire to utilize a system like that of Purtill is not enough to motivate him to develop it, even though he believes it "conforms quite well to our intuitions about temporal processes as well as to our ordinary ways

19. Hasker, *God, Time, and Knowledge*, 122.

20. Hasker, *God, Time, and Knowledge*, 123–24.

21. Sanders mentions that there are at least five views on this matter available to open theists. See Sanders, *God Who Risks*, 335–36.

22. See Prior, "Formalities of Omniscience," reprinted in *Papers on Time*, 26–44. Also, see Seymour, "Advantages of All-Falsism."

23. Purtill, "Fatalism and the Omnitemporality," 188–89.

of talking about them." In spite of all this, Hasker concludes against using any alternative and sticks to a traditional understanding because he thinks "it is much better to employ a more neutral system of logic—in this case, traditional two-value logic with omnitemporal truth values."[24]

Now, there is no reason for someone who isn't committed to LFOT to affirm Purtill's argument. That is, we should deny that the omnitemporality of truth together with the unchangeability of the past entails fatalism, at least so long as we think that fatalism is the doctrine whereupon "there is nothing which we can do now which will make any statement about the future either true or false."[25] The omnitemporality of truth might entail some variety of determinism, but even if this is true, it would be a mistake to conclude that the omnitemporality of truth entails fatalism, for determinism is not the same as fatalism. Insofar as determinism is concerned, certain actions are what *determine* their effects; so there is a way to interpret causation into what it means to "make" something true or false. Said differently, the truth-maker for some proposition about the future is just the set of events that determine the truth-value of that proposition.[26] For instance, the fact that it was true yesterday that I would be typing today is made true by the fact that I willfully decided (freely, according to the compatibilist) to type today. So, my decision to type, even if alethically determined, plays a significant role in causing the truth-value of the proposition "Ben will type tomorrow" to be true yesterday. Because something I freely do makes the proposition true, fatalism turns out to be false. Rather, some type of agent-causation proves to be a more faithful interpretation of reality—at least if the Aristotelian version of truth fails and the omnitemporality of truth holds.

Now, this is no comfort to those who reject compatibilism as an adequate understanding of freedom (among whom are all open theists),

24. Hasker, *God, Time, and Knowledge*, 125. It is here that Hasker adds in a footnote his denial of the success of Purtill's argument concerning fatalism and the omnitemporality of truth: "I therefore do not agree with Purtill that the omnitemporality of truth, together with the unchangeability of the past, entails fatalism. The answer to this contention is found in the distinction between hard and soft facts—a distinction that Purtill considers but rejects for (in my opinion) inadequate reasons." Hasker, *God, Time, and Knowledge*, 125n10.

25. Purtill, "Fatalism and the Omnitemporality," 185.

26. That is, this understanding of truth-makers best suits a realist/correspondence theory of truth, which is the overwhelming majority position. The theory that I have in mind is articulated by Alston, *Realist Conception of Truth*, and more recently by Rasmussen, *Defending the Correspondence Theory*.

for they maintain that freedom is incompatible with determinism.[27] Nonetheless, I offer this clarification for those who see no way to escape Purtill's charge that fatalism follows from the omnitemporality of truth. This type of compatibilism, though, does nothing to save us from theological incompatibilism, because offering compatibilistic responses to the DFF is already a capitulation tantamount to acknowledging that *significant* freedom (i.e., LFW) cannot exist together with the omnitemporality of truth and the unchangeability of the past.

But, this inconsistent set is exactly the set of beliefs required by LFOT. If compatibilism is not a live option (and it isn't for any open theist), then it *does* seem that the omnitemporality of truth, because of the unchangeability of the past, precludes the ability to do otherwise. In fact, Hasker admits as much:

> The claim that "You can't change the past" seems to be one that expresses a powerful intuition—one that is common both to philosophers and to the philosophically unsophisticated. To interpret this claim as the claim that one cannot alter omnitemporal truth values is extremely unfortunate. Such an interpretation is mistaken, first of all, because many of those who make the claim have never heard of omnitemporal truth values and cannot be supposed to be talking about them. But more fundamentally, it is mistaken because the result of this interpretation is to create a symmetry between past and future, when the intuitive point of the expression is precisely the opposite. Omnitemporal truth values are *by definition* unchangeable, so to interpret the claim in terms of such truth values inevitably trivializes it.[28]

Hasker continues by affirming the exact basis for what open futurists utilize as a critique of the idea that any PCFC could presently be true.[29] The past cannot be changed because it is a "concrete totality of events and processes," but the future is not, for it is a realm of possibilities whose outcome is largely dependent on our own free choices. Therefore, a temporal asymmetry exists between the past and the future. As a result, because "the concrete totality of future events *does not yet exist*," the question of changing the future does not arise. But why should we think that PCFC—propositions that describe events which don't presently exist—presently

27. For a powerful argument in favor of this position, see Van Inwagen, *Essay on Free Will*.

28. Hasker, *God, Time, and Knowledge*, 125–26.

29. A similar view is expressed by Tuggy in "Roads to Open Theism."

possess truth-values? All open theists, to date, defend presentism as the correct ontology of time, whereupon the only reality that exists is at the present. Accordingly, the past no longer exists, and the future does not yet exist. If future contingent events are not part of what presently exists as a concrete totality (as all open theists maintain), we are left wondering what makes PCFC true or false in the first place. That is, we are left wondering how LFOT accounts for what the truthmakers are that make these PCFC true at all. Said differently, there seems to be a grounding objection against LFOT. Apart from some response to the grounding objection, it seems that OFOT is much more plausible than LFOT.[30]

Hard Facts and Soft Facts

In an effort to show why LFOT fails, I will next show how Hasker's denial of a distinction between hard and soft facts fails to accomplish what he needs it to achieve in order to eliminate the successful defense of the compatibility of freedom and foreknowledge offered by the hard fact/soft fact distinction. After showing why Hasker's denial of a hard fact/soft fact distinction fails, I provide an example to show why logical fatalism looms if advocates of LFOT insist on their version of theological incompatibilism. The example I provide also precludes those who defend LFOT from adopting Linda Zagzebski's arguments that the DFF is relevantly different from the problem of logical fatalism. If my argument succeeds, it forces the open theist to choose between: (1) concluding that humans lack significant freedom (a *highly* unlikely result); or (2) concluding against the view of LFOT regarding the existence of truth-values for PCFC. Said differently, if my argument is successful, then OFOT is the only tenable version of open theism, because (if my argument succeeds) LFOT is incoherent.

In order to clarify why LFOT fails, we must first endeavor to understand what is meant by the terms "hard fact" and "soft fact."[31] Those

30. Hasker, *God, Time, and Knowledge*, 126. This is especially true when we consider the way that theological incompatibilists reject Molinism as a legitimate solution to the dilemma of freedom and foreknowledge, and usually do so because middle knowledge is susceptible to the same grounding objection that defenders of LFOT fall prey to when they articulate an open futurist defense of future contingency.

31. There now exists a rather long literature on hard facts and soft facts. Although a bit dated, the best introduction to that literature is still Fischer's introduction to *God, Foreknowledge, and Freedom*, 1–56. Also of significant interest are the following: Freddoso, "Accidental Necessity and Logical Determinism"; Hasker, "Foreknowledge and

who defend such a distinction appeal to the idea that different propositions correspond either solely to the past (hard facts), or to something about the past as that past thing/event pertains to the future (soft facts). For example,

> (1) John had a cup of tea at lunch,

expresses a hard fact, whereas

> (2) it was true at 6:00 a.m. this morning that John would have a cup of tea at lunch,

uttered at 6:01 a.m., qualifies as a soft fact.[32] This is so because although (2) expresses something about the past, the past event described in (2) simultaneously refers to what was at that time a future event. Theological compatibilists who appeal to a hard fact/soft fact distinction argue that we have some power over the veracity of soft facts, even if they involve past events. Bruce Reichenbach offers the most succinct and lucid account of the compatibilist's strategy concerning hard and soft facts:

> The objector contends that no one has the power to act so that the past would be different than it was. Though this is true in a nonrelational sense—one cannot alter facts about the past which have no intrinsic relation to the present [i.e., hard facts]—it is not true in a relational sense. For example, I have the power to act so that Martin Luther was born exactly 502 years before I wrote this paragraph by writing it on November 10th, 1985. However, I also have the power to act so that Martin Luther was not born exactly 502 years before I wrote this by delaying my writing. Here I have the power to act so that the past is different than it was, because what is brought about is relationally dependent on the present. Of course, my power is limited. I do not have it in my power to act so that, by writing this now, Martin Luther landed on the moon 502 years before I wrote this. My power relates only to the part having to do with me. But this is what is involved with respect to God's foreknowledge. What God knows about the acts of a person is relationally dependent

---

Necessity"; Hasker, "Hard Facts and Theological Fatalism"; Hoffman and Rosenkrantz, "Hard and Soft Facts"; Plantinga, "On Ockham's Way Out"; Widerker, "Two Forms of Fatalism"; Widerker and Zemach, "Facts, Freedom, and Foreknowledge." These articles have been collected together, along with others, in Fischer, *God, Foreknowledge, and Freedom*.

32. Hasker, *God, Time, and Knowledge*, 82. One might alternatively consider, instead of (2), the following: It was true yesterday that I will leave work tomorrow at 5:00 p.m.

> on what the person who is the object of that knowledge does. Thus in this relational sense a person has the power to act so that the past is what it is, that is, that God truly believes something about the present. Consequently, there is no contradiction between my human freedom and divine foreknowledge.[33]

Regardless of whether one finds the distinction between hard facts and soft facts useful in settling issues pertaining to the DFF, we can all agree with Hasker that a fact is truly "hard" only if it does not depend on any future truth, future event, or future anything. Hard facts, then, are "future-indifferent propositions—propositions that are wholly about the past and the present, and that are such that their truth or falsity cannot be affected by anything that happens in the future."[34] So, a simple account of hard facts yields something like this:

> (3) An elementary proposition is future-indifferent IFF it is consistent with there being no times after the present, and also with there being times after the present.[35]

But, Hasker believes that theistic commitments preclude the existence of any genuinely future-indifferent propositions.

> If God is a metaphysically necessary being (i.e., exists in all possible worlds) and is also essentially everlasting (as compatibilists suppose), then we immediately get the result that no proposition whatever is future-indifferent, for any proposition metaphysically entails "God exists," which in turn entails the existence of times after the present.[36]

33. Reichenbach, "God Limits His Power," 110–11. Reichenbach uses the same example in "Hasker on Omniscience," 91. Cf. Hasker, *God, Time, and Knowledge*, 79; as well as Hasker's reply to Reichenbach, "Hardness of the Past."

34. Hasker, *God, Time, and Knowledge*, 83.

35. Hasker, *God, Time, and Knowledge*, 84. Cf. Hughes, "No Way Out?" 50–51.

36. Hasker, *God, Time, and Knowledge*, 86. Hasker's argument is inconclusive for at least two reasons. First, why should we suppose that God is essentially everlasting? Not all compatibilists suppose that God is essentially everlasting; rather, some compatibilists continue to defend divine timelessness, despite its contemporary unpopularity. Second, if God is timeless, there is nothing that any proposition necessitates (metaphysically speaking) concerning the existence of future times. This is so because no proposition about the past requires that God continue sustaining the universe (or time). Hasker begs the question against divine timelessness by presupposing the necessity of divine temporality as well as a number of positions concerning the metaphysics of time (i.e., time was created at the beginning of the universe, etc.). And, all of this stands regardless of whether or not God exists of necessity.

In all fairness, I must note that Hasker takes up the question of divine timelessness

Hasker goes on to insist that, "if the consistency mentioned in [(3)] is understood as *metaphysical* consistency, the distinction between hard and soft facts collapses."[37] I should note that even though this maneuver fails to accomplish what Hasker thinks it does, even if it did work, the move isn't available for Hasker because he denies that God is a necessary being.[38] Besides this, even if Hasker were to change his mind and embrace divine necessity, he is committed to other theological beliefs that entail the same conundrum.

> If, on the other hand, God's existence is not thought to be logically necessary, it is still reasonable to suppose that in a theistic universe *every contingent being has essentially the property, "being created by God."* And so, given God's essential everlastingness, we get the result that any proposition entailing the existence of contingent beings likewise metaphysically entails the existence of God and hence of future time. Furthermore, any proposition describing an event of the past, present, or future entails that God will *remember* that event for all time to come—so, no such proposition can be future-indifferent.[39]

Of course, Hasker's account precludes an analogical understanding of divine memory; rather, it presupposes divine temporality—a position not shared by many theological compatibilists.[40]

---

later in *God, Time, and Knowledge*, specifically chapter 8, "Is 'God is Timeless' Intelligible?," and chapter 9, "Is God Timeless?" As mentioned, at the time of writing *God, Time, and Knowledge*, Hasker believed that divine timelessness would solve the freedom/foreknowledge dilemma, were it true. Of course, Hasker rejects divine timelessness on other grounds. However, because he fails to discuss the issues involved in divine atemporality as they relate to hard facts and soft facts, the points I make above are crucial to understanding how LFOT is mistaken regarding hard facts/soft facts and the omnitemporality of truth.

37. Hasker, *God, Time, and Knowledge*, 87.

38. See Hasker, "Analytic Philosophy of Religion." I take up the issue of divine necessity as it relates to the freedom/foreknowledge dilemma again in chapter 5, where I discuss these issues at length.

39. Hasker, *God, Time, and Knowledge*, 86; emphasis added.

40. Consider, for example, the most recent defense of divine timelessness, offered by Helm, *Eternal God*. Despite his lucid defense of divine timelessness, Helm is an incompatibilist, but not of the open theist variety. Rather, Helm concludes against our possession of LFW. For a sampling of recent literature supporting the idea that divine timelessness *does* eliminate the dilemma of freedom and foreknowledge, see Green and Rogers, "Time"; Rogers, *Anselm on Freedom*; Rogers, "Anselmian Eternalism"; Rogers, "Necessity of the Present"; Rogers, "Omniscience, Eternity, and Freedom"; Rota, "Problem for Hasker."

But advocates of LFOT will not succeed by denying the distinction between hard and soft facts, at least not if such a denial relies on divine necessity and/or essential everlastingness. Supposing that God is metaphysically necessary *and* in time, the distinction between hard and soft facts does collapse, but it collapses in the direction of soft facts. According to Hasker, if we deny divine timelessness, no proposition can be genuinely future-indifferent, for every proposition entails the existence of times after the present. It follows, then, that all propositions are soft facts.[41] Furthermore, all that the compatibilist needs in order for her defense against theological incompatibilism to succeed is the existence of soft facts; she does not need hard facts, although such would require her to either deny the principle of the fixity of the past, or at least significantly rework what it means to say that past events are unalterable.

One major contributor to the contemporary discussions of hard facts and soft facts is David Widerker. He maintains that the distinction between hard facts and soft facts is enough to avoid what he calls non-theological fatalism (NTF), but the distinction is not successful in eliminating the threat of theological fatalism (TF). However, Widerker's position entails that free agents enjoy counterfactual power over the past:

> We can say that the error committed by the fatalist in (NTF) consists in his incorrect application of the principle of the fixity of the past. Given the fact that Jack pulls the trigger at *t*10, we may perfectly agree with the fatalist that it was always true that he would do so. But this does not mean that it was not within Jack's power to do otherwise. On the contrary. What our discussion of (NTF) has shown is that it was *Jack* who, by acting in the way he did, brought that state of affairs about. To the extent that it was within his power not to pull the trigger at *t*10, it also was within his power to bring it about that it was not always true that he would do so. The sense in which Jack might be said as a result to have power over the past is, as we have seen, a completely innocuous one.[42]

For those who affirm the absolute fixity of the past by denying any possibility of backwards causation and/or counterfactual power over the past, there is no such thing as "a completely innocuous" sense of power over the past. On the contrary, any power over the past is problematic,

41. This is all the more true if, as I defended in chapter 1, God is metaphysically necessary.

42. Widerker, "Two Forms of Fatalism," 105. Cf. Van Inwagen, *Essay on Free Will*, 42.

for no such power exists. Hence, the dilemma for LFOT remains, so long as its advocates deny that humans possess power (or counterfactual power) over the past. But does LFOT require the fixity of the past? To this question we now turn.

Counterfactual Power Over the Past

For those who deny Ockhamism and/or the possibility of counterfactual power over the past, abandoning the principle of the fixity of the past is quite unattractive.[43] All theological incompatibilists, including open theists, affirm that what once was contingent becomes necessary *per accidens*. For instance, at some previous time it was not necessary that I drop the ball; but having done so, I cannot now bring it about that I have not, in fact, dropped the ball; my dropping the ball has become accidentally necessary. Given the fixity of the past, what are we to make of propositions about the past which also concern future contingents (i.e., those propositions purported by some to be soft facts)? Why exactly is it that the omnitemporality of truth does not entail fatalism?

Hasker believes that the transfer of necessity principle applies such that if a syllogism is necessary (in some sense), it follows by distribution that if its premises are necessary (in the same sense), then the conclusion is also necessary (in the same sense).

$\Box\,(p \rightarrow q)$

$\Box\,p$

$\Box\,p \rightarrow \Box q$[44]

Given this account of the transfer of necessity and the fixity of the past, all past events are now accidentally necessary.[45] Thus, the conclusion of some syllogism is also accidentally necessary in virtue of the fact that it is entailed by something that has become accidentally necessary.

43. Cf. Ockham, *Predestination*; Adams, *William Ockham*; Plantinga, "On Ockham's Way Out." By fixity of the past, I mean the unchangeability of the past—"the doctrine that there is nothing which we can do now which will make any statement about the past either true or false, that is, the past is beyond our control." Purtill, "Fatalism and the Omnitemporality," 185.

44. For a more extensive discussion of the transfer of necessity, see Zagzebski, *Dilemma of Freedom*, 7–9.

45. I have quite a bit more to say about the different types of necessity at work in the DFF, but I reserve further comment until chapter seven.

Hence, if defenders of LFOT wish to continue maintaining that PCFC presently possess truth-values, and they simultaneously hold to the omnitemporality of truth (which they do), they should conclude that a proposition such as

> (4) it was true yesterday that I spoke truly to my wife when I told her (yesterday) that I will leave work tomorrow at 5:00 p.m.,

entails the necessity of my leaving work at 5:00 p.m. tomorrow. This establishes that the mere fact of the omnitemporality of truth entails a problem of logical fatalism quite independent of divine foreknowledge. This dilemma stems from the principle of the fixity of the past; I cannot presently bring it about that it was not the case that I spoke truly to my wife yesterday that I would leave work tomorrow at 5:00 p.m.

We must note that it being true yesterday that I spoke truly to my wife in saying that I will leave work tomorrow at 5:00 p.m. does not describe an event. Events take place at times. Hence, when we say that some state of affairs obtained yesterday, and that (because PCFC have truth-values) it was true yesterday that I would leave work tomorrow at 5:00 p.m., it follows that what was true yesterday is not an event, but rather a proposition—namely,

> I will leave work tomorrow at 5:00 p.m.

Given the omnitemporality of truth—which, we recall, entails that propositions do not *become* true, nor do they *become* false, nor can they *change* from being true to being false (or vice versa) even if the truth-makers of the propositions exist in the future—if it is true today that I will leave work tomorrow at 5:00 p.m., it was certainly true yesterday as well, and for as long as time has been around.[46] After it comes to pass tomorrow that I leave work at 5:00 p.m., it will likewise forever be true that I left work at 5:00 p.m. on the day represented by the indexical "tomorrow."

But some philosophers don't think that propositions are true at times.[47] Consider Zagzebski's summary of this position as it regards the problem of logical fatalism set in contrast to theological fatalism:

46. I am careful to say "for as long as time has been around" rather than everlastingly true, or eternally true, for saying such likely entails various metaphysical commitments concerning the nature of time that I need not commit myself to in order for the central thesis of this chapter to succeed. Readers who favor one view of time over another should make any necessary substitutions to make them happy without worry of any damage done to my argumentation.

47. Among others, Van Inwagen defends this view in *Essay on Free Will*, 34–43.

> A proposition is not tied to moments of time as an event is. Its truth is usually thought to be either timeless or omnitemporal. If omnitemporal, then if true at one time, it is true at all times, and there is no asymmetry between past and future. If timeless, then it is not true at moments of time at all and, again, there is no asymmetry between past and future. So there is not, or at least should not be, a temptation to think of propositions as becoming fixed [i.e., becoming accidentally necessary] at some point in time as there is with events. . . . I do not mean to say there is no reason *at all* to fear that the past truth of propositions is now accidentally necessary, but rather that God's past beliefs are not nearly as easy to exclude. And that is why the argument for theological fatalism is more serious [than the argument for logical fatalism].
>
> It seems to me, then, that past truth does not threaten fatalism to the extent threatened by divine foreknowledge. This is because past truth is not an event or state of affairs that becomes "fixed" once it occurs or obtains, or if it *is* an event/state of affairs, it is so only marginally or ambiguously. The argument for logical fatalism, then, does not seriously threaten [anyone's actions] with accidental necessity.[48]

If this account of propositions not being true at times is correct, then it initially seems that LFOT succeeds, and, alternatively, it also seems that divine timelessness offers another solution. However, when one considers issues that arise with regard to the grounding of these truth-values, we can see that either open theism is unmotivated because alternative solutions to the dilemma of freedom and foreknowledge (namely, Molinism) preserve exhaustive definite foreknowledge, or LFOT is saddled with problems that render it self-referentially incoherent. But before we explore the grounding objection as it relates to LFOT, we ought to first explore Hasker's use of proper names and the philosophy of language involved in his defense of LFOT.

Does a distinction between hard facts and soft facts, then, alleviate tensions raised by the logical problem of fatalism? Hasker says yes. Recall that he thinks the hard fact/soft fact distinction saves us from the fatalism that looms given Purtill's argument. But, because Hasker is wrong about divine necessity, this move fails.[49] I note again that Hasker believes

48. Zagzebski, *Dilemma of Freedom*, 27–28.

49. Hill argues against Hasker that a distinction between hard facts and soft facts does not collapse if God enjoys existence of necessity. See Hill, *Divinity and Maximal Greatness*, 78–88.

that if God is a necessary being, the distinction between hard facts and soft facts collapses. Given my defense of divine necessity in chapter 1,[50] I maintain that Hasker cannot appeal to the distinction between hard facts and soft facts that he thinks is important to the preservation of LFW because Hasker is wrong in denying that God is metaphysically necessary. Furthermore, given Hasker's account of hard facts and soft facts, appealing to some distinction between them entails the abandonment of perfect being theology, for surely a being is more perfect if that being exists of necessity than if that same being exists contingently. Furthermore, because the central thrust of my entire project is distinctly Anselmian in nature, I conclude that the perfect being theologian, when seeking to overcome the DFF, must reject open theism as a legitimate option. Besides this, if this chapter accomplishes nothing else, it points out that the success of LFOT hinges on denying God's necessary existence. Of course, this entails denying Anselmian conceptions of God's maximal greatness, which is surely not a position many theists are willing to take.

Hard Facts and the Philosophy of Religious Language

Some will undoubtedly suggest that denying divine necessity is not a problem, and that Hasker is able to save a distinction between hard facts and soft facts by distinguishing between references to "God" and references to "Yahweh." Whereas references to "God," according to Hasker, involve all of the properties and metaphysical attributes he possesses, references to "Yahweh" do not. Instead, the ancient Hebrews used this name in referring to their God

> with no thought or connotation of such metaphysical attributes as essential omniscience, essential everlastingness, and the like. . . . We will take care to avoid importing into the name's significance such metaphysical notions as essential everlastingness. We will use the name, as the ancient Hebrews did, simply as a nonconnotative proper name referring to that individual who in fact was, and is, the God of Abraham, Isaac, and Jacob.[51]

50. That is, if Hasker denies that God is a necessary being, he owes us an explanation of why God as creator does not entail that God is a necessary being. This is especially true given the arguments of William Lane Craig and Brian Leftow, who both maintain that cosmological arguments show God to be a necessary being. See Craig, *Kalam Cosmological Argument*; Leftow, "Necessity."

51. Hasker, *God, Time, and Knowledge*, 92.

Armed with this understanding, Hasker believes that he can avoid the use of God-talk in constructing a DFF and thereby eliminate an appeal to the fact that God-talk necessitates the lack of future-indifference. Thus, instead of

> (7) God has always believed that Clarence will have a cheese omelet tomorrow,

Hasker invites readers to see the dilemma formulated with

> (8) Yahweh has always believed that Clarence will have a cheese omelet tomorrow.[52]

According to Hasker, (8) is a future-indifferent proposition. Because Judeo-Christian theists suppose that (8) is true, it follows that (8) is a hard fact.

Hasker continues by suggesting what all Judeo-Christian philosophical theologians believe:

> (9) If Yahweh exists, Yahweh is God.

After introducing this idea, Hasker immediately notes,

> This proposition is not conceptually necessary; its truth is not implied by the meanings of the terms in which it is expressed. And the proposition will not be future-indifferent, because its consequent conceptually entails God's existence. But [(9)] assuredly is a *metaphysically* necessary truth: it expresses an *essential property* of Yahweh. There is no possible world in which Yahweh exists but is not God; no one, not even God himself and certainly no human being, could bring it about that Yahweh exists but is not God. So although [(9)] is not a future-indifferent proposition, it is, in virtue of (H6) [Any conceptually or metaphysically necessary truth is a hard fact], a hard fact.[53]

With all this in view, Hasker offers the following argument, which he believes is a version of the DFF comprised entirely of hard facts.

> (8) Yahweh has always believed that Clarence will have a cheese omelet tomorrow.

> (9) If Yahweh exists, Yahweh is God.

52. Regarding (7) and (8), as well as the other numbered propositions in this section, I utilize Hasker's exact wording. Only the numeration has been changed.

53. Hasker, *God, Time, and Knowledge*, 93. (H6) taken from Hasker, *God, Time, and Knowledge*, 89.

Hasker is careful to remind us of another step in his argumentation, namely, his commitment to the idea that

> (A2) necessarily, if God has always believed that a certain thing will happen, then that thing will happen.

Hasker maintains that (8) and (9) together entail that

> (C3) God has always believed that Clarence will have a cheese omelet tomorrow.

And, of course, (C3), together with (A2), entails that

> (10) Clarence will have a cheese omelet tomorrow.

According to Hasker, the fact that (10) is entailed by a set of hard facts makes (10) itself a hard fact, and this is enough to remove LFW from Clarence.[54] Here I wish to make two points in order to show why Hasker's argumentation fails, the first of which is quite short, the second rather lengthy.

First, Hasker fails to apply the logical law of hypothetical syllogism to his argument. If *p* entails *q*, and *q* entails *r*, then, by hypothetical syllogism, *p* entails *r*. Suppose we agree with Hasker that "if Yahweh exists, Yahweh is God" and that this is metaphysically necessary. If Hasker is right, then "Yahweh is God" expresses an essential property of Yahweh. To restate the obvious, it follows from all this that if Yahweh exists, then Yahweh is God. Assuming, as we have throughout this project in analytic theology, that Christianity is true, Yahweh does exist, so it follows that Yahweh is God; and if it is true that Yahweh is God, and that Yahweh exists, it must also be true that God exists. However, if "God exists" entails that "God is essentially everlasting," then it follows, assuming Christianity is true, that "If Yahweh exists, then God is essentially everlasting." This is enough to show that (8) does not qualify as a hard fact, for despite Hasker's protestations to the contrary, (8) does not turn out to be a genuinely future-indifferent fact, and is therefore not a hard fact.

This brings up a second point, which concerns Hasker's philosophy of language. It is not possible to substitute "God" for "Yahweh" unless we claim that "God" and "Yahweh" have the same referent (in which case both "God" and "Yahweh" are proper names). Hasker wants to use "God" to refer to the God of the philosophers, but he uses "Yahweh" to refer to the God of Abraham, Isaac, and Jacob. If the substitution he makes is

54. Hasker, *God, Time, and Knowledge*, 93–94.

legitimate, then both "God" and "Yahweh" have the same referent and the distinction between the two that he makes won't hold. This is so because all the properties that God has, surely Yahweh has as well, if it is true that Yahweh is God. According to Hasker, Yahweh is God—and "Yahweh's being God" is an essential property of "Yahweh." At minimum, Hasker owes us an argument for why we should take "Yahweh" as something different from "God," especially when he wants to simultaneously use the principle of substitution to bring "God" into play from "Yahweh."

But it does seem that Hasker uses the principle of substitution, and he seems to be using it in an invalid way. Names (such as "Yahweh") are signs that signify objects, and as a sign, a name refers directly to the object itself. When we say that the meaning of a name is the object itself, we mean that the referent exhausts the meaning of the name. That is, the semantic content (i.e., literal meaning) of a name such as "Yahweh" is the object itself. When a religious person speaks of Yahweh, she is not necessarily referring to all the properties of the object.[55] But Hasker seems to agree with the consensus view, which is the neo-Millian position advocated by Saul Kripke,[56] in which a name refers directly to an object, without mediation. Simply put, "God" just means God, and "Yahweh" just means Yahweh. That is, the religious person refers solely to the object and not to all the properties that the object possesses when he says "Yahweh." If Hasker wishes to use the name "Yahweh" in this way but wants to use the name "God" in some other way, he owes us an explanation of how he is using this religious language—it won't do for him to simply assert names and, by some sleight of hand, substitute "God" for "Yahweh."

Another way to think about this is to consider the phenomenon that what a person means is not always what they convey with their speech. Sometimes a person's language conveys more (or less) than the sum total of the definitions of the words comprising a sentence would initially suggest. Perhaps the ancient Hebrews didn't mean to incorporate notions of metaphysical necessity and/or essential everlastingness into their claims about Yahweh. But if Yahweh is God, then claims about Yahweh can imply more than a speaker intends. That is, even though

55. Perhaps someone could say that on certain conceptions of the Fregean neo-descriptivist view, proper names pick out all of the properties of the referent, but not even Frege himself defended this view. See Frege, "On Sense and Reference," reprinted in *Meaning and Reference*, 23–42; Frege, "Thought," 325–45.

56. Mill, *System of Logic*. Cf. Kripke, *Naming and Necessity*. See also Soames, *Beyond Rigidity*; Hughes, *Kripke*.

Hasker intends (8) to be a soft fact, in fact (8) is a hard fact, because we know that Yahweh is an essentially everlasting being even if the ancient Hebrews didn't know this or intend this when they spoke of Yahweh. Accordingly, we can now see that (8) is a hard fact.[57]

Also, the neo-Millian view understands identity (which is picked out by proper names) to be both reflexive and transitive. So, if Clark Kent is Superman, then Superman is Clark Kent. And, if Clark Kent is Superman, and if Superman is the Man of Steel, then Clark Kent is the Man of Steel. Similarly, if Superman is faster than a speeding bullet, then Clark Kent is faster than a speeding bullet (and so is the Man of Steel!). Additionally, the metaphysical issues involved in the way language refers to things do not depend on whether or not someone is aware of the relationships between Clark Kent, Superman, and the Man of Steel. So, if Lois Lane refers to Clark Kent, then she simultaneously refers to Superman even if she does not intend to do so. That is, nothing hangs on Lois Lane's knowledge of whether Clark Kent is Superman when she says, "Clark Kent is an excellent reporter, but he never seems to be around whenever Superman saves the day." Even though she believes Clark Kent and Superman are two different people, her language is best interpreted, not according to what she intends but rather according to what is true. Because Clark Kent and Superman are not two different people, those who know the truth understand that when Lois Lane speaks of Clark Kent, she is simultaneously speaking of Superman despite her ignorance of the fact that Clark Kent is Superman.

By parallel reasoning, whether they realized it or not, when the ancient Hebrews spoke of Yahweh they were referring to a being who is essentially everlasting—at least we must conclude this if we, like Hasker, maintain that Yahweh is God and that God is an essentially everlasting being. Thus, when people say

> (8) Yahweh has always believed that Clarence will have a cheese omelet tomorrow,

they imply, whether they realize it or not, that

> (11) an essentially everlasting being has always believed that Clarence will have a cheese omelet tomorrow.

57. For a more detailed account of conversational implicature, see Grice, *Studies*, especially his chapter on "Presupposition and Implicature," 269–82.

Obviously, by Hasker's standards, (11) is not a hard fact. Neither, then, is (8) a hard fact, at least not as long as we maintain that Yahweh is God and that God is an essentially everlasting being.

With all this in view, if Hasker maintains that "God" and "Yahweh" do not refer to the same object, Christians are left struggling to understand the following theological claims: (a) Jesus is God; and (b) Yahweh is God. So understood, if Jesus is God, then it is also true that God is Jesus. Additionally, if it is true that Jesus died on the cross, then it is also true that God died on the cross. But the transitivity of identity entails that Yahweh also died on the cross, at least if we conclude that Jesus is Yahweh.[58] But this account demands further explanation concerning the Trinitarian relationships within the Godhead. If this view does not hold, we are left with serious questions about the identity of Jesus.[59] Of course, it is best to agree with the neo-Millian position regarding names of God, especially given the alternative of Fregean neo-descriptivism. But the identity issues this view raises cannot be solved except insofar as such a solution prevents the sort of DFF Hasker offers as a means of escaping the issues surrounding hard facts and soft facts.

Perhaps Hasker could avoid these problems if he were to affirm that "God" is not a name at all, but rather is a count noun used to pick out one thing of a kind. This would mean that someone uses "God" in the same way that "lion" is used when someone says, "Simba is a lion." Thus, "God" actually has some meaning outside of monotheistic religion, such that "Zeus is God" is a coherent expression, as is "Hercules is the son of a god." But of course, this seems to entail the predication of divine attributes to Yahweh when someone says, "Yahweh is God." As a result, such a view will not save Hasker's argument.

The real question here is whether or not "God" is a rigid designator. If "God" is a rigid designator (which makes sense, given the idea that "God" is a name), the term "God" picks out the same thing in all worlds.

58. Contemporary New Testament scholarship certainly supports the claim that Jesus is rightly identified as the Incarnation of Yahweh. See Bauckham, *Jesus and the God of Israel*.

59. I do not mean to suggest by this line of argumentation that all Christians must understand "Jesus is God" as an identity statement, for there are other issues that present on such an account. For instance, Daniel Hill has brought to my attention that the transitivity of identity also requires that if Jesus is God, and if the Father is God, then one may be forced to conclude wrongly that Jesus is the Father. To be clear, I deny that Jesus is the Father, but topical and space constraints preclude any further investigation into the doctrine of the Trinity at this juncture, lest we move too far afield of our present concerns.

As I discussed in chapter 1, following Peter van Inwagen, we do best to interpret "God" as referring to whatever there is one of in Anselmian monotheism. Accordingly, "God," when used in the Christian sense, picks out the divine Being. But this view raises as many questions as it solves, at least for Hasker. For instance, how are we to distinguish between the semantic content (strictly the object/referent) and the pragmatic content, which involves speech-act theory—the things that I intend with the language?[60] If Hasker means to include the pragmatic content of divine attributes when he uses the name "God" (which makes the most sense given the context of his argument) he owes us a much more serious explanation as to *why* the name "God" includes pragmatic content of divine attributes while "Yahweh" does not. That is, the gloss on language his argument suggests demands more explanation.

Perhaps the best route is to deny altogether that "God" is a name, and to assert that it is, rather, a predicate. This avoids all the problems I've raised against Hasker's use of "God" as a name. However, unfortunately for Hasker, it brings us right back to where we started. On this view, Hasker predicates divinity to Yahweh with the expression "Yahweh is God." But if this is Hasker's intention, it follows that (8) is not a hard fact, for if "Yahweh is God" is meant to predicate divinity to Yahweh, it follows that "Yahweh" possesses all the properties of divinity—including metaphysical necessity and/or essential everlastingness.

I have sought to find some way to make sense of Hasker's use of religious language. Despite my best efforts, I am unable to see how Hasker's commitment to the fact that "Yahweh is God" allows him to deny that Yahweh possesses all the divine attributes, including those attributes which prevent (7) from qualifying as a genuinely future-indifferent proposition. Therefore, if (7) does not qualify as a hard fact, it seems to follow that neither does (8) qualify as either a future-indifferent proposition or (from some other rationale) a hard fact. That is, I defend this at least as long as one maintains that "Yahweh" refers to the being who is God.[61]

60. It has been brought to my attention that this is not uncontroversial. Generally speaking, one usually takes the semantic content of language to include the sense of the expression. However, if the expression is a proper name (as is the case in our present concern), things get tricky because of the nature of designation involved with proper names. Thanks to Daniel Hill for bringing this to my attention.

61. I am especially grateful to Justin Grace for many conversations on the issues related to the philosophy of religious language, as well as his helpful feedback on a draft of this section. I should also note that I found his dissertation quite helpful, especially as it relates to how divine names function semantically. See Grace, "Referring to God."

The Grounding Objection and Limited Foreknowledge Open Theism

When discussing grounding objections and their relation to the DFF, philosophers have grown accustomed to thinking that Molinism must be center stage. I intend to show that if the grounding objection undermines Molinism, it also undermines LFOT. I do not intend to defend Molinism. Rather, I intend to show that if one's metaphysical commitments enable LFOT to be a coherent system (in that it preserves a genuinely libertarian conception of human freedom), then open theism is unmotivated because those same metaphysical commitments will undoubtedly provide a foundation for Molinism, which stands as an alternative account of divine omniscience that preserves exhaustive definite foreknowledge of future contingents. Presumably, on any standard Anselmian perfect being theology, a being who enjoys exhaustive definite foreknowledge of future contingents is thought to be superior to a being who lacks such knowledge. Accordingly, given such an analysis, the Molinist position should be favored over an open theistic response, all else being equal.

Molinists suggest that God, in virtue of what is called middle knowledge, has exhaustive knowledge of what free agents would do in various circumstances, even if those circumstances are different than the ones that actually obtain.[62] God is said to know the truth-values of all counterfactuals of creaturely freedom (CCFs). On the basis of such knowledge (called divine middle knowledge), God is able to govern the universe in a way that preserves meticulous providence and exhaustive definite foreknowledge. The most prominent objections to divine middle knowledge are offered by those who employ some version of what is known as the grounding objection.[63] The grounding objection states that there don't ex-

62. A complete analysis of Molinism is well beyond the scope of this project. However, the major works on the subject include Dekker, *Middle Knowledge*; Flint, *Divine Providence*; Freddoso, Introduction; Hill, *Divinity and Maximal Greatness*, 104–24.

63. Hasker argues against Molinism by suggesting that the CCFs that drive Molinist conceptions of divine foreknowledge and providence cannot possibly be up to the agents that these CCFs are about. Although this objection initially looks like something other than the grounding objection, Eef Dekker and Tom Flint both argue that Hasker's argument parallels, or offers a "twist," on the standard grounding objection, and Hasker himself concedes that his argument includes a variant of the "no grounds" objection. Basinger et al., *Openness of God*, 4; Flint, *Divine Providence*, 138. Taking it on good authority, then, I anticipate that the arguments that I offer concerning grounding will serve equally well as defeaters for Hasker's anti-Molinist arguments. Should they fall short, still other objections to his anti-Molinist arguments will prove useful, especially Cunningham, "Hasker's Anti-Molinist Argument," 200–222.

ist any grounds to the truth of the counterfactuals of creaturely freedom that enable Molinism to solve the DFF.[64] Because the truths of the CCFs are thought to be contingent (which is necessary to avoid determinism), worries arise as to how Molinists can fend off accusations of violating the Principle of Sufficient Reason (PSR).

In order to capture a very technical issue in as plain a way as possible, the PSR suggests that everything must have a reason or a cause, or, more specifically, that all contingent facts must have explanations.[65] Therefore, there is an answer to the question "Why is it that . . . ?" for any contingent truth. If the cause or foundation of one contingent truth is another contingency, the PSR suggests that we avoid both circular reasoning and infinite regress because any such line of questioning bottoms out, eventually, in some necessary truth.[66]

It is important to note that we are dealing with contingent truths and not necessary truths, because Molinists affirm that CCFs are contingently true. Additionally, defenders of LFW insist that there is nothing that is necessary about the sorts of future contingents that open theists say God has no knowledge about. For instance, if Abby is free with respect to whether or not to drink orange juice with her breakfast tomorrow, then it is both up to Abby whether or not she drinks the orange juice, and Abby presently has the ability to bring it about that she drinks the orange juice, and Abby also has the ability to bring it about that she refrains from drinking the orange juice. So understood, there is nothing necessary about Abby's drinking (or refraining from drinking) the orange juice; rather, it is contingent.

So consider the following proposition:

<Abby will freely drink orange juice tomorrow with her breakfast.>

Let's suppose that this proposition is true, and let's further suppose, as advocates of LFOT would have us believe, that God is unable to know such a truth. Accordingly, there exists a truth about a future contingent event that God doesn't know.

64. Dekker, *Middle Knowledge*, 44–52; Flint, *Divine Providence*, 121–37; Freddoso, Introduction, 68–74.

65. Cf. Pruss, *Principle of Sufficient Reason*.

66. One important advocate of LFOT, van Inwagen, objects to the PSR because he fears it leads to modal collapse. Van Inwagen, *Essay on Free Will*, 202–4. However, Tomaszewski has argued against Van Inwagen's position cogently in his article "Principle of Sufficient Reason." See also Pruss, *Principle of Sufficient Reason*, 97–125.

If it is true that Abby will freely drink orange juice with her breakfast, it is false that she will not drink orange juice with her breakfast. Advocates of LFOT do not take themselves to be Geachians, whereupon a proposition can be true at some time and can change to be false at some later time.[67] Since this view entails the mutability of future contingent truths, it denies the alethic settledness of the future, and is incompatible with the omnitemporality of truth, which is an important component of the LFOT system.

It would be enough to criticize such an understanding by discussing Peircean semantics as opposed to Ockham's semantics with regard to the linguistic function of "will" and "will not" as these words function in the proposition in question. Some thinkers maintain that "will" and "will not" imply a type of determinism (perhaps even causal determinism).[68] However, advocates of LFOT deny this, so I'll reserve comment on these matters until later.[69] Suffice it to say, and this is obvious, but it is very important to note: If it is true that Abby *will* drink the orange juice, then it is true that she is going to drink the orange juice. And if Abby *won't* drink the orange juice, then it is true that she is not going to drink the orange juice.

Those who believe that employing the hard fact/soft fact distinction enables one to escape the logical problem of fatalism maintain that it can be true at t_1 that Abby will drink the orange juice at t_3, and yet at t_2, Abby can bring it about that she refrains from drinking the orange juice at t_3. Perhaps Geach would insist that at t_1 it *was* true that Abby was going to drink the orange juice, but then things changed, and perhaps such an analysis makes sense, given that we are committed to taking tense seriously. But, as already noted, LFOT forbids this analysis. Furthermore, if Abby actually ends up refraining from drinking the orange juice at t_3, any statements prior to t_3 predicting that she would actually drink the orange juice fail to accurately correspond to the state of affairs that actually obtains at t_3. I take it as obvious that we intend statements about the future to map onto the *future*, and that we intend these statements to map accurately. When speaking about the future, it is very uncommon that

67. Geach suggests this possibility in light of the metaphysics of prevention. So, it is true to say, "The plane is going to crash," but it is also true to say, "The plane was going to crash until the pilot prevented the crash." Todd, "Geachianism."

68. Cf. Rhoda's essays and articles: "Fivefold Openness"; "Generic Open Theism"; "Case for Open Theism."

69. I take up these issues again and address them at length in chapter 6.

someone intends to refer to the present state of affairs in light of possible futures. All this to say, Geach's analysis of prevention and indeterminism is impressive, and certainly more complex than I have space to cover here, but Geachianism won't help defenders of LFOT because we are concerned with *definite* foreknowledge given the omnitemporality of truth.

So, if it is true that Abby will drink the orange juice tomorrow, then Abby drinks the orange juice. If it were the case both that it is true that Abby will drink the orange juice tomorrow, and yet Abby somehow ends up refraining from drinking the orange juice, this amounts to a logical contradiction. We should not interpret the sentence "Abby will freely drink orange juice tomorrow with her breakfast" to be predicting something about the tendency of which possible world might obtain in the future in light of present tendencies; rather, we take such a sentence to be a prediction about what possible world is actually going to obtain tomorrow.

But I have suggested that the grounding objection cuts against LFOT, so we need to turn our attention to the issue of truth. I am strongly committed to realism about truth, but as far as I can tell, one needn't endorse one particular theory of truth (e.g., axiomatic, deflationary, correspondence) to see why the grounding objection poses a problem for LFOT. Before anyone could reasonably conclude that God lacks exhaustive definite foreknowledge, one ought to examine alternative proposed solutions to the DFF and rule out the possibility of their success. Open theists (including defenders of LFOT) have consistently ruled out Molinism on the basis of the grounding objection. But, as we shall now see, that sword cuts two ways. Open theists who reject the most contemporary articulations of Molinism do so because they find unsatisfactory the denial of TSB that renders Trenton Merricks's formulation of Molinism immune from the grounding objection.[70] But, because open theists reject the denial of TSB, for the sake of philosophical consistency it must be the case that whatever alternative system they suggest will have to meet whatever standards are required by TSB.

On any standard understanding of propositions, PCFC expressed by sentences such as "Abby will freely drink orange juice tomorrow with her breakfast," if they are true at all, are true in virtue of something. What is it that grounds the truth of the proposition <Abby will freely drink orange juice tomorrow with her breakfast>? Three different ontologies of time (four-dimensionalism, growing-blockism, and presentism) have

70. Merricks, "Truth and Molinism." See also Merricks, *Truth and Ontology*, especially 146–55.

resources that could provide grounding for the truth-values of PCFC. On a four-dimensionalist understanding of time, the future is ontologically real, and a future state of affairs that includes Abby's drinking the orange juice sufficiently grounds the truth of the proposition in question. However, advocates of LFOT consistently reject B-theoretic approaches to time, including four-dimensionalism, for at least two reasons. First, they insist that there is something ontologically privileged about the present such that tense doesn't ultimately reduce to "earlier than," "later than," or "simultaneous with" relations. Second, they argue that if the future is real, then it follows that it is not only alethically settled, but is also causally and ontologically settled, which obviously undermines free will, and therefore eliminates any motivation for open theism (e.g., the future is not epistemically open).

But perhaps there is a way around this worry. Suppose that LFW enables us to choose between which of multiple B-theoretic time series obtains. On such a view, there are multiple time series that are equally real, but it is up to us which one is actualized. That is, it is within our power to bring it about that some particular time series obtains. The reason that this solution fails is that it requires that one simultaneously maintain two incompatible positions. On the one hand, it requires that the advocate of LFOT posit some particular B-series that gives rise to a future state of affairs that serves as the ontological ground of the truth-value of the proposition <Abby will freely drink orange juice tomorrow with her breakfast> (and this means that such a B-series is real, and fixed) while simultaneously saying that some alternative B-series could become actualized and thereby serve to ground a different truth-value for the same proposition.

Now, we must consider the main idea that gives rise to a distinction between hard facts and soft facts. Assuming temporal asymmetry as understood by the defender of LFOT, the past is fixed such that there is nothing that anyone can do to change it, whereas the future is thought to be causally open yet alethically settled. Part of what drives this commonsense conception is that whatever serves to ontologically ground the truth-values of propositions about the past has either come and gone, or obtains now at the present. Either way, it is too late to do anything about it, which is why these facts are thought to be fixed, or hard. Soft facts, on the other hand, are indexed both to the past (or present) and the future. But if the grounding objection serves as a defeater of Molinism, so too will it raise questions as to what serves to ground the truth-values of PCFC, even if we call those PCFC soft facts.

The suggestion that some B-series serves to ground the truth-values of PCFC together with the idea that a different B-series could obtain amounts to the claim that some ontology of the actual world can become a different ontology of the world, all while remaining the same possible world; but this is absurd, for such amounts to a logical contradiction. To see why, consider that if we have the ability to rearrange the ontological furniture of the universe as demanded by this proposed solution, there is no good reason to think that one couldn't do so in such a way that changes the truth-values of propositions about the past. Responses to this controversial claim that include restating claims about temporal asymmetry amount to begging the question, or it is an *ad hoc* way of avoiding the problem. Therefore, if some B-series is sufficient to ontologically ground the truth-values of PCFC, then changes to which B-series is actual counts as an ontological change, and this is a change to something that is *hard*. Therefore, this amounts to the claim that the world is a certain way, and is fixed in this way so as to ground the truth-values of PCFC, but can be unfixed so as to become different. All told, we can rule out any B-theoretic approaches to time as serving to ground the truth-values of PCFC, which leaves two A-theoretic approaches.

The alternative A-theoretic ontologies of time that we must consider are growing blockism and presentism. Presentism is championed by all open theists, but there wouldn't be anything incoherent about an open theist appealing to growing blockism instead. On both growing-blockism and presentism, the future isn't ontologically real, so future states of affairs cannot serve to ground the truth-values of PCFC.

Because the future isn't ontologically available to ground the truth-values of PCFC on either growing blockism or presentism, advocates of LFOT need to look to something in the present that grounds the truths in question. Those who favor growing blockism could argue that something in the past grounds the truth-values of PCFC, but since presentist accounts will mirror whatever moves are made here by growing blockists, and because contemporary advocates of LFOT are presentists, in what follows I will focus on presentism.

Assuming presentism, the only time that exists is the present—there is no past, and there is no future, ontologically considered. Therefore, there must be some state of affairs that obtains in the present state of affairs that secures the truth-value of PCFC. But notice that, assuming any version of open theism, whatever state of affairs obtains in the present (or obtained in the past) that serves to ontologically ground the truth-values of PCFC guarantees that outcome. This is true because, in any given possible world, once the present arrives, it is too late for something else to obtain at one and the same moment in that same possible world. In any given world, at any given present moment, the state of affairs that is the present cannot be any other state of affairs in that same world at that same moment, lest a contradiction arise. To see why this is the case, consider the fact that once the past has occurred in a given possible world, on the thesis of the fixity of the past, the past cannot later become a different past because whatever has obtained cannot be changed once it has obtained. The same holds true for the present. In any given possible world, once the present state of affairs obtains, it is fixed, and cannot in one any the same present moment be some different state of affairs, on pains of contradiction. Therefore, we do well to note that the present lies on the side of the past with respect to temporal asymmetry.

Consider what would be the case if some state of affairs grounds the truth that Abby will freely drink orange juice tomorrow with her breakfast, yet Abby is free to refrain from drinking orange juice tomorrow. That would mean that at $t1$, some state of affairs obtains that grounds the proposition in question, but at some later moment, a different state of affairs obtains which grounds a different truth-value for the same proposition. Obviously, if a later state of affairs obtains that gives rise to a different outcome, then it is false to say that whatever prior state of affairs had obtained truly *grounded* the truth-value of the proposition in question—after all, a different truth-value for the same proposition can obtain.

So this proposed solution fails for two reasons. First, the advocate of LFOT is equivocating about whether some future event really "will" or "will not" happen, at least so long as they continue insisting that some PCFC are omnitemporally true, yet we have the ability to bring it about at some future moment that they are false. Second, the ontological changes required to make sense of LFOT amount to rearranging the ontological furniture of the universe, but this should be impossible, for the ontological arrangements that give rise to omnitemporal truths are rightly understood to be sufficiently hard, or fixed. Therefore, assuming that such ontological rearranging is possible at all, there is no good reason to embrace temporal asymmetry without either begging the question or positing some reason that is exceedingly *ad hoc*.

To restate things, if it is presently true that Abby will freely drink orange juice tomorrow with her breakfast, yet it is within Abby's power to refrain from drinking the orange juice tomorrow, then it is within Abby's ability to bring it about that what was true was not, in fact, true. Given the ontologies that can make sense out of this, we are left without a good reason to see why counterfactual power over the past cannot also be applied to hard facts. Suppose that Abby has the ability to bring it about that, if she were to refrain from drinking the orange juice, it would have been the case that the ontology that would have been actual would be an ontology that would have grounded the truth of the proposition <Abby will freely refrain from drinking orange juice with her breakfast tomorrow>. Given that whatever ontology obtained in the past is sufficiently hard, and that we cannot rearrange the ontological furniture of the universe, we have no good reason to see why such counterfactual powers couldn't apply equally to God's past beliefs. If Abby is free with respect to what ontology obtained, then she is also free with respect to what God believed. If it is presently true that Abby will freely drink orange juice tomorrow with her breakfast, and it is also true that God presently believes that Abby will freely drink the orange juice tomorrow with her breakfast, and it is also true that it is within Abby's ability to refrain from drinking the orange juice tomorrow with her breakfast, then Abby has counterfactual power such that if Abby were to refrain from drinking the orange juice, she has it within her power to bring it about that God always believed she would refrain from drinking the orange juice with her breakfast.

We have seen that any proposal that satisfies the worries of those who argue against Molinism by way of the grounding objection, regardless of which ontology of time is being considered, either fails to preserve genuine freedom, or it amounts to rearranging the ontological furniture of the universe in an unacceptable manner. Therefore, once issues stemming from the grounding objection have been addressed, LFOT is either self-defeating or unmotivated. So long as advocates of LFOT are unwilling to embrace open futurism, they cannot argue in a philosophically consistent way against Molinism by way of anything akin to the grounding objection. Therefore, on any temporal ontology that makes LFOT coherent, it is either the case that genuine freedom (as understood by the libertarian) is eliminated (and so LFOT is false), or Molinism is available as an equally plausible means of diffusing tensions raised by the DFF. Consequently, since the arguments above demonstrate that LFOT is either self-defeating or unmotivated, those who find defenses of traditional understandings of divine omniscience to be unsatisfactory in light of the DFF should embrace some type of open futurism.[71]

Conclusion

I have shown that LFOT, because of its commitment to the omnitemporality of truth, either entails fatalism despite its denial of divine foreknowledge, or leaves alternative responses to the DFF with sufficient metaphysical foundations so as to render LFOT unmotivated. Because advocates of LFOT, like all open theists, affirm both the libertarian view that free will requires the ability to do otherwise, and that humans have free will, advocates of LFOT should endorse Peter Geach's view that the truth-values of PCFC can change (and thereby give up omnitemporality of truth), or they should embrace OFOT, which defends the alethic openness of the future. In light of the philosophy of language as it concerns divine names, I argued that Hasker's attempt to provide a distinction between hard facts and soft facts fails. Furthermore, apart from such a distinction, Purtill's argument for fatalism (or at least determinism) from the omnitemporality of truth holds, at least if one denies the possibility of counterfactual power over the past. Thus, if one wishes to defend open theism as a means of preserving significant freedom in response to the DFF, it seems that denying divine foreknowledge necessitates the alethic openness of the future.

71. Various articulations of open future open theism have been defended by Hess, Rhoda, Todd, Tuggy, and Zimmerman. I reserve further comment on these types of open theism for another chapter.

5

When Does God Learn?

Open Theism, Simultaneous Causation, and Divine Knowledge of the Present[1]

In order to construct a *reductio ad absurdum*, let us grant that open theists are right to conclude in the face of the dilemma of freedom and foreknowledge (DFF) that God lacks exhaustive definite foreknowledge. From this assumption, I will show that open theism's response to the DFF requires not only a conclusion against divine foreknowledge, but also that God lacks knowledge of the present. I take as obvious that this is an undesirable conclusion for any theist. Hence, if my argument holds, open theism should be rejected.

It has become somewhat customary for pieces of analytic philosophy to begin with a section of prolegomena in which terms are defined and parameters set, but I won't follow that convention in this chapter. Rather than frontloading a sizeable section of prolegomena, wisdom dictates that I discuss the technicalities concerning different types of necessity along the way rather than expect readers to remember everything aforementioned while simultaneously navigating the already challenging terrain that comprises those philosophical puzzles of divine foreknowledge and human freedom. That said, for those who benefit from a road map, allow me to offer an outline of how my argument progresses. I begin by discussing the modal claims involved in traditional articulations of the DFF. In so doing, I explain how certain open theistic articulations of theological incompatibilism rely on fallacies of modal logic. I go on to explain how open theists (and other theological incompatibilists) can

1. A much shorter version of this has been published as Arbour, "When Does God Learn?"

avoid those mistakes. While discussing these matters, I pay special attention to two claims offered by different types of open theists.

First, I respond to the claim that God is not a necessary being (represented by William Hasker and perhaps others as well) and note the problems such open theists will face that stem from fallacies involving modal logic. Second, I respond to the claim that propositions concerning future contingents (PCFC) are either all false or lack truth-values (à la Dale Tuggy, Alan Rhoda, and other defenders of open future open theism [OFOT]).[2] Following conventional use as established by metaphysicians of modality, the term "possible world" denotes a maximally specified state of the way things could be, which includes a complete and total world history (and therefore the future).[3] All theists who defend omniscience—including defenders of limited foreknowledge open theism (LFOT) who redefine omniscience to offer weaker, modal accounts thereof maintain that God, as part of his natural knowledge (which includes knowledge of counterfactuals)[4]—possesses exhaustive knowl-

2. That OFOT entails denying that there exists an actual world is based upon the consensus that possible world theory involves making claims about a maximally coherent state of affairs as an account of the world, which incorporates a complete and total world history, including the way things will be (i.e., the future). Cf. Tuggy, "Roads to Open Theism." An advocate of OFOT might respond by suggesting that her conception of the world is maximally descriptive insofar as there are no truths or further state of affairs concerning the future to include with any description of the past and present, so thereby qualifies as maximally descriptive. However, this is a non-standard account of possible worlds and the metaphysics of modality, so the burden is on the open theist to demonstrate why such non-standard accounts of possible worlds still fall under the same semantic domain in the long literature where "possible worlds" clearly means something different.

Whereas thus far I have been arguing uniquely against what I call LFOT, the following argument, in my estimation, cuts just as poignantly against what I call OFOT as it cuts against LFOT. Recall that advocates of LFOT maintain that at least some PCFC are presently true (yet the truth-values of these propositions are unknown to God). Advocates of OFOT, on the other hand, deny that any PCFC are presently true. The following argument doesn't concern itself with the ontological status of PCFC and the metaphysics of future time, although I have dealt with the first of these issues in chapter four and will take up the latter in chapter 6.

3. To clarify, this is the way that the vast majority of metaphysicians use the possible world language. Given that there is a standard definition of the semantic content of "possible world" in the discourse concerning the metaphysics of modality, those who dissent from the conventional terminology owe us an explanation of why they do so.

4. Quite a bit turns on how one understands counterfactuals of creaturely freedom (CCFs). Perhaps God knows CCFs concerning the future that open theists call "might" counterfactuals. Or perhaps God knows even the stronger CCFs that include what someone "would" or "would not" do in a particular possible world, yet God lacks knowledge of which possible world will become actual. For my present purposes, this

edge of all modalities, and thereby knows every truth about all possible worlds. However, if the future is open (i.e., contingent, and therefore undetermined, as understood by advocates of open theism, especially OFOT), the answer to the question "Which world will obtain?" is not settled.[5] Rather, according to the open theist, humans play a creative role in bringing about which possible world is real by the free choices we make. This, of course, entails the very strange idea that God, despite divine knowledge of all the possible worlds that can obtain, does not actually know which world has been created. This also raises questions regarding the use of possible world discourse in OFOT's account of the DFF. The inability on the part of open theists (defenders of LFOT and OFOT alike) to adequately respond to the problems involved with fallacious modal logic require them to import other "weaker" forms of necessity (which I call ontological necessity) into their articulation of the incompatibility between divine foreknowledge and human freedom.[6]

---

is unimportant, so I won't explore further any of those implications at this juncture. Regardless, both traditional theists and open theists believe that God possesses knowledge of all modalities, which is enough to guarantee that God knows the details of all possible worlds, even if (as the defender of OFOT must maintain) God doesn't know which world will obtain.

5. For an in-depth analysis of what open futurism means to different open theists, see Rhoda, "Generic Open Theism"; Rhoda, "Fivefold Openness," 69–93. Also, cf. Kodaj, "Open Future."

6. Tom Crisp appreciates that a distinction between strong necessity (modal necessity, or broadly logical necessity—something is true in all possible worlds) and weak necessity (that is, necessary in the actual world, given certain truths about the way things are but not true in all possible worlds) would count heavily against the anti-existentialism argument from presentism, but Crisp doubts that anyone "has been able to produce an informative analysis of weak necessity." See his essay "Presentism," 228. I hope that my account overcomes his concerns. For a detailed account of the type of argument which concerns Crisp in the immediate context of his essay, see Fine, "Plantinga on the Reduction."

I make no claim of originality in making use of the term "ontological necessity." However, I employ the term very differently than other articulations of ontological necessity some readers may be familiar with. So, for instance, I hope to make clear that I do not use ontological necessity in the same way that Swinburne does in *Christian God*, 118–22. However, my use of the term is similar to that of Green and Rogers, who utilize the term in "Time, Foreknowledge." Also, D. K. Johnson, who uses the term in a very similar way to my own understanding of the term in his article "God, Fatalism, and Temporal Ontology." A key difference is that, as I understand it, ontological necessity serves as an umbrella term to denote any type of necessity weaker than modal necessity. The two varieties of ontological necessity I discuss in this chapter are accidental necessity (AN) and consequential necessity (CN). I will not explore whether the category of ontological necessity as I understand it encompasses other forms of necessity (such as causal necessity, temporal necessity, or some other variety of necessity). I do not mean

In order to better accommodate the claims of open theists so as to put forward a stronger *reductio*, in what follows, I develop a metaphysical category of necessity called ontological necessity. Ontological necessity, I maintain, is like metaphysical necessity in that it is weaker than modal necessity, which describes what is necessary in a broadly logical sense. What is modally necessary, or logically necessary, is true in all possible worlds. Open theists maintain that a certain type of necessity attaches to some events/propositions even if these events/propositions are not modally necessary, that is, these events do not obtain in all possible worlds.

I will develop my account of ontological necessity in much greater detail later. Presently, I wish to clarify that ontological necessity can take multiple forms, either accidental necessity or consequential necessity.[7] However, even if we allow weaker forms of necessity a seat at the table in aiding our understanding of the DFF, problems remain. This is so because all traditional articulations of the DFF—even versions of the DFF involving these alternative "weaker" forms of necessity—include at least some truths that are broadly logically necessary. For example, even when one considers articulations of the DFF that don't involve logical necessity, it seems that those who take the DFF as sufficient grounds for theological incompatibilism about divine foreknowledge and human freedom understand the meta-argument of the DFF to be sound in all possible worlds. In light of this reality, I propose an understanding of the relationship between modal necessity and ontological necessity. Building on Thomas Flint's recent analysis of varieties of accidental necessity, I explain why theological incompatibilists are unable to employ some versions of accidental necessity in arguments for open theism. This leaves other forms of accidental necessity available, which I maintain are really varieties of consequential necessity. Consequential necessity, then, is the only type of necessity available to the open theist for motivating open theistic responses to the DFF. This established, I conclude by showing how utilizing consequential necessity in formulating the DFF allows for a non-open theistic response/solution to the DFF.[8] Furthermore, and more importantly,

to limit ontological necessity as being interpreted as *only* these, but AN and CN are the only two possible interpretations I take up. I leave further explanation of this question to be taken up by others.

7. I define and elaborate upon the nature of both accidental necessity and consequential necessity later in this chapter.

8. I discuss this solution, which I call possible world Ockhamism, in more detail in chapter 6. Such a solution is bolstered if God is timeless, as Green, Rogers, and Rota all contend. For those arguments, see Green and Rogers, "Time"; Rogers, "Anselmian

utilizing consequential necessity in formulating the DFF forces the open theist to concede not only that God lacks knowledge of the truth-values of PCFC, but also that God lacks knowledge of the truth-values of propositions concerning *present* contingents. That is, if arguments for open theism succeed, God must lack knowledge of all present truths involving free will as understood by the libertarian (LFW).

Defining the Dilemma of Freedom and Foreknowledge

Up to this point, my defense of divine omniscience and my arguments against open theism have required only a cursory understanding of the DFF. At this juncture, however, because of the nature of the technicalities of the modal logic employed in this *reductio*, allow me to clarify by elaborating on the nature of the DFF.[9] Historically, the DFF has led many to puzzle as to how the following three truths comprise a coherent set:

1. God's knowledge is infallible, and thus cannot be wrong.
2. God knows at *t1* that an agent *S* will freely do an action *A* at *t3*.
3. *S* is free to refrain from doing *A* at *t3*.[10]

Eternalism"; as well as Rogers, "Necessity of the Present"; Rota, "Problem for Hasker"; Rota, "Eternity Solution."

9. Much of what follows is heavily indebted to Zagzebski's account of the DFF as articulated in chapter 1 of her *The Dilemma of Freedom and Foreknowledge*. I have taken the liberty of changing numeration of premises, as well as the wording of propositions in a few places, but I trust my representations are faithful to Zagzebski's intent.

One specific change I make is changing "believes" in (2) to "knows." I do this so as to focus on the metaphysical issues involved in the DFF, and also to avoid getting entangled in epistemological concerns about divine beliefs vs. divine knowledge. I maintain that such issues are off topic for three reasons: first, because versions of the DFF could be so formulated as to avoid these issues; second, because I do not think dealing with any of the epistemological issues gets at the metaphysical issues involved in the DFF. So, because extended deliberations on the epistemology of divine knowledge leave us with the same conundrum in the end, I won't bother prolonging an already lengthy chapter with additional discussions of such here. This stated, for my present purposes, I use "God knows" and "God believes" (or similar tensed versions of such) interchangeably.

10. For those unfamiliar with the demarcations, the prefix "*t*" denotes time, and the numeric markers denote chronological progression such that *t1* is prior to *t2* which is prior to *t3*, and so on. We skip *t2* in the argument so as to allow for the possibility of times in between *t1* and *t3*—that is, although *t3* is after *t1*, it is not immediately subsequent to *t1*. Some philosophers utilize time markers such as these where *t2* denotes the present. In this chapter, I follow the most contemporary literature in denoting the present with t_{α}.

It is easy to see where the dilemma lies. Most libertarians believe free will entails the ability to do otherwise, and they insist that accounts of freedom that fail to preserve such ability fail to preserve moral responsibility. Thus, if *S* is free with respect to *A* at *t3*, then it is within *S*'s power at *t3* to either do *A*, or to refrain from doing *A*. But if it is within *S*'s power to refrain from doing *A* at *t3*, then it is within *S*'s power at *t3* to bring it about that God was wrong in believing at *t1* that *S* would do *A* at *t3*. But this is obviously inconsistent with God's being an infallible knower. Some have suggested that this does not require that *S* have at *t3* the ability to bring it about that God was wrong, but rather that were *S* to refrain from doing *A* at *t3*, it would have been the case that God believed that *S* would have refrained from doing *A* at *t3*.[11] But such an ability (power, or counterfactual power over the past) strikes many—including all open theists—as counterintuitive, for the past is fixed such that it cannot be changed.[12] The common intuition of temporal asymmetry—that the past is relevantly different from the future, such that we can causally affect what happens in the future while we cannot presently causally affect the past—entails that we lack what some suggest is necessary to preserve both free will and divine foreknowledge. That is, we cannot presently cause things that compose history to have been different than they in fact were. Because open theists believe humans possess LFW, and because they are not persuaded that any solutions to the DFF succeed in eliminating the tension raised by the DFF, open theists conclude that it is impossible for God to know any true PCFC. Hence, open theists reject (2)—that is, they deny that God knows, or believes, at *t1* that *S* will do *A* at *t3*.[13] Nonethe-

11. This ability has sometimes been called counterfactual power over the past and is associated with Ockhamism. There exists a significant amount of literature on the subject, but a few pieces that stand out are chapter 6, "Counterfactual Power over the Past," in Hasker, *God, Time, and Knowledge*, 96–115; Plantinga, "On Ockham's Way Out." For an excellent introduction to the issues surrounding counterfactual power over the past, see also Mavrodes, "Is the Past Unpreventable?" Cf. Ockham, *Predestination*.

12. Henceforth, I refer to this difference as temporal asymmetry, which refers to the idea that we can affect, determine, and impact the future in a way that we cannot presently affect, determine, or impact the past.

13. This does not necessarily entail that God is in time. Even if God is timeless, it would be true at *t1* that God knows/believes (timelessly) that I will do *S* at *t3*. Cf. Van Inwagen, "Omniscient Being," 218–20. Much debate exists as to whether divine timelessness presents a genuine solution to the DFF, but I won't engage that literature here for the simple reason that I am presupposing open theism for the sake of argument. Although some non-open theists affirm that God is in time (e.g., Craig, Plantinga, Wessling), as far as I know, all open theists defend some version of divine temporality. Whether such a temporality is essential to the divine nature (à la Wolterstorff)

less, open theists maintain both (1) and (3)—that God's knowledge is infallible and that we enjoy LFW.

To ensure that I am not mischaracterizing the argument for open theism, let us consider what exactly is meant by LFW. Hasker offers a definition of LFW that I believe is representative of all open theists:

> (FW) N is free at *T* with respect to performing $A =_{df}$ It is in N's power at *T* to perform *A*, and it is in N's power at *T* to refrain from performing *A*.[14]

With this understanding of LFW, Hasker offers two arguments for open theism. The first argument:

> (A1) Necessarily, God has always believed that Clarence will have a cheese omelet tomorrow morning. (Premise: the necessity of the past)
>
> (A2) Necessarily, if God has always believed that a certain thing will happen, then that thing will happen. (Premise: divine infallibility)
>
> (A3) Therefore, necessarily, Clarence will have a cheese omelet tomorrow.[15]

Call this version of the DFF presented by Hasker the accidental necessity version. Because Hasker is concerned about the type of necessity

---

or accidental (à la William Lane Craig) is irrelevant. Hasker at one time thought that divine timelessness, if true, would offer a solution to the DFF, but he later changed his mind. For the first view, see Hasker, *God, Time, and Knowledge*, 144–85; for the second, see Hasker, "Absence."

14. Hasker, *God, Time, and Knowledge*, 66. Hasker later clarifies and further nuances his libertarian account of free will in defining it as follows: (FW') N is free at *T* with respect to performing $A =_{df}$ It is in N's power at *T* to perform *A* and it is possible at *T* for N to exercise that power, and it is in N's power at *T* to refrain from performing *A*, and it is also possible at *T* for N to exercise *that* power. Hasker, *God, Time, and Knowledge*, 138.

15. Hasker, *God, Time, and Knowledge*, 68. This argument perfectly parallels the argument Zagzebski offers, although Hasker's argument isn't given in the first person but is instead about Clarence, and the generic action *A* is Clarence's having a cheese omelet instead. Although defenders of LFOT and OFOT disagree on the ontological status of PCFC, they agree that open theism is the proper response to the DFF. Taking Hasker's arguments, then, as representative of all open theists is in no way unfair or uncharitable to defenders of OFOT, for their arguments against the compatibility of foreknowledge and LFW do not differ from those articulated by Hasker, regardless of what metaphysical differences may exist between these groups on other matters. As far as I can discern, the differences between defenders of LFOT and OFOT have no bearing on the argument I offer here.

involved in the argument (an issue I discuss at length later), he offers a second argument:

> (B1) It is now true that Clarence will have a cheese omelet for breakfast tomorrow. (Premise)
>
> (B2) It is impossible that God should at any time believe what is false, or fail to believe anything that is true. (Premise: divine omniscience)
>
> (B3) Therefore, God has always believed that Clarence will have a cheese omelet for breakfast tomorrow. (From 1,2)
>
> (B4) If God has always believed a certain thing, it is not in anyone's power to bring it about that God has not always believed that thing. (Premise: the unalterability of the past)
>
> (B5) Therefore, it is not in Clarence's power to bring it about that God has not always believed that he would have a cheese omelet for breakfast. (From 3,4)
>
> (B6) It is not possible for it to be true both that God has always believed that Clarence would have a cheese omelet for breakfast, and that he does not in fact have one. (From 2)
>
> (B7) Therefore, it is not in Clarence's power to refrain from having a cheese omelet for breakfast tomorrow. (From 5,6) So Clarence's eating the omelet tomorrow is not an act of free choice.[16]

Call this version of the DFF the consequential necessity (CN) version.

To restate their position, open theists conclude that God lacks foreknowledge of future contingents because of an alleged incompatibility between divine foreknowledge and LFW. Believing that we possess LFW, open theists therefore conclude against divine foreknowledge of future contingents in the face of the DFF.[17] The DFF is strengthened by the transfer of necessity principle.[18]

> *Transfer of Necessity Principle 1 (TNP 1)*
>
> $\Box_w \Phi$

16. Hasker, *God, Time, and Knowledge*, 69.

17. Although LFW serves as a premise in *God, Time, and Knowledge*, Hasker has offered numerous defenses of LFW in numerous articles, and also in chapter 4, "Free Will and Agency," in Hasker, *Emergent Self*, 81–109.

18. Zagzebski, *Dilemma of Freedom*, 7–9.

$\Box (\Phi \rightarrow \Psi)$

Therefore, $\Box_w \Psi$

Transfer of Necessity Principle 2 (TNP 2)

$\Box_w \Phi$

$\Box (\Phi \leftrightarrow \Psi)$

Therefore, $\Box_w \Psi$[19]

The use of these transfer of necessity principles in the DFF is owed to the law of distribution, which dictates that operators can be distributed across a conditional, so long as they are distributed to both the antecedent and the consequent. Thus, for *TNP 1*,

$\Box (\Phi \rightarrow \Psi)$

after distribution, becomes

$\Box\Phi \rightarrow \Box\Psi$

Or, for *TNP 2*,

$\Box (\Phi \leftrightarrow \Psi)$

becomes

$\Box\Phi \leftrightarrow \Box\Psi$

What might be required in order for either *TNP 1* or *TNP 2* to apply to the DFF? The crucial premise of the DFF is divine infallibility. Zagzebski succinctly summarizes the matter in a discussion of divine omniscience, which she maintains entails divine infallibility.[20] Recall that there are two ways of understanding divine infallibility: either God is accidentally infallible (which opens the possibility of God having incorrect beliefs in other possible worlds) or God is essentially infallible (whereby in all worlds in

19. Zagzebski, *Dilemma of Freedom*, 7. In clarifying the nature of the transfer of necessity principles, Zagzebski immediately continues, "*W*-necessity may be any sort of necessity, but accidental necessity (the necessity of the past) is the sort of necessity relevant to our dilemma. The idea behind these two principles is that a necessity weaker than logical necessity can be transferred by strict implication (or strict equivalence) from the antecedent to the consequent of the conditional." Recall also that the box symbol "□" denotes modal necessity—true in all possible worlds. Fischer makes use of the same overall concept in formulating one of the three basic forms of the DFF in the introduction to *God, Freedom, and Foreknowledge*, 6, but he calls this the Principle of the Transfer of Powerlessness.

20. I share Zagzebski's opinion that omniscience entails infallibility, as I discussed in chapter 2, where I defend (D11) omniscience.

which God exists, it is impossible that he hold incorrect beliefs). Because Anselmian monotheism maintains that God is a maximally great being who exists of necessity, and because essential infallibility is obviously superior to accidental infallibility, Anselmians conclude that God is infallible in all the worlds at which God exists, which is all of them. Additionally, perfect being theology requires not only that God know all truths, but also that God cannot be wrong about any truth, or fail to know any truth that counts as true from the divine perspective.[21]

So,

> *A* is *omnisicient* ↔ *A* knows the truth value of every proposition.[22]

Although she has not, to date, defended the view as thoroughly as I have, Zagzebski believes that God's omniscience is an essential property, such that

> *A* is *essentially omniscient* ↔ It is impossible that *A* exist and fail to know the truth value of any proposition.[23]

Since we are working with (D11) omniscience, which is compatible with all that Zagzebski says, let us go on to clarify what exactly divine infallibility entails. Following Zagzebski, let us say that

21. (D11)—For every being, *x*, *x* is omniscient if and only if, for every type of belief state, *B*, if *x* is in a token of *B* then *x*'s token of *B* has as object a truth, and if *x* is not in a token of *B* then if *x* were in a token of *B* then *x*'s token of *B* would have as object a falsehood; and, *x* enjoys all cognitive perfections such that everything known by *x* is known perfectly and, therefore, infallibly.

We must go further, though, in our understanding of divine infallibility. Not only is God essentially infallible, such that he is infallible in all the worlds in which he exists, but God is necessarily infallible, for God is a necessary being. According to Anselmian perfect being theology, there is no world in which God can be wrong about any truth. Hence, whatever God believes must be true. This is enough to guarantee the dilemma I raise for open theists. But, some open theists (such as Hasker) deny that God is a necessary being. In order to show that the argument I offer against open theism still succeeds, I demonstrate below how the force of the argument cuts against open theism even on understandings of God as a contingent being.

22. Zagzebski, *Dilemma of Freedom*, 4. This definition of omniscience differs from my own, but it is entailed by my definition, so we can utilize Zagzebski's formulation in the present circumstances to ensure continuity with her thought without worry about coherence throughout the project.

23. Zagzebski, *Dilemma of Freedom*, 5. Per the arguments I have offered in chapter 1, God is a necessary being. Thus, God's being necessary, and essentially omniscient, entails that God is necessarily omniscient, such that the "exist" aspect to Zagzebski's definition is redundant.

> *A* is *infallible* ↔ *A* cannot make a mistake in his beliefs. For any proposition *p*, if *A* believes *p* is true, *p* is true. If *A* had believed *p* was true, *p* would have been true.[24]

If infallibility is a great-making property—as it certainly is, given the fact that (D11) omniscience includes infallibility, and omniscience is indubitably a great-making property—then infallibility must be an essential property of the divine nature, such that

> *A* is *essentially infallible* ↔ It is impossible that *A* fail to be infallible. For any proposition *p*, if *A* believes *p* at any time in any world, *p* is true in that world.[25]

Given divine infallibility, the impossibility language seems to empower the application of the transfer of necessity principle to the DFF. After all, the impossibility of one thing makes its negation necessary. Thus, if God infallibly believes *p*, then ~*p* is impossible (at least in that world), or so some would argue. I will show that such an assumption (which open theists want to maintain) creates insurmountable problems for open theists who maintain that God knows all present realities. Before turning to discuss those issues, let me take a moment to examine possible objections to the doctrine of essential divine infallibility.

Someone who fails to carefully interpret Zagaebski might charge her with incoherence. If God is a necessary being, then God's omniscience entails knowledge of all modalities. So, God's knowledge of world-indexed properties makes it such that propositions concerning world-indexed properties are true in all worlds. Consider: let us call this world *alpha*, and let us suppose for a moment that this world is the only world in which some person, say, John Lennon, exists. If God knows all truths, then even in those worlds in which John Lennon does not exist, God knows that John Lennon exists in *alpha*. Someone might wrongly conclude from hasty reasoning that this is incoherent, making the proposition "John Lennon exists" true in all worlds, including those worlds in which John Lennon does not exist. Two remarks of clarification will alleviate any tension.

First, if John Lennon exists at all in any world, then it is true that John Lennon exists *simpliciter*, so it is not false to say, nor is it wrong to believe "John Lennon exists" even if the one believing such a proposition

24. Zagzebski, *Dilemma of Freedom*, 5.

25. Zagzebski, *Dilemma of Freedom*, 5.

says or believes such from a world in which John Lennon does not exist. Secondly, it seems to me that given perfect cognitive faculties, divine knowledge is absolutely precise with respect to modalities, such that John Lennon's existence is indexed to specific worlds. On this account, the proposition God believes is "John Lennon exists in *alpha*," which is true in all worlds. Hence, God's knowledge of such in all worlds is not problematic. It would only be a problem if God were to believe that "John Lennon exists in some world other than *alpha*," but the modal character of even the strongest definitions of omniscience does not require that God know this, so infallibility and omniscience remain unscathed. So, with this understanding of divine infallibility, let us return to the DFF.

Modal Necessity and the Dilemma of Freedom and Foreknowledge

The DFF, as outlined above, rests on the necessary truth that, given divine infallibility, "If God knows at $t1$ that an agent S will perform action A at $t3$, then agent S will perform action A at $t3$"; symbolized as

(4) $\Box\,(G^{t1}SA^{t3} \rightarrow SA^{t3})$[26]

Those subscribing to LFW deny that an action is free if it is necessary because an action's necessity eliminates the ability to do otherwise and the ability to do otherwise is essential to the principle of alternative possibilities (PAP).[27] After distribution, then, open theists are concerned that the necessity operator attaching to the consequent of the conditional eliminates freedom in

(5) $\Box\, G^{t1}SA^{t3} \rightarrow \Box\, SA^{t3}$

However, it only follows from (5) that an agent S performs some action A at $t3$ of necessity if it is also necessary at $t1$ that God believes at

26. In the antecedent, the superscripts denote the time at which things occur. So, the first superscript ($t1$) denotes the time at which God knows what God knows. The second superscript ($t3$) denotes the time at which the object of God's knowledge will occur.

27. A libertarian might retort that an action can *now* be accidentally necessary, even if it was a free action *when performed*. However, if accidental necessity precludes the ability to do otherwise with respect to the past, I fail to see why it doesn't preclude the ability to do otherwise in the present, for the present lies on the side of the past with respect to temporal asymmetry. Once the present obtains, it cannot any longer be different than it is at one and the same present moment, on pains of contradiction.

$t1$ that an agent *S* performs some action *A* at $t3$. Generating the necessity of the antecedent proves rather difficult for the open theist. Even if divine infallibility entails "It is necessary that, 'If God knows *p*, then *p*,'" we cannot conclude that *p* is necessary unless God necessarily knows *p*.[28] Since *p* is not true in all possible worlds, it is not the case that God knows that *p* is true in all possible worlds, and we should not conclude that God knows *p* of necessity (except perhaps that God's knowledge of *p* is accidentally necessary). But we should certainly not think that *p* is necessary in any other sense of necessity—modal, logical, metaphysical, nomological, ontological, consequential, or otherwise) at $t1$ such that God knows at $t1$ that *p* of non-accidental necessity.[29] This is so for at least two reasons. First, if God is not a necessary being (as some open theists want to maintain), then God does not exist in/at all possible worlds.[30] Obviously, in the worlds in/at which God does not exist, God does not know *p*. Second, unless *p* is a metaphysically necessary truth, then there are worlds in which God knows ~*p*. And if *p* is presumed to be a necessary truth, then a theological

28. At times, I will use a variable, such as *p* or *x*, to abbreviate some longer thing that God knows, such as "an agent *S* will perform some action *A* at some time *t*." Any time such an abbreviation is used, I do so in order to demonstrate that divine knowledge is the issue, and not the time of such knowledge. Also, I take up the issues of world-indexed knowledge later in the chapter.

29. Such invalid reasoning is based on a common modal fallacy, known today as Sleigh's fallacy. Robert Sleigh first noted how some people attempt to argue from "Necessarily, either *p* or *q*" together with "Not *p*" to "Necessarily, *q*." Symbolized, this invalid inference is the attempt to argue from "$\Box(p \vee q)$" and "$\sim p$" to "$\Box q$." Cf. Plantinga, "Self-Profile," 24–25. The argument from $\Box\ (p \rightarrow q)$ together with p does not yield $\Box q$. In order to generate $\Box$q by way of a (modal) *modus ponens* move, $\Box p$ is needed. But denying that God is a necessary being eliminates this possibility. If there are worlds in which God does not exist, then it simply isn't true that in all possible worlds God knows *p*. Thus, if God is a contingent being, then it is not the case that $\Box p$, and the strongest versions of the DFF remain unmotivated.

30. Again, I make use of the in/at distinction to preserve the notion of divine transcendence. Cf. Adams, "Actualism and Thisness." Also, Anselmianism naturally lends itself to defenses of the idea that God is a necessary being, especially when we consider the role and function of Anselmian intuitions in Plantingian modal ontological arguments. However, Hasker denies a Plantingian metaphysics of modality, and along with it the notion of God as a necessary being. His reasoning (briefly) is as follows: Hasker rejects Plantinga's metaphysics of modality because it grants divine necessity, which in turn supports divine simplicity. Divine simplicity bolsters divine timelessness, which Hasker believes needs be rejected in order to proffer open theism. (This is all Hasker's line of thinking; I am not making any claims that he himself has not already made in the material cited immediately below.) So, Hasker's denial of divine necessity is motivated by his affirmation of open theism. See Hasker, "Analytic Philosophy of Religion," 438–40.

incompatibilist is guilty of begging the question against the possibility of coherence between freedom and foreknowledge by postulating from the start that the "free" action known by God is necessary. But if *p* is metaphysically necessary, then *p* cannot be free by definition. Either way, it is not the case that God necessarily knows *p*. Again, inferring "Necessarily *p*" from "Necessarily, if God knows that *p*, then *p*" and "God knows that *p*" is fallacious and therefore invalid reasoning.[31]

But Hasker does not think that the DFF requires modal necessity. Hasker avoids making the modally erroneous error in two ways. The first, which I discuss immediately below, involves his rejection of divine necessity. The second, which I take up later, deals with his assertion that weaker forms of necessity raise the same problems that modal necessity raises in the DFF.

Instead of relying on modal necessity in explaining why open theism is the proper response to the DFF, Hasker insists that the dilemma regards divine omniscience, which exists in all worlds in/at which God exists. Thus, although Hasker does believe that the statement "If God knows *p*, then *p*" is a modally necessary truth, he thinks that it is acceptable to distribute a weaker version of necessity across the syllogism rather than distributing the necessity operators equally. If we grant that weaker, non-broadly logical conceptions of necessity are plausible, we must understand what relationship, if any, exists between modal/logical necessity and what I deem "weaker" versions of necessity, which, we recall, I refer to as "ontological" necessity.[32]

31. It is worth mentioning that appealing to God's natural knowledge (i.e., divine knowledge of all modalities and possibilities) could generate a world-indexed type of knowledge, and then perhaps it is necessary that God knows *x*, if *x* is tied to a specific world. If God is a necessary being, and if God is essentially omniscient, thereby possessing complete knowledge of all possible worlds, then in all worlds God necessarily knows that *x* is true at all worlds *w* in which *x* is true. But God's natural knowledge of *x* at *w* worlds is not enough to guarantee that any of the *w* worlds obtain. So if divine foreknowledge creates a dilemma between itself and freedom, it must be divine knowledge of the actual world (i.e., part of what philosophers call God's free knowledge). Additionally, this line of reasoning requires that we understand God to be a necessary being—a claim Hasker rejects.

32. Recall that I take this term—ontological necessity—from D. K. Johnson who uses the term in "God, Fatalism, and Temporal" 435–54. Green and Rogers use Anselmian eternalism to refute Johnson's argument for open theism while utilizing the same terminology. See Green and Rogers, "Time." A reminder: I argue that ontological necessity should be understood as either accidental necessity or consequential necessity, both of which allow theological compatibilists to respond to the claims of open theism adequately. Again, my use of the term is dissimilar from that of Swinburne in *Christian God*.

Someone attempting to evade the concern that I raise might retort that in all worlds at which God exists, God cannot (a) fail to be omniscient; and (b) fail to be infallible.[33] That is, if God exists in *w*, then in *w* God knows all truths. Thus, in *w*, because God cannot fail to be omniscient or fail to be infallible in *w*, God must know all the truths of *w*, and presumably all the truths of other worlds in which God exists.[34] The maneuver renders divine omniscience a world-indexed property.

What might this move accomplish? An example will help explain. Call this world—the actual world that we live in—*alpha*. Assume that God exists in *alpha*. In *alpha*, God is omniscient and infallible. Thus, in *alpha* God cannot fail to know any truths, including *p*. From the fact that God cannot fail to know *p*, some argue that *p* follows necessarily, especially given the law of non-contradiction such that both *p* and ~*p* cannot both be possible simultaneously. If it is a necessary condition of contingency that *p* be possible and that ~*p* be possible, then the impossibility of ~*p* from God's infallibly knowing *p* renders *p* necessary (in at least some sense). Going still further, open theists argue that as a necessary truth, *p* cannot be free in the libertarian sense.

Now, this argument moves much too fast, but consider what it would mean if the argument successfully alleviated the tension I raise. If the argument succeeds, then it follows that everything that God knows would be necessarily true. How one understands the type of necessity is certainly important, but according to open theists, any type of necessity is sufficient to eliminate the sort of contingency that is vital to LFW.[35] Therefore, no open theist could employ this line of reasoning, for doing so would prove self-defeating on other fronts.

33. The (D11) understanding of omniscience that I propose already entails divine infallibility, but I separate these ideas here just in case some people reject the doctrine of omniscience I defend in chapter 2. The reason for doing so is to show that the arguments I raise here against open theism are not necessarily dependent on (D11) omniscience.

34. Those who reject divine necessity might be inclined to argue that God can know the truths of worlds in which God does not exist, but I don't see how any such argument could succeed, for lack of access on the part of God to those worlds in which God doesn't exist. In all fairness, just as we can know necessary truths about worlds in which we do not exist, surely God could know that all necessary truths are true in the worlds in which God does not exist. But this isn't enough to preserve divine omniscience.

35. Any type of necessity save accidental necessity, which open theists admit is a type of necessity that now attaches to some past event, but this type of necessity doesn't preclude that some past action was committed freely in the past.

Furthermore, besides the problem noted above, even granting that such an argument succeeds in the first place would be a mistake. At best, this argument reveals that it follows from God's infallible knowledge of *p* in *alpha* that "if God infallibly knows that *p* in *alpha*, then in *alpha*, *p*." And just because *p* is true in *alpha* does not mean that *p* is true in other possible worlds; that is, *p* isn't necessarily true. As long as *p* is thought to be contingently true, there is as least one world in which ~*p* is true. Said differently, unless ~*p* is incoherent, there exists at least one possible world in which *p* is false. Certainly it is true that in *alpha*, *p* is certain to obtain, given God's knowledge of *p* in *alpha*, but this is not enough to guarantee that *p* is necessary in all worlds, even though divine knowledge of *p* in *alpha* necessitates that *p* must obtain in *alpha*. Recall that the chief premise of the DFF involves the idea that in all worlds (i.e., necessarily in the broadly logical sense), if God knows *p*, then *p*. But in order for the necessity operator to distribute properly, the operator in question must comprise either a concept of modal/logical necessity, or some weaker form of necessity. If one takes modal/logical necessity to imply and/or include accidental necessity, the distribution of this lesser or "weaker" form of world-indexed necessity allows for numerous responses to the DFF, to which I turn now.[36]

Ontological Necessity

Perhaps modal necessity isn't even the main issue when it comes to the DFF, such that focusing on divine necessity or other matters related to those issues raised above constitutes an exercise in missing the point.[37]

36. For more thoughts concerning the conundrums regarding God's status as a necessary being that plague defenders of both LFOT and OFOT, see additional "Coda" at the end of this chapter.

37. In what follows I discuss the second way Hasker avoids the potential problems created by modal necessity, namely, by specifically denying that modal necessity is the issue. Referring to his (A)-type argument from accidental necessity, Hasker notes, "The first premise makes assumptions about the relation of God's knowledge to events in time, and these assumptions need to be made explicit so they can be examined. But the most serious deficiency of argument (A) concerns the modal operator in the first premise. 'Necessarily' here does not refer to logical necessity, as it does in the second premise; it is not claimed that God has the belief in question in all possible worlds. Rather, 'necessarily' in the first premise refers to the 'necessity of the past' [accidental necessity]: God's having held this belief *now* necessarily because it has *already happened*. And it is this necessity that is, as it were, transmitted across the entailment stated in the second premise so as to appear again in the conclusion." Hasker, *God, Time, and Knowledge*, 68.

If so, there must be something else motivating the DFF besides modal necessity.[38] If divine necessity and the modal necessity it could carry along aren't the issue, then it must be divine infallibility that drives the DFF. That is, because it is a necessary truth (in the broadly logical sense) that "if God knows *p*, then *p*," theological incompatibilists might be arguing that all truths that are known by God that involve a decision and/or action of an agent cannot be free in the libertarian sense. In fact, it might be that divine infallibility guarantees as much. Since God cannot be wrong, it is absolutely impossible for anything that God knows to be false. Additionally, because God is omniscient, there are no truths that God fails to know.[39]

In light of these ideas, we can run another argument—the dilemma of freedom and divine *infallibility*. It runs as follows:

> (6) Necessarily, if God believes *p*, then *p*. (premise: divine infallibility)
>
> (7) No one has the ability to bring it about that God is wrong. (from [6])
>
> (8) God believes *p*. (Premise)
>
> (9) It is not possible that *p* be false. (from 6, 7, and 8)[40]

38. Weaker forms of necessity can and do motivate alternative forms of the DFF. However, I find responses to these weaker forms of the dilemma successful, so I am not persuaded by open theists that theological incompatibilism wins the day. However, in light of Hasker's denial that God is a necessary being, I want to go to extreme lengths to show that his arguments against theological compatibilism fail. I will set aside the fact that this means ignoring the defense of God as a necessary being that I defended in chapter 1; and never mind the fact that Hasker has yet to answer the question as to what makes divine existence contingent—that is, what God's existence depends upon (which violates the Principle of Sufficient Reason [PSR]). Let's grant yet another premise (undesirable as it might be to perfect being theologians) to Hasker for the sake of constructing this *reductio*.

39. For reasons discussed in chapters 1, 2, and 3, philosophers and theologians who subscribe to perfect being theology agree that omniscience is an essential component of God's nature. So we can go further in saying not only that there are no truths that God fails to know, but also that it is impossible that there be a truth unknown to God. I am not aware of any arguments that grant any reason to take seriously the idea that God just so happens to be omniscient—that God is accidentally omniscient. On such a view, there are worlds in which God exists, yet is not omniscient. Regardless, so long as God is omniscient in the actual world, then all of the argumentation in this chapter holds.

40. One might object by making the Ockhamist move in claiming that it might be possible to do something such that, were one to do it, God wouldn't have believed what God actually believes. However, because open theists do not concede such a possibility because of the hardness of God's beliefs, we needn't consider that option here.

(10) Thus, it is ontologically necessary that *p*.

If it is ontologically necessary (ON) that *p*, then *p* must be true. But if *p* must be true (à la [10]), then it is not possible for *p* to be false. Even if the "is not possible" in (9) does not entail logical necessity, it at least follows from this that *p* is ON. If *p* is ON, this means that in any world in which "God knows that *p*" is part of divine free knowledge, then in those worlds ~*p* cannot obtain. After all, God's free knowledge is dependent on what type of world God creates, and if God has chosen to actualize a state of affairs in which *p* is true, it obviously follows that ~*p* is false. This fits perfectly with the intuition of theological incompatibilists who argue that for any proposition *p* describing an outcome involving an agent's decision, the fact that ~*p* cannot obtain is sufficient to remove alternative possibilities, and thereby eliminate genuine freedom.[41]

Perhaps what I am calling ON (hereafter symbolized [**ON**]) is what Tomis Kapitan has in mind when he discusses why the theological compatibilists reject arguments for incompatibilism about freedom and foreknowledge. Theological compatibilists often object that the arguments put forward by incompatibilists are based on the "egregious" modal error known as Sleigh's fallacy. He writes,

> This disturbs Hunt who feels that one commits an "egregious" fallacy upon reasoning from P and □ (P → Q) to □Q. Fallacious? The reasoning is central to the doctrine of relative modality according to which a consequence of a set of propositions itself possesses a certain sort of necessity, a necessity relative to that set and, thus, *distinct from* the necessity of the consequence relation. The doctrine cannot be dismissed lightly. The everyday *cans, cannots, mights,* and *maybes* we use in planning, predicting, and ruminating about the past express some such relative modality, for example, those of the negligent student who concludes in his eighth semester that he *cannot* graduate at the end of his fourth year because of his past failure to meet all the distribution requirements. If this "cannot" expresses necessity then there is more than meets the eye in the inference from

41. To be fair, the fact that ~*p* cannot obtain *now* does not eliminate the possibility that *p* was performed with genuine freedom when done in the past. William Alston may be working with a similar idea, which might be called situationally based logical necessity, or, as Alston puts it, "S-logical necessity," wherein a given situation logically entails some outcome, even if the entailment is something other than causal determinism. See Alston, "Divine Foreknowledge and Alternative Conceptions," reprinted in *Divine Nature and Human Language*, 162–77.

> P and □ (P → Q) to □Q, and it takes more than expressions of bewilderment to undermine it.[42]

For now, let ON denote the type of necessity that attaches to a set of propositions apart from logical necessity. That is, given a set of criteria, other things become necessary, even though that necessity isn't enough to guarantee that some truth is true in all possible worlds. So, given the truth of divine infallibility, if God knows *p*, then *p* is ON, even if *p* is not true in all possible worlds. Symbolized,

(G*p* → (<u>ON</u>)*p*)

It seems that this is a necessary truth, and not just in the sense of being ON. Therefore, we conclude that

□ (G*p* → (<u>ON</u>)*p*).

Accidental Necessity

One way of avoiding the issue of logical necessity in arguments concerning the DFF is to apply an interpretation of ON along the lines of what the medievals called necessity "*per accidens*," or accidental necessity as expressed in the contemporary literature.[43] Accidental necessity (AN, hereafter symbolized by (AN)) is so named because it involves a different type of necessity than logical necessity. For example, there are no worlds in which it is false that 2 + 2 = 4, so this is a necessary truth in the strongest sense—it is logically necessary. But, if we do not have power to change the past, then there are certain truths that are now necessary, even if they were at one time undetermined (contingent), and since these truths aren't logically necessary, they aren't true in all possible worlds. For example, in this world, it is true, and cannot now be made false, that Socrates drank the hemlock, so we say that it is AN that Socrates drank the hemlock.[44] However, there are a great many possible worlds in which

42. Kapitan, "Acting," 292.

43. For an introduction to the medieval understanding of necessity *per accidens*, see Zagzebski, *Dilemma of Freedom*, 15–32. Flint notes that Alfred Freddoso was the first to anglicize the term by calling it "accidental necessity" (rather appropriately, it seems to me) in the preface of Luis de Molina, *On Divine Foreknowledge*. Flint notes this in his essay "Varieties of Accidental Necessity."

44. Swinburne offers this definition of AN: "A statement *p* is accidentally necessary at a time *t* if and only if *p* is true and it is not coherent to suppose that any agent by his

it is false that Socrates drank the hemlock—for example, all the worlds in which Socrates was executed some other way, not to mention the worlds in which Socrates does not exist as a concrete particular.

Open theists utilize AN in constructing the DFF. In any argument for openness accounts of theological incompatibilism, a premise is put forward concerning our lack of power over the past on the basis of temporal asymmetry, which is the metaphysical basis for accidental necessity. Thomas Flint has recently offered an analysis of different articulations of AN that elicit different responses from those who maintain that freedom and foreknowledge are compatible, depending on what variety of accidental necessity is used when constructing arguments about the DFF.[45] Although Flint identifies nine different versions of AN, the key difference between these types of AN allows all of them to be categorized into two groups: versions of AN which focus on the fixity of what is AN, or versions which focus on the fact that what is now AN was previously contingent. I now turn to show why arguments for open theism based on any type of AN in the DFF do not succeed.

Zagzebski has argued compellingly that the medieval notion of AN precludes this version of necessity from being transferred to the consequent of a conditional by way of the transfer of necessity principle. The reason that the transfer of necessity principle doesn't apply is due to the fact that the AN operator cannot transfer to the consequent of conditionals involved in the DFF. The reason that AN cannot be transferred to the consequent of these conditionals is because AN is a type of necessity that is relevant only to past events.[46] Suppose that God foreknew at *t*1 that an agent *S* will perform some action *A* at *t*3. Now suppose that at t_α (the present) it is now AN that God believed at *t*1 that an agent *S* would perform some action *A* at *t*3. The open theist suggests that the transfer of necessity principles outlined above allow for the distribution of the AN operator to

action at *t* can make *p* false, although it is coherent to suppose that at some other time an agent could make *p* false. Given the logical impossibility of backward causation for which I argued in the previous chapter [72–95, especially 81–90] all and only true statements about the past have this kind of necessity because it is not coherent to suppose that they can be made false by present action (whereas it is coherent to suppose that they could at some earlier time have been made false by action then); statements about the future are not thus necessary." Swinburne, *Christian God*, 116.

45. Cf. Flint, "Varieties of Accidental Necessity." It bears mentioning that in this essay Flint is concerned specifically with how the Molinist ought to respond to the dilemma of freedom and foreknowledge, depending on which version of AN is in play, but I see no reason why only Molinists are in a position to make use of his findings.

46. Zagzebski, *Dilemma of Freedom*, 32.

the consequent of the syllogism such that even at t_α (the present) it is AN that some agent *S* will perform some action *A* at *t*3 (in the future). But, if Zagzebski is right (and I think her exegesis of the medievals is correct in ascertaining that, at least for them, AN applies uniquely to events in the past), then no future action can be AN by definition.

But theological incompatibilists (especially open theists) insist that such a maneuver, while perhaps technically correct in virtue of the definition of AN, doesn't get at the logic of what the transfer of necessity principle is all about. So, even if we say that the consequent—"some agent *S* will perform some action *A* at *t*3"—isn't AN, it must be necessary in at least *some* way, otherwise the transfer of necessity principle is invalid. In light of this reasoning, open theists can go one of two routes. The first involves finding a way to redefine AN so as to allow the AN operator to transfer to PCFC. The second is to suggest that the type of necessity that applies to the consequent of the conditional in question still matters, even if it isn't AN. Let us examine both of these possibilities.

If we appropriate some of Flint's definitions and the way that he categorizes the different varieties of AN, we can see that attempts to allow AN to affix to PCFC entail that the version of AN in view switches from one type (one which focuses on the fixity of the past event) to another (one which emphasizes the former contingency of the AN event). However, this fails because it is unfaithful to the transfer of necessity principle. The distribution of necessity operators must be consistent; as stated, the transfer of necessity principle will not allow one type of necessity to be transferred to the antecedent and some other type to the consequent. So any attempt by open theists to save their argument cannot rely on this approach.

Furthermore, we must restate that the DFF includes at least one logically necessary truth. Recall that in all possible worlds, if God knows at *t*1 that some agent *S* will perform some action *A* at *t*3, then that agent *S* will perform that action *A* at *t*3.[47]

(11) $\Box\,(G^{t1}SA^{t3} \rightarrow SA^{t3})$

47. In all of the following, I do not mean to suggest that God is temporal in stating that "God knows at *t*1 . . ." However, this statement could accommodate that belief, so I offer it as written to accommodate those who defend divine temporality as either an accidental property of God (e.g., William Lane Craig) or as an essential property of the divine nature (e.g., Nicholas Wolterstorff). But, the statement could just as easily be interpreted to accommodate divine atemporality as "It is true at *t*1 that God knows . . ."

I have already noted that the transfer of necessity principles only allow for the distribution of the same type of necessity. Thus, logical necessity needs be transferred. So, from (11), the transfer of necessity principle grants

(12) $\Box\, G^{t1}SA^{t3} \rightarrow \Box\, SA^{t3}$

But perhaps there is a good reason to think that logical necessity entails some weaker form of necessity which can be distributed according to the transfer of necessity principle.

If something is necessary in all worlds, then it is certainly necessary in some specific world *w*. And if ON (which can be interpreted according to one type of AN) is a weaker form of necessity that designates a world-indexed type of necessity such as metaphysical or nomological necessity, then any logically necessary truths will be at least ON. Whether or not ON truths count as also being AN depends on which version of AN is in play. If we are discussing versions of AN which emphasize the fixity of whatever is AN, then a logically necessary truth could also be AN.[48] However,

> If what one wishes to emphasize is the *temporal* aspect of the truths in question—the fact that at some time the propositions in question *come* to be true, and *come* to be fixed—then one should (as Freddoso does) specify that only metaphysically contingent propositions can be accidentally necessary.[49]

Because logical necessities are not contingent at all, if one wishes to utilize AN to emphasize that the act *becomes* necessary, then it won't work to see logical necessity as entailing AN. So, we can see that if any *p* is logically necessary, then *p* is at least ON, and might be AN, but it depends on which version of AN is in play. It seems, then, that logical necessity entails AN such that we can distribute AN from logical necessity, provided that it is the same type of AN that distributes across both the antecedent and the consequent of the syllogism. But, since we cannot utilize versions of AN that emphasize that an event *becomes* necessary, the only versions of AN that can be distributed are those which focus on fixity of the events in question.

48. Flint notes as much in "Varieties of Accidental Necessity." For a defense of versions of AN on which metaphysically necessary truths turn out to also be AN, see Plantinga, "On Ockham's Way Out," 261.

49. Flint, "Varieties of Accidental Necessity," 48.

If we take the former route by distributing the version of AN which focuses on the fixity of the event, then we are working with a version of AN that is materially equivalent to consequential necessity, which I discuss more below. Briefly, given this type of AN, we can see that because we lack the ability to change the past, for any moment later than *t*1, it is now accidentally necessary (fixed) that God believed that some agent *S* would perform some action *A* at *t*3. As a result of distribution, it is equally fixed that some agent *S* will perform some action *A* at *t*3. This fixity is sufficient to eliminate any LFW on the part of that agent *S* in regards to that action *A* at *t*3, or so argue theological incompatibilists. But if this version of necessity is sufficient to eliminate LFW in regards to future contingents (and thereby provide open theists the motivation to deny that God enjoys exhaustive definite foreknowledge), then (as I argue below) it is also sufficient to eliminate LFW at the present. Of course, by parallel reasoning, since open theists desire to defend LFW, this would provide open theists with motivation for denying that God enjoys exhaustive definite knowledge of the present. If open theists remain consistent, they will continue to preserve LFW no matter what the consequence, and this will lead them to deny divine knowledge of the present.

But what about the other variety of AN that emphasizes former contingency? Although this version of AN, by definition, cannot apply to PCFC, what if there is some way for this version of AN to be distributed across the syllogism? The only way that this could be is if we reinterpret the central claim of the DFF to be an AN truth. Thus,

(11) (<u>**AN**</u>) $(G^{t1}SA^{t3} \rightarrow SA^{t3})$

If this were the case, we could acknowledge that (although it might have been otherwise) God did in fact believe at *t*1 that that agent *S* would perform that action *A* at *t*3 in such a way that God's belief is fixed and unchangeable. As a result, although it is not logically or metaphysically necessary (and therefore could be different), it is now the case that at *t*3 some agent *S* will perform some action *A* in a way that is presently fixed. Two remarks are in order here. First, if it is AN that God believed at *t*1 that that agent *S* would perform that action *A* at *t*3 in the sense that it was at one moment contingent and then became necessary, we should ask, "When exactly did God come to believe this?" Given (D11) omniscience and the omnitemporality of truth, God has always believed what God believes, so there was never a time when God did not believe that some agent *S* would perform some action *A* at *t*3. Since there was never a movement from contingency to necessity in God's beliefs, distributing this alternative conception of AN proves to be quite problematic.[50] Second (and perhaps obviously), if it is possible that some agent *S* will perform some action *A* at *t*3, then we need still more clarification in regards to the type of *necessity* that is driving the DFF. To this we now turn.

Consequential Necessity

Perhaps we still haven't identified the root of the open theist's claims. Divine infallibility seems to be doing a lot of metaphysical work in that it seems to entail a certain type of necessity. That is, whatever God knows, it cannot fail to be so. This need not be understood in such a way that everything that God knows is logically necessary. For instance, God knows that Socrates lived in Greece, but it certainly could have been otherwise. But the fact that God cannot be wrong about what God knows is sufficient to guarantee that no person has the power to do anything such that God was, is, or will be incorrect about anything, ever. Accordingly, if God knows that some agent *S* will perform some action *A* at *t*3, then *S* does not have the power to refrain from performing action *A* at *t*3, for that power would entail that *S* has the ability to bring it about that God is not infallible, which is an untenable position. So understood, the open theist suggests that if God knows *p*, then it is ON that *p*. Let us call this type of ON consequential necessity (CN, hereafter symbolized by (CN))—it follows as a consequence of God's infallibly knowing *p*, that *p* is CN.[51]

50. One might wonder about still other alternative conceptions of accidental necessity according to which AN does not require any movement from contingency to necessity. Were anyone to push such a line of reasoning, I would respond in two ways: first, we need an account of what exactly such AN would look like, and second, by definition, it wouldn't count as genuine AN since the movement from contingency to necessity is exactly the idea that this version of AN is trying to capture.

51. It is important to note that consequential necessity is not the same as causal necessity. That *p* follows necessarily from God's infallible knowledge of *p*, does not mean that God's knowledge of *p* is the cause of *p*. Instead, the ground of God's knowledge of *p* could be *p*, such that if *p*, then necessarily God infallibly knows *p*, given the defense of divine omniscience I have offered in chapter two.

Consequential necessity, as I understand it, does bear an affinity to what Swinburne calls natural necessity. See *Christian God*, 117. However, Swinburne's understanding of natural necessity overlaps in some ways with causal necessity, which is a concern. But, because I am persuaded by Anscombe that causation does not entail determination, I deny that the affinity in view requires that consequential necessity entails causal necessity. See Anscombe, *Causality and Determination*.

To revisit an earlier point, I am not suggesting that open theists are guilty of Sleigh's modal fallacy.[52] I am not suggesting that open theists arrive at the conclusion that anything God knows is CN by way of reasoning

$\mathbf{N}^* \ (\mathrm{G}p \rightarrow p)$

$\mathrm{G}p$

Thus, $\mathbf{N}^* \ (p)$

where **N*** denotes necessity of any kind. Rather, I want to grant to theological incompatibilists, including open theists, a premise that they find compelling. Given divine infallibility, there is a type of necessity that attaches to anything God knows, so we should posit as a premise

$\mathrm{G}p \rightarrow (\underline{\mathbf{CN}})\ p$[53]

Although CN does follow logically from divine infallibility, it ought not be confused with logical necessity. The fact that CN is not modal necessity implies that it is world-indexed, such that

If God knows that p in world $w \rightarrow (\underline{\mathbf{CN}})\ p$ in world w

This is enough to rule out the possibility of $\sim p$ in w. Because open theists assert that PAP must be in place for an agent to be free in the libertarian sense with respect to some action, then any free act must lack the property of being CN at the time. And, given open theism as a response to the DFF, if an action is free in the libertarian sense, then God cannot possess knowledge of such at the time, for divine knowledge entails that the object of divine knowledge is CN. Hence, we have

$(p)\ (\mathrm{LFW})\ p \rightarrow \sim \mathrm{G}p$

or

$(p) \sim \sim \mathrm{G}p \rightarrow \sim (\mathrm{LFW})\ p$

To simplify, the rule of double negation allows us to state

52. For more on Sleigh's modal fallacy, see Plantinga, "Self-Profile," 25–27; Plantinga, "It's Actual."

53. This, then, best captures the concern I noted earlier of Kapitan. See Kapitan, "Acting," 292. One might think that this captures the notion of "If p, then it must be the case that q," where the "must" means something stronger than strict implication or entailment. The fact that "if p, then necessarily q," properly captures the notion that "if p, then it cannot be false that q." It is this idea that open theists push in motivating their understanding of divine knowledge. Necessarily, if God knows p, then it cannot be false that p. But this is true of anyone's knowledge, at least so long as knowledge is factive.

$(p)\ Gp \rightarrow \sim (LFW)\ p$

Of course, even on open theism God can possess knowledge of actions that *were* done freely. These actions, now already committed, are presently fixed because they are AN, assuming we lack any sort of power to change the past. Thus, these actions are not presently free in that no one possesses the power to bring it about that any of these actions did not occur, even if they were free when originally performed. So it would be wrong for anyone to conclude that God cannot know about any actions that *were* done freely. We should conclude only that, given open theism, God lacks knowledge of any events which are presently free, whether free in the immediate present, or free in that they will be performed freely in the future.

Even though this sort of CN is a world-indexed type of necessity, we should suppose that the conditional represented above is a logically necessary truth, such that in all worlds, if God exists in/at a world and knows *p* in that world, then *p* is CN in that world. So

$\Box\ ((w)Gp \rightarrow (\underline{\mathbf{CN}})\ (w)p)$

But if CN—or any other type of ON such as AN, or even some other variety of ON yet to be identified—is sufficient to eliminate LFW at the time, then open theists find themselves having to deny quite a bit more than divine foreknowledge. And now we will see why.

We need to remember that logical necessity, being the strongest and broadest category of necessity, entails weaker forms of necessity. That is, if something is logically necessary (true in all possible worlds), then it is at least ON (in which case it must be true in this world). Thus:

$\Box\ (p) \rightarrow (\underline{\mathbf{ON}})\ (p)$

and

$\Box\ (p \rightarrow q) \rightarrow (\underline{\mathbf{ON}})\ (p \rightarrow q)$

Recall also that ON can be interpreted as either AN or CN, provided that we work with the proper conception of AN. So:

$(\underline{\mathbf{ON}})\ (p \rightarrow q) \rightarrow \{[(\underline{\mathbf{AN}})\ (p \rightarrow q)]\ \mathrm{v}\ [(\underline{\mathbf{CN}})\ (p \rightarrow q)]\}$

So, it follows that we can reinterpret

$\Box\ ((w)Gp \rightarrow (\underline{\mathbf{ON}})\ (w)p)$

as

$(\underline{\text{ON}})\ ((w)\text{G}p \to (\underline{\text{ON}})\ (w)p)$

If we allow the transfer of necessity principle to do its work here, we distribute the operator such that

$(\underline{\text{ON}})\ (w)\text{G}p \to (\underline{\text{ON}})(\underline{\text{ON}})\ (w)p$

S4 allows us to remove multiple operators, so we are left with

$(\underline{\text{ON}})\ (w)\text{G}p \to (\underline{\text{ON}})\ (w)p$[54]

We now can remove the operator to come back

$(\underline{\text{ON}})\ ((w)\text{G}p \to (w)p)$[55]

Now, it is not exactly a radical idea to postulate that God knows the present. But, given divine infallibility, whatever God knows about the present in this world is ON in this world. But this means that if God knows at t_α that some agent *S* is performing some action *A* at t_α, then the action *A* done by agent *S* at t_α is CN at t_α, and therefore not free at t_α. Of course, open theists affirm that actions performed in the present need be done freely in order for moral responsibility to supervene on such actions (such as when we presently choose to do something—the present is the moment when the decision is made, presumably with the ability to choose differently (i.e., LFW)). But, since open theists insist that any type of ON (be it CN or AN, or some other variety that eliminates PAP) is sufficient to eliminate LFW, open theists are forced to choose between one of two options: (a) God lacks knowledge of all present truths involving LFW; or (b) we lack LFW at the present.

As Michael Rota has recently pointed out, Hasker cannot gloss his definition of LFW to accommodate this concern, for if Hasker jettisons the fact that we possess LFW in the present, he defeats his own case for theological incompatibilism.[56] Denying that we have LFW at present

54. Recall that S4 is the system of modal logic in which repeating identical modal operators can be reduced to one appearance. Symbolized, S4 allows for: $\Diamond\Diamond p \to \Diamond p$ as well as $\Box\Box p \to \Box p$. In this case, I maintain that S4 legitimately applies to weaker forms of necessity.

55. Again, consequential necessity is a type of ontological necessity, so (ON) could easily be replaced with (CN) in the foregoing, as well as with (AN), provided that the right type of accidental necessity is in view.

56. Rota defends Anselmian eternalism as a solution to the DFF in "Problem for Hasker." Rota is building on the work of Rogers. See her "Anselmian Eternalism"; and also her "Necessity of the Present."

Two things make the argument I offer here different than those arguments offered

offers another response to the DFF, namely, Augustinian compatibilism, or, for those who want to press the matter further in that direction, theological determinism.[57] But this road obviously eliminates any motivation for open theism. Besides this, Hasker is committed to the notion that this response raises serious concerns as to the problem of evil,[58] and, we recall, Hasker also denies that divine timelessness offers any help in responding to the DFF. Furthermore, Hasker's definition of LFW specifically states that in order for an agent to perform some action freely, then one must have the ability to do otherwise. Assuming Hasker's preferred ontology of time, namely, presentism, the only time that exists is the present. Therefore, the only time that anyone can be free is the present, and the only time anyone can perform any given action is the present. So, according to Hasker, an agent must possess LFW at t_α to be free since that is the only time available for anyone to be free in the first place. Recall Hasker's definition of free will:

> (FW) N is free at *T* with respect to performing $A =_{df}$ It is in N's power at *T* to perform *A*, and it is in N's power at *T* to refrain from performing *A*.[59]

by Rota and Rogers. First, I have not set out to defend Anselmian eternalism as a response to the DFF, which is their motivation. Secondly, whereas they have stated that Hasker's denial of their solution requires that God lack knowledge of the present, I argue that Hasker's position requires this lack of divine knowledge regardless of whether he considers Anselmian eternalism a solution. This is so because even if Anselmian eternalism does provide a solution to the DFF, Hasker denies divine timelessness, so such a solution would have little, if any, appeal to him.

57. Here I have in mind the work of Derk Pereboom, who affirms incompatibilism about freedom and determinism, as well as incompatibilism between freedom and foreknowledge, yet is a theist who affirms both divine foreknowledge and metaphysical determinism. Therefore, as a hard determinist, Pereboom denies that humans are free at all, much less in the libertarian sense. See Pereboom, *Living Without Free Will*; Pereboom, "Free Will."

58. For more on Hasker's take on open theism as it relates to the problem of evil, see his *Providence, Evil, and the Openness of God*, as well as his *The Triumph of God over Evil.* For a specific take on his concerns about theological determinism, see his exchange with Helm, "Does God Take Risks?"

59. Hasker, *God, Time, and Knowledge*, 66. Hasker later clarifies and further nuances his libertarian account of free will in defining it as follows: (FW') N is free at *T* with respect to performing $A =_{df}$ It is in N's power at *T* to perform *A*, and it is possible at *T* for N to exercise that power, and it is in N's power at *T* to refrain from performing *A*, and it is also possible at *T* for N to exercise *that* power. Hasker, *God, Time, and Knowledge*, 138.

Symbolized, my argument against God's ability to know the present, given open theism, runs as follows:

$\Box\ (G^{t\alpha}p \rightarrow (CN)\ p^{t\alpha})$

God's omniscience requires that God knows all reality, such that in all worlds in which God obtains, it cannot be the case that God fails to know all truths about the present, since no matter what metaphysic of time one adopts, the present is ontologically real.[60] So there is something ON about God's knowledge of the present—God cannot fail to have it. Thus,

$(\underline{ON})\ G^{t\alpha}p$

But once we have this in place, it follows by way of *modus ponens* that

$(\underline{CN})\ p^{t\alpha}$

Recall that open theists insist that ON, because it is enough to eliminate PAP, precludes LFW at the time of the action. Thus, in order to preserve LFW, open theists should conclude that God lacks knowledge of the present. However, despite their willingness to abandon the theological heritage of Christianity in denying divine foreknowledge, open theists are unwilling to admit that openness responses to the DFF logically entail that God also lacks knowledge of the present.[61] Open theists attempt to escape this conundrum by asserting that God knows the present directly, and that the source of divine knowledge is the event itself. So, if an action occurs at the present, then God at the present knows the present action. Symbolized, this would mean

60. Defenders of OFOT cannot respond by saying that God does not know the present in the way they might when it comes to denying that God knows the truth-values of PCFC. This is so because, while they might want to argue that presentism either entails all-falsism for PCFC, or it precludes the existence of truth-values for PCFC, presentism *guarantees* that the present exists, and therefore all actions which take place in the present certainly possess truth-values. And if God is omniscient, then God knows those truth-values.

61. I find it extremely interesting that theologically motivated open theists (e.g., Boyd, Pinnock, and Sanders) are reluctant to deny God's knowledge of the present. The hermeneutic these theologians endorse requires a *prima facie* reading of Scripture; it is this same method of interpretation open theists point to in an effort to show biblical support for the fact that God lacks knowledge of future contingents. However, when pressed, this same hermeneutic can also show that God lacks knowledge of the present (Gen 3:9) and even that God lacks exhaustive knowledge of history (Gen 3:11; 18:20–21).

$(p^{t\alpha} \rightarrow G^{t\alpha}p^{t\alpha})$

This symbolism should not be interpreted as suggesting that God learns the present as it comes into being, such that the present happens, and God learns about it as soon as it happens, but divine knowledge of these events obtains temporally subsequent to these events actually happening. This understanding wouldn't actually yield God's knowledge of the present, for on such an account, by the time God knows, the event wouldn't qualify as part of the objective present (on any A-series account of time), but rather would be history. So, we shouldn't interpret God's direct knowledge of the present as though the event takes place temporally prior to God's knowing. That interpretation would entail God's coming to learn the present immediately after it happens; thus God doesn't know the present per se but rather comes to learn history as immediately as possible. No, for Hasker, there is no temporal succession between a present event and God's knowledge of such an event. Instead, the symbolization above should be interpreted as representing logical priority rather than temporal succession. The logical priority means that God's knowledge at t_α of p at t_α is dependent upon the action being performed such that if p did not take place at t_α, then God would not know p. So, unsurprisingly,

$\sim p^{t\alpha} \rightarrow \sim G^{t\alpha}p^{t\alpha}$

or

$\sim p^{t\alpha} \rightarrow G^{t\alpha} \sim p^{t\alpha}$[62]

Presumably, this all saves the possibility of LFW in the present. But direct knowledge is still knowledge, so it is still infallible if God's, and therefore still renders the event known CN. And, if this works to save LFW in the present, Rota and Rogers have pressed the point in asking why it won't do to save timeless foreknowledge of LFW in the same way. But I wish to press the point differently, showing that regardless of how the open theist responds to Anselmian timelessness, their position still demands that God lacks knowledge of the present.

If an omniscient God exists, then God cannot fail to know all truths about a particular world.[63] And all theists agree that God exists. So, be-

62. These two assertions parallel one another, given the version of (D11) omniscience I propose, for not only does God not believe anything that is false (divine infallibility), but it is also true that God believes all truths, and ~ p at t_α is a truth.

63. Careful open theists retort that omniscience entails only that God cannot fail to know all logically knowable truths, but this point is irrelevant so long as open theists

cause God exists in this world, he cannot fail to know all truths about it, including truths about the present.[64] So there is a type of necessity that attaches to the proposition "If some agent *S* performs some action *A* at t_α, then God knows at t_α that that agent *S* performs that action *A* at t_α." Symbolized, we get

$(\underline{\text{ON}})\ (p^{t\alpha} \rightarrow G^{t\alpha}p^{t\alpha})$

By interpreting the ON as CN, we get

$(\underline{\text{CN}})\ (p^{t\alpha} \rightarrow G^{t\alpha}p^{t\alpha})$[65]

and after distributing the operator,

$(\underline{\text{CN}})\ p^{t\alpha} \rightarrow (\underline{\text{CN}})\ G^{t\alpha}p^{t\alpha}$

As a consequence of divine omniscience, God cannot fail to know the present. So

$(\underline{\text{CN}})\ G^{t\alpha}p^{t\alpha}$

Now we have enough to generate the dilemma more clearly. If God is omniscient as described by (D11), then we have good reason to believe that God knows the present. But we have already seen from (6)–(10) that whatever God knows is ON, at least if we utilize the premise that open theists agree is required to properly interpret all that divine infallibility entails.

$Gp \rightarrow (\underline{\text{CN}})\ p$

When we insert tense into the syllogism, we find

$G^{t\alpha}p^{t\alpha} \rightarrow (\underline{\text{CN}})\ p^{t\alpha}$

---

wish to maintain that knowledge of present reality is logically knowable. Should they decide otherwise, my point is already granted—that open theism's response to the DFF dilemma requires that God lacks knowledge of the present because such knowledge is logically impossible.

64. All theists conclude at minimum that God exists in this world. Those open theists who deny that God is a necessary being won't affirm that God exists in/at all worlds, but even those such as Hasker will concede at least that God exists in the actual world. This is the universal premise of theism.

65. I have defended above the idea that ON can be interpreted as either AN or CN. I have argued above why AN is either inapplicable to the DFF, or logically equivalent to CN. Assuming my argument holds, I use will use CN as the proper interpretation of ON in what follows.

If, as the open theist wishes to maintain, God at the present knows what is presently occurring, then we conclude

$$(\underline{\text{CN}})\, p^{t\alpha}$$

by way of a simple *modus ponens* move. But the open theist must conclude that divine knowledge precludes LFW, because whatever God knows is CN at the time in virtue of divine infallibility. Therefore, if God knows the present, then an action done at the present cannot be free, even if God's knowledge of the present is direct. This is so because the transposition of

$$\text{G}p \rightarrow (\underline{\text{CN}})\, p$$

gets us

$$\sim (\underline{\text{CN}})\, p \rightarrow \sim \text{G}p$$

That is, the only way that an event can avoid being CN is that it remain unknown to an infallible knower such as God. If some event remains significantly free (i.e., if LFW presently plays some part in the event such that the event in question is not yet determined), then God cannot know it; infallible knowledge of such would be sufficient to eliminate PAP. Hence, if the decisions made by free agents in the present are not ON (whether AN or CN is irrelevant), then God cannot know them, given the open theist's response to the DFF.

Having run the argument symbolically with the various forms of necessity, let us instantiate the claims according to Hasker's consequentialist argument (the [B]-type argument) in order to show why God lacks knowledge of the present.

> (B1*) It is now true that Clarence is presently eating a cheese omelet for breakfast, and Clarence does so freely. (Premise)
>
> (B2*) It is impossible that God should at any time, including the present, believe what is false, or fail to believe anything that is true. (Premise: divine omniscience)
>
> (B3*) Therefore, God presently believes that Clarence is presently eating a cheese omelet (freely) for breakfast. (From 1,2)
>
> (B4*) Once God has (presently) come to believe a certain thing, it is not in anyone's power to bring it about that God does not believe that thing. (Premise: the unalterability of the present, for

surely the present lies on the side of the past with respect to temporal asymmetry, as described above)

(B5*) Therefore, it is not in Clarence's power to bring it about that God presently believes that Clarence is not presently eating a cheese omelet (freely) for breakfast. (From 3,4)

(B6*) It is not possible for it to be true both that God believes that Clarence is presently eating a cheese omelet for breakfast, and that Clarence is not, in fact, presently eating a cheese omelet (freely) for breakfast. (From 2)

(B7*) Therefore, it is not in Clarence's power to refrain from presently eating a cheese omelet (freely) for breakfast. (From 5,6) So Clarence's present act of eating the omelet for breakfast is not an act of free choice.[66]

Simultaneous Causation

Having dealt with and dismissed all other possible solutions, only one option remains available for the open theist. Perhaps God knows the present instantaneously, such that any present action or event is the cause, simultaneously, of God's knowledge of the present. Although this maneuver preserves the logical priority of the present event as the cause of God's present knowledge of the event, such a position comes at a tremendous cost: affirming simultaneous causation. Space constraints preclude a summary of the massive literature that exists on the metaphysics of simultaneous causation, or the even larger body of literature covering causation in general.[67] However, a few remarks are in order to clarify why this option is not a viable path for theological incompatibilists who affirm divine knowledge of the present while simultaneously defending open theism as the proper response to the DFF. I will first summarize why affirming simultaneous causation is so problematic. I go on to show why the only escape left available for open theists requires that they affirm simultaneous causation. Finally, I cover the views concerning simultaneous causation of three significant open theists: Richard Swinburne, Peter van Inwagen, and

66. I take the structure of this argument directly from Hasker, *God, Time, and Knowledge*, 69.

67. Of the many articles and monographs on the subject of causation and simultaneous causation specifically, the best, recent book-length treatment of the subject is Tooley, *Time, Tense, and Causation*.

William Hasker in order to show that open theism faces insurmountable problems with respect to simultaneous causation, the metaphysics of time, God's knowledge of the present, and LFW.

First, Richard Swinburne (who we recall defends LFOT) explicitly denies the possibility of simultaneous causation in *The Christian God*. While discussing the metaphysics of time, Swinburne goes into great detail in describing his third principle, which he calls the causal theory of time. He takes it to be beyond dispute that the future is contingent, that we can causally affect the future. But, Swinburne develops a proof that an effect cannot precede its cause, for such would be tantamount to circular causation, which he takes to be obviously false, especially given the account of causation he believes is necessary for Christian theism. In order to better understand the context of Swinburne's comments, I quote him at length:

> Causation in a circle is not logically possible. If A causes B, B cannot cause A (or cause anything which by a longer circle causes A). For what causes what is logically contingent—"anything can produce anything," wrote Hume. [Footnote 17 on page 82 in Swinburne, *Christian God*] Let us put the point in this way: a sufficiently powerful being could, it is logically possible, alter the laws of nature in such a way that some event had, instead of its normal effect at a certain time, one incompatible with that normal effect. So if causation in a circle were logically possible and A caused B and B caused A, a sufficiently powerful being at the moment of B's occurrence could have altered the laws of nature so that B caused not-A; in which case A would have (indirectly) caused A not to occur—which is absurd. So since manifestly the future is causally affectible, the past is not. It follows that backward causation is impossible—causes cannot be later than their effects. It follows too that simultaneous causation is impossible. For if simultaneous causation were possible and A caused B simultaneously, and B caused C simultaneously, then, by Hume's principle cited earlier, it would be logically possible that B could have had, instead of its normal effect, not-A. That logically impossible conjunction of causal sequences is, given Hume's principle, only rendered impossible if we suppose simultaneous causation itself to be impossible. Hence, given that causes and effects are events which last for periods of time [which Swinburne has defended in the previous chapter on causation of *Christian God*, 51–71], any effect (which has a beginning) must begin at an instant later than its cause begins;

> and any effect (which has an end) must end at an instant later than its cause ends.[68]

Swinburne understands simultaneous causation to be logically equivalent to backward causation, which, if it were possible, would entail that power over the past is coherent, and therefore (logically) possible. If power over the past is possible, then Ockhamism presents a successful response to the DFF, and open theism would prove unnecessary.

In his *Critique of Pure Reason*, Kant offers the standard example still used today by many to support the possibility of simultaneous causation. In fact, Kant claims that "the great majority of efficient natural causes are simultaneous with their effects."[69] He asks readers to consider a ball that falls and comes to lie on a cushion, thereby forming a hollow. Kant contends that the hollow forms simultaneously as the falling ball comes into contact with the cushion. Swinburne's compelling reason why one should reject Kant's articulation of the possibility of simultaneous causation is worth quoting at length:

> But Kant gives no argument in favour of the claim that these are simultaneous, let alone in favour of his wide general claim; and he seems to have casually supposed that where he was unable to observe a time interval between the ball beginning to exert its gravitational force (concentrated at the ball's centre of gravity) and the first depression of the cushion, there was in fact no interval. But Kant's casual supposition was mistaken; special relativity can now tell us the length of that very small interval. In the Middle Ages it was generally supposed that light had an infinite velocity, and Newton and his successors supposed the force of gravity to act with infinite velocity; and infinite velocity involves the simultaneity of cause and effect. The Special Theory of Relativity has the consequence that all causal action is propagated with finite velocity. But, if my arguments in the text [of my chapter on time] are correct, it did not need special relativity with its empirical foundation to show this; it follows from logical considerations alone. It did of course need empirical considerations to show that the velocity of light is the fastest signal. Hume, by contrast, had an argument to show the logical impossibility of simultaneous causation (*Treatise*, 1. 3. 2). He argues that cause and immediate effect must be as close as possible. (If an earlier event causes a later event separated

68. Swinburne, *Christian God*, 82.

69. Kant, *Critique of Pure Reason*, A213/B260, 213.

> from it by an interval of time, it can only do so via a chain of close events which connect the two.) And how close is close? If cause and effect could be simultaneous, argues Hume, they would be; and then all effects would be simultaneous with their causes and that would lead to 'the utter annihilation of time'. So cause and effect cannot be simultaneous, and the requirement of closeness will have to be satisfied by mere contiguity of time. But Hume gives no argument as to why if nature allows one effect to be simultaneous with its cause, it has to allow all so to be. My claim in the text is that the *Treatise* contains the resources for a much stronger argument.[70]

Let us ignore for a moment that Ockhamism likely solves the DFF if simultaneous causation is metaphysically similar enough to backwards causation as to allow for power over the past, or counterfactual power over the past (as Swinburne contends).[71] Recall that open theism is working with a very precise definition of LFW:

> (FW') N is free at *T* with respect to performing $A =_{df}$ It is in N's power at *T* to perform *A* and it is possible at *T* for N to exercise that power, and it is in N's power at *T* to refrain from performing *A*, and it is also possible at *T* for N to exercise *that* power.[72]

The precision of this definition proves to be quite problematic for the open theist, precisely because it *requires* the possibility of simultaneous causation. Let us suppose that God is somehow able to know in the very same present moment our present actions. God, because he is omnipotent, might have the ability to do what we cannot do.[73] That is,

70. Swinburne, *Christian God*, 6, 245.

71. In a recent article, Alicia Finch and Michael Rea argue compellingly that Ockhamism is only a solution for those who reject presentism. Open theists already reject Ockhamism on the grounds that the distinction it makes between hard/soft facts is untenable. Given that open theists put forward presentism as the accurate metaphysic of time, it is unlikely that they will opt for Ockhamism as a legitimate solution to the DFF, even if they become persuaded that their arguments against the hard/soft fact distinction fail. Finch and Rea, "Presentism."

72. Hasker, *God, Time, and Knowledge*, 138.

73. I am not suggesting that God possesses the power to do what is logically impossible. Recall the Thomistic principle that I utilize in chapter 2 when defining omnipotence: "If A is an impossible task, then the fact that a given being cannot perform A does not imply that that being is not omnipotent." Wielenberg, "New Paradox," 262. Thus, I mean only to say that perhaps given our limitations, simultaneous causation is impossible for us in a way that it is not in the divine economy. This possibility is even more likely, it seems, when one considers all that might be involved if God is outside of time.

perhaps by some miraculous demonstration of perfect cognitive power, our present actions are all that is needed to ground the truth of the various propositions in question, and therefore cause (simultaneously) God's knowledge of the present.[74] If our present actions aren't causally necessary for God's knowledge of the present, we are saddled with grounding objections concerning truthmakers for true propositions about present actions. But even granting all this, we encounter yet another problem for those insisting on the above conception of LFW. And now we can see why.

Even if it is possible for simultaneous causation to occur in the divine economy because God is omnipotent, this does not save LFW from problems that arise regarding the necessity of the present. It is impossible that someone could, as a free agent, be the determining cause of some action at the present moment, yet at the same simultaneous moment decide to act differently than she is acting, especially when we recognize that such decision making implies change, and therefore temporal duration, even if only for the briefest duration of time.[75] Recall that once the present obtains, it is AN, for surely the present lies on the side of the past with respect to temporal asymmetry. As stated in the previous chapter, in any given world, at any given present moment, the state of affairs that is the present cannot be any other state of affairs in that same world at that same moment, lest a contradiction arise. Again, remember that once the past has occurred in a given possible world, given the fixity of the past, the past cannot later become a different past because whatever has obtained cannot be changed once it has obtained. The same holds true for the present. In any given possible world, once the present state of affairs obtains, the present is fixed, and cannot in one any the same present

74. Of course, given that God is continually learning the present, and is everlastingly going to continue to do so, it counts against this view that God is actually performing a miracle, at least so long as rarity is part of what constitutes the miraculous. Personally, I find Alston's articulation of the miraculous rather compelling, and don't think it should count heavily against something being a miracle even if it is a rather common occurrence. Alston, "God's Action." I raise the concern only because mine is the minority view concerning the miraculous, so many will find that I am being overly charitable to the open theist in granting such possibilities to God as described above. However, in keeping with the intent of this chapter, I seek to grant as much as possible to the open theist in order to show that, even granting so many suppositions, their view remains untenable.

75. This problem is even more severe if one is working with agent-causal models of LFW, although as best I can tell the same problems would obtain for event-causal libertarians.

moment be some different present state of affairs, on pains of contradiction. Therefore, we conclude that the present lies on the side of the past with respect to temporal asymmetry.

That is, once the present has arrived, it is not logically possible for it to be other than it is *in the same present moment in the same possible world*.[76] But, in order for us to possess the kind of LFW which open theists insist humans enjoy, we must be able to render what has become AN (e.g., the present) different than it is, which is, of course, absurd. It may have been possible at some moment prior to the present for an agent to act in such a way so as to bring it about that either *p* or ~*p*. But once *p* obtains in the present moment, because it is logically impossible that *p* and ~*p* at one and the same moment in the same possible world, we note that the present shares with the past the property of being AN. Recall that indeterminists maintain that AN does not eliminate the contingent nature of whatever state of affairs is in view, for *p* could have been different. That is, there is nothing about *p* that is necessary, in the logical or metaphysical sense. Rather, what renders ~*p* now impossible is the principle of the fixity of the past. Therefore, once *p* obtains in the present moment, it is no longer possible that ~*p* in that same moment, in that same possible world, on pains of contradiction.

Suppose that an agent *S* chooses to do some action *A* at t_α. That is, in the present moment, *S* is choosing to do *A*. Now, in order for *S* to be free at t_α with respect to *A*, then it must be possible—*at the exact same moment*—that S refrain from choosing to do *A* and that S possess the power to exercise such a choice. But, this requires that the present—having arrived, thereby being AN in that it cannot change—can be different than it in fact is. This is different than saying that it *could* have been different, but has become AN. No, in order for the definitions of LFW offered by open theists to succeed, it must be possible for an agent *S* to presently decide to do *A* and, having (presently) decided to do *A*, an agent *S* must be able to simultaneously cause himself to chose otherwise. But clearly this is impossible, for once the present arrives, it cannot be other than what it is, unless one is willing to deny the law of identity. This is because

76. I acknowledge that *p* & ◇~*p* is not a formal contradiction. However, given a particular possible world, and standard tense logic, and a particular moment, the modal possibility operator cannot be understood to denote broadly logical possibility. What I am talking about is whether in a specific possible world, at some specific present moment, one state of affairs can obtain, while it still being possible at that same specific moment in that same specific possible world for another different state of affairs to obtain. *That*, I maintain, *would* constitute a contradiction.

of the specific type of necessity, namely AN, that attaches to the present once it obtains. Given the AN of the present, it is no longer possible that the same present moment be different than it is (in the same possible world). Given the fact that open theists (especially Swinburne) have argued against the possibility of simultaneous causation, it is evident that they should abandon the working definition of LFW.[77]

Some might maintain that it is possible for an agent *S*, in one and the same present moment, to decide to do *A*, and then deliberate and decide to refrain from doing *A* in such a way that the latter decision is not simultaneous with the first. While this option would alleviate the tensions created by the impossibility of simultaneous causation, it rests upon a misunderstanding of what constitutes the present. For presentists, the present is the moment that divides the past from the future.[78] As this boundary, it is the very smallest time-slice that could possibly exist. Suggesting that there would be time for choosing something other than one already chooses is to suggest that the smallest possible time slice is actually larger than it is, for I can certainly conceive of a time-slice

77. I should mention that William Lane Craig has vociferously defended simultaneous causation, believing it to be necessary in order to defend the doctrine of *creatio ex nihilo* as well as certain versions of the cosmological argument (including the Kalam argument I utilize in chapter 1). A series of essays on the subject, introduced by Craig, can be found in Craig and Smith, *Einstein*. Cf. Craig, "Professor Grünbaum on Creation"; Craig, "Response to Grünbaum."

It seems to me that Craig's concerns can be addressed apart from simultaneous causation by way of divine timelessness, at least so long as one takes such a view, which Craig does not (for other reasons not directly related to the "simultaneous" causation of the universe). Additionally, I believe that Craig makes a category mistake in supposing that the creation of the world is an instance of simultaneous causation. That is, Craig equivocates when discussing God's relation to time at the "moment" of creation. Craig defends the idea that time was created along with the universe (at the same moment), and that, upon the creation of time, God simultaneously entered into time while "simultaneously" causing the universe. The mistake, as I see it, lies in failing to understand timeless causation. So, even for those who deny divine timelessness in favor of divine accidental temporalism, it is best to suppose instead that God timelessly caused the universe (and time) and upon its creation, God entered time. This approach eliminates the temporal mechanics of causation which present problems for simultaneous (and backwards) causation, while also preserving the metaphysics of time that are necessary to allow for coherent defenses of the Kalam cosmological argument and *creatio ex nihilo*. Said differently, a timeless cause that produces a tensed effect is not the same as a temporal cause simultaneously producing a temporal effect.

For more on this topic, see the comments of both Helm and Craig in Craig, *God and Time*, 47–52, 65–67, 84–86. Special thanks to Daniel Hill for helping me think clearly about this matter. Personal conversation with author, Aug. 6, 2011.

78. Swinburne, *Christian God*, 81. Cf. Crisp, "Presentism."

so small that it would not allow for time to move from one decision to another, and surely this smaller time-slice must be what serves as the boundary between the past and the future. Hence, even this method does not allow for the open theist to escape the fact that simultaneous causation must not only be possible, but an incredibly common—nay, constant—reality, at least so long as one wishes to maintain that God possesses exhaustive knowledge of the present.

Peter van Inwagen takes a different account of causation from that of Swinburne. Van Inwagen denies that causation exists at all if causation is understood as a relation between events. Instead he believes that causal relations (such as pushing and pulling) hold between substances, not events.[79] Regardless, he insists that causal influence never moves at a speed greater than light.[80] This leads me to conclude that causation, according to van Inwagen, obtains over time as a process, and necessarily so, such that one substance cannot exert causal influence over another so as to produce an effect simultaneously.

Hasker, in contrast to both Swinburne and van Inwagen, does not deny the possibility of simultaneous causation. He argues that Swinburne's account must proceed as follows:

> There are two objects, A and B. A is able to exert some sort of causal power on B, bringing about some unspecified change in B. A has two relevant states: *causing*, when it is exercising the causal power in question, and *not-causing*, when it is not. B also has two relevant states: *allowing*, the state in which it allows A to exercise power on B, and *preventing*, which prevents A from exercising such power.

79. Personal communication with author, Sept. 5, 2011. Although he did not say as much, I am inclined to think that Van Inwagen believes this distinction is necessary to preserve agent causal models of freedom, as opposed to event causation, which, according to him, entails determinism.

80. Cf. Van Inwagen, "Plantinga's Replacement Argument," 200n16. I should note that this article is not principally about causation, but when discussing Plantinga's now-famous "replacement" argument concerning identity over time with respect to the mind-body problem for materialists, Van Inwagen has a great deal to say about his account of causation. "There cannot be two 'adjacent' intervals (two intervals such that a certain mathematical instant *t* is the least upper bound of one them [*sic*] and the greatest lower bound of the other) such that *x* is not a part of Alice at any instant that belongs to the earlier interval and is a part of Alice at every instant that belongs to the later one. Assimilation, whatever else it may be, is a causal process, and causal processes take time." Van Inwagen, "Plantinga's Replacement Argument," 195. Van Inwagen reiterated these points to me in personal communication, Sept. 5, 2011.

> Now, suppose B is in *allowing*, and A goes into the state *causing*. Then all goes smoothly, and A produces the appropriate changes in B. On the other hand, if B is in *preventing*, A cannot go into *causing*, and A produces no change in B.
>
> Now, suppose causation is instantaneous. B is in *allowing*, and A goes into *causing* at t. But the instantaneous effect of this is that B goes into *preventing*, again at t, and A exerts no causal power on B. So A, by exerting causal power on B, causes it to be the case that A never exerts any causal power on B. Call this the *self-negating causation* sequence (SNC). SNC is obviously impossible. But the only way to forestall it, according to Swinburne, is to deny the possibility of instantaneous causation.
>
> I reply, SNC can be blocked without denying instantaneous causation. The problem with SNC is that B is said to go into *preventing at t*, the very time at which A's causal action begins. But this means that *there is no interval of time subsequent to t* during which A's causal action can occur. And since before t A is in *not-causing*, there is no interval at all during which A is in *causing*. But Swinburne would agree that there is no sense to the idea of a causal action which occurs at a single point in time but neither before nor after that point. So the description of SNC is incoherent: to restore coherence, we must suppose that B goes into *preventing* at some time *after* t, and the paradox disappears.
>
> SNC requires B to be in *allowing* at t, so as to enable A to be in *causing* at t. But it also requires B to be in *preventing* at t, so as to prevent A from causing B to change. But a scenario that requires B to be in two contradictory states simultaneously is obviously out of the question, and creates no problems for instantaneous causation as such.[81]

Hasker believes simultaneous causation can escape the sort of paradox Swinburne raises by showing that SNC requires something (B) to be in two contradictory states at the same time. If this is a problem for the object being affected by a cause, then it must certainly be a problem also for a cause to be in two contradictory states at the same time. But this is exactly what is required in order to preserve open theism given its definition of LFW. Suppose the present has arrived such that God knows that some agent *S* is doing some action *A*. If *S* is free with respect to *A* in the present, it must be in *S*'s power, while he is doing *A*, to

81. This quotation, and all other positions attributed to Hasker in what follows, come from personal communication, Aug. 31, 2011, and are offered with his permission.

simultaneously refrain from doing *A* in the present—*even though the present has arrived such as to accidentally necessitate* S*'s doing* A, *thereby guaranteeing that God knows that* S *is doing* A. Of course, if *S* has this power, it is the case that the present has already obtained and a state of affairs that includes *S*'s doing *A* is part of reality, and that such a state of affairs is AN. Nonetheless, *S* has the power to refrain from doing *A* such that were *S* to exercise such a power that a *different* state of affairs would result, and this state of affairs (including ~*A*) would obtain in one and the same present moment, in one and the same possible world where a contradictory state of affairs has already obtained and become AN. But, as previously stated, I deny that any person has the power to bring about a logical contradiction, which would be the case here. Said differently, *S* cannot have the power to bring about two mutually exclusive, contradictory states at one and the same moment: doing *A* at the present moment, in the actual world, while simultaneously refraining from *A* at the same present moment, in the same actual world.

Additionally, if *S* has this power, then *S* has the power to bring it about that at the present, God is not infallible.[82] Suppose again that the present has arrived such that, because God knows the present, God knows that some agent *S* is doing some action *A*. So, God believes that *S* is doing *A*, yet at the very time that *S* is doing *A*, *S* is free to refrain from doing *A*. It follows that *S* has the power to bring it about that what God believes is not true, which is obviously untenable. So even with the admission of the possibility of simultaneous causation, Hasker does not avoid the dilemma of how God can know the present on the terms established by open theism.[83]

82. This is sufficiently analogous to counterfactual power over the past in a way that those who deny the possibility of such should also deny counterfactual power over the present. This is important to stave off objections of the form: perhaps *S* has the ability to do something such that, were *S* to do it, God would have presently believed something different from what God actually believes at present.

83. Both space and the subject matter preclude a more detailed investigation of this matter, so I offer a brief sketch of one additional problem involved in the issues pertaining to time and causation. Hasker maintains that many types of causation are real, and not all causation is simultaneous. Given presentism, however, this position is untenable. If the only moment of time that exists is the present, then the only time at which causation can occur is the present. To be clear—the presentist affirms the passing of time, and all presentists agree that the persistence of objects through time comes by way of endurance rather than by perdurance. But it does not make sense to say that an effect can obtain apart from a cause, nor does it make sense to say that a cause can obtain without producing some effect. Now, given presentism as the correct metaphysic of time, the only objects that exist do so in the present. So, if a cause is to have an effect,

Conclusion

What possible explanation could be given for the fact that an omniscient being lacks knowledge of the present—knowledge that we possess ourselves?[84] Lacking any compelling answer to this question, we should conclude against open theism's response to the DFF, recognizing that openness responses to the DFF entail far more serious consequences than originally intended. As it turns out, philosophically driven open theism requires not only redefining omniscience such that God lacks foreknowledge, but also that God does not know any truths about the present reality involving LFW. This is so because, as Hasker notes, open theists tend to be more willing to hedge against divine knowledge in denying that God knows certain things—things which they insist are logically unknowable—than they are willing to deny LFW of humanity.[85]

---

it must have its effect on an object existing at the same time as the cause, for no other objects exist. And, if one wants to say that causation that produces change obtains over time, such a position, given presentism, requires that one defend the difficult view that a currently non-existent object has caused (in the past, when it existed) a currently existing object to experience, currently, some effect. Hasker is a presentist, but he denies that all causation is simultaneous—taking instead something like that just described above as the accurate understanding of causation over time. Because his account of open theism is motivated in part by presentism, I find that even his concession of the possibility of simultaneous causation is not enough for him to avoid the full force of the conundrum open theism faces with respect to the question of when God comes to learn what once was future. Given presentism, apart from a concession that all causation is simultaneous, I do not see how Hasker can affirm that God knows the present. But as I have shown, utilizing simultaneous causation to escape this conundrum creates other insurmountable problems, so that won't do either. Of course, this same argument applies not only to Hasker, but also to any other presentist—including Zimmerman—who denies that all causation is simultaneous.

84. It occurs to me that one might argue that we do not (cannot?) know the actual present. One might argue that certain brain states occur, and only after they occur do we become aware of them, even if our consciousness of these brain states is almost instantaneously thereafter. However, this strikes me as counterintuitive to what is meant by commonsensical understanding of our knowing about what is presently happening. I leave further exploration of this matter to those interested in the intersection(s) of the metaphysics of time, philosophy of mind, and epistemology. Suffice it to say for now that even if humans lack the ability to know the present, I see no reason to attribute such a lack of perfection to an omniscient God. Recall that (D11) omniscience requires that God know all knowable truths. Hence, if propositions concerning the present reality possess truth-values, and if the present is knowable, then an omniscient God must know them. Perhaps Hasker would accept this line of argument and suggest that the present is not knowable, thereby preserving his understanding of divine omniscience. But I take it as obvious that it is undesirable, and seemingly impious, to suggest that God does not know the present.

85. Consider the following passage from Hasker, taking up the issue of responding

Hence, if, as I have shown, it is logically impossible for God to know aspects of the present reality involving LFW, then open theists (so long as they are consistent) will go on to conclude against the idea that God possesses exhaustive knowledge of the present.

I set out to accomplish several important things in this chapter. I began by explaining how the strongest versions of the DFF involve premises that involve modal claims, and the issues in modality upon which the DFF turns are improperly motivated by open theism, regardless of whether one approaches the issues from the perspective of LFOT or OFOT. Having shown as much, I turned to weaker articulations of the DFF, arguing briefly that alternatives to open theism prove equally successful in addressing the tension for omniscience raised by the DFF. I went on by developing an understanding of ON, which is weaker than logical necessity, but is exactly what must motivate the DFF, at least the version(s) of the DFF that open theists have in mind. I went on to show how even the most plausible candidate—understanding ON as CN—allows for the creation of a logically equivalent problem: the dilemma of freedom and *knowledge*. This dilemma requires that we understand either: (1) that God lacks knowledge of any of the present reality involving LFW or (2) that humans lack LFW in the present. Because openness advocates seek to preserve LFW at all costs (even by offering a highly attenuated conception of omniscience), it seems that they are stuck with denying that God enjoys exhaustive definite knowledge of the present.

I concluded by discussing the prospects for open theists to avoid the conundrum I raise against them by considering the possibility of simultaneous causation. Given Swinburne's explicit denial of the possibility of simultaneous causation, I take it as obvious that my argument, at minimum, puts the open theist on the horns of a dilemma: open theists must either acknowledge that God does not know the present, but rather comes to learn of history as immediately as logically possible; or open theists may change their position regarding simultaneous causation. Taking either of these to be undesirable consequences of open theism, and because there

to his arguments (A) and (B) by denying LFW. "Both (A) and (B) conclude to a denial of libertarian free will. In fact, however, relatively few incompatibilists accept this conclusion. Rather, incompatibilists tend to adopt modified conceptions of omniscience so as to avoid the deterministic outcome." Hasker, *God, Time, and Knowledge*, 73. To restate what I already discussed in chapter four, Hasker is simply wrong on this point. Throughout the history of Christian faith, the vast majority of incompatibilists have denied LFW in order to preserve the most robust conception of omniscience rather than accommodate omniscience towards LFW.

may be still other consequences even more radical than those discussed in this chapter that remain thus far unforeseen, I suggest that philosophers and theologians alike close the door on open theism even if they remain unwilling to endorse some other response to the DFF.

Coda

When discussing the issues of modal logic involved in the DFF, we must remember that properly Anselmian conceptions of the divine nature lead to the conclusion that God is a necessary being. Initially, it might seem that divine necessity has nothing to do with divine knowledge of the present, but this is a mistaken intuition. Note that Hasker cannot appeal to divine necessity in order to motivate the modal moves required to construct a strong form of the DFF because he denies that God is a necessary being. While critiquing Plantinga for not spelling out what exactly necessity is, Hasker denies Plantingian metaphysics of modality because it establishes divine necessity.[86] Hasker rejects divine necessity because it supports the doctrine of divine simplicity; and Hasker feels compelled to undermine divine simplicity because that doctrine supports divine timelessness; and Hasker rejects divine timelessness in order to defend open theism. So, Hasker denies that God is a necessary being in order to defend open theism. But insurmountable articulations of the DFF do not hinge on divine necessity. So, even if Hasker (or any other open theist) were to affirm divine necessity, the argument(s) are not any more secure. Rather, such a move fails to provide open theists a solution to the problem of divine knowledge of the present for one of two reasons, which I detail below.

First, if God is a necessary being, then one of the necessary conditions is met in order to generate the truth of "Necessarily, God believes *p*"—the part that can only be satisfied by a necessary being. But only this part is satisfied, for it is absurd to suggest that there are no worlds in which God knows ~*p* while simultaneously positing the idea that *p* is an action performed freely. Suggesting that it isn't absurd simply begs the question against theological compatibilism. But perhaps we can bring

86. Hasker, "Analytic Philosophy of Religion," 440. I find it rather ironic that Hasker charges Plantinga with not spelling out exactly what necessity is (which Plantinga acknowledges in the first chapter of *The Nature of Necessity*) while Hasker puts forward an understanding of necessity that is merely pragmatic, so he doesn't actually tell us what necessity is any more than Plantinga does.

world-indexed properties back into play by stipulating that "Necessarily, God believes that an agent *S* will perform an action *A* in world *alpha*." Thus, in all worlds, God believes something about *alpha*, namely, that agent *S* does *A* in *alpha*, which brings me to the second response.

Perhaps the antecedent is satisfied, but this is so only if there is a truth-value for God to know about that proposition concerning the future *p*. The only escape from the problems of logical fatalism, which I discussed in chapter 5, is to opt for OFOT, but this won't work either. Defenders of OFOT either affirm all-falsism about PCFC by denying that any PCFC are presently true (a position that I discuss in detail in the next chapter), or they deny that the principle of bivalence applies to PCFC and thereby deny that there are any truth-values for PCFC. Either way, God couldn't know any *p* where *p* concerns a future contingent—in *alpha* or in any other world. Thus, given OFOT, the antecedent to the conditional cannot exist, much less be necessary, so the DFF remains improperly motivated.

Besides this, if defenders of OFOT were to affirm that some PCFC are true, they would actually be defending LFOT, and thereby fall prey to all the arguments I offered against that position in chapters three and four. Additionally, making such an argument requires that there is an actual world, where possible world includes a complete and total world history (including the future), which is a position those who subscribe to OFOT deny. I discuss this more in the next chapter, but suffice it to say that defenders of OFOT believe instead that the non-existence of an actual world is a necessary component of our possession of LFW.[87] If there were an actual world with truth-values concerning the future, the future wouldn't be contingent, or so they insist.[88]

In light of this, then, we see that OFOT's denial of divine foreknowledge is not so much motivated because there is some contradiction between freedom and foreknowledge. Instead, OFOT is based on a particular understanding of the metaphysics of time, namely, an aberrant conception of truth-makers given presentism. But once these metaphysical positions are assumed, defenders of OFOT are guilty of begging the question against theological compatibilists—at least so long as we are discussing responses to the DFF properly and not focusing

87. Tuggy makes a similar point in "Roads to Open Theism."

88. Here it seems that defenders of OFOT believe that the mere existence of truths about the future renders those events necessary, which is the problem of logical fatalism that I discussed in the last chapter.

strictly on the metaphysics of time. And of course, in this chapter I *am* discussing the open theist's response to the DFF, so I won't pay any more attention at this juncture to arguments favoring open theism that are not motivated as responses to the DFF.[89]

89. Again, I discuss those arguments and how they relate to perfect being theology in the next chapter. I raise these issues here only to show that the arguments I offer in this chapter succeed against both LFOT and OFOT, albeit for very different reasons.

6

Lord Even over Time

A Few Worries About the Systematic Metaphysics of Open Future Open Theism[1]

It seems prudent to clarify exactly which version(s) of openness theology I will argue against in this chapter by explaining what exactly differentiates open future open theism (OFOT) from limited foreknowledge open theism (LFOT). One way to differentiate types of open theism involves the principle of bivalence and the law of the excluded middle. Some open theists affirm that some propositions concerning future contingents (PCFC) are presently true; these thinkers include Greg Boyd, Keith DeRose, William Hasker, Alan Rhoda, Richard Swinburne, and Peter van Inwagen. Other open theists deny that the principle of bivalence applies to PCFC. Instead, they prefer some probabilistic, multivalent approach to the truth-values of PCFC; among these thinkers are Craig Bourne, J. R. Lucas, Richard Purtill, Dale Tuggy, and Dean Zimmerman.

Another way to categorize openness theologies also relates to truth. Some open theists (notably Hasker, Swinburne, and van Inwagen, whom I argued against in chapters 4 and 5) defend LFOT—wherein divine omniscience does not entail knowledge of all truths. This is so because on LFOT, bivalent truths about future contingents are omnitemporal; that is, the truth-values of PCFC do not change as the future becomes present and fades into the past. According to LFOT, these truths are unknown to God, but this poses no problem for divine omniscience because knowledge of such truths is metaphysically impossible, even for perfect beings. LFOT differs substantially from OFOT, for the latter rejects the omnitemporality of truth.

1. A condensed version of this can be found in Arbour, *Essays Against Open Theism*.

OFOT comes in two varieties. Defenders of each version of OFOT affirm that divine omniscience entails knowledge of all truths, so they stand against LFOT's redefining omniscience in modal terms.[2] However, advocates of OFOT affirm divine knowledge of all truths for different reasons. According to Alan Rhoda's articulation of OFOT (hereafter Rhodanian OFOT), all PCFC involving "will" or "will not" language are false. This position, which is sometimes called all-falsism, is thought to preserve the principle of bivalence for PCFC, whereas an alternative articulation of OFOT championed by Dean Zimmerman (hereafter Zimmermanean OFOT) denies that the principle of bivalence applies to PCFC. Either way, defenders of OFOT deny that God possesses exhaustive definite foreknowledge. In fact, both types of OFOT require denying that God possesses any foreknowledge of future contingents whatsoever.[3]

In this chapter, I will not address LFOT since I have already offered two different arguments against that position in chapters 4 and 5. Here I am concerned only with OFOT. Both versions of OFOT, I maintain, should be rejected, but not because they are incompatible with Anselmian perfect being theology. In what follows, I summarize both the Zimmermanean and Rhodanian articulations of OFOT, and I demonstrate why they each ought to be rejected along the way. Next, I argue against OFOT by showing that the way that philosophy of time drives OFOT is incompatible with any contemporary systematic metaphysics. I continue by offering a type of Anselmian argument against OFOT, but I show why this sort of argument won't accomplish what it needs to in order to rule out OFOT on entirely Anselmian grounds. However, I do show with this type of argument that OFOT is dubious because of the metaphysics of time it requires, and it turns out on the basis of this type of argument that the metaphysics of time needed to motivate OFOT faces even more serious problems than those I raise against it in the section about systematic metaphysics. I conclude by discussing a theological counterexample to

2. But note that for those who affirm divine knowledge of all truths, it is vacuously true that God knows all that it is logically possible to know.

3. Although both Zimmermanean and Rhodanian versions of OFOT affirm theological incompatibilism—the belief that divine foreknowledge and creaturely free will are incompatible—advocates of OFOT motivate their understandings of open theism by way of the metaphysics of time rather than strictly as a response to the dilemma of freedom and foreknowledge (DFF). However, proponents of OFOT agree with the arguments for the incompatibility of freedom and foreknowledge. Because I have already discussed those arguments in detail in earlier chapters, I won't discuss those issues here. Rather, I focus on the issues that advocates of OFOT have used to motivate their various positions.

OFOT that serves to demonstrate that even if a logically coherent systematic metaphysics could be developed to make sense of OFOT, such a metaphysics is not what has obtained in the actual world. Therefore, Christians who defend the idea that God is the being ultimately responsible for the creation of the world should not appeal to OFOT as the proper response to the dilemma of freedom and foreknowledge (DFF).

Zimmermanean Open Future Open Theism, Presentism, and Bivalence

Dean Zimmerman is the leading proponent of the version of OFOT that denies that the principle of bivalence applies to PCFC. Zimmerman maintains that the underdetermined nature of the future (hereafter open futurism), together with metaphysical presentism requires that we abandon a bivalent understanding of PCFC. That is, PCFC should not be understood as either true or false in light of the alethic openness for the future. Rather, Zimmerman suggest that we adopt a multi-valued, probabilistic logic.[4] Zimmerman argues that if someone is free in the libertarian sense with respect to some action to be performed in the future, then there cannot currently exist a bivalent truth-value for the proposition that corresponds to that future contingent. If the action in question were determined to come about, then bivalent truth-values could be assigned to any proposition about said action. However, that such an action would be determined eliminates the contingency that is needed to preserve the freedom thought to be associated with the action, and therefore any moral responsibility for that action. Believing that humans do enjoy freedom as understood by the libertarian (LFW), Zimmerman and others of his ilk conclude that the principle of bivalence does not apply to PCFC.

The Zimmermanean take on OFOT is also motivated in part by the view that truth supervenes on being. Given presentism, only present things exist, so there can be no "truth" of the matter (in the bivalent sense) about future contingencies because the future does not yet exist.[5]

4. Zimmerman's work on presentism and open futurism includes, but is not limited to:" "A-Theory of Time"; "A-Theory of Time, Presentism"; "Presentism and the Space-Time"; "Privileged Present"; and "Temporary Intrinsics and Presentism." Others who defend this position include Tuggy and Purtill. See Tuggy, "Roads to Open Theism"; Purtill, "Fatalism and the Omnitemporality."

5. As I discussed in chapters 4 and 5, this is a good reason to reject LFOT. Note that this problem does not arise for the past, given the principle of the fixity of the past.

However, according to Zimmermaneans, that the principle of bivalence doesn't apply to PCFC doesn't mean that indeterministic truth predicates cannot be applied to PCFC.[6] Rather, Zimmermaneans reject standard logics and advocate instead for Polish-style, fuzzy, multi-valued logic.[7] This allows for taking character and psychological tendencies into account so as to make sense of probabilities while preserving the indeterminacy of future contingents. On such a view, if Abby prefers orange juice to apple juice, given the choice between the two for breakfast, taking probabilities into account, it makes sense to say that it is 85 percent true that Abby will drink orange juice with her breakfast tomorrow.[8]

It doesn't make much sense to say that it is 85 percent true that Abby will drink orange juice with her breakfast tomorrow. Rather, what seems intuitive rests on probabilities, such that it is 100 percent true that there is presently an 85 percent chance that Abby will have orange juice with her breakfast tomorrow. Note that bivalence is preserved on this analysis, although the contingent nature of probability theory has been taken into account. If this is what Zimmerman and others of his ilk want to preserve, then there is no reason to abandon the principle of bivalence, for alternative interpretations of probability theory offer what he wants (contingency) without abandoning the universal applicability of the principle of bivalence. Nonetheless, Zimmerman isn't the only philosopher to have suggested a multi-valued logic,[9] and Craig Borne has attempted to work out the details of some of these issues in his book *A Future for Presentism*.[10]

This all stems from the asymmetry thesis, which states that the future is open in a way that the past is not. Rhoda gives reasons for this in his "Presentism, Truthmakers, and God." Of course, there are good reasons for rejecting this "problem" for presentism. Tom Crisp has argued for an ersatz way to ground the truth of future contingents, even on presentism, in his article "Presentism and the Grounding Objection." Cf. Craig, "Middle Knowledge." For the sake of argument, however, I will ignore this solution and grant the problem so as to construct alternative responses to Zimmermanean OFOT.

6. For more on this, see Łukasiewicz, "Many-Valued Systems."

7. For a greater understanding of what this requires, see Haack, *Deviant Logic, Fuzzy Logic*; Bolc and Borowik, *Many-Valued Logics* (both volumes). The best introduction to this material can be found online. See Gottwald, "Many-Valued Logic."

8. It will be clear why rounding 85 percent (or 99.99 percent) up to 100 percent won't do once we examine what presentism demands concerning how one should interpret the semantic content of "will" and "will not" statements, which I discuss in the next section.

9. For example, see Lucas, *Future*; Tuggy, "Roads to Open Theism"; Purtill, "Fatalism and the Omnitemporality."

10. Bourne, *Future for Presentism*.

Nonetheless, those who want to follow Zimmerman should recognize that abandoning the principle of bivalence, even if only with respect to PCFC, is a steep price to pay for preserving OFOT, and isn't necessary given the Rhodanian alternative (discussed below). But even if the Rhodanian alternative weren't available, it would still be wrong to go the way of Zimmerman and others. Many philosophers believe that the principle of bivalence is universal; that is, necessarily, all propositions are either true or false and not both. Call this view necessary bivalentism. If this holds, then Zimmermanean articulations of OFOT are obviously false. On necessary bivalentism, for any proposition, necessarily, that proposition is either true or false, and not both. If a sentence does not have a bivalent truth-value, then that sentence does not express a proposition. This view not only necessitates the falsity of Zimmermanean OFOT, but it also avoids the conundrum for bivalentism posed by the Liar paradox.[11]

If this holds, then Zimmermanean articulations of OFOT are false, and necessarily so. But why should anyone hold to necessary bivalentism? One reason stems from understandings of contemporary systematic metaphysics. On standard interpretations thereof, four categories play the most foundational/fundamental role in shaping one's understanding of reality: properties, causation, laws of nature, and modality. On this account, truth and themes related to it (such as bivalence) are best understood as subcategories of the metaphysics of properties. Because properties are one of the most fundamental categories of a systematic metaphysics, it seems odd that aspects of metaphysics less fundamental to a systematic metaphysics (in the case of Zimmerman's interpretation of OFOT, time and free will) would impact one's understanding of the more foundational components related to properties (in this specific case, truth and bivalence).[12] Rather, one would expect the flow to move from the more fundamental aspects of systematic metaphysics to the derivative components entailed by the more fundamental components. In the case of Zimmermanean OFOT, this seems to be reversed. Zimmermaneans

11. The Liar paradox has many variations. The easiest way to understand what is at issue in the paradox is to consider the sentence "This sentence is not true" and grapple with whether or not the sentence can be true (or not). On my view, this sentence does not express a proposition. I don't pretend that this view is uncontroversial, or that things proceed as neatly and easily as suggested here, for there are responses against this view, but further comments would lead us too far afield of our present concerns. For more on ideas related to my proposed solution, see Glanzberg, "Against Truth-Value Gaps."

12. I take up the issue of systematic metaphysics in a bit more detail when discussing Rhodanian OFOT later in this chapter.

would do well to work out their metaphysics first and then turn their attention to the DFF, rather than determine that OFOT is the correct response to the DFF, then turning their attention to provide the metaphysics to make sense out of that response. That is, philosophical theologians should not work the other way around. Besides all this, it just strikes most people not only as counterintuitive, but also as obviously false, that any proposition could be anything other than 100 percent true or 100 percent false. How could something ever be 61.29 percent true?

To recap, the cost associated with fuzzy, multi-valued logics is too high a price to pay, and no one has offered a systematic metaphysics that could make sense of the Zimmermanean version of OFOT, so this interpretation of OFOT needs be rejected.[13] Additionally, given non-multivalent logics together with both the law of the excluded middle and the law of non-contradiction, the principle of bivalence holds for all propositions, entailing that all propositions are necessarily either true or false, and this includes PCFC. Therefore, if any version of OFOT is to succeed, it must preserve the principle of bivalence. Because Rhodanian articulations of OFOT purport to do just this, I now turn to that understanding of OFOT.

Rhodanian Open Future Open Theism, Presentism, and Bivalence

Alan Rhoda contributes prolifically to the literature on OFOT, and stands as the leading defender of what I have called Rhodanian OFOT,[14] but he is certainly not the only defender of the version of OFOT that bears his name. However, because his recent work on the subject plays such a prominent role in contemporary discussion of open theism, and because he has published more on this topic than his counterparts, I will focus my interaction on his literature, taking his numerous

13. Or, more modestly, defenders of OFOT should be much less confident in their articulation of theology proper and their response to the DFF until someone provides a systematic metaphysics that makes sense of this novel interpretation of reality. Without a systematic metaphysics to undergird this understanding of open futurism, defends of OFOT ought to proceed much more cautiously, and they should pay more attention to the numerous critiques of openness theology that have come from both philosophers and theologians, both contemporary and historic.

14. Rhoda's published work on OFOT includes: "Generic Open Theism"; "Case for Open Theism"; "Fivefold Openness." He also co-authored with Boyd and Belt the article "Open Theism, Omniscience." He has claimed all of the positions I attribute to him in these works; I have verified this with him in numerous personal conversations.

contributions to be representative of a version of OFOT that differs from the Zimmermanean version discussed above.[15]

According to Rhodanian OFOT, all PCFC involving "will" and "will not" language are false. Obviously, this avoids the multi-valued logic required by Zimmermanean OFOT. But determining whether Rhoda's understanding of the falsity of PCFC preserves bivalence requires a more detailed examination of his position. In what follows, I discuss Rhoda's understanding of the semantic force of the wording of PCFC in the light of both presentism and the correspondence theory of truth (both of which Rhoda affirms). I go on to show how the metaphysics of modality required by Rhodanian OFOT entails that free agents possess power over the actual world, which allows Ockhamism to settle any tensions created by the DFF. Finally, I conclude my critique of Rhodanian OFOT by showing that refuting the Ockhamist solution I propose, given all that is required by Rhodanian OFOT, requires a wholesale revision of contemporary systematic metaphysics.

One way Rhodanian OFOT purports to preserve bivalence for PCFC involves appealing to a Peircean understanding of the semantic content of PCFC. This linguistics is rather complicated, and depends on two issues related to the metaphysics of time. First, the Peircean believes that the A-theory of time is correct, which means that time is fundamentally tensed and explanations thereof cannot be reduced to "earlier-than," or "later-than" relations. Rather, there is something important about the present, or the "now-ness," that precludes the possibility of a B-theory of time. Furthermore, Peirceans motivate their understanding of the semantic force of PCFC by way of presentism, which is the combination of the A-theory of time together with an ontology which maintains that everything that exists is present, or, said differently, the only time that things exist is the present.[16] I now turn to explain the difference between

15. The two other scholars that figure most prominently in this school of open theism are Boyd and DeRose. See also Johnson, "God, Fatalism, and Temporal."

16. Describing the various options in the philosophy of time is an incredibly difficult task facing contemporary metaphysicians, especially when writing for non-specialists. Unfortunately, a deep investigation into such would take us too far afield of the central thrust of this project, so I must unfortunately presuppose that the reader is generally aware of contemporary work on the philosophy of time, at least since McTaggart first introduced the distinction between what he labeled the A-series and the B-series. For non-specialists on the issues, I recommend Crisp, "Presentism"; Rea, "Four-Dimensionalism." For more on presentism in particular, I highly recommend the collection of essays in Magalhaes and Oaklander, *Presentism*; Bourne, *Future for Presentism*; Zimmerman, "A-Theory of Time, Presentism."

a Peircean understanding of the semantic content of PCFC, given presentism, and its Ockhamistic alternative.

The difference between Ockhamistic and Peircean understandings of PCFC turns on how each school of thought interprets "will" or "will not" in statements such as "Abby will drink orange juice tomorrow with her breakfast." Suppose that Abby is free with respect to whether or not she drinks orange juice tomorrow; that is, whether or not she actually drinks orange juice tomorrow with her breakfast is presently contingent; it is underdetermined by either her character and/or the laws of nature. According to the Ockhamist, it makes perfect sense to speak of the fact of what will or will not occur tomorrow with reference to Abby's drinking the orange juice (or refraining from doing so, as the case may be)—*even though the event is contingent*. Thus, for the Ockhamist, even though it is up to her whether or not she drinks the orange juice, there is still a truth as to which of the two possible outcomes obtains (as a matter of fact).[17]

But the Peircean rejects the Ockhamistic analysis of "will" and "will not" language. For the Peircean, it makes absolutely no sense at all to say, "Abby will drink orange juice tomorrow with her breakfast," unless the "will" is interpreted with strong causal force such that the drinking of the orange juice is no longer contingent. That is, according to the Peircean, the proposition referred to by the utterance "Abby will drink orange juice tomorrow with her breakfast" cannot presently be both true and genuinely contingent. Rather, the Peircean explains that any statements truthfully asserting what will or will not happen in the future do not refer to what will contingently occur, but rather to what will happen of necessity—what is determined—given the state of affairs that has obtained at the time of the assertion in question. Again, the reality to which such a proposition points is presently determined, at least on a Peircean understanding of "will" and "will not" language. Instead of using language that leads to confusion with respect to the status of the future (that is, whether or not it is determined to occur), when referring to future contingents,

---

It also bears mentioning that, presumably, the same semantics would hold for the growing block theory of time, but in light of Trenton Merricks's rather devastating critique of it, and also because no open theists to date defend growing blockism, I pay no attention to that view here. See Merricks, "Good-Bye Growing Block."

17. How this fact obtains is rather controversial, especially given presentism, such that there is no future. These worries are raised by Rhoda et al., "Open Theism."

the Peircean asserts with subjunctive language, "I might drink orange juice tomorrow with my breakfast, but I might not."[18]

It is this last phrase—"but I might not" (entailed by the Ockhamistic interpretation of PCFC that use "will" or "will not")—that leads Peirceans to avoid "will" and "will not" language. On the Peircean account, talk of what will or will not occur is to assert with a probability of either 1.0 or 0.0 what is going to happen in the future. For the Peircean, any use of "will" and "will not" language in propositions about the future fails to preserve contingency at all. Rather, "will" and "will not" language points to alethic settledness instead of alethic openness. In order to preserve the genuinely contingent nature of future actions, Peirceans deny that it makes sense to speak of what "will" or "will not" happen when discussing future contingents.

Initially, it might appear that a Peircean understanding of the semantic content of PCFC requires an abandonment of the principle of bivalence, which we are reminded requires that all propositions are either true or false. But such is not the case, for all PCFC using counterfactual language such as "might" and "might not" are bivalently true even if the action in question to which the proposition points has a probability between 0.0 and 1.0. But what of propositions using "will" and "will not" language?

Peirceans contend that all assertions concerning future contingents which employ "will" and "will not" language are false.[19] Call this thesis "all-falsism." At first, it seems like this leads to an obvious contradiction. After all, it is absurd to suggest that "Abby will drink orange juice tomorrow with her breakfast" is false while simultaneously maintaining that it is also false to assert, "Abby will not drink orange juice with her breakfast." However, Peirceans maintain that "will" and "will not" sentences refer to

18. Of course, synonyms for "might" or "might not" will work just as well, as will adverbial modification to "will" and "will not" language, even when those synonyms and/or adverbial modification denote strong probabilities, so long as they do not raise the probability to 1.0, which would eliminate the contingency of the future by making it situationally, even if not metaphysically or logically, necessary. So, for example, statements like "I will almost certainly drink orange juice tomorrow with my breakfast" still count as PCFC, according to the Peircean, while pure Ockhamistic assertions about the future do not count as PCFC, but rather as propositions concerning actions presently determined to occur in the future.

19. Building on work originally put forward by A. N. Prior, Amy Seymour has recently begun to defend this idea, which she calls all-falsism. See her "Advantages of All-Falsism." Cf. Prior, *Past, Present, and Future*; Prior, *Papers on Time and Tense*.

propositions that are not contradictories, but rather are contraries.[20] A Lewisian square of opposition showing how counterfactuals ought to be understood bears this out.

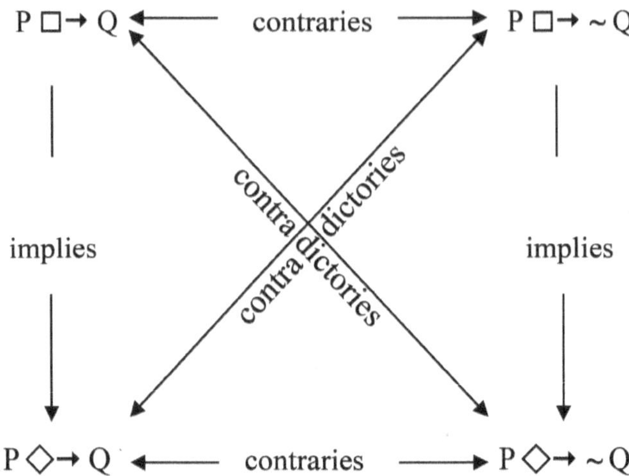

On this account (which is endorsed by open theists), "would" counterfactuals are represented by □⦿ whereas "might" counterfactuals are represented by ◇⦿.[21] If Q would obtain given P, then it is false to say that ~Q might obtain given P. The Peircean semantic takes "will" and "will not" statements to be logically equivalent to "might" counterfactuals insofar as "will" and "will not" statements should be understood as contraries rather than contradictories.

On the Peircean view, propositions can change in truth-value over time such that at one time something may be false, whereas at another time it may be true. Thus, consider three moments of time, *t1*, *t2*, and *t3*, and let *t3* be the moment at which Abby does or does not drink orange juice tomorrow with her breakfast. According to the Peircean, at *t1*, if Abby's drinking orange juice tomorrow is genuinely contingent, it is false to assert that she will do so. However, perhaps a certain state of affairs obtains at *t2* so as to remove the contingency regarding her

20. Daniel Hill has brought to my attention that the fact that these sentences are contraries (strictly subcontraries) rather than contradictories makes no difference: they still cannot both be false, just as David Lewis's "P ◇→ Q" and "P ◇→ ~Q" cannot both be false.

21. This figure is taken from Moreland and Craig, *Philosophical Foundations*, 53. It represents the views of David Lewis as expressed in his *Counterfactuals*.

drinking orange juice tomorrow with her breakfast (at *t3*). Perhaps her character has been so concretized as to remove her ability to choose otherwise which wasn't true at *t1*, or perhaps the laws of nature bear on her behavior at *t2* in such a way as to necessitate her drinking the orange juice and this wasn't true at *t1*. Regardless of how the contingency is removed, at *t2* it could be true to assert that Abby will drink orange juice tomorrow with her breakfast (at *t3*) because at *t2* the event in question would no longer be a future contingent, but rather an action determined to take place in the future. Thus, for the Peircean, one and the same proposition can change truth-value over time.[22]

It's worth mentioning that the Peircean understanding of the semantic content of PCFC hinges on fairly complicated metaphysical theories, namely, the conjunction of truth-maker theory (which Rhoda ties to the correspondence theory of truth) and not only an A-theory of time, but also metaphysical presentism.[23] Given such a combination, there are two ways in which one can make sense of all-falsism. The first supposes that PCFC actually refer to the future, whereas the second suggests that PCFC only seem to be about the future. I will examine each of these in turn.

Metaphysical Arguments

Peirceans sometimes motivate their contention that all PCFC involving "will" and "will not" language are false by pointing out that, on presentism, the future does not exist. Given that truth supervenes on being—a common assumption defended by the vast majority of contemporary philosophers—it seems presentism precludes the possibility of the existence of truths for future contingents. That is, according to Peirceans, presentism demands not only the causal openness of the

22. Of course, any view which denies the omnitemporality of truth faces an uphill battle. Rhoda et al. discuss this in their article "Open Theism." However, I won't discuss those issues here for two reasons. First, the omnitemporality of truth has been defended by the vast majority of philosophers throughout history, and I tend to agree with what has already been written in response to detractors elsewhere. But secondly, in order to strengthen the key arguments I put forward in this chapter, I want to assume for the sake of argument that the Peircean understanding of the semantic content of PCFC is correct.

23. None of these views enjoy unanimous support from academic scholars, whether philosophers or theologians, much less the combination of all of them. Nonetheless, I will continue assuming these views in the spirit of charity, not least because both philosophical and theological defenses of each of these positions have been offered by leading academic figures.

future, but also alethic openness.[24] Of course, things that are presently determined to occur in the future are true in virtue of the fact that such truths are grounded in present realities, namely, states of affairs that presently obtain. But such is not the case for future contingents; so, on presentism, Peirceans insist that it cannot be true that some given future contingent will or will not occur. Because Peirceans affirm the principle of bivalence, even as it pertains to PCFC, the only option left is to say that all PCFC involving "will" and "will not" language are false.

But this move preserves bivalence only in a technical sense. We have already examined one sentence that presents us with a puzzle for how we might make sense of bivalentism as a necessary truth. Let us now consider another. Suppose someone says, "The present king of France is bald." Has the person spoken truthfully, or falsely? While many philosophers believe this sentence lacks a truth-value, many other philosophers believe this sentence is false in virtue of reference failure; that is, because there is no present king of France, it cannot be true that he is bald.[25] Therefore, given the principle of bivalence, we are left to conclude that the statement is false.[26]

As aforementioned, reference failure falsehood preserves bivalence only in the most technical manner and doesn't really get at what staunch defenders of necessary bivalentism wish to assert. After all, the way in which the sentence "The present king of France is bald" is false differs significantly from the way in which the sentence "Ben Arbour is not interested in open theism" is false. Given a correspondence theory of truth, the first sentence has no corresponding state of affairs that could serve to determine the truth or falsity of the sentence by way of correspondence. But the second sentence does. The first sentence predicates baldness to

24. For more on the notion of alethic openness, see Rhoda, "Fivefold Openness."

25. Neo-Meinongians will likely maintain that our ability to speak about the present king of France entails that there is such a being, even if that being doesn't exist, so the statement may be true if understood along a neo-Meinongian schema of interpretation. However, such a view represents an extreme minority report among contemporary philosophers, and for that reason I won't pursue it further here. For what it's worth, I agree with what is known as the realist interpretation of fictional objects. On this account, the lack of an actual, concrete existence of a present king of France would still entail the falsehood of the sentence. The development of my own views owes mostly to Van Inwagen's essay "Quantification and Fictional Discourse." For more on this position, as well as an argument against my view, see Everett, "Against Fictional Realism," and the literature discussed therein.

26. One could also argue that the sentence fails to express a proposition such that it doesn't have a truth-value at all.

a non-actual entity, so the overall sentence is said to be false in virtue of reference failure; there is no corresponding state of affairs that could even potentially serve to validate the truthfulness of the sentence. The second sentence, however, is false precisely because there *is* a corresponding state of affairs that *invalidates* the statement. Thus, when the metaphysics of presentism is utilized to show how language games concerning reference failure preserve the principle of bivalence, even as it concerns PCFC involving "will" and "will not" language, we end up not so much with bivalence, but a strange form of trivalence.[27] This trivalence, if you will, is due to the fact that false statements are understood to be false in a very different manner than the notion of falsehood as traditionally understood by correspondence theorists of truth.[28]

But yet another issue merits attention. Rhoda and others who defend a version of OFOT, which purports to preserve universal application of the principle of bivalence, often mistakenly assume that the correspondence theory requires truth-maker theory. However, these thinkers have failed to interact at all with Trenton Merricks's rather compelling analysis against truth-maker theory, *and Merricks defends a version of the correspondence theory of truth.*[29] Furthermore, Craig and Hunt have pointed out specific places in which Rhoda et al. make this mistake, as well as other problems in what should be regarded as the most articulate defense of Rhodanian OFOT.[30] If correspondence theory does not require truth-maker theory, then the worries raised by Rhoda et al. can be avoided altogether, and other portions of the metaphysical

27. For a useful, even if somewhat dated, discussion of some of these issues, see Ayer, *Language, Truth and Logic*, especially 87–102.

28. Unfortunately, delving any more deeply into the philosophical issues surrounding theories of truth would take us too far afield of a more focused discussion of OFOT. Besides this, given that I am a realist about truth à la Alston, *Realist Conception of Truth*, and given that many philosophers maintain that a realist position about truth requires some version or other of a correspondence theory of truth, and given that Rhodanian OFOT itself defends correspondence theory, it doesn't seem that delving into alternative conceptions of truth is necessary. For those who might wish to pursue these issues in more detail, minimalists about truth defend a view in which realism about truth does not require correspondence theory. Cf. Horwich, *Truth*. An introductory articulation of still other conceptions of truth, even beyond realism, can be found in Kirkham, *Theories of Truth*.

29. Merricks, *Truth and Ontology*. For an alternative perspective, see Armstrong, *Truth and Truthmakers*. Cf. also Craig, "Middle Knowledge" and the literature discussed therein.

30. Craig and Hunt, "Perils." Their critique is directed principally against Rhoda et al., "Open Theism," but it also addresses Tuggy's "Roads to Open Theism."

underpinning of OFOT are seriously compromised. This significantly undermines at least some of the motivation for Rhodanian OFOT. Obviously, if this is true, then Rhodanian OFOT's popularity will wane and other more attractive alternatives will come into vogue.

Semantic Arguments

Defenses of Rhodanian OFOT based on the semantics of PCFC also involve the metaphysics of time. As we have seen, Rhoda and others sometimes argue for all-falsism because PCFC lack a corresponding state of affairs to serve as a truth-maker. But they also say that PCFC involving "will" and "will not" language are not about the future at all, but rather only *seem* to be about the future. Although the proposition expressed by the sentence "Abby will drink orange juice tomorrow with her breakfast" seems to be about the future, it is actually about the present. Because the future doesn't exist (on presentism, anyway) the proposition expressed by the sentence above is actually something like, <It is presently the case that Abby will drink orange juice tomorrow with her breakfast>. That PCFC are actually about the present is thought to lend support to the idea that some truths about the future, either non-bivalent probabilistic truths or bivalent determined truths, can be grounded in present realities, which obviously fits well with presentism. However, given the causal force of "will" and "will not" language on a Peircean semantic, truths about the future must be determined, and therefore are not contingent.[31]

This understanding of all-falsism is coherent, but while it makes sense logically, it entails a hefty set of problems. I will discuss these issues further below. But before discussing the problems in systematic metaphysics entailed by Rhodanian OFOT, I wish to register disagreement with all-falsism in general, for it seems obviously false, at least given the metaphysics of modality and the theory of possible worlds entailed by OFOT. The Peircean understanding of all-falsism is built on the A-theory of time, which insists that we take tense seriously when

31. Given three times, *t1*, *t2*, and *t3*, perhaps at *t1* some action which may or may not take place at *t3* is contingent. But, if some state of affairs obtains at *t2* which removes the contingent nature of the action in question to take place at *t3*, then at *t2* the action is no longer considered contingent, for as of *t2* it is determined to occur. Regardless, for Rhodanian OFOT, if an event is presently contingent, then it is false to speak of whether it will or will not occur. If it is presently determined, then it no longer makes sense to speak of the action as contingent *even if there was previously a time when the action was undetermined.*

seeking to understand the semantic content of tensed propositions. Assuming the A-theory, we cannot reduce tense in statements to relations of priority and succession, as B-theorists are wont to do. Therefore, once we consider the linguistic concerns involved in taking tense seriously, let us consider modal assertions of the sort, "In 2014, possibly, Barack Obama is president of the United States." Since the sentence is indexed to 2014, the "is" must be taken as denoting the present in 2014. If this sentence were uttered in 2012, we cannot say that this sentence expresses a proposition about an earlier present such that the locution could be properly interpreted as representing the following proposition: <It is presently possible that in 2014 Barack Obama will be president of the United States>. The proposition in view is tensed to 2014, not to the present.[32] Failing to affirm that such a proposition is genuinely about the future, then, amounts to a failure to take tense seriously. Furthermore, failure to affirm that such a proposition is true entails denying that there is a possible world in which (at that world) it is presently 2014 and Barack Obama is president of the United States. But why should we deny the possibility of such a world, especially given the idea that, in the actual world, it is presently possible for Barack Obama to be president of the United States in 2014? Such a question is meant to show that unless we abandon the common sense understanding of modality used to make sense of possible world discourse, this proposition should count as true.[33] Therefore, all-falsism is false.

But another interesting conclusion follows from the Peircean semantic. To date, open theists have distinguished themselves from classical theists by denying that God enjoys exhaustive definite foreknowledge (EDF). However, in order to preserve omniscience, as it turns out,

32. To clarify: the sentence "In 2014, possibly, Barack Obama is president of the United States" does not express the same proposition as <It is presently possible that in 2014 Barack Obama will be president of the United States>. Whereas the former is indexed to 2014, the latter is indexed to whichever moment the present is at the time someone expresses the proposition (presumably some moment in 2012). The word "presently" serves to do this indexing in the latter, but the word "presently" isn't part of the sentence in question.

33. Observant readers will note that the success of OFOT hinges upon a type of equivocation also present in defenses of LFOT. Advocates of OFOT insist that we utilize common sense understandings of various issues only when it suits them. When common sense understandings of possible world discourse, the metaphysics of modality, and language cut against OFOT, we are told to eschew elementary, wrong-headed understandings driven by common sense in favor of more enlightened, yet terrifically complicated, understandings of the same.

defenders of OFOT who employ Peircean semantics must affirm that God has EDF. The term "definite" in EDF is thought to rule out the possibility of Geachianism, upon which PCFC can change both from false to true and from true to false. On such a view, God could have exhaustive foreknowledge, but it wouldn't be definite, for at one moment God could know that Abby will drink the orange juice tomorrow, while at some later time it might become false that she will do so.[34]

Given this understanding of "definite" it is easy to see why defenders of openness theology would want to clarify the type of knowledge about the future that God doesn't have. However, as it turns out, according to open theists who think that "will" and "will not" language entails definiteness about the future, God does enjoy definite foreknowledge. That is, anything that will or will not be the case is known by God, because if it will be the case (or even if it will not), such an event is determined and therefore isn't contingent. In fact, open theists are happy to acknowledge that everything about the future that is determined is known by God. But if God knows everything (exhaustively) about what will or will not happen (definitely) in the future (foreknowledge), then God does have exhaustive definite foreknowledge. For all the things that are definite about the future, God knows all of these truths. So what distinguishes OFOT from classical theism?

Things get tricky here for defenders of OFOT because there is no way for them to quantify over what God does not know. Whereas defenders of the traditional view can deny that Peircean semantics are the right way to understand "will" and "will not" locutions and thereby affirm that God knows what will contingently happen in the future, denying Peircean semantics isn't an option for advocates of Rhodanian OFOT. Recall that Rhoda maintains that anything that *will* happen in the future cannot be contingent. If the causal force of "will" is correct, as the Peircean insists, then defenders of OFOT cannot distinguish their view of divine foreknowledge from that of traditional theism by saying something to the effect of, "On the traditional view, God knows what will happen in the future, whereas according to OFOT, God does not know what will happen in the future," for, as we have seen, God *does* know whatever *will* and whatever *will not* happen in the future. It's also

34. Geach understood as much to be required by a proper analysis of the metaphysics of prevention. Consider: the plane *was* going to crash, but the pilot intervened to prevent the catastrophe. For more on this see both Geach, *Providence and Evil*; Todd, "Geachianism."

worth mentioning that attempts to get around this problem by articulating things differently will fail because of conversational implicature. Therefore, it won't do to say, "God lacks knowledge of what is going to be the case," or "God doesn't know what is going to happen," or anything of this sort, for these locutions turn out to be logically equivalent to "God doesn't know what will happen."

Additionally, it won't do to cash out the differences strictly in positive terms by saying something such as, "On classical theism, God is thought to have exhaustive foreknowledge of future contingents, whereas on OFOT, God does not have exhaustive foreknowledge of future contingents." This won't work because if God is omniscient, God must know all modalities in virtue of divine natural knowledge. That is, God knows the entire spectrum of possibilities that can obtain—there is no limit to this aspect of divine knowledge, even on open theism, regardless of which version (LFOT, OFOT, either Zimmermanean or Rhodanian). This also won't work because defenders of OFOT don't take future contingents to be possibilities covered by divine natural knowledge and suggesting as much would amount to equivocation. So, again, we are left wondering exactly how OFOT distinguishes itself from classical theism with respect to what God doesn't know.[35]

Some open theists will be glad to know that I understand this, especially since on presentism there isn't anything in the future to quantify over. For these thinkers, my point will serve to elucidate the claim that the debates about the extent of divine foreknowledge are not a debate about omniscience, per se, or even the DFF, but rather a debate about ontology and the metaphysics of time. I'm happy to acknowledge this point, but more needs to be said. One need not adopt a neo-Meinongian outlook to affirm that the sentence "There are no square circles" is a coherent statement of fact. Even Meinong did not think that square circles have being. That is, quantifying over the non-existent makes sense, even if we deny that square circles have being.

35. This is not to suggest that there are no distinctions between the metaphysical systems that undergird classical theism or OFOT, for certainly one can differentiate between them in that if A is a free agent, then, according to classical theism, there is (now or timelessly) a truth about what A will freely do tomorrow, and according to OFOT there isn't. However, insofar as open theism is thought to be a novel interpretation of divine omniscience, it is difficult to see how advocates of OFOT are able to distinguish their view in regards to divine knowledge. It seems, rather, that the differences between classical theism and OFOT hinge on metaphysical differences that have implications for divine knowledge, but, as it turns out, there may not be any way to describe what knowledge God lacks on OFOT that God enjoys according to classical theism.

Interestingly, even if one defends presentism and understands this to motivate (or even entail!) OFOT, there is no way for such a person to quantify over that which God does not know.

It also won't do for defenders of OFOT to say something like, "On open theism, God knows all truths about the past and present, as well as all truths about the future that are entailed by the past and the present, whereas the traditional view affirms not only that God enjoys complete knowledge of the past and present, and truths about the future that are entailed by the past and present, but also truths about the future that are not so entailed." Whereas the Ockhamist can interpret the phrase "but also truths about the future that are not so entailed" without understanding "are not" with the force of causal determinism, this interpretation isn't available to the Peircean. On Rhodanian OFOT, for any PCFC *p*, although both *p* and ~*p* are presently false, one of the two disjuncts will become true, but it is presently undetermined which of these two disjuncts will become true in the future. So, although the disjunction "Either Abby will drink orange juice with her breakfast tomorrow, or Abby will not drink orange juice with her breakfast tomorrow" is presently false, on OFOT, the disjunction will become true, and there's no problem interpreting "will" in the previous phrase along the lines of Peircean semantics. So, when asked to describe what God doesn't know about the disjunction, defenders of OFOT should respond that God knows that, presently, the disjunction is false, since both of the disjuncts are false. Additionally, on OFOT, God knows that the disjunction will become true, because one of the disjuncts will become true (assuming that a future time obtains in which Abby is able to drink orange juice with her breakfast tomorrow, or refrain from so doing). So, when pressed about what God doesn't know in regards to the disjunction, the defender of OFOT has to say something like, "God doesn't know whether it is 'Abby drinks orange juice with her breakfast tomorrow' or 'Abby does not drink orange juice with her breakfast tomorrow' that will obtain." And here again we find the use of "will" problematic for the same reasons discussed above.

Rhodanian open theists initially might want to acknowledge the point, but counter by equivocating on the meaning of "will" and "will not." Perhaps they want to use "will*" and "will not*" to describe the contingency that's at issue. Of course, this move only solves the problem by backing things up a bit. If the Peircean semantic holds, it must be employed equally under all circumstances in which tense is in play. Therefore, if a defender of OFOT wants to use "will*" to avoid the problem I raise here, why can't the Ockhamist use "will*" to preserve contingency from the start, thereby eliminating any motivation for Peirceanism and/or all-falsism in the first place?

This seems like a puzzle that needs to be solved in order for OFOT to distinguish itself from classical theism, unless the only difference between open theism and classical theism is ontological presentism, which certainly doesn't seem to be what open theists think. If there's no way to describe these issues coherently because the future doesn't exist, then the conversation is over, and we shouldn't concern ourselves with OFOT at all. If advocates of OFOT suggest that the conversation is important, since this is a novel way to think about Anselmianism while avoiding the troubles presented by the DFF, then they owe us a coherent way of talking about these matters. Apart from this, there's no reason to continue the conversation, and we should default to the traditional understanding of divine foreknowledge, since at least it offers a coherent analysis of what God knows and what God doesn't know.

But suppose that issues in philosophy of language are ancillary to what is really at issue. That is, suppose that metaphysical issues involving the nature of time are the fundamental categories upon which everything in the debates concerning the extent of divine foreknowledge turns, at least insofar as OFOT is concerned. How should a Christian think through those issues?

The Metaphysics of Modality, Possible Worlds, and Open Future Open Theism

Does God Know Which Possible World Is the Actual World?

Before discussing in great detail the problems in systematic metaphysics required by OFOT, we should note briefly that according to OFOT, there is no such thing as the actual world.[36] This is true for both Zimmermanean OFOT (wherein PCFC lack bivalent truth-values) and for Rhodanian OFOT (wherein all PCFC involving "will" and "will not"

36. Tuggy acknowledges as much in his "Roads to Open Theism." Additionally, in personal conversation, Rhoda has confirmed that he shares this view. To be perfectly clear, on this point nothing hinges on whether one understands "actual" in a technical sense as did David Lewis such that which world is actual is merely a world-indexed property.

language are false). It has become standard in possible world discourse to describe a possible world as a maximally consistent state of affairs.[37] But, on OFOT, there is no actual world because a maximally consistent state of affairs necessarily includes a complete and total world history—*including a particular future*. After all, bracketing out theological claims that require the existence of future times, there isn't anything logically impossible about the current state of affairs being consistent both with the existence of a future, or with its being consistent with the end of time at whatever moment comes immediately after you conclude reading this sentence. Therefore, the present state of affairs is logically compatible with a great many possible worlds such that, on OFOT, it is impossible to determine which possible world picks out the actual world. This problem isn't merely a subjective epistemological conundrum, for it applies even to God if OFOT is true, since the lack of ontological status of the future means that there is no actual future, but rather only possible futures. But this renders modal actualism (the view defended by Plantinga) false, for the standard account of a possible world includes a particular future. To restate what seems shocking, given the contingent, open nature of the future on the metaphysics of time and the metaphysics of modality required by OFOT, technically speaking, if there is an actual world, it is not the same as the world that will eventually obtain, and it is very non-standard to think that whichever possible world obtains in the future is a different possible world than the one that obtains presently. Furthermore, on OFOT, God does not know which of many possible worlds God will obtain, leading to the untoward conclusion that God doesn't know which world he has created.[38]

This is not to say that we are not real, or that what we perceive to be reality is, in fact, an illusion. Rather, what I am suggesting is that OFOT requires a deviant understanding of modal metaphysics and a non-standard account of possible world semantics. Therefore, insofar as anything requires one to make use of possible world discourse in responding to various issues related to philosophical theology and philosophy of religion (e.g., theodicies/defenses against the problem of

37. This is true regardless of which position one takes in regards to the debate in the metaphysics of modality over the ontological status of possible worlds. So, for Plantinga (who represents a view known as modal actualism) as much as for Lewis (a modal concretist), a possible world necessarily includes a complete and total world history. See Plantinga, *Nature of Necessity*; Lewis, *Plurality of Worlds*.

38. To understand more clearly why this is so, see Rhoda, "Fivefold Openness."

evil), defenders of OFOT find themselves at a significant disadvantage. Additionally, we should be exceedingly cautious in understanding what advocates of open futurism do and do not mean when they appeal to possible worlds in making distinctions between actuality and possibility, for these thinkers mean something significantly different than what the vast majority of thinkers do when they employ standard semantics regarding the metaphysics of modality in discourse about possible worlds. In fact, it seems that OFOT requires a wholesale revision of modal metaphysics in order to accommodate aberrant notions of what exactly constitutes the real "world." This is all because, according to OFOT, whichever world ends up obtaining in actuality is up to us. Therefore, at the present moment, if anything about the future is genuinely contingent, there is no actual world. Instead, the reality which we inhabit is perfectly compatible with a great many possible worlds. Again, reality might include time(s) beyond the very instant you read this (e.g., a future), and reality might not include any time(s) beyond your reading this. On open futurism, in fact, reality definitely does not include any times beyond your reading this, though reality might be compatible with there being times beyond your reading this.

It doesn't make sense to speak of a world, even a possible world, as perhaps including times beyond the present, and perhaps not, because each possible world (as a maximally consistent state of affairs which possesses a complete and total world history) is something like a set of true propositions.[39] Furthermore, each possible world is made up of properties essential to that world, properties such as moments of time obtaining beyond your reading this, or the opposite. Hence, no world—not even the actual world (if there is such a thing)—can be said to lack both a given property and its opposite. Said differently, in each and every possible world, every proposition is either true or false, and the truth or falsity of any given proposition is essential to that respective possible world.[40] As

39. It won't do for the defender of OFOT to say that the set of true propositions that accurately describe the actual world doesn't include any propositions about the free future. Consider the following proposition: <Possibly, Jones cuts his grass tomorrow>. If Jones is free with respect to cutting his grass tomorrow, then this expresses a true proposition about the free future.

40. The open theist might object that this begs the question against any version of open theism that denies the principle of bivalence. Were someone to argue in this way, two replies are in order. First, there are independent reasons for rejecting the rejection of the principle of bivalence that I've already canvassed. Second, the metaphysics of modality and the semantics of possible worlds that I am using is considered the standard approach. For anyone who wishes to employ a non-standard account of modality and

an example, consider that every single possible world it is either the case that Abby drinks orange juice tomorrow with her breakfast or it is not the case that Abby drinks orange juice tomorrow with her breakfast, even if the latter holds because Abby doesn't exist in/at that world.[41]

Of course, it isn't uncommon for open theists to utilize standard possible world semantics in working out of whichever version of open theism they defend.[42] But standard articulations of the metaphysics of modality simply aren't available for OFOT. In fact, it is fair to say that on OFOT, God created the heavens and the earth, but not even God knows which possible world has been actualized.[43] To illustrate why this is so, recall that on OFOT (and on LFOT, for that matter), agents who enjoy LFW are the cause of their own actions, at least with respect to those actions of which they are rightly said to be significantly free. If those actions are undetermined, and if the outcome of those actions shapes which possible world is the actual world, then free agents causally determine which world is the actual world, or, more precisely, free agents play a role in causally determining which of the many possible worlds that are presently metaphysically possible best represent reality. In virtue of divine natural knowledge, God enjoys knowledge of all modalities, and therefore knows all of the possible worlds that "could" be, for God knows

possible worlds discourse, we are owed an explanation of why the standard understandings won't work, and we are owed an accounting of what alternative is being offered. The argument that, on OFOT, the standard understandings won't work makes headway, but the alternative understanding where a possible world simply refers to the set of all fixed/determined truths fails to do justice to the most robust accounts of modal metaphysics offered by contemporary philosophers. To my knowledge, no alternative analysis of possible worlds and modal metaphysics has been developed which satisfies our intuitions about the proper way to describe, not only the way things are but captures a complete a total world history (including the future).

41. I won't engage the discussion of the difference between existing in or at a given world, for such a discussion has no bearing on the points I make in this chapter. For those interested in those matters, see Adams, "Theories of Actuality," 211–31; Adams, "Actualism and Thisness," 3–41.

42. This is especially true when open theists of both the LFOT camp and the OFOT camp begin to delve into issues of divine providence, and all the more when dealing with the problem of evil. See Hasker, *Providence*; Hasker, *Triumph of God*.

43. The same can be said for LFOT, but Hasker, Swinburne, and Van Inwagen (because they affirm that future contingents are presently true) can say that there is such a thing as the actual world. Hence, God created the actual world, but God isn't sure which of all the possible worlds is the actual one. At this juncture, it is worth mentioning that an open theistic doctrine of creation, on both LFOT and OFOT, bears a significant amount of similarity to that of process theology, despite how much open theists might wish it weren't so.

all possibilities. God knows what will happen if Abby chooses to drink orange juice tomorrow with her breakfast, and God also knows what will happen if Abby refrains from doing so. Call world *alpha* a world in which Abby drinks the orange juice, and call world *beta* a world that is otherwise identical to *alpha*, but in *beta* Abby refrains from drinking orange juice with her breakfast tomorrow. On OFOT, God knows that, presently, both *alpha* and *beta* are possible worlds that might represent reality, but God lacks knowledge as to which "world"/reality will obtain.[44]

A very interesting feature of open futurism is that the issue of which world obtains isn't settled until either time ends, or until contingency is removed from everything that presently makes up what we call the future (i.e., determinism becomes true of all future events). In fact, since possible world essentialism offers the most resources in discussing what is or is not a feature of any given world, we should also include modality among the properties of any given world. Therefore, if a state of affairs obtains at time $t1$ in some world *alpha* such that at some later time t^*, some event E can either occur or not occur (that is, E is indeterminate), we should note that the possible world that obtains at $t1$ is a different world than the one that obtains at t^* when event E either occurs or does not. That is, on open futurism, because time plays such a fundamental role in that metaphysics, the passage of time and the elimination of contingency that stems from accidental necessity entails that we are constantly moving from occupying one world to a different world.[45] It goes without saying that this highly complicates discussions of endurance, perdurance, and the ontology of where/when/how beings exist across time and across multiple possible worlds. If simplicity is a desideratum of philosophy and theology, as Ockham's razor suggests, we have good reason to reject open futurism for the problems that it creates for other related metaphysical issues.

A (Very) Brief Introduction to Systematic Metaphysics

Systematic metaphysics is systematic theology's philosophical cousin. To better understand the comparison, consider the way that some systematic theologies organize the presentation of Christian doctrine

44. Note that God cannot know which world will obtain, for the causal force of "will" on the Peircean semantic eliminates the contingency at issue, as discussed above.

45. This problem that I raise is something that stems from the modal anti-realism that rises from open futurism. See Kodaj, "Open Future."

around key themes of the Christian religion. Some systematic theologies involve an organization of key themes around what are perceived to be the more foundational elements of a given tradition's understanding of Christian theology such that certain doctrines push and pull and drive and influence a thinker's understanding of other doctrines.[46] The same idea is present in systematic metaphysics.

In the quest to identify the most foundational elements of a metaphysical system, metaphysicians identify common areas that do the pushing and pulling of, for, and in other areas of metaphysics.[47] Contemporary systematic metaphysicians agree that four areas are the most foundational elements of any metaphysical system. These four areas are: properties, laws of nature, causation, and modality. The basic idea of systematic metaphysics is that philosophy in general, and metaphysics in particular, is not a buffet from which a person can select at random whatever variety of ideas they wish.[48] Instead, there are relations between ideas such that certain views won't hold together.

Even though there are more than two options for each of the four foundational metaphysical categories, let us suppose briefly that each of the four most fundamental aspects of systematic metaphysics allows for only one of two positions. So, for example, with respect to the laws of nature, suppose that one could hold to a weaker Humean view where the laws merely explain reality, or alternatively, one could hold a stronger view in which the laws of nature actually do some pushing and pulling in determining what happens in the actual world. Suppose also that parallel dualistic conceptions of each of the other three foundational areas in systematic metaphysics exist. Now, suppose that each of the four areas is

46. To consider but one contemporary example, see Michael Horton's four-volume series on covenantal dogmatics: *Covenant and Eschatology*; *Lord and Servant*; *Covenant and Salvation*; and *People and Place*.

47. The key figures in contemporary systematic metaphysics are David Armstrong, Alexander Bird, Jonathan Jacobs, Alexander Pruss, and the late David Lewis. Depending on who one is talking to, a few other names might be added into this group, notably Van Inwagen and Lowe. Of course, there are a great many other philosophers who have significant things to say about the individual areas that comprise systematic metaphysics. The names I've listed here are those who work on systematizing these other areas of metaphysics.

48. The most accessible introduction to systematic metaphysics is Armstrong's *Sketch for a Systematic Metaphysics*. This is a condensed version of his elaborate metaphysical system which he works out in much greater detail in *A World of States of Affairs*, but that volume is directed at professional philosophers and is academically accessible only for those who come to the book with a significant background in metaphysics.

assigned letters which represent the respective possible options *A* or *B*, *C* or *D*, and so forth. Hence, someone could be an *ACEG*, or perhaps an *ACEH*, or even a *BDFG*, etc., similar to a Myers-Briggs personality test. Systematic metaphysicians maintain that these four foundational categories of metaphysics exert power in determining what options are live in secondary categories of metaphysics, categories such as the philosophy of time, personal ontology, free will, etc.[49]

For example, in systematic metaphysics, if someone holds to causal determinism, it would be inconsistent—nay, incoherent—for that person to defend a libertarian conception of free will. Systematic metaphysicians assert that the combination of more foundational elements (in this case, that person's understanding of the laws of nature and causation) precludes the possibility of a person having the ability to do otherwise.[50]

Let us now turn to the systematic metaphysics of OFOT. At minimum, whatever metaphysics of modality OFOT requires must allow for at least some actions/events to be contingent (namely, those actions for which we are said to have LFW), even if others are necessary. Whatever version of the metaphysics of modality one endorses entails a particular understanding of possible worlds; that is, possible world theory stems from the metaphysics of modality.[51] Now recall also that, on OFOT, free agents play a role in determining which possible world is in fact reality.[52] So, OFOT requires that the metaphysics of modality allow for one

49. In all fairness, there is some debate about what categories should be considered fundamental in systematic metaphysics, and how many categories should be admitted as fundamental, not to mention debates about methodology for determining these matters. Most notably absent from my list is substance, but it seems to me that this is acceptable for the simple reason some philosophers defend the idea that there are no substances, but rather only bundles of properties. Although I don't endorse this thesis, I want to minimize ontological commitment for the sake of the arguments presented in this chapter.

50. Of course, there are also relations between the foundational aspects of systematic metaphysics and not merely between them and other areas of metaphysics. For example, it is difficult to see how the metaphysics of modality could be anything except deterministic if the laws of nature and causation were as described above, *unless* the laws of nature and the nature of causation were themselves contingent.

51. I've already mentioned Plantinga's *The Nature of Necessity* and David Lewis's *On the Plurality of Worlds*. But, for more on the metaphysics of modality and how possible world theory stems from it, see Divers, *Possible Worlds*; Loux, *Possible and the Actual*; Plantinga, *Essays in the Metaphysics*; Pruss, *Actuality, Possibility, and Worlds*.

52. Again, it is tempting to say that free agents play a part in determining which world is the actual world, but on OFOT there is no such thing as the actual world. Hence, I use the term "reality" to denote what would normally be called the actual world.

to exercise power over the actual world. But, as I show below, OFOT's understanding of the metaphysics of modality (and the theory of possible worlds that flows from it) presents us resources to solve the DFF by way of Ockhamism. Efforts to eliminate such solutions, which would be necessary to preserve adequate motivation for OFOT in the first place, entail a wholesale revision of systematic metaphysics. I now explain why this is the case.

Consider again two possible worlds, *alpha* and *beta*, identical to each other in every way except that in *alpha*, Abby freely drinks orange juice tomorrow with her breakfast, whereas in *beta*, Abby freely refrains from drinking orange juice tomorrow with her breakfast. According to OFOT, in order for Abby to be genuinely free with respect to drinking the orange juice tomorrow with her breakfast, both of these possible worlds are metaphysically possible, given that tomorrow arrives and that Abby is free with respect to drinking orange juice with her breakfast. This fits nicely with the metaphysics of modality required by OFOT. But there is nothing incoherent about divine foreknowledge if it is up to Abby whether *alpha* or *beta* obtains. In *alpha*, God infallibly knows that Abby will drink the orange juice, whereas in *beta*, God infallibly knows that she will refrain. Furthermore, we can even say that in *alpha* it is consequentially necessary that Abby drinks the orange juice, whereas in *beta* it is consequentially necessary that she refrain from doing so.[53] Even this does not pose a problem for divine foreknowledge so long as it is up to Abby whether *alpha* or *beta* obtains.

Defenders of OFOT will likely object that divine foreknowledge of future contingents precludes the ability in humans to determine whether *alpha* or *beta* obtains, for such an ability amounts to power to change the past. But this is mistaken. In *alpha*, God has always believed that Abby would drink the orange juice, and in *beta*, God has always believed that she would refrain. The ability to causally determine whether *alpha* or *beta* obtains in no way allows for changing the past, because the past is part of a complete and total world history and is therefore indexed to a particular possible world. If Abby brings it about that *alpha* is the possible world that represents reality, then Abby brings it about that God has always believed that she would drink the orange juice. Similarly, if Abby brings it about

53. Recall that consequential necessity is the special type of ontological necessity that follows from a given state of affairs arising. Recall also that Alston sometimes referred to this same notion as S-logical necessity to denote the kind of logical necessity that follows given a particular situation.

that *beta* is the possible world that represents reality, then she brings it about that God has always believed that she would refrain from drinking the orange juice. Thus, given the metaphysics of modality required by OFOT (and the theory of possible worlds that stems from it), a person's power to determine which possible world represents reality allows for what I call "possible world Ockhamism." Possible world Ockhamism differs from standard articulations of Ockhamism in that, on standard Ockhamism, the focus is on counterfactual power over the past within the same world, whereas possible world Ockhamism suggests that free agents have counterfactual power over which possible world obtains, with times being fixed within each respective, indexed world.[54]

At this juncture, defenders of OFOT will likely object that I've missed the point of the principle of the fixity of the past with respect to which possible worlds are metaphysically available. On OFOT, the only possible worlds that are metaphysically available are worlds that share a complete and total world history up to the present moment.[55] That is, the future is causally open in a way that the past is not. Modality does not reduce simply to the two categories of contingent and necessary. Rather, the metaphysics of modality required by OFOT is linked to an understanding of time that affirms the fixity of the past. The results of this combination of modality and time yield versions of necessity that involve time, such as accidental necessity, which itself rests upon the principle of the fixity of the past.[56] Furthermore, there are other types of necessity, such as the view that some event in the future (which doesn't yet exist on a presentist ontology) is necessary in virtue of present realities which determine a given outcome (e.g., metaphysical necessity, ontological necessity, consequential necessity, etc.). But why should anyone adopt such a view when possible world Ockhamism allows for a type of theological compatibilism to navigate around the tensions

54. I owe to Mark D. Linville some of the ideas in the preceding section. Although he fails to adequately pursue the details and nuances of an alternative to power over the past Ockhamism, an inchoate version of possible world Ockhamism can be found in his "Divine Foreknowledge and the Libertarian."

55. Perhaps this is what the diagrams are intended to communicate in Rhoda et al., "Open Theism." Unfortunately for them, these diagrams conflate the ontology of existence (on presentism) with the metaphysics of A-theory, an issue that Craig and Hunt raise and explain in great detail in their article "Perils." Kane, who I am told is an open theist (but of which variety I'm not sure), calls this the "garden of forking paths," and insists that it is necessary to preserve free will. See Kane, "Beginning the Discussion."

56. To be clear, this is not unique to OFOT, or even open theism in general.

raised by the DFF? To see how possible world Ockhamism helps in avoiding open theism as a response to the DFF, consider a parallel argument offered by David Lewis for the compatibility of determinism and a libertarian conception of free will.

Lewis maintained that if the laws of nature causally determine what an agent will choose, it is still within the agent's power to choose to do otherwise. Of course, her choosing to do otherwise entails that she exercises counterfactual power over the laws of nature such that the laws of nature would be different than they, in fact, are if she, in fact, does otherwise.[57] A great many philosophers find this claim far from obvious and go further in asserting that Lewis's argument requires a Humean view of the laws of nature, which many philosophers maintain is not in keeping with a common sense understanding of what the laws of nature are. Regardless of whether or not anyone finds Lewis's argument persuasive, his argument rests on the idea that we enjoy counterfactual power over the laws of nature. For Lewis, this isn't a problem because counterfactual power is weaker than actual power, so he is able to avoid straightforward contradiction.

Now, to consider the parallel, recall that on OFOT, we do not merely enjoy the weaker counterfactual power over which possible world obtains. No, on OFOT humans possess actual power to determine which one of the many possible worlds obtains. Whereas counterfactual power implies only that agents have the ability to bring it about that some state of affairs *would* have been true, *were* some agent to have performed some given action, actual power doesn't refer to what *could* happen, but rather to what *does* happen when agents causally bring about whatever state of affairs obtains. If humans really possess this power, which is entailed by the metaphysics of modality required by OFOT to be coherent at all (and the theory of possible "worlds" that flows from that metaphysics of modality), why should anyone believe that the only worlds that are metaphysically available must share an identical world history? Remember, there is no such thing as an actual world on OFOT, and we play a part in causally determining which of many possible worlds best correspond to reality. Hence, there is no good reason to deny possible world Ockhamism as a solution to the DFF, *even if we affirm the principle of the fixity of the past*. If a person's actions determine which world is real, there is no problem with affirming that in *alpha* it has always been the case that

57. Lewis, "Are We Free?"

God believed that Abby would freely drink the orange juice, and that in *beta* it has always been the case that God believed that Abby would not drink the orange juice. If it is up to Abby whether or not she drinks the orange juice (that is to say, Abby enjoys LFW with respect to drinking the orange juice), then Abby's decision determines whether *alpha* or *beta* is the actual world, and thereby determines what God has always believed without impugning the principle of the fixity of the past.[58]

Defenders of OFOT will almost certainly dismiss this solution, insisting that possible world Ockhamism still fails to take seriously the fundamentality of time and the principle of the fixity of the past. On a certain reading of the metaphysics of modality and the theory of possible worlds that stems from it, I am willing to grant such a claim. If defenders of OFOT were to claim that time is so fundamental an aspect of reality, and were they to assert also that presentism requires that the only possible worlds that are metaphysically available at any given time t^* share an identical world history up to and including time t^*, then one could argue that possible world Ockhamism fails.[59] However, such an admission requires the advocate of OFOT to assert that time is more fundamental to systematic metaphysics than modality *simpliciter*, for time determines what is metaphysically available, which has obvious implications for the metaphysics of modality (and OFOT's view of possible worlds).

Obviously, this amounts to a radical departure from the majority opinion among systematic metaphysicians. Such a move requires the addition of time as a fifth category of systematic metaphysics alongside properties, causation, the laws of nature, and modality. In fact, it seems that time isn't merely a fifth category, but rather is something more

58. Defenders of OFOT will retort that when they speak of the fixity of the past, they mean to imply that it is now impossible for Abby now to determine what God believed in the past. But this is no worry, for Abby has no such power on possible world Ockhamism. God always believed in *alpha* that Abby would drink orange juice, and God always believed in *beta* that Abby would refrain from drinking orange juice. And, it is within Abby's power to bring it about that *alpha*, or that *beta*, obtains.

59. Of course, the success of such an argument would hinge on a rejection of a distinction between hard facts and soft facts, as well as other arguments against divine timelessness. But these two things together lend an incredible amount of support to possible world Ockhamism and, to date, have not been defeated (at least by consensus opinion of academic philosophers). Cf. Green and Rogers, "Time"; Rogers, "Necessity of the Present"; Rogers, "Omniscience, Eternity, and Freedom"; Stump and Kretzmann, "Eternity"; Stump and Kretzmann, "Eternity, Awareness, and Action"; Timpe, "Truth-Making and Divine Eternity." For the most recent work that comes close to offering a dissenting view by arguing against traditional Ockhamism (but fails to deal with possible world Ockhamism), see Todd, "Prepunishment and Explanatory Dependence."

foundational to metaphysics than modality and causation, for the nature of time, according to OFOT, is the basis for any understanding of whatever the actual "world"/reality is, what types of causation can and cannot obtain, and what the nature of im/possibility is in reality (i.e., the metaphysics of modality). Can anyone offer a systematic metaphysics that makes time more foundational to reality than modality and causation? Could such a project succeed? In a word, maybe. Open theism is a relatively new research project, so it remains to be seen whether such a reformulation provides a coherent expression of reality, or whether it exchanges one set of problems for another larger, more complex set of (insurmountable?) problems. Suffice it to say that defenders of open theism, especially open future varieties thereof, need to provide a coherent account of the metaphysics that makes possible such a non-traditional view of God and reality in order to make sure that the project is viable in the first place. At this juncture, at least four points deserve further attention.

First, defenders of OFOT regularly make use of our common-sense understanding of the world around us in order to motivate their positions regarding the philosophy of time, namely, the A-theory, and presentism in particular. However, when it comes to how we ordinarily use "will" and "will not" language when expressing PCFC, we are told to abandon common sense and ordinary language philosophy in favor of the much more complicated Peircean semantics. But not even philosophical theologians can have their cake and eat it too. Defenders of OFOT, whether Zimmermaneans or Rhodanians, cannot insist that we play by rules they employ only when it suits them, especially since they want to eschew these same rules when following them would undermine OFOT. It simply won't do for defenders of OFOT to appeal to common sense on the one hand while cautioning against such reasoning when it cuts against them.

This leads to a second issue, which is related to the first. If OFOT allows for the use of possible world discourse at all (and especially as it concerns the metaphysics of modality), then OFOT needs to provide some explanation of what reality is. Of course, in order to make sense of any such claims, until some plausible account of possible worlds that accords with OFOT emerges that satisfies our intuitions about the proper way to describe not only the way things are, but also captures a complete a total world history (including the future), whatever reality turns out to be needs to be cashed out in terms of standard possible world discourse semantics. If OFOT cannot provide such an account, we should first recognize that an even more radical departure from systematic metaphysics is necessary even beyond what I have already shown is required—namely, one that involves a wholesale revision of possible world-based metaphysics of modality.[60]

Third, let us suppose that the sort of revisions that OFOT requires for systematic metaphysics in general and the metaphysics of modality in particular (and whatever theory of possible worlds stems from that metaphysics of modality) somehow render possible world Ockhamism unsuccessful and thereby save OFOT from various defeaters. Even if these revisions can accomplish all this (a claim that is far from obvious and certainly yet to be demonstrated), OFOT remains saddled with other problems. Perhaps philosophers should pay more attention to time as a fundamental metaphysical category; perhaps all the work in powers metaphysics to date is mistaken in denying that time is fundamental because the nature of time itself is contingent; perhaps time is necessary for the metaphysics of modality to properly appropriate both the metaphysical category of causation and alternative versions of necessity (such as accidental necessity, ontological necessity, and consequential necessity discussed in chapter five). Even still, it seems that OFOT must choose between two horns of a dilemma.

The first horn leaves open theism unmotivated because there is a way God could infallibly know which possible world will eventually correspond to the actual world without such knowledge hinging on any sort of necessity that compromises LFW.[61] This is because the type of necessity that distributes from "Necessarily, (If God knows *x*, then *x*)" to the corresponding conditional "If God necessarily knows *x*, then necessarily *x*" gives us a false antecedent. Allow me to explain.

On any version of the metaphysics of modality that is consistent with both theism and a theory of possible worlds such that more than one possible world is metaphysically available (i.e., more than one possible world could obtain, and there are real differences between those

60. One way this could happen is found in Jacobs, "Powers Theory of Modality." But, Jacobs isn't an open theist, and his view of modality will not allow for OFOT.

61. In the previous chapter, I discuss several types of necessity, including logical necessity, ontological necessity, consequential necessity, and accidental necessity. I was careful to show how, and under what circumstances, each version undermines LFW. However, I also showed that if any of the versions of necessity involved in the DFF eliminate LFW, then it follows that God does not know the present. I won't rehash those arguments here, but rather remind the reader that substituting one version of necessity for another won't help an open theist escape the problems at hand.

worlds), it is obviously false that God necessarily knows (in the broadly logical sense) whatever God would need to know in order to motivate strong forms of the DFF. Said differently, it is obviously false that God, as part of divine free knowledge, necessarily (in the broadly logical sense) knows something *as part of the actual world*, because the existence of the actual world is contingent. That is, even though God has knowledge of all modalities as part of divine natural knowledge, and necessarily so, God does not necessarily know (in the broadly logical sense) which possible world is the actual world as a part of divine free knowledge.[62] This is all the more true given that OFOT entails denying that there is an actual world (on the standard semantics of discourse about possible worlds in which a possible world is a maximally consistent state of affairs with a complete and total world history, including a future). On possible world Ockhamism, there are a great many worlds in which God, instead of knowing *x*, knows ~*x*.[63]

This obviously generalizes over matters concerning future contingency such that in *alpha*, God knows some given future contingent which renders an event such as Abby's freely drinking orange juice tomorrow with her breakfast consequentially necessary, and in *beta* God knows its negation, thereby making it consequentially necessary that Abby freely refrain from drinking the orange juice. This is all that is needed to show that it is false to assert that "Necessarily (in all possible worlds), God knows *x*." But this is precisely the way that many formulations of the DFF are stated. Therefore, the conditional used by OFOT to motivate these versions of DFF is vacuously true because it has a false antecedent, which, in turn, eliminates any strength of the form of the DFF by rendering the argument unsound.

And this brings us to the second horn of the dilemma that defenders of OFOT face. Regardless of which of the various weaker conceptions of necessity defenders of OFOT use to rescue their arguments for theological incompatibilism, such as either accidental necessity or consequential necessity (both versions of ontological necessity I offered in chapter 5), open theists are against the ropes, for these varieties of ontological necessity either allow for an escape for theological compatibilists

62. Here I am assuming modal actualism. If one were to adopt a Lewisian view of modal concretism, whereupon all possible worlds are real, not just as divine ideas or abstractions but as concrete particulars, what I am suggesting would be false.

63. The same is true *mutatis mutandis* for defenders of LFOT such as Hasker who denies that God is a necessary being.

(such as possible world Ockhamism, or perhaps some other response to the DFF), or create insurmountable problems for the open theist, namely, that God cannot know the present.

I hope that by including this argument readers can more easily see that the conclusions I draw against open theism's ability to affirm divine knowledge of the present apply just as strongly to OFOT as they do for LFOT. But this dilemma raises even more serious problems for OFOT than it does for LFOT. Recall that defenders of LFOT are content to redefine omniscience in modal terms such that, according to these thinkers, God does not need to know all truths in order to count as omniscient. But this is not the case for OFOT. Because defenders of OFOT defend the thesis that truth supervenes upon being (TSB), and because the future doesn't exist on presentism, it poses no problem for robust articulations of omniscience (even by (D11) standards) that God lacks knowledge of which future contingents "will*" obtain.[64] For both Zimmermaneans and Rhodanians, no such truths exist, and for Rhodanians, all PCFC are false. However, neither of these options is available with respect to present realities, for clearly the present exists on presentism, so there are true bivalent truth-values for propositions about the present. But, on the reformulations in the systematic metaphysics of modality (and the theory of possible worlds that stems from it) of OFOT required to avoid possible world Ockhamism, as I argued in the last chapter, it turns out that God cannot know certain truths that do exist, namely, truths about the present that involve free will.

Fourth, and finally, let us continue supposing (apart from any supporting evidence) that all of the radical revisioning of systematic metaphysics succeeds against each argument I've offered, including the issues of necessity just mentioned, OFOT suffers from massive confusion with regard to its conflating temporal modality with metaphysical modality.[65] Although the two concepts might be related,[66] contemporary

64. Here I use "will*" in an attempt to charitably explain the contingent nature of what is at issue. It's worth mentioning again that a solution to these problems can be found in denying TSB by appropriating arguments that Merricks makes in *Truth and Ontology*. Such a move would help OFOT avoid some of the problems that I raise, but the same move eliminates much of the motivation for OFOT in the first place.

65. Cf. Craig and Hunt "Perils," as well as Ulrich Meyer's very helpful essay "Time and Modality."

66. It is a disputed matter as to what relation temporal modality has with metaphysical modality. For an account of similarity, see Rini and Cresswell, *World-Time Parallel*. See also Meyer, "Time and Modality."

philosophers of time all agree that one cannot simply substitute metaphysical modality for temporal modality, nor can one switch back and forth between the two as though they express the same concepts. The relationship(s) between/among the metaphysics of modality, temporal modality, modal logic, tense logic, and the metaphysics of time are extremely complicated. For too long, open theists in general, and defenders of OFOT in particular, have rested on (an) assumed philosophical system(s) that is/are far from obvious.

Put simply, the systematic metaphysics that open theism requires has yet to be adequately developed, and might not even be tenable at all. For all we know, no such metaphysics exists, for whatever would be required to make sense of OFOT might be self-referentially incoherent. I am not suggesting this is the case, but no one can make this judgment until a philosophical system is developed and put forward. When confronted by these sorts of calls for a systematic metaphysics that makes sense of open-futurism advocates of OFOT have responded by talking about how intuitive open-futurism is to everyday people in much the same way that they affirm LFW. Insofar as systematic metaphysics is concerned, when defenders of OFOT have responded at all, they have done so in an *ad hoc* manner about which of a number of metaphysical commitments OFOT affirms and rejects. If I have accomplished nothing else in this chapter, I hope that I have exposed the need for defenders of OFOT to develop a much more thorough account of systematic metaphysics that makes sense of the claims of OFOT, nay, even calling for it, while simultaneously providing adequate metaphysical motivation to eliminate and avoid alternative proposed solutions to the DFF (such as possible world Ockhamism).

A Fallacious Anselmian Argument Against Open Future Open Theism

We have seen that OFOT is motivated not so much as a response to the DFF as much as it is the logical response to the DFF given the outworking of the metaphysics of time championed by open theists, namely, the A-theory of time, and specifically presentism. One easy way to defeat OFOT is to reject presentism.[67] Since others have critiqued this view

67. Alternative conceptions of open theism could probably be reformulated on growing-blockism, but no open theist, to date, defends growing-blockism as the correct A-theoretic understanding of the ontology of time.

of time, I won't delve any more deeply into the metaphysical issues involved in analyzing the rightness or wrongness of presentism than I already have.[68] Although I deny that presentism is correct, I won't simply dismiss OFOT on those grounds. Instead, in what follows I continue to grant open theists as many presuppositions as necessary, for the sake of argument (and in the interests of charity), to show other problems with this view of divine knowledge. Therefore, let us assume that presentism is defensible and sound.

In this section, I will offer what might seem to be good arguments for incompatibilism about Anselmian perfect being theology and OFOT. However, I will demonstrate how defenders of OFOT can defeat this argument, but only by putting themselves in a place that necessitates that they respond to these Anselmian criticisms by placing themselves in the line of fire of other criticisms I've already discussed concerning the lack of a systematic metaphysics that would render OFOT coherent in the first place.

Suppose that it is true that the combination of presentism and LFW yields OFOT. If this much is true, defenders of OFOT must defend the idea that presentism is logically necessary in order to escape what initially seems to be a conundrum. Any argument against OFOT that rests entirely on Anselmian grounds requires showing that defenders of OFOT must choose at most two of the following three: the Anselmian conception of God, presentism, and LFW. After I explain the argument and offer an analysis of the dialectic between defenders of OFOT and defenders of classical theism concerning this argument, I will show why the argument against OFOT fails.

Recall that the Anselmian conception of God precludes any sort of ontological kenotic move, not only for Christology, but also as regards theology proper.[69] But one might think that OFOT entails divine self-limitation, which is metaphysically impossible if we conceive of God as the being than which none greater can exist. Thus, just as various

68. A number of important critiques of presentism have been published. Among the most important are: Oaklander, *Ontology of Time*; Sider, *Four Dimensionalism*; Le Poidevin, *Travels in Four Dimensions*. For a more introductory critique, see Rea, "Four-Dimensionalism."

69. There is a long literature on kenotic theology (and kenotic Christology in particular) that I won't interact with here. Suffice it to say that functional kenoticism seems compatible with maximal greatness, whereas real change in the ontology of a being from maximal greatness to anything other than maximal greatness poses obvious problems for perfect being theology.

articulations of LFOT offered by Hasker, Swinburne, and van Inwagen fail in light of Anselmian perfect being theology, OFOT might fail for the same reason. That is, any theist who maintains that God is the greatest of all possible beings cannot affirm open theism, in either its limited foreknowledge expression or its open future expression.

An adequate explanation requires a deeper investigation into other concepts of divine epistemology. Within the divine mind, we must distinguish between natural knowledge and free knowledge. God's natural knowledge includes knowledge of all necessities and knowledge of all possibilities, whereas God's free knowledge includes knowledge of what exists, or, as many prefer, what is "actual."[70] Now, given that Rhoda insists that "the open theist wants to say that God has *maximal* knowledge," an Anselmian might argue that if some logically possible metaphysics of time could allow at least some PCFC to be true in the bivalent sense, then if God creates at all, a maximally great being must actualize a world in which the metaphysics of time make possible divine foreknowledge of future contingents.[71] Said differently, if God could have a "type" of knowledge available only in some particular type of possible world but not available in the actual world, the concept of divine maximal greatness precludes that what is thought to be the actual world is even metaphysically possible since in such a world God lacks maximally possible knowledge. Call this the maximal knowledge argument from the Anselmian thesis. If God were thought to choose to actualize such a world by limiting divine knowledge, it's obvious that such a decision is a type of kenotic move that amounts to some kind of divine limitation, which is clearly incompatible with the Anselmian conception of God.[72]

But defenders of OFOT are bound to object: there are lots of worlds that are logically possible, but not actual, and in a great many of those

70. As I noted in chapter 1, David Lewis and others who defend modal concretism understand the term "actual" in a rather technical fashion such that it refers to what is real in a given possible (yet truly extant) world. That is, actualization is a world-indexed property. While ordinary language might allow for alternative understandings of "actual," I'll do my best to avoid equivocation, given that so much of the debates concerning OFOT hinges on a proper understanding of the metaphysics of modality.

71. Rhoda notes that this stems from "the commitment to theism. Consequently, if it is *possible* for God to know something he must know it." Rhoda, "Generic Open Theism," 227–28.

72. This Anselmian conception of theology proper has important implications for properly understanding the *parousia*, which I take up later. Suffice it to say, I maintain the kenotic Christologies are not compatible with classic interpretations of Anselmian theism.

worlds it seems God would have a different type of knowledge. After all, one might suggest that God could have created a world with one more person, or other beings (say, elves, for instance), so divine free knowledge could always contain "more" facts (quantitatively) than God currently knows. If divine maximal greatness precludes the possibility of divine self-limitation, then maximal greatness necessitates either that God create a world in which God knows all that can possibly be known *as part of divine free knowledge*, or maximal greatness entails a Lewisan metaphysics of modality whereupon all logically possible worlds exist as concrete particulars. But, unless we are willing to go so far as to say that this world includes the existence of elves, or affirm modal concretism, it is obviously possible that God could know more as part of divine free knowledge than God actually knows with regard to what is actual in this world. Thus, the maximal knowledge argument fails.

Two replies. First, nothing seems to render metaphysically impossible God's actualizing a world with more people, and such would result in God knowing the truth-values of propositions about what would correspond to the actual world as part of divine free knowledge. But, it isn't at all clear that God would know more truths quantitatively were God to create such a world. It is true that in a world with elves, God would know <The world has elves>, but it is also true that in the actual world, God knows <There are no elves>. So the issue in question is not precisely the *quantity* of God's free knowledge but rather the *quality* of knowledge. The Anselmian could concede that God could know as real (that is, as actual, instantiated, concrete in virtue of divine free knowledge) truths that God currently does not know, but it doesn't necessarily follow that God would know more truths than God actually knows. So, despite initial appearances, it likely isn't the case that divine free knowledge could be "larger" than it actually is. Because divine knowledge includes knowledge of all modalities, including these potentialities (even if they aren't actualized), God knows the same number of truths regardless of what kind of world God creates. As an example, let us consider one fictional object/being who exists as an unactualized divine idea; we can call him uncreated-Joe.

If God is omniscient, God has knowledge of uncreated-Joe because God knows the truth-values of all propositions concerning uncreated-Joe in virtue of divine natural knowledge of all the possible worlds in which uncreated-Joe exists as an actualized, concrete particular. Unless we follow Lewis's modal concretism (which is contrary to the modal actualism that defenders of OFOT have thus far sought to maintain) we presume that all of the worlds in which uncreated-Joe exists as a concrete particular are not part of what obtains as concrete reality. That is, since no world in which uncreated-Joe obtains as a concrete particular has been actualized by God, uncreated-Joe is not actual in the sense that he does not exist as a concrete particular. What God knows about uncreated-Joe is different than what God would know about him if God had known Joe as a creature who enjoys the status of being part of the actual world as an instantiated, truly extant, concrete particular. But God does not genuinely lack any knowledge (*quantitatively*) of uncreated-Joe in this counterexample any more than God lacks knowledge of any other part of the realm of possibilia.

The second reply goes as follows. OFOT demands that, one way or another, PCFC are never true, for on the OFOT interpretation of PCFC, the truth of such propositions would entail that those truths are determined, thereby eliminating the contingent nature of whatever is being discussed in PCFC.[73] But the arguments employed by defenders of OFOT that seek to show that God is genuinely omniscient in the Anselmian sense break down when one considers the limitations placed on divine knowledge that stem from openness understandings of creation. If God enjoys the same kind of freedom that open theists insist that humans enjoy, then it is true that prior to creating a world, God had a choice about what kind of world to create.[74] Since no one is arguing that deterministic worlds are metaphysically impossible, God could have created a world in which no beings possess the type of LFW that demands the ability to do otherwise. If this is true, then Anselmians might conclude against LFW by arguing that OFOT articulations of theological incompatibilism about freedom and foreknowledge are simply incompatible with Anselmian perfect being theology. This is so because at creation, God has a choice to either create a world in which God knows the future, or a world in which God does not know the future. A divine decision to create a world in which agents possess LFW requires that God does not enjoy a type of knowledge that is otherwise available were God to decide to create a world in which agents lack LFW. What could serve as motivation for God

73. This is true for both Zimmermanean and Rhodanian articulations of OFOT.

74. This is true regardless of what position one takes on the issue of God's relation to time. For those who think God is in time, the phrase "prior to creation" can be interpreted temporally. For those who defend either traditional divine timelessness or accidental divine temporalism (the view defended by William Lane Craig), the phrase "prior to creation" can be interpreted logically instead of chronologically.

to choose against having a category of knowledge that we implicitly think it would be better to have than to not have?

Were God to actualize a world that lacks indeterminism (thereby ensuring that agents lack LFW), then one could defend the combination of an A-theoretical view of time and metaphysical/ontological presentism, together with the idea that God experiences time (a view defended by all open theists) and preserve exhaustive definite foreknowledge.[75] This is because in such a world there would be no future contingents, but rather only determined future events, whose truths could be grounded in present reality. Thus, in order to defend OFOT, one must already have defeated solutions to the DFF that rely on compatibilist understandings of freedom since compatibilism makes a type of divine knowledge possible that isn't available to God *at all* if God creates a world in which presentism is true and human beings possess LFW. This understanding of what is at stake concerning limitations to divine knowledge given which possible world God creates differs substantially from what was at stake concerning uncreated-Joe. The idea is that God could actualize uncreated-Joe, but doesn't, and this doesn't impugn divine omniscience since God still has extensive knowledge of uncreated-Joe in virtue of divine knowledge of all possibilia. So, even if God lacks knowledge of uncreated-Joe as an actualized concrete particular, the reason that God lacks such knowledge is because it is logically impossible—it is a contradiction—for an uncreated being such as uncreated-Joe to exist as a concrete particular. But notice that whereas that type of knowledge is logically impossible for God to enjoy as part of divine free knowledge of the actual world (since we assume that the actual world includes agents who enjoy LFW), it is not logically impossible for God to enjoy exhaustive knowledge of what will obtain in the future as part of divine free knowledge *simpliciter* (for there are worlds in which agents lack LFW, and God can certainly know what will obtain in those worlds). All this is to say, the *quality* of knowledge that God has in virtue of the mode of divine knowledge is significantly different on OFOT, and the concept of God's essentially being omniscient and maximally knowing, as demanded by Anselmian monotheism, poses problems for uncritically accepting the radical modifications to divine knowledge required by OFOT.

75. Interestingly, the same understanding of the world (no indeterminism, together with some A-theoretical understanding of time in that world) could obtain, with the same benefits of timeless foreknowledge, even if God were timeless and did not experience the passing of time.

In fact, it is only because of a divine choice that God cannot know what will* happen in the future, namely, a divine choice to actualize a world in which: (a) agents enjoy LFW; and (b) metaphysical presentism obtains. But again, why would God want to limit the scope of divine knowledge in this way when there are other possible worlds that God could actualize that don't require this type of self-imposed limitation?

But this type of Anselmian argument ultimately fails to defeat OFOT because God's natural knowledge of all possible worlds renders the extent of divine knowledge the same regardless of which world God creates. If God is essentially omniscient, and maximally so, the extent of divine knowledge doesn't hinge on what sort of world God creates. If God creates a world in which it is metaphysically impossible for God to know as part of divine free knowledge the truth-values of PCFC, this doesn't technically limit divine knowledge, because even on OFOT God still knows (in virtue of divine natural knowledge of all modalities) all the truth-values of future contingents in all possible worlds in which these same PCFC do have truth-values (perhaps because the nature of time is different in those worlds, thereby making it logically possible for some future event to be both contingent yet true). That is, in much the same way that God knows the truth-values concerning uncreated-Joe because of divine natural knowledge of all modalities (which entails perfect knowledge of all possible worlds in which Joe exists as a concrete particular), the defender of OFOT can respond that even if the world God created precludes divine foreknowledge of future contingents, this in no way entails that God does not know the truths of the future in alternative, possible but non-concrete worlds.

Suppose for the sake of argument that three different worlds are possible, and suppose also that God is essentially omniscient. Regardless of which (if any) world God creates, divine knowledge of the other two worlds remains in virtue of the exhaustive nature of divine natural knowledge of all possibilia, even if God chooses not to actualize these other possible worlds. Those who defend OFOT, therefore, will object that divine natural knowledge renders the maximal knowledge argument moot in adjudicating for or against OFOT, for God's knowledge remains equal regardless of what type of world is instantiated.

This counterargument seems quite strong. However, upon further analysis, this objection, in order to have any teeth, actually requires a Lewisian understanding of modal concretism that defenders of OFOT have thus far rejected. Recall that Lewis believes that all possible worlds do, in fact, exist—not just as divine ideas, but rather as instantiated, concrete realities. That is, all possible worlds are real, and we live in one particular world, which is but one of the many genuinely extant worlds. Other possible worlds are not mere possibilities. This metaphysics of modality is the only way that anyone could say God's total, complete knowledge is the exact same regardless of which world we inhabit.[76] God's knowledge of other possibilities, so long as they aren't instantiated, is different in at least the mode by which God knows them. God's knowledge of uncreated-Joe is different from God's knowledge of you and me, for we actually exist in the real world whereas uncreated-Joe does not. God's free knowledge of you and me differs from divine natural knowledge of uncreated-Joe because God knows you and me as genuinely existing beings and not merely as possibilia. I argued above that the quantity of divine knowledge is not the issue, and that God's knowledge of potentialities need not be considered as a serious objection to the threat that the maximal knowledge argument poses for OFOT. Is there an equivocation in now suggesting that there is a significant difference?

Recall that the Anselmian argument suggests that quantity is not the issue, but quality is. There is a real and significant difference between the mode of God's knowing something as real versus God's knowing something merely as potential, and the issue of mode can be understood as an issue of the quality of divine knowledge. Given that God could always create a world with one more person in it, or one more tree, it follows that the sorts of worlds metaphysically available to God are potentially infinite. But, there are good reasons for rejecting the existence of *actual* infinities, so we shouldn't be concerned that such potentially infinite possibilities impugn maximal knowledge, and therefore Anselmian conceptions of divine omniscience.[77]

In responding to arguments concerning the *amount* of divine knowledge, my point is not that such differences don't matter at all, but that quantitative differences of this variety don't pose a serious threat to God's being essentially and maximally omniscient. Instead, it would be

76. Because "actual" is an indexical term on modal concretism, God's knowledge of what is actually the case will depend on which world is actual. However, my contention is that God transcends all the worlds and has complete knowledge of all truths in all worlds. This is why the mode of divine knowledge (natural vs. free) is the same in all cases, because, on modal concretism, there are no aspects of possibilia that don't exist as concrete particulars in some world that exists concretely.

77. For a sampling of some of these reasons, see Craig, *Kalam Cosmological Argument*, 20–29, 69–95.

categorical, or qualitative, differences in divine knowledge that do matter. If it is possible that God could have created a world with one more person (or a world with elves), it seems that God could have also created a world with two more people (or a world with both elves and unicorns). And so it goes for a world with three more people, etc. (and a world with a combination of unicorns, elves, and ents, etc.). But, assuming the impossibility of an actual infinite, these quantitative considerations need not be taken into account when considering divine omniscience, for doing so would entail the suggestion that God knows the impossible, which amounts to predicating absurdity to God.[78] As I argued in the last chapter, it is not self-limitation on the part of God that prevents God from knowing the unknowable, for divine self-limitation is metaphysically impossible given God's maximal greatness, as established by Anselmian perfect being theology. Rather, the reason that divine knowledge of an actually infinite amount of truths isn't possible (even for God) is precisely because the very existence of an actual infinite is itself a metaphysical impossibility. Therefore, to suggest that God might know what is metaphysically impossible is incoherent. Therefore, one of the pillars of an OFOT defeater of the Anselmian maximal knowledge argument is unmotivated.

That said, with respect to categories of knowledge, the manner in which God knows any given truth does seem to be significant. We have already seen that truth-values with respect to the future are available for God to be known as "real" (i.e., instantiated) if God creates a world in which agents lack LFW, yet OFOT entails that no such truths exist as part of the actual world given the fact that God chose to create a world in which agents *do* enjoy LFW, and this world is one in which the metaphysics of time precludes the existence of truths about future contingents. But, according to OFOT, this means that God's decision to create this world entails that an entire category of knowledge (viz., propositions concerning contingent future events) is inaccessible to God as "real."

OFOT cannot escape the charge that God's knowledge is not as *qualitatively* robust as it could be, thus meaning that the decision to create a world in which agents enjoy LFW is a decision resulting in God's self-limitation of divine knowledge, which is metaphysically impossible

78. That God could know the unknowable seems as ludicrous as the idea that God can draw four-sided triangles, or that God can create a rock so heavy that he cannot lift it, or that God can make it such that he both exists and does not exist at the same time. Of course, this claim should be met with agreement from all open theists, who assert that God can only know what is logically knowable. As noted earlier, the Anselmian insists that this is true but trivially so.

given the Anselmian conception of maximal greatness. Hence, Anselmians might argue that OFOT must: (i) abandon the idea that agents enjoy the sort of LFW that demands they have the ability to do otherwise; (ii) recognize that there is some flaw in the arguments for theological incompatibilism about freedom and foreknowledge; (iii) abandon metaphysical presentism in favor of some alternative conception of time; or (iv) deny that God is the greatest of all possible beings. But, OFOT requires (i), (ii), and (iii), so OFOT should be rejected by those who maintain that (iv) God is the greatest of all possible beings.

Conceding Anselmian Perfect Being Theology to Defenders of Open Future Open Theism

Having said all this, yet another counterargument can be offered on behalf of OFOT. Doesn't the same argument that I've just offered against OFOT cut just as deeply against classical theism? Yes, it does, and this is why OFOT cannot be eliminated on Anselmian grounds alone. Let's continue assuming modal actualism (the view that only one possible world is concrete—the actual world—and all other possible worlds are real only in the sense that they are part of the realm of possibilia). If modal actualism is true, then even on classical theism, divine knowledge of truths about other worlds isn't real in the same way that Anselmians might argue that, on OFOT, divine knowledge of future contingents in other possible worlds isn't real. Furthermore, on modal actualism, God could not have actualized more than one world, so God could not have had better knowledge than he has about the different possible worlds.[79] By contrast, the defender of OFOT admits that God could have actualized a world in which he could have had better knowledge than he does, namely, a deterministic world. Accordingly, this type of argument against OFOT should be abandoned.

If we grant for the sake of argument that OFOT is the right way to respond to the DFF, we should also grant that there might be overriding reasons that serve to adequately motivate God's decision to create a world in which agents enjoy LFW—*even if that decision entails that God lacks exhaustive definite foreknowledge of which future contingents will* obtain in the actual world.*[80] Perhaps LFW is a good in and of itself,

79. Thanks are due to Daniel Hill for helping me clarify my thinking on this point.

80. Here, again, I use the "will*" in an effort to charitably represent what is at issue.

or perhaps it is instrumentally valuable insofar as it makes salvation possible in some way that isn't metaphysically possible apart from genuine cooperation, or synergism.[81] Of course, at this point, we are well beyond thinking through the DFF. But it's important to say that Anselmian arguments against OFOT don't seem to have the teeth that they do when offered against LFOT.

It seems that the argument above, after analysis, gives us strong reasons to think that there are different types of worlds available to God, and if God is free with respect to what kind of world to actualize, then the content of divine free knowledge will be different depending on what kind of world God chooses to instantiate. Even if God's decision concerning what world to create entails that some type of knowledge doesn't obtain as part of divine free knowledge, this doesn't impugn omniscience, given the scope of truth that exists in open future worlds.[82] *Therefore, it's important that I mention that OFOT* does *seem to be compatible with maximal greatness and Anselmian perfect being theology*. However, granting the logical compatibility of Anselmian perfect being theology and OFOT does not by any means suggest that OFOT is true, or that Christians have good reasons for taking it as the correct account of theology proper. For the remainder of this chapter, I will offer non-Anselmian-style arguments against OFOT.

On the Modality of Open Future Open Theism's Metaphysics of Modality

It seems that defenders of OFOT want to suggest both that time is such a fundamental aspect of reality as to require rethinking all of systematic metaphysics and that time itself is what precludes divine knowledge of certain truths. That is, these two suggestions don't intuitively fit well with the Anselmian conception of divine maximal greatness. Rather, what fits more neatly with the Anselmian thesis is that since the nature

81. So, for instance, Stump, "Atonement and Justification."

82. One could argue that omniscience is impugned because on OFOT God doesn't know in the actual world whether Abby will drink the orange juice (assuming that Abby is free with respect to drinking the orange juice), whereas God does know this in a world where agents lack the ability to do otherwise. However, on OFOT, were God to believe that Abby will (or will not) drink the orange juice, God would believe something that is false, which is obviously incompatible with divine infallibility. So such an argument begs the question against OFOT's account of PCFC.

of time itself is contingent, whatever metaphysics of time God chooses to instantiate should lend support to the maximal knowledge argument instead of raising any tensions for it. Of course, as we've seen, this doesn't constitute a proof against OFOT, but it does raise a worry, which, together with the other arguments I've offered, tends towards a cumulative case argument against OFOT.

Recall that defenders of OFOT will likely retort that I've failed to realize that God's knowledge is still no different, for as long as God is essentially omniscient, then it doesn't matter whether or not what God knows falls under divine natural knowledge or divine free knowledge.[83] If God's knowledge of the entire realm of possibilia includes knowledge of everything that could happen such that God has exhaustive knowledge of all possible worlds, then the fact that God lacks a type of knowledge doesn't impugn divine omniscience because God created this world and not some other world in which God could know truths about the future. It may be the case that PCFC aren't true in this world, but this does not amount to a limitation on divine knowledge any more than God's decision to actualize a world in which uncreated-Joe doesn't exist as a concrete particular amounts to a limitation of divine omniscience.[84]

The response above saves OFOT from being defeated on entirely Anselmian grounds, and it would count as a devastating blow against my thesis if it were possible for God to create a world in which God lacked knowledge of an entire category of truths available to God in other worlds. However, because divine omniscience is an essential and not accidental or contingent property of God, defenders of OFOT should take seriously the idea that the type of possible world in which OFOT is true might be metaphysically impossible (that is, worlds in which both metaphysical presentism is true and agents enjoy LFW). As we have seen, God exists necessarily (i.e., in/at all possible worlds), and in all those worlds God is omniscient, and maximally so. Thus, in all worlds, God possesses the maximum amount of knowledge God could possibly have. Ultimately, the reason that God cannot create the type of world demanded by OFOT is because such a world is a state of affairs in which God's knowledge is limited because of a decision to create a world in which presentism is true and agents enjoy LFW.

83. To see the problem, consider that on OFOT, God won't know which world is actual, given a standard understanding of possible worlds.

84. But it would certainly be a limitation of divine omniscience if God didn't know whether or not uncreated-Joe were actual.

Tom Crisp, one of the leading defenders of metaphysical presentism, has argued compellingly that presentism is a contingent truth.[85] Thus, because presentism isn't a necessary truth concerning the metaphysics of time, it follows that if presentism (together with Anselmian perfect being theology and LFW) entails OFOT, and if OFOT is a limitation of divine knowledge, then such worlds are metaphysically impossible, given the Anselmian conception of divine maximal greatness. Because any self-limitation of God is self-referentially incoherent, the idea that God would create a universe which entails that God does not possess exhaustive knowledge of what will* happen in the future is unacceptable. Of course, this problem is exacerbated all the more when we consider that there are good reasons to think that presentism (if true at all) is contingently true. Therefore, alternative conceptions of time are genuine metaphysical possibilities available for God that preserve exhaustive definite foreknowledge. Furthermore, there are still other alternatives that include presentism coupled together with alternative conceptions of human freedom (viz., compatibilism, semi-compatibilism, or other conceptions of LFW which don't demand PAP).

I am not suggesting that God lacks freedom with respect to what sort of world God could instantiate. That is, I'm not arguing that God needed to create a world in which B-series views of time were instantiated, for this would make any A-theory of time (including presentism) metaphysically impossible.[86] Rather, I am arguing that presentism, together with theological incompatibilism about freedom and foreknowledge, once properly understood, entails a counterintuitive approach to divine omniscience, even if it doesn't entail any divine self-limitation, strictly speaking. At least, I don't know of anyone who would intuitively think that God lacks knowledge of which future contingents will* and will not* obtain when initially considering all that falls under the domain of divine omniscience. Of course, OFOT only makes sense if it is true that presentism renders impossible any truths about future contingents.[87] Such

85. For more on the contingent nature of presentism, see Crisp, "Presentism."

86. Nor am I endorsing Ted Sider's arguments that presentism is necessarily false, although I do find them rather persuasive. Sider, *Four Dimensionalism*, especially 11–52.

87. As noted in Crisp, "Presentism," 90n407, Tom Crisp has argued compellingly against this by offering an ersatz way around the problem. Therefore, Crisp disagrees with Rhoda et al. that presentism, when conjoined with LFW, entails all-falsism. See Crisp, "Presentism and the Grounding." Of course, if presentism is false (a view that I defend), none of this matters.

an analysis does not mean that God limits the scope of divine knowledge directly by simply choosing to not know truths about PCFC in the way that some theologians have suggested.[88] However, the fact that PCFC lack true truth-values is determined by something else under God's control, namely, God's decision of what type of time to actualize. Thus, if OFOT follows from the conjunction of presentism and LFW, what would otherwise be intuitively affirmed as part of divine omniscience is limited indirectly by the decision to instantiate a particular metaphysics of time together with a particular metaphysics of free will. As has now been demonstrated, this is so counterintuitive that defenders of OFOT need to offer accounts of why God would make such a choice, and they need to provide a systematic metaphysics to make sense of all this, and show how it does not amount to any sort of divine self-limitation. But even if all this could be done, there are other theological reasons that one shouldn't endorse OFOT. Let's consider one of them.

A Theological Defeater for Open Future Open Theism

Although OFOT might not be defeated on Anselmian grounds alone, this doesn't mean that there are not other good theological arguments against it. I want to offer a theological example that shows that OFOT doesn't fit with traditionally accepted views about seemingly unrelated matters in Christian doctrine. Before I show why this is the case, let me make a few observations about the metaphysics of free will as understood by a libertarian. Suppose that some event *E* is counterfactually dependent on some action *A* such that if *A*, then *E*, and if ~*A*, then ~*E*. Given any version of open theism, if *A* or ~*A* is underdetermined (that is, if *A* is contingent), then God cannot know whether *A* or ~*A*. But, it follows from this that neither can God know whether *E* or ~*E*, for *E* is likewise contingent since *E* remains counterfactually dependent on *A*, and *A* is underdetermined. But, in Scripture we find examples of divine knowledge of future contingents that are counterfactually dependent on the free choices of human agents, and nothing about this changes even if we assume a libertarian understanding of moral responsibility.

88. Consider Pinnock's view that God chooses to limit divine knowledge to allow for genuine freedom. Pinnock, "God Limits His Knowledge." Consider also Tom Oord's view that God involuntarily limits divine knowledge since God is constrained by the divine nature itself to create beings with significant freedom. Oord, *Uncontrolling Love of God*.

Numerous biblical texts could serve to fill in for the variables I've laid out in the argument above, but I will focus on just one. In a passage known as the Olivet Discourse—a passage that has been hotly debated as it concerns not only eschatological themes but also Christological controversies—Jesus makes it unequivocally clear that neither angels, nor humans, nor even Jesus himself knows when Christ will return. But Jesus also makes it unequivocally clear that the Father does know both the day and the hour that this event will come to pass. However, we know that the *parousia* is counterfactually dependent upon the completion of the Great Commission. In the immediate context of this surprising assertion, Jesus had just proclaimed that "the Gospel of the Kingdom will be preached throughout the whole world as a testimony to all nations, *and then the end will come*."[89] We know from numerous other texts that Christians bear moral responsibility for evangelism, that is, the proclamation and spread of the gospel (cf. Ezek 3:18; 33:8; Matt 28:19–20; Acts 20:26–27). To make things even clearer, that the *parousia* is counterfactually dependent upon human actions is reaffirmed by the apostle Peter when he makes it clear that we are to labor, not only in actively waiting on the day of God but we actually play a part in hastening its arrival (2 Pet 3:11–12). Given a *prima facie* reading of 2 Pet 3, the day and the hour of Christ's return is presently contingent, for it is counterfactually dependent on human obedience to the Great Commission. However, Jesus plainly asserts that this contingent future event is known by God. Is there a way that open theists can make sense of such a counterexample to their beliefs?[90]

Perhaps open theists could retort that God has set up a contingency plan just in case humans, by their disobedience, fail to fulfill the conditions necessary for the *parousia* to occur by some given time. They might even cite texts in the book of Revelation that seem to indicate that angelic beings will preach the gospel to the ends of the earth prior to the consummation of all things. But even if those apocalyptic texts should be understood along those lines of interpretation, such does not alleviate the tensions created by a proper interpretation of Matt 24. The "end" that is to come upon the completion of the task of the proclamation of the gospel to all nations in Matt 24 is not the consummation of all

89. Matthew 24:14, translation and emphasis mine.

90. Another obvious example that could fill the variables is Peter's threefold denial of Christ after Jesus was arrested. See Matt 26:33–35; Mark 14:39–31; Luke 22:33–34; John 13:36–38.

things, but rather is more properly interpreted as the beginning of the end, as the context makes clear.[91] Hence, appeal to alternative schematics to explain divine foreknowledge of one specific future contingent, namely, the *parousia*, fails to account for the way that the context of the pericope in question makes clear that *humans* are the agents that bring about these things. Apart from some divine decree that renders certain future events not contingent, but determined, I fail to see how an open theist can account for divine (fore)knowledge of the time of the *parousia*. Of course, appealing to the determination of said event won't satisfy a broadly openness hermeneutic, whereupon a divine command obviously necessitates human responsibility, which, in turn, requires significant freedom and the ability to do otherwise. Left without any alternative responses to this conundrum, I conclude that divine knowledge of the day and the hour of the return of the Son (and other contingent events that are counterfactually dependent on actions for which we bear moral responsibility) constitutes a powerful theological defeater for all versions of open theism, including OFOT.

Conclusion

In this chapter, I began by offering a nomenclature of various articulations of open theism as well as a taxonomy to aid readers in differentiating between these different versions of open theism. As I argued against two different versions of OFOT, I repeatedly sought to charitably grant various presuppositions to defenders of OFOT for the sake of argument. It's worth mentioning again that the easiest way to defeat OFOT is to deny presentism, for without this metaphysics of time, OFOT doesn't even get off the ground.[92] However, in order to avoid being too simplistic, I argued against Zimmermanean open theism by pointing out the cost of rejecting the principle of bivalence for PCFC. I went on to explain how Rhodanian OFOT differs from its Zimmermanean counterpart. I argued that it fails because the Peircean semantic that it requires is self-referentially incoherent, for defenders of OFOT deny that God enjoys

91. Please note that such a position does not necessitate a dispensational hermeneutic for Matthew's Gospel, nor does it require a premillennial eschatology.

92. Perhaps one could argue that OFOT could be based on a growing-block theory of time. However, in light of Trenton Merricks's rather devastating critique of growing-blockism, I don't think such an approach to saving OFOT merits much attention. See Merricks, "Good-Bye Growing Block."

what classical theists call exhaustive definite foreknowledge (including knowledge of future contingents), but on Peirceanism, it's quite clear that God *does* enjoy exhaustive definite foreknowledge. After discussing issues in systematic metaphysics that are pertinent to OFOT, I noted that defenders of OFOT need to provide a coherent metaphysical system before we can take the position seriously, for the whole project seems to be improperly motivated by an account of time being more fundamental to reality than the metaphysics of modality. On the basis of some of these issues in systematic metaphysics, I then attempted an Anselmian-style argument against OFOT, but I showed why that argument ultimately fails. Therefore, I concluded by arguing against OFOT by raising a theological conundrum against it. All told, OFOT might be compatible with Anselmian perfect being theology, but there are many other reasons that it should be rejected.

Conclusion

What should we think about open theism? Many of those interested in philosophy of religion will no doubt continue to focus their attention on this relatively recent development in theology proper and its novel interpretations of divine omniscience. This is especially true for those working within the subdiscipline that has come to be known as analytic theology. However, throughout this project, I have endeavored to show that open theism does not merit the attention it has received because openness theology faces serious problems that make it highly unattractive, despite the fact that its advocates insist on its superiority as a response to the dilemma of freedom and foreknowledge (DFF).

This thesis began by appealing to Anselmian perfect being theology as a means of analytically adjudicating between competing understandings of divine omniscience. I went on to critique understandings of maximal greatness that yield a being that is less than omniperfect. This critique of contemporary understandings of Anselmianism forestalls some of the ways that open theists might want to suggest modal accommodations of divine knowledge as less than absolute omniscience.

After arguing that the traditional understanding of omniperfection is what Anselmian monotheism entails, I briefly surveyed the literature on both omnipotence and omniscience, thereby paving the way to turn my attention to open theism. I offered a new definition of omniscience that fits more naturally with Anselmian intuitions, and argued that this understanding of omniscience does a better job of overcoming several concerns raised by those dubious about traditional articulations of omniscience.

In the next two chapters, I offered arguments against limited foreknowledge open theism (LFOT). In chapter 3, I concluded that modal reformulations of omniscience fail to preserve what is important about divine knowledge for perfect being theologians. Contrary to Van Inwagen's argument, omnipotence and omniscience are dissimilar in that an inability to know what is logically unknowable does not preserve omniscience if there are facts unknown to God. Whereas omnipotence concerns potentiality, knowledge of all truths does not. In chapter 4, I proved that the omnitemporality of truth generates problems along the lines of logical fatalism independently of divine foreknowledge (or lack thereof), which cuts against the versions of openness theology championed by Hasker, Swinburne, and Van Inwagen.

In chapter 5, I demonstrated that open theism entails that God lacks knowledge of present truths involving significant freedom, which is obviously a very untoward consequence. I carefully showed that this problem faces, not only LFOT but also open future open theism (OFOT). Although I maintain that this argument provides sufficient reason to reject any and all forms of open theism, I went on in the final chapter to critique various articulations of OFOT on four different grounds. First, the cost associated with Zimmermanian OFOT is too high in that it entails the rejection of the principle of bivalence, and it therefore requires multivalent logic, which is inferior to simpler ontologies of truth. Second, I showed that although one version of OFOT preserves the application of the principle of bivalence to propositions concerning future contingents, the Peircean semantics this requires renders OFOT unable to differentiate itself from classical articulations of divine foreknowledge. Third, I demonstrated that the systematic metaphysics required to properly motivate OFOT require that time be included as a more fundamental aspect of reality than can be justified. Fourth, I argued that OFOT fails to account for scriptural and theological data that are important to Christians.

For all these reasons, I maintain that openness theology ought to be rejected. I have been careful to avoid suggesting that any particular solution to the DFF is the right way to respond to this philosophical puzzle, so readers should not understand my rejection of open theism to entail a commitment to simple foreknowledge, or Molinism, or Calvinism, or divine timelessness, or any other response. Moreover, I have also been careful to avoid appeals to any particular conception of time, whether A-theoretic or B-theoretic in nature, nor have I suggested any particular ontology of time (presentism, growing blockism, four-dimensionalism, or moving spotlightism). In light of this rather aporetic conclusion, I am deeply persuaded that the DFF will remain a perennial issue in philosophical theology. However, I am equally persuaded that open theism should not remain a live option for Christians seeking to preserve significant freedom in the face of the DFF while simultaneously holding on to Anselmian perfect being theology. To clarify, I don't see why open theism should continue to be taken so seriously by analytic theologians until someone demonstrates why my arguments are unsuccessful in establishing their conclusions.

Afterword

Two traits that characterized Ben Arbour were his passion for Nicene theological orthodoxy and his jubilant love for people. For all of his brilliance, Arbour was also an irrepressible extrovert with a strong pastoral sensibility, and he took great joy in connecting fellow believers and ministering to them, especially in the intellectual realm. He somehow made the oft-lonely business of philosophical pursuits a richly social affair, which had the effect of uniting people of disparate philosophical and theological persuasions and making his passion for orthodoxy wonderfully contagious. I am a better person for this, as are countless others whose lives were touched by Ben Arbour.

On robust display in this book are Arbour's immense analytical skills, powerfully enhanced by his keen philosophical intuitions and a truly Socratic tactical genius. Anyone who regularly engaged Ben Arbour in philosophical dialogue knows that his favorite argumentative strategy was *reductio ad absurdum*. Not surprisingly, this book features several forceful *reductio* arguments against open theism that place significant burdens of rebuttal upon its proponents to demonstrate the plausibility of their view. I would like to highlight what, to my mind, are the three most significant such arguments in Arbour's case against open theism. Arbour's first *reductio* concerns Nagasawa's claim that Anselmian theism does not entail divine omniperfection. Specifically, Arbour demonstrates that Nagasawa's reformulation of Anselmian theism entails the possibility of polytheism—the existence of multiple maximally great beings, an implication that is inconsistent with traditional conceptions of Anselmian theism. Consequently, Arbour maintains we should conclude that Nagasawa is mistaken in thinking that a maximally great being may be less than omniperfect. I believe Arbour's argument succeeds, and this is significant for purposes that go well beyond this particular project, as his critique of Nagasawa's claim preserves the soundness of Anselmian theism as a philosophical-theological methodology.

Another major *reductio* argument deployed by Arbour appears in chapter 5, where he argues that if open theism is true, then God does not know the present. This seems to follow from the fact that on open theist assumptions there must be a slight time lag between a given event, say Sally doing X, and God's knowledge of this event, since God's knowledge would naturally be causally dependent upon the occurrence of the event, given standard open theist assumptions, including the impossibility of simultaneous causation. But since no open theist would grant that God lacks knowledge of the present, this implication appears to be an effective *reductio* of their view. In the foreword to this book, Elijah Hess attempts to dodge this implication by proposing that God's knowledge that Sally is doing X is not causally dependent but metaphysically dependent on the event, since what God knows here is a proposition, and propositions, as abstract entities, do not bear causal relations. While this is an interesting move on Hess's part, it unfortunately misconstrues how, again given open theist assumptions, God must come to know that Sally is doing X. If it is an actual state of affairs in the world, then it cannot be a purely propositional kind of knowing. It must somehow be perceptual. And perceptual knowledge *is* causal in nature. So Hess's attempt to reconstrue God's knowledge of present realities in non-causal terms in order to evade the force of Arbour's *reductio* fails.

A third reductio argument deployed by Arbour appears in chapter 6 and is leveled specifically at open future open theism (OFOT). If OFOT is true, Arbour claims, then God does not know which world he has created, and in fact there *is* no actual world. Since the "actual world" would include a completely comprehensive world history, from beginning to end, and we have not arrived at the end of history, not even God can know which among many possible worlds he has actualized. In fact, as Arbour points out, "The issue of which world obtains isn't settled until either time ends, or until contingency is removed from everything that presently makes up what we call the future." Arbour could have pressed this point even further by noting that, since humans will retain their libertarian freedom in the eschaton and biblical orthodoxy affirms that the kingdom of God will proceed endlessly into the future, it follows that God will *never* know the actual world. After all, given these assumptions, however far we progress into the future there will always be more contingent events yet to be determined by acts of libertarian free will that God cannot know until they come to pass.

These three *reductio* arguments are as important as they are powerful, and it is my hope that they will receive their due attention in scholarly discussions of open theism in the future. But I equally appreciate other observations Arbour makes along the way that are somewhat tangential to his main project. One of these regards how open theists are wont to accuse classical theists of allowing their conception of God to be corrupted by Greek philosophy. Astutely, Arbour notes that open theists never actually argue for this significant historico-philosophical claim. Rather, he says, "That traditional Christian readings of Scripture have been unduly influenced by Greek philosophy is not a conclusion *for* which open theists argue but rather an assumption *from* which they argue." Arbour points out that this charge leveled by open theists against traditional theism seems to suggest that open theists are themselves immune to imposing their own philosophical assumptions on Scripture. Arbour goes on to note some of the philosophical assumptions that open theists bring to their philosophical theology, but one important such assumption he does not highlight is actually the principal driver of their perspective, namely, the concept of libertarian free will. This definition of freedom is not to be found in Scripture, so it is clearly philosophical in nature. And it is a controversial conception of freedom at that. Compatibilist and other non-libertarian views of freedom are important rivals to the libertarian view of freedom. So, in one sense, the whole theological debate over open theism presupposes that the libertarian view is to be judged the winner of that debate. But why be so confident that libertarianism (not to mention its crucial attendant assumption, the principle of alternative possibilities) is correct such that one would be willing to scuttle major aspects of the traditional understanding of the nature of God in order to accommodate its implications? At the least, this is a theologically hazardous assumption. Open theists have often touted their belief in the "God who takes risks." In fact, it seems to me that the biggest risk-takers here are the open theists themselves.

While Arbour's book, like so much of his published work elsewhere, is primarily philosophical nature, it is informed by biblical texts and doctrinal considerations. His ultimate concerns were always practical, even pastoral. In short, Arbour's tireless aim was always to guard the sacred truths of Scripture and build the faith of fellow Christians. Fittingly, his book ends with one of the few direct theological arguments he uses to critique open theism, a defeater based on Jesus' remarks about the end of history in the Olivet Discourse. Jesus tells us that the Father knows the day and hour of Christ's return (Matt 24:36), an event that will only occur upon the completion of the Great Commission. But the preaching of the gospel around the world is something that human beings *freely* do and therefore is a matter of future contingency. This is powerful evidence that God does know future contingents, a great many of them as it turns out. Of course, this is but one instance of numerous biblical passages which underscore God's knowledge of human choices well in advance of their occurrence, from Old Testament prophecies about the fates of whole cities and nations (e.g., Jer 49:16; Ezek 26:12; Nah 1:10) to Jesus' prediction of Peter's three-fold denial of Christ (e.g., Matt 26:33–35). Such passages firmly establish God's sovereignty over the macro- as well as micro-events of history. So even though Arbour does not explicitly emphasize it here, the most significant practical upshot of his study pertains to the reasonableness of our personal trust in the sovereign Lord of Scripture. We can be confident in God's promises for the eschaton and for our individual lives, precisely because he knows the future in its entirety, and he meticulously governs all things according to his morally perfect will. This confidence was central to the faith and life of Ben Arbour, so it is no surprise that he would devote several years of research and writing to its philosophical defense. I suspect that Arbour would be (or, if I may, *is*) pleased to see it in print. And I am certain he would want me to reiterate his standard acknowledgment regarding all of his scholarly work and everything else he did: *Soli Deo Gloria*.

—James S. Spiegel

Bibliography

Abraham, W. E. "Is the Concept of Necessary Existence Self-Contradictory?" *Inquiry* 5 (1962) 43–47.

Abraham, William J. "The Existence of God." In *The Oxford Handbook of Systematic Theology*, edited by John Webster et al., 19–34. New York: Oxford University Press, 2007.

Adams, Marilyn McCord. "Is the Existence of God a 'Hard' Fact?" *Philosophical Review* 76 (1967) 492–503.

———. *William Ockham*. 2 vols. Notre Dame: University of Notre Dame Press, 1987.

Adams, Robert Merrihew. "Actualism and Thisness." *Synthese* 49 (1981) 3–41.

———. "Divine Necessity." *Journal of Philosophy* 80 (1983) 741–52. Reprinted in *The Virtue of Faith and Other Essays in Philosophical Theology*, 209–20. New York: Oxford University Press, 1987.

———. "Has It Been Proven That All Real Existence Is Contingent?" *American Philosophical Quarterly* 8 (1971) 284–91. Reprinted in *The Virtue of Faith and Other Essays in Philosophical Theology*, 195–208. New York: Oxford University Press, 1987.

———. "The Logical Structure of Anselm's Arguments." *Philosophical Review* 80 (1971) 28–54. Reprinted in *The Virtue of Faith and Other Essays in Philosophical Theology*, 221–42. New York: Oxford University Press, 1987.

———. "Presumption and the Necessary Existence of God." *Noûs* 22 (1988) 19–32.

———. "Primitive Thisness and Primitive Identity." *Journal of Philosophy* 76 (1979) 5–26.

———. "Theories of Actuality." *Noûs* 8 (1974) 211–31.

———. "Thisness and Time Travel." *Philosophia* 25 (1997) 405–15.

———. "Time and Thisness." *Midwest Studies in Philosophy* 11 (1986) 315–29.

———. *The Virtue of Faith and Other Essays in Philosophical Theology*. New York: Oxford University Press, 1987.

Alcoff, Linda, and Elizabeth Potter, eds. *Feminist Epistemologies*. London: Routledge, 1992.

Alston, William P. "Divine Foreknowledge and Alternative Conceptions of Human Freedom." *International Journal for Philosophy* 18 (1985) 19–32. Reprinted in *Divine Nature and Human Language: Essays in Philosophical Theology*, 162–77. Ithaca, NY: Cornell University Press, 1989.

———. *Divine Nature and Human Language: Essays in Philosophical Theology*. Ithaca, NY: Cornell University Press, 1989.

———. "Does God Have Beliefs?" *Religious Studies* 22 (1987) 287–306. Reprinted in *Divine Nature and Human Language: Essays in Philosophical Theology*, 178–93. Ithaca, NY: Cornell University Press, 1989.

———. "God's Action in the World." In *Divine Nature and Human Language: Essays in Philosophical Theology*, 197–222. Ithaca, NY: Cornell University Press, 1989.

———. "The Ontological Argument Revisited." *Philosophical Review* 69 (1960) 452–74.

———. *A Realist Conception of Truth*. Ithaca, NY: Cornell University Press, 1996.

Alter, Torin. "On Two Alleged Conflicts Between Divine Attributes." *Faith and Philosophy* 19 (2002) 47–57.

Anderson, James, and Greg Welty. "The Lord of Non-Contradiction." *Philosophia Christi* 13 (2011) 321–38.

Anglin, W. S. "Can God Create a Being He Cannot Control?" *Analysis* 40 (1980) 220–23.

———. *Free Will and the Christian Faith*. Oxford: Clarendon, 1990.

Anscombe, G. E. M. "Aristotle and the Sea Battle." *Mind* 65.257 (1956) 1–15.

———. *Causality and Determination*. New York: Cambridge University Press, 1971.

Anselm of Canterbury. *Proslogion*. In *The Major Works*, edited by Brian Davies and G. R. Evans, 82–104. New York: Oxford University Press, 1998.

The Ante-Nicene Fathers. Edited by Alexander Roberts and James Donaldson. 1885–87. 10 vols. Reprint, Peabody, MA: Hendrickson, 1999.

Aquinas, St. Thomas. *On the Eternality of the World*. Edited and translated by Ralph McInerny. London: Penguin, 1998.

———. *Summa Contra Gentiles*. 5 vols. South Bend, IN: University of Notre Dame Press, 1992.

———. *Summa Theologica*. 5 vols. Translated by the Fathers of the English Dominican Province. Westminster, MD: Christian Classics, 1981.

Arbour, Benjamin H. "Future Freedom and the Fixity of Truth: Closing the Road to Limited Foreknowledge Open Theism." *International Journal for Philosophy of Religion* 73 (2013) 189–207.

———, ed. *Philosophical Essays Against Open Theism*. New York: Routledge, 2019.

———. "Unqualified Divine Temporality and the Problem of Omnipotence." Unpublished paper presented at the Annual Congress of the Evangelical Philosophical Society, Milwaukee, WI, Nov. 14, 2012.

———. "When Does God Learn What He Learns? Open Theism, Simultaneous Causation, and Divine Knowledge of the Present." In *God, Mind, and Knowledge*, edited by Andrew Moore, 103–20. The British Society for Philosophy of Religion 2. London: Ashgate, 2014.

Arbour, Benjamin H., and Douglas K. Blount. "The Camel's Nose: Open Theism and Biblical Interpretation." *Bibliotheca Sacra* 171 (2014) 274–88.

Aristotle. *Categories and De Interpretatione*. Translated by J. L. Ackrill. New York: Oxford University Press, 1975.

Armstrong, D. M. *Sketch for a Systematic Metaphysics*. New York: Oxford University Press, 2010.

———. *Truth and Truthmakers*. Cambridge Studies in Philosophy. New York: Cambridge University Press, 2004.

———. *A World of States of Affairs*. Cambridge Studies in Philosophy. New York: Cambridge University Press, 1997.

Augustine. *Confessions*. Translated by John K. Ryan. Colorado Springs: Image, 1960.
———. *The Trinity*. Translated by Edmund Hill. Hyde Park, NY: New City, 1991.
Ayer, Alfred Jules. *Language, Truth, and Logic*. New York: Dover, 1952.
Baia, Alex. "Presentism and the Grounding of Truth." *Philosophical Studies* 159 (2012) 341–56.
Baker, Deane-Peter, ed. *Alvin Plantinga*. Contemporary Philosophy in Focus. New York: Cambridge University Press, 2007.
Barnes, Elizabeth, and Ross Cameron. "The Open Future: Bivalence, Determinism and Ontology." *Philosophical Studies* 146 (2009) 291–309.
Barr, James. *Biblical Words for Time*. 2nd ed. London: SCM, 1969.
Basil the Great. *On the Holy Spirit*. Crestwood, NY: St. Vladimir's Seminary Press, 1980.
Basinger, David. "Can an Evangelical Christian Justifiably Deny God's Knowledge of the Future?" *Christian Scholar's Review* 25 (1995) 133–45.
———. *The Case for Freewill Theism: A Philosophical Assessment*. Downers Grove, IL: InterVarsity, 1996.
———. "Divine Omniscience and Human Freedom: A Middle Knowledge Perspective." *Faith and Philosophy* 1 (1984) 291–302.
———. "Divine Omniscience and the Best of All Possible Worlds." *Journal of Value Inquiry* 16 (1982) 143–48.
———. *Divine Power in Process Theism: A Philosophical Critique*. New York: State University of New York Press, 1988.
———. "Middle Knowledge and Classical Christian Thought." *Religious Studies* 22 (1986) 407–22.
———. "Omniscience and Deliberation: A Response to Reichenbach." *International Journal for Philosophy of Religion* 20 (1986) 169–72.
Basinger, David, and Randall Basinger, eds. *Predestination and Free Will: Four Views of Divine Sovereignty and Human Freedom*. Downers Grove, IL: InterVarsity, 1986.
Basinger, David, et al., eds. *Philosophy of Religion: Selected Readings*. 3rd ed. New York: Oxford University Press, 2007.
Basinger, David, et al. *The Openness of God: A Biblical Challenge to the Traditional Understanding of God*. Downers Grove, IL: InterVarsity, 1994.
Bauckham, Richard. *Jesus and the God of Israel: God Crucified and Other Studies on the New Testament's Christology of Divine Identity*. Grand Rapids: Eerdmans, 2008.
Beard, Robert W. "Is God's Non-Existence Conceivable?" *Southern Journal of Philosophy* 18 (1980) 251–57.
———. "Professor Lucas on Omniscience." *International Journal for Philosophy of Religion* 20 (1986) 37–43.
Beebee, Helen, et al., eds. *The Oxford Handbook of Causation*. New York: Oxford University Press, 2010.
Beer, Michelle. "Temporal Indexicals and the Passage of Time." *Philosophical Quarterly* 38 (1988) 158–64.
Beilby, James K., and Paul R. Eddy, eds. *Divine Foreknowledge: Four Views*. Downers Grove, IL: InterVarsity, 2001.
Belnap, Nuel. "Branching Space-Time." *Synthese* 92 (1992) 385–434.
Belnap, Nuel, and Mitchell Green. "Indeterminism and the Thin Red Line." *Philosophical Perspectives* 8 (1994) 365–88.
Bergmann, Michael. "(Serious) Actualism and (Serious) Presentism." *Noûs* 33 (1999) 118–32.

Bergmann, Michael, and J. A. Cover. "Divine Responsibility Without Divine Freedom." *Faith and Philosophy* 23 (2006) 381–408.

Bernstein, C'Zar. "Giving the Ontological Argument its Due." *Philosophia* 42 (2014) 665–79.

———. "Is God's Existence Possible?" *Heythrop Journal* 56 (2014) 424–32. https://onlinelibrary.wiley.com/doi/10.1111/heyj.12132.

Bird, Alexander. *Nature's Metaphysics: Laws and Properties*. New York: Oxford University Press, 2007.

Black, Max. "The Identity of Indiscernibles." *Mind* 61 (1952) 153–64.

Blount, Douglas K. "An Essay on Divine Presence." PhD diss., University of Notre Dame, 1997.

———. "Togas, Tulips, and the Philosophy of Openness." *Southwestern Journal of Theology* 47 (2005) 177–89.

Boethius. *The Consolation of Philosophy*. Translated by Richard Green. New York: Pearson, 1962.

———. *De Trinitate (On the Trinity)*. Translated by H. F. Stewart and E. K. Rand. In *The Theological Tractates and The Consolation of Philosophy*. Rev. ed. LCL 287. Cambridge: Harvard University Press, 1978.

Bohm, David, and B. J. Hiley. *The Undivided Universe: An Ontological Interpretation of Quantum Theory*. London: Routledge, 1993.

Bolc, Leonard, and Piotr Borowik. *Many-Valued Logics*. 2 vols. Berlin: Springer, 1992–2003.

Bourne, Craig. "Fatalism and the Future." In *The Oxford Handbook of Philosophy of Time*, edited by Craig Callender, 41–67. New York: Oxford University Press, 2011.

———. *A Future for Presentism*. New York: Oxford University Press, 2006.

Boyd, Gregory A. "Christian Love and Academic Dialogue: A Reply to Ware." *Journal of the Evangelical Theological Society* 45 (2002) 233–43.

———. *God of the Possible*. Grand Rapids: Baker, 2000.

———. "The Open-Theism View." In *The Openness of God: A Biblical Challenge to the Traditional Understanding of God*, edited by Clark H. Pinnock et al., 13–47. Downers Grove, IL: InterVarsity, 1994.

———. *Satan and the Problem of Evil: Constructing a Trinitarian Warfare Theodicy*. Downers Grove, IL: InterVarsity, 2001.

Bray, Gerald. *The Personal God: Is the Classical Understanding of God Tenable?* Carlisle: Paternoster, 1998.

Brown, T. Patterson. "St. Thomas' Doctrine of Necessary Being." *Philosophical Review* 73 (1964) 76–90.

Cahn, Steven M. *Fate, Logic, and Time*. Atascadero, CA: Ridgeview, 1967.

Calvin, John. *Institutes of the Christian Religion*. Edited by John T. McNeill. Translated by Ford Lewis Battles. Vol. 1. Louisville: Westminster John Knox, 1960.

Cameron, Ross P. *The Moving Spotlight: An Essay on Time and Ontology*. New York: Oxford University Press, 2015.

Carlson, Erik. "Incompatibilism and the Transfer of Power Necessity." *Noûs* 34 (2000) 277–90.

Castañeda, Hector-Neri. "Omniscience and Indexical Reference." *Journal of Philosophy* 64 (1967) 203–10.

Chandler, Hugh S. "Some Ontological Arguments." *Faith and Philosophy* 10 (1993) 18–32.

Chisholm, R. M. "Agents, Causes, and Events: The Problem of Free Will." In *Agents, Causes, and Events*, edited by Timothy O'Connor, 95–100. New York: Oxford University Press, 1995.

———. "Identity Through Possible Worlds: Some Questions." *Noûs* 1 (1967) 1–8.

Chisholm, Roderick M., and Dean W. Zimmerman. "Theology and Tense." *Noûs* 31 (1997) 262–65.

Clarke, Randolph. "Libertarian Views: Critical Survey of Noncausal and Event-Causal Accounts." In *The Oxford Handbook of Free Will*, edited by Robert Kane, 356–85. New York: Oxford University Press, 2002.

———. "Toward a Credible Agent-Causal Account of Free Will." *Noûs* 27 (1993) 191–203. Reprinted in *Agents, Causes, and Events*, edited by Timothy O'Connor, 201–15. New York: Oxford University Press, 1995.

Coburn, Robert C. "Professor Malcolm on God." *Australasian Journal of Philosophy* 41 (1963) 143–62.

Code, Lorraine. "Taking Subjectivity into Account." In *Feminist Epistemologies*, edited by Linda Alcoff and Elizabeth Potter, 15–48. London: Routledge, 1993.

Conee, E. "The Possibility of Power Beyond Possibility." *Philosophical Perspectives* 5 (1991) 447–73.

Craig, William Lane. "#148 Causation and Spacetime." *Reasonable Faith with William Lane Craig*, Feb. 15, 2010. https://www.reasonablefaith.org/question-answer/p40/causation-and-spacetime.

———. "Adams on Actualism and Presentism." *Philosophia* 25 (1997) 401–5.

———. "The Caused Beginning of the Universe: A Response to Quentin Smith." *British Journal for the Philosophy of Science* 44 (1993) 623–39.

———. *The Cosmological Argument: From Plato to Leibniz*. Eugene, OR: Wipf and Stock, 2001.

———. "Creation and Big Bang Cosmology." *Philosophia Naturalis* 31 (1994) 217–24.

———. "Creation and Conservation Once More." *Religious Studies* 34 (1998) 177–88.

———. "A Critique of Grudem's Formulation and Defense of the Doctrine of Eternity." *Philosophia Christi* 19 (1996) 33–38.

———. "Divine Eternity." In *The Oxford Handbook to Philosophical Theology*, edited by Thomas P. Flint and Michael C. Rea, 145–66. New York: Oxford University Press, 2009.

———. *Divine Foreknowledge and Human Freedom: The Coherence of Theism: Omniscience*. New York: Brill, 1991.

———. "Divine Foreknowledge and Newcomb's Paradox." *Philosophia* 17 (1987) 331–50.

———. "Divine Timelessness and Necessary Existence." *International Philosophical Quarterly* 37 (1997) 217–24.

———. "Divine Timelessness and Personhood." *International Journal for Philosophy of Religion* 43 (1998) 109–24.

———. "The Eternal Present and Stump-Kretzmann Eternity." *American Catholic Philosophical Quarterly* 73 (1999) 521–36.

———. "God and the Beginning of Time." *International Philosophical Quarterly* 41 (2001) 17–31.

———. "God and Real Time." *Religious Studies* 26 (1990) 335–47.

———. "God, Time, and Eternity." *Religious Studies* 14 (1979) 497–503.

———. *God, Time, and Eternity: The Coherence of Theism II: Eternity*. New York: Springer, 2001.

———. "Graham Oppy on the *Kalam* Cosmological Argument." *Sophia* 32 (1993) 1–11.

———. "Hasker on Divine Knowledge." *Philosophical Studies* 67 (1992) 89–110.

———. "Is Presentness a Property?" *American Philosophical Quarterly* 34 (1997) 27–40.

———. *The Kalam Cosmological Argument*. Eugene, OR: Wipf and Stock, 2000.

———. "McTaggart's Paradox and the Problem of Temporal Intrinsics." *Analysis* 58 (1998) 122–27.

———. "Middle Knowledge, TruthMakers, and the Grounding Objection." *Faith and Philosophy* 18 (2001) 337–52.

———. "Omniscience, Tensed Facts, and Divine Eternity." *Faith and Philosophy* 17 (2000) 225–41.

———. *The Only Wise God: The Compatibility of Divine Foreknowledge and Human Freedom*. Eugene, OR: Wipf and Stock, 2000.

———. "On the Alleged Metaphysical Superiority of Timelessness." *Sophia* 37 (1998) 1–9.

———. "On the Argument for Divine Timelessness from the Incompleteness of Temporal Life." *Heythrop Journal* 38 (1997) 165–71.

———. "The Ontological Argument." In *To Everyone An Answer: A Case for the Christian Worldview*, edited by Francis J. Beckwith et al., 124–37. Downers Grove, IL: InterVarsity, 2004.

———. "Professor Grünbaum on Creation." *Erkenntnis* 40 (1994) 325–41.

———. "Professor Mackie and the Kalam Cosmological Argument." *Religious Studies* 20 (1985) 367–75.

———. "A Response to Grünbaum on Creation and Big Bang Cosmology." *Philosophia Naturalis* 31 (1994) 237–49.

———. Review of *Eternal God*, by Paul Helm. *Journal of the Evangelical Theological Society* 36 (1993) 254–55.

———. "The Special Theory of Relativity and Theories of Divine Eternity." *Faith and Philosophy* 11 (1994) 19–37.

———. "A Swift and Simple Refutation of the *Kalam* Cosmological Argument?" *Religious Studies* 35 (1999) 57–72.

———. "Temporal Necessity: Hard Facts/Soft Facts." *International Journal for Philosophy of Religion* 20 (1986) 65–91.

———. "The Tensed vs. Tenseless Theory of Time: A Watershed for the Conception of Divine Eternity." In *Questions of Time and Tense*, edited by Robin Le Poidevin, 221–50. Oxford: Clarendon, 1998.

———. *The Tenseless Theory of Time: A Critical Examination*. Synthese Library. Dordrecht: Kluwer Academic, 2000.

———. "Timelessness and Creation." *Australasian Journal of Philosophy* 74 (1996) 646–56.

———. "Timelessness and Omnitemporality." *Philosophia Christi* 2 (2000) 29–33.

Craig, William Lane, and David Hunt. "The Perils of the Open Road." *Faith and Philosophy* 30 (2013) 49–71.

Craig, William Lane, and J. P. Moreland, eds. *The Blackwell Companion to Natural Theology*. Oxford: Wiley-Blackwell, 2009.

Craig, William Lane, and Quentin Smith, eds. *Einstein, Relativity, and Absolute Simultaneity*. New York: Routledge, 2008.

Creel, Richard. "Can God Know That He Is God?" *Religious Studies* 16 (1980) 195–201.

Crisp, Oliver D., ed. *A Reader in Contemporary Philosophical Theology*. Edinburgh: T&T Clark, 2009.

Crisp, Oliver D., and Michael C. Rea. *Analytic Theology: New Essays in the Philosophy of Theology*. New York: Oxford University Press, 2009.

Crisp, Thomas M. "Comments on Thomas P. Flint's 'The Varieties of Accidental Necessity.'" In *Science, Religion, and Metaphysics: New Essays on the Philosophy of Alvin Plantinga*, edited by Michael C. Rea and Kelly James Clark, 54–60. New York: Oxford University Press, 2012.

———. "In Defense of Presentism." PhD diss., University of Notre Dame, 2002.

———. "On Divine Foreknowledge and Newcomb's Paradox." *Philosophia Christi* 1 (1999) 33–42.

———. "On Presentism and Triviality." *Oxford Studies in Metaphysics* 1 (2004) 15–20.

———. "Presentism." In *The Oxford Handbook of Metaphysics*, edited by Michael J. Loux and Dean W. Zimmerman, 211–45. New York: Oxford University Press, 2003.

———. "Presentism and Cross-Time Relations." *American Philosophical Quarterly* 42 (2005) 5–17.

———. "Presentism and the Grounding Objection." *Noûs* 41 (2007) 90–109.

———. "Reply to Ludlow." *Oxford Studies in Metaphysics* 1 (2004) 37–46.

Crisp, Thomas M., and Donald P. Smith. "'Wholly Present' Defined." *Philosophy and Phenomenological Research* 71 (2005) 318–44.

Cunningham, Arthur J. "Where Hasker's Anti-Molinist Argument Goes Wrong." *Faith and Philosophy* 33 (2016) 200–222.

Dainton, Barry. "Time, Passage, and Immediate Experience." In *The Oxford Handbook of Philosophy of Time*, edited by Craig Callender, 382–419. New York: Oxford University Press, 2011.

Dalmiya, Vrinda. "Why Should a Knower Care?" *Hypatia* 17 (2002) 34–52.

Dalmiya, Vrinda, and Linda Alcoff. "Are 'Old Wives' Tales' Justified?" In *Feminist Epistemologies*, edited by Linda Alcoff and Elizabeth Potter, 217–44. London: Routledge, 1993.

Davies, Brian. "Simplicity." In *The Cambridge Companion to Christian Philosophical Theology*, edited by Charles Taliaferro and Chad Meister, 31–45. New York: Cambridge University Press, 2010.

Davis, Richard. "God and Modal Concretism." *Philosophia Christi* 10 (2008) 37–54.

Davis, Stephen T. "Anselm and Question-Begging: A Reply to William Rowe." *International Journal for Philosophy of Religion* 7 (1976) 448–57.

———. "Does the Ontological Argument Beg the Question?" *International Journal for Philosophy of Religion* 7 (1976) 433–42.

———. *Logic and the Nature of God*. Grand Rapids: Eerdmans, 1983.

Deasy, Daniel. "The Moving Spotlight Theory." *Philosophical Studies* 172 (2015) 2073–89.

Dekker, Jack C. *Middle Knowledge*. Louvain: Peeters, 2000.

DeRose, Keith. "Epistemic Possibilities." *Philosophical Review* 100 (1991) 581–605.

Descartes, Rene. *Meditations on First Philosophy: In Which the Existence of God and the Distinction of the Soul from the Body are Demonstrated.* Indianapolis: Hackett, 1993.

DeWesse, Garrett J. *God and the Nature of Time.* Ashgate Philosophy of Religion Series. Burlington, VT: Ashgate, 2004.

———. "Timeless God, Tenseless Time." *Philosophia Christi* 2 (2000) 53–59.

Diekemper, Joseph. "B-Theory, Fixity, and Fatalism." *Noûs* 41 (2007) 429–52.

———. "Eternity, Knowledge, and Freedom." *Religious Studies* 49 (2013) 45–64.

———. "Logical Determinateness, Fixity, and the Symmetry of Time." *Philosophical Papers* 34 (2005) 1–24.

———. "Presentism and Ontological Symmetry." *Australasian Journal of Philosophy* 83 (2005) 223–40.

———. "Temporal Necessity and Logical Fatalism." *Proceedings of the Aristotelian Society* 104 (2004) 287–94.

———. "Thisness and Events." *Journal of Philosophy* 106 (2009) 255–76.

Divers, John. "The Modal Metaphysics of Alvin Plantinga." In *Alvin Plantinga*, edited by Deane-Peter Baker, 71–92. Contemporary Philosophy in Focus. New York: Cambridge University Press, 2007.

———. *Possible Worlds.* The Problems of Philosophy. New York: Routledge, 2002.

Dolezal, James E. *God Without Parts: Divine Simplicity and the Metaphysics of God's Absoluteness.* Eugene, OR: Pickwick, 2011.

Dombrowski, Daniel A. *Rethinking the Ontological Argument: A Neoclassical Theistic Response.* New York: Cambridge University Press, 2006.

Dowe, Phil. "Causal Process Theories." In *The Oxford Handbook of Causation*, edited by Helen Beebee et al., 185–212. New York: Oxford University Press, 2010.

———. "Process Causality and Asymmetry." In *Laws of Nature, Causation, and Supervenience*, edited by Michael Tooley, 265–82. Analytic Metaphysics 1. New York: Routledge, 1999.

Downey, James P. "On Omniscience." *Faith and Philosophy* 10 (1993) 230–34.

Dyke, Heather. "Real Times and Possible Worlds." In *Questions of Time and Tense*, edited by Robin Le Poidevin, 93–117. New York: Oxford University Press, 1998.

Edwards, Jonathan. *Freedom of the Will.* Edited by Paul Ramsey. The Works of Jonathan Edwards 1. New Haven: Yale University Press, 1957.

Egan, Andy, and Brian Weatherson, eds. *Epistemic Modality.* Oxford: Oxford University Press, 2011.

Ekstrom, Laura W. "Free Will Is Not a Mystery." In *The Oxford Handbook of Free Will*, edited by Robert Kane, 366–80. 2nd ed. New York: Oxford University Press, 2011.

———. "Libertarianism and Frankfurt-Style Cases." *Midwest Studies in Philosophy* 29 (2005) 309–22.

Erickson, Millard. *What Does God Know and When Does He Know It? The Current Controversy over Divine Foreknowledge.* Grand Rapids: Zondervan, 2003.

Everett, Anthony. "Against Fictional Realism." *Journal of Philosophy* 102 (2005) 624–49.

Farmer, Daniel Diedrich. "Defining Omniscience: A Feminist Perspective." *Faith and Philosophy* 27 (2010) 306–20.

Fields, Chase. "Perfect Being Theology: Two Worries." Unpublished paper presented at the Annual Meeting of the Evangelical Philosophical Society, Atlanta, GA, Nov. 19, 2010.

Finch, Alicia, and Michael Rea. "Presentism and Ockham's Way Out." *Oxford Studies in Philosophy of Religion* 1 (2008) 1–17.

Findlay, J. N. "Can God's Existence Be Disproved?" In *New Essays in Philosophical Theology*, edited by Anthony Flew and Alasdair MacIntyre, 49–55. New York: Macmillan, 1955.

———. "Plantinga on the Reduction of Possibilist Discourse." In *Alvin Plantinga*, edited by James E. Tomberlin and Peter van Inwagen, 145–86. Profiles 5. Dordrecht: Reidel, 1985.

Fine, Kit. *Modality and Tense*. New York: Oxford University Press, 2005.

———. "Plantinga on the Reduction of Possible Worlds to Sets of Possible Worlds." In *Alvin Plantinga*, edited by James E. Tomberlin and Peter van Inwagen, 145–86. Profiles 5. Dordrecht: Reidel, 1985.

Fischer, John Martin, et al. "Engaging with Pike: God, Freedom, and Time." *Philosophical Papers* 38 (2009) 247–70.

———. "Foreknowledge and Freedom." *Faith and Philosophy* 19 (2002) 89–93.

———. "Foreknowledge, Freedom, and the Fixity of the Past." *Philosophia* 39 (2011) 461–74.

———, et al. *Four Views on Free Will*. Great Debates in Philosophy. Oxford: Blackwell, 2007.

———. "Frankfurt-Type Examples and Semicompatibilism: New Work." In *The Oxford Handbook of Free Will*. 2nd ed., edited by Robert Kane, 243–65. New York: Oxford University Press, 2011.

———. "Freedom and Foreknowledge." *Philosophical Review* 92 (1983) 67–79.

———, ed. *God, Foreknowledge, and Freedom*. Stanford: Stanford University Press, 1989.

———. "Hard-Type Soft Facts." *Philosophical Review* 95 (1986) 591–601.

———. "Libertarianism and Avoidability: A Reply to Widerker." *Faith and Philosophy* 12 (1995) 119–25.

———. *The Metaphysics of Free Will: An Essay on Control*. Oxford: Blackwell, 1994.

———. "Molinism." In *Oxford Studies in Philosophy of Religion*, edited by Jonathan Kvanvig, 1:18–43. New York: Oxford University Press, 2008.

———. *Moral Responsibility*. Ithaca, NY: Cornell University Press, 1986.

Fischer, John Martin, and Neal Tognazzini. "Omniscience, Freedom, and Dependence." *Philosophy and Phenomenological Research* 88 (2014) 346–67.

Fischer, John Martin, and Patrick Todd. "The Truth About Foreknowledge." *Faith and Philosophy* 30 (2013) 286–301.

Fitzgerald, P. "Stump and Kretzmann on Time and Eternity." *Journal of Philosophy* 82 (1985) 260–69.

Flew, Antony, and Alasdair MacIntyre, eds. *New Essays in Philosophical Theology*. New York: Macmillan, 1955.

Flint, Thomas P. "Compatibilism and the Argument from Unavoidability." *Journal of Philosophy* 84 (1987) 423–40.

———. "Divine Providence." In *The Oxford Handbook of Philosophical Theology*, edited by Thomas P. Flint and Michael Rea, 262–85. New York: Oxford University Press, 2009.

———. *Divine Providence: The Molinist Account*. Ithaca, NY: Cornell University Press, 1998.

———. "Hasker's *God, Time, and Knowledge*." *Philosophical Studies* 60 (1990) 103–15.

———. "In Defence of Theological Compatibilism." *Faith and Philosophy* 8 (1991) 237–43.

———. "Middle Knowledge and the Doctrine of Infallibility." *Philosophical Perspectives* 5 (1991) 373–93.

———. "Omniscience." In *The Routledge Encyclopedia of Philosophy*, edited by Edward Craig, 7:107–12. London: Routledge, 1998.

———. "The Problem of Divine Freedom." *American Philosophical Quarterly* 20 (1983) 255–64.

———. "Risky Business: Open Theism and the Incarnation." *Philosophia Christi* 6 (2004) 213–33.

———. "The Varieties of Accidental Necessity." In *Science, Religion, and Metaphysics: New Essays on the Philosophy of Alvin Plantinga*, edited by Kelly Clark and Michael Rea, 38–54. Oxford: Oxford University Press, 2012.

Flint, Thomas P., and Alfred J. Freddoso. "Maximal Power." In *The Existence and Nature of God*, edited by Alfred J. Freddoso, 81–113. University of Notre Dame Studies in the Philosophy of Religion 3. Notre Dame: University of Notre Dame Press, 1983.

Flint, Thomas P., and Michael C. Rea, eds. *The Oxford Handbook of Philosophical Theology*. New York: Oxford University Press, 2009.

Forbes, Graeme. "Logic, Logical Form, and the Open Future." *Philosophical Perspectives* 10 (1996) 73–92.

Forgie, J. William. "The Modal Ontological Argument and the Necessary *a posteriori*." *International Journal for Philosophy of Religion* 29 (1991) 129–41.

Forrest, Peter. "General Facts, Physical Necessity, and the Metaphysics of Time." *Oxford Studies in Metaphysics* 2 (2006) 137–52.

Francks, Richard. "Omniscience, Omnipotence, and Pantheism." *Philosophy* 54 (1979) 395–99.

Frankfurt, Harry G. "Alternate Possibilities and Moral Responsibility." *Journal of Philosophy* 66 (1969) 828–39.

———. "The Logic of Omnipotence." *Philosophical Review* 73 (1964) 262–63.

Freddoso, Alfred J. "Accidental Necessity and Logical Determinism." *Journal of Philosophy* 80 (1983) 257–78.

———. "Accidental Necessity and Power over the Past." *Pacific Philosophical Quarterly* 63 (1982) 54–68.

———, ed. *The Existence and Nature of God*. University of Notre Dame Studies in the Philosophy of Religion 3. Notre Dame: University of Notre Dame Press, 1983.

———. Introduction to *On Divine Foreknowledge (Part IV of the Concordia)*, by Luis de Molina. Translated with notes by Alfred J. Freddoso. Ithaca, NY: Cornell University Press, 1988.

Frege, Gottlob. "On Sense and Reference." Reprinted in *Meaning and Reference*, edited by A. W. Moore, translated by Max Black, 23–42. Oxford: Oxford University Press, 1993.

———. "Thought." In *Logic and Philosophy: Selected Readings*, edited by John B. Shartley and John E. Smith, translated by A. M. Quinton and Marcelle Quinton, 325–45. Boston: Allyn and Bacon, 1970.

Fretheim, Terence E. *The Suffering of God: An Old Testament Perspective*. Philadelphia: Fortress, 1984.

Gale, R. *On the Nature and Existence of God*. Notre Dame: University of Notre Dame Press, 1991.

Ganssle, Gregory. "Atemporality and the Mode of Divine Knowledge." *International Journal for Philosophy of Religion* 34 (1993) 171–80.

———. "Does the B-Theory of Time Entail Fatalism? A Reply to Hasker." *International Philosophical Quarterly* 35 (1995) 217–18.

———. "God's Knowledge of the Future." Unpublished paper presented at the Society of Christian Philosophers' Eastern Regional Meeting, Apr. 1998.

———, ed. *God and Time: Four Views*. Downers Grove, IL: InterVarsity, 2001.

Ganssle, Gregory E., and David M. Woodruff, eds. *God and Time: Essays on the Divine Nature*. New York: Oxford University Press, 2002.

Geach, Peter. "Can God Fail to Keep Promises?" *Philosophy* 52 (1977) 93–95.

———. *Providence and Evil*. New York: Cambridge University Press, 1977.

Geisler, Norman L. *Creating God in the Image of Man? The New "Open" View of God—Neotheism's Dangerous Drift*. Minneapolis: Bethany House, 1997.

———. "The Missing Premise in the Ontological Argument." *Religious Studies* 9 (1973) 289–96.

Gellman, Jerome. "The Limits of Maximal Power." *Philosophical Studies* 55 (1989) 329–36.

———. "Omnipotence and Impeccability." *New Scholasticism* 51 (1977) 21–37.

———. "The Paradox of Omnipotence, and Perfection." *Sophia* 14 (1975) 31–39.

Glanzberg, Michael, "Against Truth-Value Gaps." In *Liars and Heaps: New Essays on Paradox*, edited by J. C. Beall, 151–94. New York: Oxford University Press, 1990.

Goldstein, Sheldon. "Bohmian Mechanics." In *Stanford Encyclopedia of Philosophy*, edited by Edward N. Zalta and Uri Nodelman, Mar. 4, 2013. https://plato.stanford.edu/archives/spr2013/entries/qm-bohm/.

Gottwald, Siegfried. "Many-Valued Logic." In *Stanford Encyclopedia of Philosophy*, edited by Edward N. Zalta and Uri Nodelman. https://plato.stanford.edu/archives/win2025/entries/logic-manyvalued/.

Gould, Paul, ed. *Beyond the Control of God? Six Views on the Problem of God and Abstract Objects*. New York: Bloomsbury, 2014.

Grace, Justin. "Referring to God: Whom Do Christians Worship and What Do Muslims Talk About?" PhD diss., Southwestern Baptist Theological Seminary, 2011.

Green, Jeffrey, and Katherin Rogers. "Time, Foreknowledge, and Alternative Possibilities." *Religious Studies* 48 (2012) 151–64.

Grice, H. Paul. *Studies in the Way of Words*. Cambridge: Harvard University Press, 1989.

Grim, Patrick. "Against Omniscience: The Case from Essential Indexicals." *Noûs* 19 (1985) 151–80.

———. "Impossibility Arguments." In *The Cambridge Companion to Atheism*, edited by Michael Martin, 199–214. New York: Cambridge University Press, 2007.

———. "In Behalf of 'In Behalf of the Fool.'" *International Journal for Philosophy of Religion* 13 (1982) 33–42.

———. "Logic and the Limits of Language." *Noûs* 22 (1988) 341–67.

———. "On Omniscience and a 'Set of All Truths': A Reply to Bringsjord." *Analysis* 50 (1990) 271–76.

———. "Plantinga's God." *Sophia* 18 (1979) 35–42.

———. "Some Neglected Problems of Omniscience." *American Philosophical Quarterly* 20 (1983) 265–76.

Grünbaum, Adolf. "Some Comments on William Craig's 'Creation and Big Bang Cosmology.'" *Philosophica Naturalis* 31 (1994) 225–36.

Haack, Susan. *Deviant Logic, Fuzzy Logic: Beyond the Formalism*. Chicago: University of Chicago Press, 1996.

———. "On a Theological Argument for Fatalism." *Philosophical Quarterly* 25 (1975) 156–59.

Hall, Christopher, and John Sanders. *Does God Have a Future? A Debate on Divine Providence*. Grand Rapids: Baker Academic, 2003.

Harnack, Adolf von. *History of Dogma*. 7 Vols. Eugene, OR: Wipf and Stock, 1997.

Harrison, C. "The Ontological Argument in Modal Logic." *Monist* 54 (1970) 302–13.

Hartshorne, Charles. *Anselm's Discovery: A Re-Examination of the Ontological Proof for God's Existence*. LaSalle, IL: Open Court, 1965.

———. *The Logic of Perfection*. LaSalle, IL: Open Court, 1962.

———. "The Logic of the Ontological Argument." *Journal of Philosophy* 58 (1961) 471–73.

———. "The Meaning of 'Is Going to Be.'" *Mind* 74 (1965) 46–58.

———. "Necessity." *Review of Metaphysics* 21 (1967) 290–96.

———. *Omnipotence and Other Theological Mistakes*. Albany: SUNY Press, 1984.

Hasker, William. "The Absence of a Timeless God." In *God and Time: Essays on the Divine Nature*, edited by Gregory E. Ganssle and David M. Woodruff, 182–206. New York: Oxford University Press, 2002.

———. "Analytic Philosophy of Religion." In *The Oxford Handbook of Philosophy of Religion*, edited by William J. Wainwright, 421–46. New York: Oxford University Press, 2005.

———. "The Antinomies of Divine Providence." *Philosophia Christi* 4 (2002) 361–76.

———. "Divine Knowledge and Human Freedom." In *The Oxford Handbook of Free Will*, edited by Robert Kane, 39–54. 2nd ed. New York: Oxford University Press, 2011.

———. *The Emergent Self*. Ithaca, NY: Cornell University Press, 1999.

———. "Eternity and Providence." In *The Cambridge Companion to Christian Philosophical Theology*, edited by Charles Taliaferro and Chad Meister, 81–91. New York: Cambridge University Press, 2010.

———. "The Foreknowledge Conundrum." *International Journal for Philosophy of Religion* 50 (2001) 97–114.

———. "Foreknowledge and Necessity." *Faith and Philosophy* 2 (1985) 121–57.

———. *God, Time, and Knowledge*. Cornell Studies in Philosophy of Religion. Ithaca, NY: Cornell University Press, 1989.

———. "Hard Facts and Theological Fatalism." *Noûs* 22 (1988) 419–36.

———. "The Hardness of the Past: A Reply to Reichenbach." *Faith and Philosophy* 4 (1987) 337–42.

———. "Is There a Second Ontological Argument?" *International Journal for Philosophy of Religion* 13 (1982) 93–101.

———. "Middle Knowledge: A Refutation Revisited." *Faith and Philosophy* 12 (1995) 223–26.

———. *Providence, Evil, and the Openness of God*. London: Routledge, 2004.

———. "Theological Incompatibilism and the Necessity of the Present." *Faith and Philosophy* 28 (2011) 224–29.

———. *The Triumph of God over Evil: Theodicy for a World of Suffering*. Downers Grove, IL: InterVarsity Academic, 2008.

———. "Yes, God Has Beliefs!" *Religious Studies* 24 (1988) 385–94.

Hasker, William, et al. *Middle Knowledge: Theory and Applications*. Frankfurt: Lang, 2000.

Hasker, William, et al., eds. *God in an Open Universe: Science, Metaphysics, and Open Theism*. Eugene, OR: Pickwick, 2011.

Hatch, Edwin. *The Influence of Greek Ideas on Christianity*. New York: Harper and Brothers, 1957.

Hays, J. Daniel. "Does God Have Ears? Anthropomorphism, Revelation, and Historicity in the Old Testament." Unpublished paper presented at the Annual Meeting of the Evanglical Theological Society, Atlanta, GA, Nov. 19–21, 2003.

———. "Does Systematics Drive Old Testament Exegesis? Or Can God Still Change His Mind? Questions of Method." Unpublished paper presented at the Annual Meeting of the Evangelical Theological Society, Toronto, Canada, Nov. 20–22, 2002.

Hazen, Allen. "One of the Truths about Actuality." *Analysis* 39 (1979) 1–3.

Helm, Paul. "The Augustinian-Calvinist Response." In *Divine Foreknowledge: Four Views*, edited by James K. Beilby and Paul R. Eddy, 124–33. Downers Grove, IL: InterVarsity, 2001.

———. "Divine Timeless Eternity." *Philosophia Christi* 2 (2000) 21–27.

———. "Does God Take Risks?" In *God, Time, and Eternity: The Coherence of Theism II*, edited by W. L. Craig and P. K. Moser, 218–41. Dordrecht: Kluwer, 2001.

———. "Eternal Creation: The Doctrine of the Two Standpoints." In *The Doctrine of Creation*, edited by Colin Gunton, 29–45. Edinburgh: T&T Clark, 1997.

———. *Eternal God: A Study of God Without Time*. Oxford: Clarendon, 1988.

———. *Eternal God: A Study of God Without Time*. 2nd ed. New York: Oxford University Press, 2010.

———. *The Providence of God*. Contours of Christian Theology. Downers Grove, IL: InterVarsity, 1994.

Helseth, Paul Kjoss, et al., eds. *Beyond the Bounds: Open Theism and the Undermining of Biblical Christianity*. Wheaton, IL: Crossway, 2003.

———. "The Trustworthiness of God and the Foundation of Hope." In *Beyond the Bounds: Open Theism and the Undermining of Biblical Christianity*. Edited by John Piper et al. Wheaton, IL: Crossway, 2003.

Henle, Paul. "Uses of the Ontological Argument." *Philosophical Review* 70 (1961) 102–9.

Hess, Elijah. "Arguing from Molinism to Neo-Molinism." *Philosophia Christi* 17 (2015) 331–52.

———. "Reconciling Divine Foreknowledge and Human Freedom." Unpublished paper.

Hick, John. "Necessary Being." *Scottish Journal of Theology* 14 (1961) 353–69.

Hill, Daniel. *Divinity and Maximal Greatness*. London: Routledge, 2005.

———. "A New Definition of 'Omnipotence' in Terms of Sets." In *New Waves in Philosophy of Religion*, edited by Yujin Nagasawa and Erik J. Wielenberg, 1–21. London: Palgrave MacMillan, 2009.

Hirsch, Eli. "Rashi's View of the Open Future: Indeterminateness and Bivalence." *Oxford Studies in Metaphysics* 2 (2006) 111–36.

Hoefer, Carl. "Causation in Spacetime Theories." In *The Oxford Handbook of Causation*, edited by Helen Beebee et al., 687–706. New York: Oxford University Press, 2010.

———. "Time and Chance Propensities." In *The Oxford Handbook of Philosophy of Time*, edited by Craig Callender, 68–90. New York: Oxford University Press, 2011.

Hoffman, Joshua. "Can God Do Evil?" *Southern Journal of Philosophy* 17 (1979) 213–20.

Hoffman, Joshua, and Gary S. Rosenkrantz. *The Divine Attributes*. Exploring the Philosophy of Religion. Oxford: Blackwell, 2009.

———. "Hard and Soft Facts." *Philosophical Review* 93 (1984) 419–34.

———. "The Omnipotence Paradox, Modality, and Time." *Southern Journal of Philosophy* 18 (1980) 473–79.

———. "Omnipotence Redux." *Philosophy and Phenomenological Research* 49 (1988) 283–301.

Hogg, David S. *Anselm of Canterbury: The Beauty of Theology*. Burlington, VT: Ashgate, 2004.

Holmes, Stephen R. "The Attributes of God." In *The Oxford Handbook of Systematic Theology*, edited by John Webster et al., 54–71. New York: Oxford University Press, 2007.

Holmes, Stephen R., and Murray A. Rae, eds. *The Person of Christ*. New York: T&T Clark, 2005.

Horton, Michael S. *Covenant and Eschatology: The Divine Drama*. Louisville: Westminster John Knox, 2002.

———. *Covenant and Salvation: Union with Christ*. Louisville: Westminster John Knox, 2007.

———. *Lord and Servant: A Covenant Christology*. Louisville: Westminster John Knox, 2005.

———. *People and Place: A Covenant Ecclesiology*. Louisville: Westminster John Knox, 2008.

Horwich, Paul. *Truth*. 2nd ed. New York: Oxford University Press, 1998.

Hudson, Hud. "Omnipresence." In *The Oxford Handbook of Philosophy of Religion*, edited by Thomas P. Flint and Michael C. Rea, 199–216. Oxford: Oxford University Press, 2009.

Huffman, Douglas S., and Eric L. Johnson, eds. *God Under Fire: Modern Scholarship Reinvents God*. Grand Rapids: Zondervan, 2002.

Hughes, Christopher. *Kripke: Names, Necessity, and Identity*. Oxford: Oxford University Press, 2004.

———. "No Way Out?" In *Reason, Faith and History: Philosophical Essays for Paul Helm*, edited by M. W. F. Stone, 47–68. London: Ashgate, 2008.

———. *On a Complex Theory of a Simple God: An Investigation in Aquinas' Philosophical Theology*. Cornell Studies in Philosophy of Religion. Ithaca, NY: Cornell University Press, 1989.

Iseminger, Gary. "Foreknowledge and Necessity." *Midwest Studies in Philosophy* 1 (1976) 5–11.

Ismael, Jenann. "Temporal Experience." In *The Oxford Handbook of Philosophy of Time*, edited by Craig Callender, 460–82. New York: Oxford University Press, 2011.

Jacquette, Dale. "Conceivability, Intensionality, and the Logic of Anselm's Modal Argument for the Existence of God." *International Journal for Philosophy of Religion* 42 (1997) 163–73.

Jackson, Frank. "Epiphenomenal Qualia." *Philosophical Quarterly* 32 (1982) 127–36.

———. "What Mary Didn't Know." *Journal of Philosophy* 83 (1986) 291–95.

Jacobs, Jonathan. "A Powers Theory of Modality: Or, How I Learned to Stop Worrying and Reject Possible Worlds." *Philosophical Studies* 151 (2010) 227–48.

Jaggar, Alison. "Love and Knowledge: Emotion in Feminist Epistemology." *Inquiry* 32 (1989) 151–76.

Johnson, Daniel M. "The Sense of Deity and Begging the Question with Ontological and Cosmological Arguments." *Faith and Philosophy* 26 (2009) 87–94.

Johnson, David Kyle. "God, Fatalism, and Temporal Ontology." *Religious Studies* 45 (2009) 435–54.

Johnson, Elizabeth A. *She Who Is: The Mystery of God in Feminist Theological Discourse.* New York: Crossroads, 1992.

Jowers, Dennis, ed. *Four Views on Divine Providence.* Grand Rapids: Zondervan, 2011.

Kane, Robert. "Beginning the Discussion: The A–Z of Free Will and Determinism." In *The Oxford Handbook of Free Will*, edited by Robern Kane, 3–44. New York: Oxford University Press, 2005.

———. "Introduction: The Contours of Contemporary Free Will Debates." In *The Oxford Handbook of Free Will*, edited by Robert Kane, 3–41. New York: Oxford University Press, 2005.

———. "Introduction: The Contours of Contemporary Free-Will Debates (Part 2)." In *The Oxford Handbook of Free Will*, edited by Robert Kane, 3–35. 2nd ed. New York: Oxford University Press, 2011.

———. "The Modal Ontological Argument." *Mind* 93 (1984) 336–50.

———, ed. *The Oxford Handbook of Free Will.* New York: Oxford University Press, 2005.

———, ed. *The Oxford Handbook of Free Will.* 2nd ed. New York: Oxford University Press, 2011.

———. "Rethinking Free Will: New Perspectives on an Ancient Problem." In *The Oxford Handbook of Free Will*, edited by Robert Kane, 381–404. 2nd ed. New York: Oxford University Press, 2011.

———. *The Significance of Free Will.* New York: Oxford University Press, 1996.

———. "Two Kinds of Incompatibilism." *Philosophy and Phenomenological Research* 50 (1989) 219–54.

Kant, Immanuel. *Critique of Pure Reason.* Translated and edited by Paul Guyer and Allen W. Wood. Cambridge: Cambridge University Press, 1998.

Kapitan, Tomis. "Acting and the Open Future: A Brief Rejoinder to David Hunt." *Religious Studies* 33 (1997) 287–92.

Keene, G. B. "A Simpler Solution to the Paradox of Omnipotence." *Mind* 69 (1960) 74–75.

Keller, Simon. "Presentism and Truthmaking." *Oxford Studies in Metaphysics* 1 (2004) 83–104.

Keller, Timothy. *The Reason for God: Belief in an Age of Skepticism.* New York: Dutton, 2008.

Kelsey, David H. "The Human Creature." In *The Oxford Handbook of Systematic Theology*, edited by John Webster et al., 121–39. New York: Oxford University Press, 2007.

Kenny, Anthony. "Divine Foreknowledge and Human Freedom." In *Aquinas: A Collection of Critical Essays*, edited by Anthony Kenny, 254–70. Modern Studies in Philosophy. Garden City, NY: Doubleday, 1969.

———. *The God of the Philosophers.* Oxford: Clarendon, 1979.

———. *Will, Freedom, and Power.* Oxford: Blackwell, 1975.

Khamara, E. J. "Eternity and Omniscience." *Philosophical Quarterly* 24 (1974) 204–19.

———. “In Defence of Omnipotence.” *Philosophical Quarterly* 28 (1978) 215–28.

Kneale, Martha. “Eternity and Sempiternity.” *Proceedings of the Aristotelian Society* (1968–69) 223–38.

Kodaj, Daniel. “Open Future and Modal Anti-Realism.” *Philosophical Studies* 168 (2014) 417–38.

Konyndyk, Kenneth. *Introductory Modal Logic*. South Bend, IN: University of Notre Dame Press, 1986.

Koons, Robert C. “Defeasible Reasoning, Special Pleading, and the Cosmological Argument: A Reply to Oppy.” *Faith and Philosophy* 18 (2001) 192–203.

———. “Dual Agency: A Thomistic Account of Providence and Human Freedom.” *Philosophia Christi* 4 (2002) 397–410.

Kretzmann, Norman. *The Metaphysics of Theism*. Oxford: Clarendon, 1997.

———. “Omniscience and Immutability.” *Journal of Philosophy* 63 (1966) 409–21.

Kripke, Saul. *Naming and Necessity*. Cambridge: Harvard University Press, 1981.

Kuhn, Thomas S. *The Structure of Scientific Revolutions*. 4th ed. Chicago: University of Chicago Press, 2012.

Kutach, Douglas. “The Asymmetry of Influence.” In *The Oxford Handbook of Philosophy of Time*, edited by Craig Callender, 247–75. New York: Oxford University Press, 2011.

Kvanvig, Jonathan L. “Adams on Actualism and Presentism.” *Philosophy and Phenomenological Research* 50 (1989) 289–98.

———. “The Analogy Argument for a Limited Account of Omniscience.” *International Philosophical Quarterly* 29 (1989) 129–37.

———. “Closure and Alternative Possibilities.” In *The Oxford Handbook of Skepticism*, edited by John Greco, 456–84. New York: Oxford University Press, 2008.

———. “Closure Principles.” *Philosophy Compass* 1 (2006) 256–67.

———. “Coherentism and Justified Inconsistent Beliefs: A Solution.” *Southern Journal of Philosophy* 50 (2012) 21–41.

———. “Contrastivism and Closure.” *Social Epistemology* 22 (2008) 247–56.

———. “Hasker on Fatalism.” *Philosophical Studies* 65 (1992) 91–101.

———. “The Incarnation and the Knowability Paradox.” *Synthese* 173 (2010) 89–105.

———. *The Intellectual Virtues and the Life of the Mind: On the Place of the Virtues in Contemporary Epistemology*. Savage, MD: Rowman & Littlefield, 1992.

———. “Omniscience and Eternity: A Reply to Craig.” *Faith and Philosophy* 18 (2001) 369–76.

———. *The Possibility of an All-Knowing God*. New York: St. Martin’s, 1986.

———. “Unknowable Truths and the Doctrine of Omniscience.” *Journal of the American Academy of Religion* 57 (1989) 485–507.

La Croix, Richard R. “Failing to Define Omnipotence.” *Philosophical Studies* 34 (1978) 219–22.

———. “The Impossibility of Defining ‘Omniscience.’” *Philosophical Studies* 32 (1977) 181–90.

Le Poidevin, Robin. *Change, Cause, and Contradiction: A Defence of the Tenseless Theory of Time*. London: MacMillan, 1991.

———. *The Images of Time: An Essay on Temporal Representation*. New York: Oxford University Press, 2007.

———, ed. *Questions of Time and Tense*. Oxford: Clarendon, 1998.

———. *Travels in Four Dimensions: The Enigmas of Space and Time*. New York: Oxford University Press, 2005.

Le Poidevin, Robin, and Murray MacBeath, eds. *The Philosophy of Time*. Oxford Readings in Philosophy. New York: Oxford University Press, 1993.

Leftow, Brian. "Anselmian Polytheism." *International Journal for Philosophy of Religion* 23 (1988) 77–104.

———. "Anselmian Presentism." *Faith and Philosophy* 26 (2009) 297–319.

———. "Aquinas, Divine Simplicity, and Divine Freedom." In *Metaphysics and God*, edited by Kevin Timpe, 21–38. London: Routledge, 2009.

———. "Aquinas on God and Modal Truth." *Modern Schoolman* 82 (2005) 171–200.

———. "Aquinas on Omnipotence." In *The Oxford Handbook of Aquinas*, edited by Eleanore Stump and Brian Davies, 187–98. New York: Oxford University Press, 2012.

———. "Eternity and Simultaneity." *Faith and Philosophy* 8 (1991) 148–79.

———. *God and Necessity*. New York: Oxford University Press, 2012.

———. "Individual and Attribute in the Ontological Argument." *Faith and Philosophy* 7 (1990) 235–42.

———. "A Latin Trinity." *Faith and Philosophy* 21 (2004) 304–33.

———. "A Modal Cosmological Argument." *International Journal for Philosophy of Religion* 24 (1988) 159–88.

———. "Necessity." In *The Cambridge Companion to Christian Philosophical Theology*, edited by Charles Taliaferro and Chad Meister, 15–30. New York: Cambridge University Press, 2010.

———. "Omnipotence." In *The Oxford Handbook to Philosophical Theology*, edited by Thomas P. Flint and Michael C. Rea, 167–98. New York: Oxford University Press, 2009.

———. "The Ontological Argument." In *The Oxford Handbook on Philosophy of Religion*, edited by William Wainwright, 80–115. New York: Oxford University Press, 2005.

———. "Perfection and Necessity." *Sophia* 28 (1989) 13–20.

———. "Swinburne on Divine Necessity." *Religious Studies* 46 (2010) 141–62.

———. "Time, Actuality, and Omniscience." *Religious Studies* 26 (1990) 303–22.

———. *Time and Eternity*. Cornell Studies in the Philosophy of Religion. Ithaca, NY: Cornell University Press, 1991.

———. "Timelessness and Foreknowledge." *Philosophical Studies* 63 (1991) 309–25.

———. "Why Perfect Being Theology?" *International Journal for Philosophy of Religion* 69 (2011) 103–18.

Leibniz, Gottfried Wilhem. *Discourse on Metaphysics and the Monadology*. Translated by George R. Montgomery. Mineola, NY: Dover, 2005.

———. *Theodicy*. Translated by E. M. Huggard. New York: Cosimo Classics, 2010.

Lewis, David. "Anselm and Actuality." *Noûs* 4 (1970) 175–88. Reprinted with postscript in *Philosophical Papers* 1:1–25. New York: Cambridge University Press, 1983.

———. "Are We Free to Break the Laws?" *Theoria* 47 (1981) 113–21.

———. "Attitudes *De Dicto* and *De Se*." *Philosophical Review* 88 (1979) 513–43.

———. *Counterfactuals*. Oxford: Wiley-Blackwell, 1973.

———. "Counterfactual Dependence and Time's Arrow." *Noûs* 13 (1979) 455–76.

———. *On the Plurality of Worlds*. Oxford: Wiley-Blackwell, 2001.

———. "Ordering Semantics and Premise Semantics for Counterfactuals." *Journal of Philosophical Logic* 10 (1981) 217–34.

———. "Tensed Qualifiers." *Oxford Studies in Metaphysics* 1 (2004) 3–14.

Lewis, Delmas. "Eternity Again: A Reply to Stump and Kretzmann." *International Journal for Philosophy of Religion* 15 (1984) 73–79.

———. "Eternity, Time, and Tenselessness." *Faith and Philosophy* 5 (1988) 72–86.

Linville, Mark D. "Divine Foreknowledge and the Libertarian Conception of Human Freedom." *International Journal for Philosophy of Religion* 33 (1993) 165–86.

Littlejohn, Clayton. "Concessive Knowledge Attributions and Falibilism." *Philosophy and Phenomenological Research* 83 (2011) 603–19.

Loss, Roberto. "Free Will and the Necessity of the Present." *Analysis* 69 (2009) 63–69.

Loux, Michael J. *The Possible and the Actual: Readings in the Metaphysics of Modality.* Ithaca, NY: Cornell University Press, 1979.

Lucas, Bill. "The Logic of Omniscience." PhD diss., University of Texas at Austin, 1981.

Lucas, John Randolph. *The Future: An Essay on God, Temporality, and Truth.* Oxford: Basil Blackwell, 1989.

Ludlow, Peter. "Presentism, Triviality, and the Varieties of Tensism." *Oxford Studies in Metaphysics* 1 (2004) 21–36.

Ludlow, Peter, et al., eds. *There's Something About Mary: Essays on Phenomenal Consciousness and Frank Jackson's Knowledge Argument.* Cambridge, MA: MIT Press, 2004.

Łukasiewicz, Jan. "Many-Valued Systems of Propositional Logic." In *Polish Logic 1920–1939*, edited by Storrs McCall, 40–65. New York: Oxford University Press, 1967.

Lycan, William G. "Two—No, Three—Concepts of Possible Worlds." *Proceedings of the Aristotelian Society* 91 (1990–91) 215–27.

MacDonald, Scott, ed. *Being and Goodness: The Concept of God in Metaphysics and Philosophical Theology.* Ithaca, NY: Cornell University Press, 1991.

MacFarlane, John. "Future Contingents and Relative Truth." *Philosophical Quarterly* 53 (2003) 321–36.

Mackie, J. L. *The Cement of the Universe: A Study of Causation.* Clarendon Library of Logic and Philosophy. New York: Oxford University Press, 1980.

———. "Evil and Omnipotence." *Mind* 64 (1955) 200–212.

———. *The Miracle of Theism: Arguments For and Against the Existence of God.* New York: Oxford University Press, 1982.

Malcolm, Norman. "Anselm's Ontological Arguments." *Philosophical Review* 69 (1960) 41–62.

Mann, William. "Definite Descriptions and the Ontological Argument." *Theoria* 33 (1967) 211–29.

———. "Divine Attributes." *American Philosophical Quarterly* 12 (1975) 151–59.

———. "The Ontological Presuppositions of the Ontological Argument." *Review of Metaphysics* 26 (1972) 260–77.

———. "The Perfect Island." *Mind* 85 (1976) 417–21.

———. "Ross on Omnipotence." *International Journal for Philosophy of Religion* 8 (1977) 142–47.

Manson, Neil A., ed. *God and Design: The Teleological Argument and Modern Science.* New York: Routledge, 2003.

Markosian, Ned. "A Defense of Presentism." *Oxford Studies in Metaphysics* 1 (2004) 47–82.

Martin, Timothy John. "Significant Responsibility Amidst Robust Providence: A Defense of Reformed Molinism as a Rapprochement Between Divine Election and Metaphysical Human Freedom." PhD diss., Southwestern Baptist Theological Seminary, 2010.

Mavrodes, George. "Defining Omnipotence." *Philosophical Studies* 32 (1977) 191–202.

———. "Is the Past Unpreventable?" *Faith and Philosophy* 1 (1984) 131–46.

———. "Some Puzzles Concerning Omnipotence." In *Philosophy of Religion: Selected Readings*, edited by David Basinger et al., 146–49. 3rd ed. New York: Oxford University Press, 2007.

Maydole, Robert E. "The Ontological Argument." In *The Blackwell Companion to Natural Theology*, edited by William Lane Craig and J. P. Moreland, 553–92. Oxford: Wiley-Blackwell, 2009.

McCabe, Herbert. *God Matters*. London: Chapman, 1987.

McCall, Storrs. "A Dynamic Model of Temporal Becoming." *Analysis* 44 (1984) 172–76.

———. "Objective Time Flow." *Philosophy of Science* 43 (1976) 337–62.

McCall, Thomas, and Michael C. Rea. *Philosophical and Theological Essays on the Trinity*. Oxford: Oxford University Press, 2009.

McCann, Hugh. "Divine Sovereignty and the Freedom of the Will." *Faith and Philosophy* 12 (1995) 582–98.

———. "Sovereignty and Freedom: A Reply to Rowe." *Faith and Philosophy* 18 (2001) 110–16.

McClelland, R. T., and R. J. Deltete. "Divine Causation." *Faith and Philosophy* 17 (2000) 3–25.

McDermott, Gerald R., ed. *The Oxford Handbook of Evangelical Theology*. New York: Oxford University Press, 2010.

McGrath, Alister E. "Faith and Tradition." In *The Oxford Handbook of Evangelical Theology*, edited by Gerald R. McDermott, 81–95. New York: Oxford University Press, 2010.

McGrath, P. J. "Does the Ontological Argument Beg the Question?" *Religious Studies* 30 (1994) 305–10.

———. "The Modal Ontological Argument—A Reply to Kane and Morris." *Mind* 95 (1986) 373–76.

———. "The Refutation of the Ontological Argument." *Philosophical Quarterly* 40 (1990) 195–212.

McKim, Vaughn R., and Charles C. Davis. "Temporal Modalities and the Future." *Notre Dame Journal of Formal Logic* 17 (1976) 233–38.

McTaggart, John McTaggart Ellis. *The Nature of Existence*. Vol. 2. New York: Cambridge University Press, 1927.

———. *Some Dogmas of Religion*. New York: Greenwood, 1968.

———. "The Unreality of Time." *Mind* 18 (1908) 457–84.

Meister, Chad, and Paul Copan, eds. *The Routledge Companion to Philosophy of Religion*. New York: Routledge, 2007.

Mele, Alfred R. "Causation, Action, and Free Will." In *The Oxford Handbook of Causation*, edited by Helen Beebee et al., 554–74. New York: Oxford University Press, 2010.

Mele, Alfred, and M. P. Smith. "The New Paradox of the Stone." *Faith and Philosophy* 5 (1988) 283–90.

Merricks, Trenton. "Good-Bye Growing Block." In *Oxford Studies in Metaphysics*, edited by Dean Zimmerman, 2:103–10. New York: Oxford University Press, 2006.

———. "Persistence, Parts, and Presentism." *Noûs* 33 (1999) 421–38.

———. "Truth and Freedom." *Philosophical Review* 118 (2009) 29–57.

———. "Truth and Molinism." In *Molinism: The Contemporary Debate*, edited by Ken Perszyk, 50–72. Oxford: Oxford University Press, 2011.

———. *Truth and Ontology*. New York: Oxford University Press, 2009.

Metcalf, Thomas. "Omniscience and Maximal Power." *Religious Studies* 40 (2004) 289–306.

Meyer, Ulrich. *The Nature of Time*. New York: Oxford University Press, 2013.

———. "Time and Modality." In *The Oxford Handbook of Philosophy of Time*, edited by Craig Callender, 91–121. New York: Oxford University Press, 2011.

Miller, B. *A Most Unlikely God*. Notre Dame: University of Notre Dame Press, 1996.

Millican, Peter. "The One Fatal Flaw in Anselm's Argument." *Mind* 113 (2004) 437–76.

Mill, John Stuart. *A System of Logic, Ratiocinative and Inductive: Being a Connected View of the Principles of Evidence, and the Methods of Scientific Investigation*. Edited by J. M. Robson. Collected Works of John Stuart Mill 7. Toronto: University of Toronto Press, 1973.

Molina, Luis de. *On Divine Foreknowledge: Part IV of the Concordia*. Translated Alfred J. Freddoso. Ithaca, NY: Cornell University Press, 2004.

Moore, Andrew. "Reason." In *The Oxford Handbook of Systematic Theology*, edited by John Webster et al., 394–412. New York: Oxford University Press, 2007.

Morris, Thomas V. *Anselmian Explorations: Essays in Philosophical Theology*. Notre Dame: Notre Dame University Press, 1987.

———. *The Concept of God*. New York: Oxford University Press, 1987.

———. "God and the World: A Look at Process Theology." In *Anselmian Explorations: Essays in Philosophical Theology*, 124–50. South Bend, IN: University of Notre Dame Press, 1987.

———. "The God of Abraham, Isaac, and Anselm." *Faith and Philosophy* 1 (1984) 177–87. Reprinted in *Anselmian Explorations: Essays in Philosophical Theology*, 10–25. South Bend, IN: University of Notre Dame Press, 1987.

———. *The Logic of God Incarnate*. Ithaca, NY: Cornell University Press, 1986.

———. "A Modern Discussion of Divine Omnipotence." In *Philosophy of Religion: A Guide and Anthology*, edited by Brian Davies, 402–14. New York: Oxford University Press, 2000.

———. "Necessary Beings." *Mind* 94 (1985) 263–72. Reprinted in *Anselmian Explorations: Essays in Philosophical Theology*, 179–93. South Bend, IN: University of Notre Dame Press, 1987.

———. *Our Idea of God: An Introduction to Philosophical Theology*. Notre Dame: University of Notre Dame Press, 1991.

———. "Perfection and Power." In *Anselmian Explorations: Essays in Philosophical Theology*, 70–75. South Bend, IN: University of Notre Dame Press, 1987.

———. "Perfect Being Theology." *Noûs* 21 (1987) 19–30.

———. "Properties, Modalities, and God." *Philosophical Review* 93 (1984) 35–55. Reprinted in *Anselmian Explorations: Essays in Philosophical Theology*, 76–97. South Bend, IN: University of Notre Dame Press, 1987.

———. "A Theistic Proof of Perfection." *Sophia* 26 (1987) 31–35.

Moskop, John C. *Divine Omniscience and Human Freedom*. Macon, GA: Mercer University Press, 1984.

Mozersky, M. Joshua. "Presentism." In *The Oxford Handbook of Philosophy of Time*, edited by Craig Callender, 122–44. New York: Oxford University Press, 2011.

Mundy, Brent. "The Metaphysics of Quantity." *Philosophical Studies* 51 (1987) 29–54.

Murray, Michael J., and Michael Rea. *An Introduction to the Philosophy of Religion*. New York: Cambridge University Press, 2008.

Nagasawa, Yujin. "Divine Omniscience and Experience: A Reply to Alter." *Ars Disputandi* 3 (2003) 94–99.

———. "Divine Omniscience and Knowledge *De Se*." *International Journal for Philosophy of Religion* 53 (2003) 73–82.

———. *The Existence of God: A Philosophical Introduction*. London: Routledge, 2011.

———. "God and Universal Value Commensurability." Unpublished paper presented at the Baylor Philosophy of Religion Conference, Waco, TX, Feb. 6, 2009.

———. "A New Defence of Anselmian Theism." *Philosophical Quarterly* 58 (2008) 577–96.

Nash-Marshall, Siobhan F. "Properties, Conflation, and Attribution: The 'Monologion' and Divine Simplicity." *Saint Anselm Journal* 4 (2007) 1–18.

Nicene and Post-Nicene Fathers. Edited by Philip Schaff and Henry Wace. 14 vols. 1893. Reprint, Peabody, MA: Hendrickson, 1999.

Normore, Calvin. "Divine Omniscience, Omnipotence, and Future Contingents: An Overview." In *Divine Omniscience and Omnipotence in Medieval Philosophy*, 3–22. Profiles 5. Dordrecht: Reidel, 1985.

O'Connor, Timothy. "Agent-Causal Theories of Freedom." In *The Oxford Handbook of Free Will*, edited by Robert Kane, 309–28. 2nd ed. New York: Oxford University Press, 2011.

———. "Agent Causation." In *Agents, Causes, and Events*, edited by Timothy O'Connor, 173–200. New York: Oxford University Press, 1995.

———, ed. *Agents, Causes, and Events: Essays on Indeterminism and Free Will*. New York: Oxford University Press, 1995.

———. "Libertarian Views: Dualist and Agent-Causal Theories." In *The Oxford Handbook of Free Will*, edited by Robert Kane, 337–55. Oxford: Oxford University Press, 2005.

———. "On the Transfer of Necessity." *Noûs* 27 (1993) 204–18.

———. *Persons and Causes: The Metaphysics of Free Will*. New York: Oxford University Press, 2000.

———. *Theism and Ultimate Explanation: The Necessary Shape of Contingency*. Oxford: Blackwell, 2008.

Oaklander, L. Nathan. "Freedom and the New Theory of Time." In *Questions of Time and Tense*, edited by Robin Le Poidevin, 185–205. New York: Oxford University Press, 1998.

———. "McTaggart's Paradox and Crisp's Presentism." *Philosophia* 38 (2010) 229–41.

———. "Time and Foreknowledge: A Critique of Zagzebski." *Religious Studies* 31 (1995) 101–3.

Ockham, William. *Opera Theologica*. Edited by Gerald Etzkorn and Francis Kelly. New York: St. Bonaventure, 1979.

———. *Predestination, God's Foreknowledge, and Future Contingents*. Translated by Marilyn McCord Adams and Norman Kretzmann. Indianapolis: Hackett, 1969.

Oden, Thomas C. *How Africa Shaped the Christian Mind: Rediscovering the African Seedbed of Western Christianity*. Downers Grove, IL: InterVarsity Academic, 2007.

Oderberg, David S. "Traversal of the Infinite, the 'Big Bang,' and the *Kalam* Cosmological Argument." *Philosophia Christi* 4 (2002) 303–34.

———. "The Tristram Shandy Paradox: A Reply to Oppy." *Philosophia Christi* 4 (2002) 351–60.

Oord, Thomas J. *The Uncontrolling Love of God: An Open and Relational Account of Providence*. Downers Grove, IL: InterVarsity Academic, 2015.

Oppy, Graham. *Arguing About Gods*. New York: Cambridge University Press, 2006.

———. "Modal Theistic Arguments." *Sophia* 32 (1993) 17–24.

———. "Natural Theology." In *Alvin Plantinga*, edited by Deane-Peter Baker, 15–47. Contemporary Philosophy in Focus. New York: Cambridge University Press, 2007.

———. "Omnipotence." *Philosophy and Phenomenological Research* 71 (2005) 58–84.

———. "Ontological Arguments." In *Stanford Encyclopedia of Philosophy*, edited by Edward N. Zalta and Uri Nodelman, July 15, 2001. https://plato.stanford.edu/archives/fall2011/entries/ontological-arguments/.

———. *Ontological Arguments and Belief in God*. New York: Cambridge University Press, 1995.

———. "Professor William Craig's Criticisms of Critiques of *Kalam* Cosmological Arguments by Paul Davies, Stephen Hawking, and Adolf Grünbaum." *Faith and Philosophy* 12 (1995) 237–50.

———. "The Tristram Shandy Paradox: A Response to Oderberg." *Philosophia Christi* 4 (2002) 335–50.

Owen, John. *Vindiciae Evangelicae, or, the Mystery of the Gospel Vindicated and Socinianism Examined* in *Works of John Owen*. Vol. 12. Edited by William H. Goold. Carlisle, PA: Banner of Truth, 1999.

Padgett, Alan G. *God, Eternity, and the Nature of Time*. London: St. Martin's, 1992.

Pannenberg, Wolfhart. *Basic Questions in Theology: Collected Essays*. Vol. 2. Minneapolis: Augsburg Fortress, 1971.

Pendergraft, Garrett. "Divine Deliberation (or Lack Thereof)." Unpublished paper presented at the Annual Meeting of the Evangelical Philosophical Society, Providence, RI, Nov. 19, 2008.

Penelhum, Terence. "Divine Necessity." *Mind* 69 (1960) 175–86.

Pereboom, Derk. "Free Will, Evil, and Providence." In *God and the Ethics of Belief: New Essays in Philosophy of Religion*, edited by Andrew Chignell and Andrew Dole, 77–98. New York: Cambridge University Press, 2005.

———. *Living Without Free Will*. New York: Cambridge University Press, 2004.

Perry, John. "The Problem of the Essential Indexical." *Noûs* (1979) 3–21.

Pike, Nelson. "Divine Omniscience and Voluntary Action." *Philosophical Review* 74 (1965) 27–46.

———. *God and Timelessness*. Eugene, OR: Wipf and Stock, 2002.

———. "Omnipotence and God's Ability to Sin." *American Philosophical Quarterly* 6 (1969) 208–16.

Pinnock, Clark. "God Limits His Knowledge." In *Predestination and Free Will: Four Views of Divine Sovereignty and Human Freedom*, edited by David Basinger and Randall Basinger, 143–62. Downers Grove, IL: InterVarsity, 1986.

———, ed. *The Grace of God and the Will of Man*. Grand Rapids: Zondervan, 1989.

———. *Most Moved Mover: A Theology of God's Openness*. Grand Rapids: Baker Academic, 2001.

Plantinga, Alvin. "Actualism and Possible Worlds." *Theoria* 42 (1976) 139–60.

———. "Appendix: Two Dozen (or so) Theistic Arguments." In *Alvin Plantinga*. Contemporary Philosophy in Focus, edited by Deane-Peter Baker, 203–27. New York: Cambridge University Press, 2007.

———. "*De Essentia*." In *Essays in the Metaphysics of Modality*, edited by Matthew Davidson, 139–57. New York: Oxford University Press, 2003.

———. "Divine Knowledge." In *Christian Perspectives on Religious Knowledge*, edited by C. Stephen Evans and Merold Westphal, 40–65. Grand Rapids: Eerdmans, 1993.

———. *Does God Have a Nature?* Milwaukee: Marquette University Press, 1980.

———. *Essays on the Metaphysics of Modality*. Edited by Matthew Davidson. New York: Oxford University Press, 2003.

———. "Existence, Necessity, and God." *New Scholasticism* 50 (1976) 61–72.

———, ed. *Faith and Philosophy: Philosophical Studies in Religion and Ethics*. Grand Rapids: Eerdmans, 1964.

———. *God and Other Minds*. Ithaca, NY: Cornell University Press, 1967.

———. *God, Freedom, and Evil*. Grand Rapids: Eerdmans, 1974.

———. "Is Theism Really a Miracle?" *Faith and Philosophy* 3 (1986) 109–34.

———. "It's Actual, so It Must Be Possible." *Philosophical Studies* 12 (1961) 61–64.

———. "Kant's Objection to the Ontological Argument." *Journal of Philosophy* 63 (1966) 537–45.

———. *The Nature of Necessity*. New York: Oxford University Press, 1974.

———. "Necessary Being." In *Faith and Philosophy: Philosophical Studies in Religion and Ethics*, edited by Alvin Plantinga, 97–110. Grand Rapids: Eerdmans, 1964.

———. "On Existentialism." *Philosophical Studies* 44 (1983) 1–20.

———. "On Ockham's Way Out." *Faith and Philosophy* 3 (1986) 235–69.

———. "Reply to the Basingers on Divine Omnipotence." *Process Studies* 11 (1981) 25–29.

———. "Self-Profile." In *Alvin Plantinga*, edited by James E. Tomberlin and Peter van Inwagen, 3–69. Profiles 5. Dordrecht: Reidel, 1985.

———. "Two Concepts of Modality: Modal Realism and Modal Reductionism." *Philosophical Perspectives* 11 (1987) 189–231.

———. "Two Dozen (or So) Theistic Arguments." In *Faith and Rationality: Reason and Belief in God*, edited by Alvin Plantinga and Nicholas Wolterstorff, 1–33. Notre Dame: University of Notre Dame Press, 1983.

———. *Warranted Christian Belief*. New York: Oxford University Press, 2000.

———. "Which Worlds Could God Have Created?" *Journal of Philosophy* 70 (1973) 539–52.

Plantinga, Alvin, and Patrick Grim. "Truth, Omniscience, and Cantorian Arguments: An Exchange." *Philosophical Studies* 71 (1993) 267–306.

Price, Huw. "The Flow of Time." In *The Oxford Handbook of Philosophy of Time*, edited by Craig Callender, 276–311. New York: Oxford University Press, 2011.

Price, Huw, and Brad Weslake. "The Time-Asymmetry of Causation." In *The Oxford Handbook of Causation*, edited by Helen Beebee et al., 414–46. New York: Oxford University Press, 2010.

Prior, A. N. "The Formalities of Omniscience." *Philosophy* 32 (1962) 119–29.

———. *Papers on Time and Tense*. Edited by Per Hasle et al. Rev. ed. New York: Oxford University Press, 2003.

———. *Past, Present, and Future*. New York: Oxford University Press, 1967.

Pruss, Alexander R. *Actuality, Possibility, and Worlds*. Continuum Studies in Philosophy of Religion. New York: Continuum, 2011.

———. "From Restricted to Full Omniscience." *Religious Studies* 47 (2011) 257–64.

———. "The Leibnizian Cosmological Argument." In *The Blackwell Companion to Natural Theology*, edited by William Lane Craig and J. P. Moreland, 24–100. Oxford: Wiley-Blackwell, 2009.

———. *The Principle of Sufficient Reason: A Reassessment*. Cambridge Studies in Philosophy. New York: Cambridge University Press, 2006.

Purtill, Richard L. "Fatalism and the Omnitemporality of Truth." *Faith and Philosophy* 5 (1988) 185–92.

Quinn, Philip. "On the Mereology of Boethian Eternity." *International Journal for Philosophy of Religion* 32 (1992) 51–60.

Rasmussen, Joshua. *Defending the Correspondence Theory of Truth*. Cambridge: Cambridge University Press, 2014.

Rea, Michael C. "Four-Dimensionalism." In *The Oxford Handbook of Metaphysics*, edited by Michael J. Loux and Dean W. Zimmerman, 246–80. New York: Oxford University Press, 2003.

———. "Presentism and Fatalism." *Australian Journal of Philosophy* 84 (2006) 511–24.

———. "Temporal Parts Unmotivated." *Philosophical Review* 107 (1998) 225–60.

Reichenbach, Bruce. "God Limits His Power." In *Encountering Evil: Live Options in Theodicy*, edited by Stephen T. Davis, 101–24. Atlanta: John Knox, 1981.

———. "Hasker on Omniscience." *Faith and Philosophy* 4 (1987) 86–92.

———. "Mavrodes on Omnipotence." *Philosophical Studies* 37 (1980) 211–14.

———. "Omniscience and Deliberation." *International Journal for Philosophy of Religion* 16 (1984) 225–36.

Restall, Gregg. "Truthmakers, Entailment, and Necessity." *Australaisan Journal of Philosophy* 74 (1996) 331–40.

Rhoda, Alan R. "The Case for Open Theism." In *God, Time, and Eternity: The Coherence of Theism II*, edited by W. L. Craig and P. K. Moser, 301–11. Dordrecht: Kluwer Academic, 2001.

———. "The Fivefold Openness of the Future." In *God in an Open Universe: Science, Metaphysics, and Open Theism*, edited by William Hasker et al., 69–93. Eugene, OR: Pickwick, 2011.

———. "Generic Open Theism and Some Varieties Thereof." *Religious Studies* 44 (2008) 225–34.

———. "The Philosophical Case for Open Theism." *Philosophia* 35 (2007) 301–11.

———. "Presentism, Truthmakers, and God." *Pacific Philosophical Quarterly* 90 (2009) 41–62.

Rhoda, Alan R., et al. "Open Theism, Omniscience, and the Nature of the Future." *Faith and Philosophy* 23 (2006) 432–59.

Rice, Richard. *God's Foreknowledge and Man's Free Will*. Eugene, OR: Wipf & Stock, 1985.

Richards, Jay Wesley. *The Untamed God: A Philosophical Exploration of Divine Perfection, Simplicity, and Immutability*. Downers Grove, IL: InterVarsity, 2003.

Robinson, Howard. "Can We Make Sense of the Notion of a Non-Physical Substance?" *Proceedings of the Aristotelian Society* 84 (1984) 127–43.

Robinson, Michael D. *Eternity and Freedom: A Critical Analysis of Divine Timelessness as a Solution to the Foreknowledge/Free Will Debate*. New York: University Press of America, 1995.

———. "Why Divine Foreknowledge?" *Religious Studies* 36 (2000) 251–75.

Rogers, Katherin. *An Anselmian Approach to God and Creation*. Lewiston, NY: Mellon, 1997.

———. "Anselmian Eternalism: The Presence of a Timeless God." *Faith and Philosophy* 24 (2007) 3–27.

———. *Anselm on Freedom*. New York: Oxford University Press, 2008.

———. "Back to Eternity: A Response to Leftow's 'Anselmian Presentism.'" *Faith and Philosophy* 26 (2009) 320–38.

———. "Eternity Has No Duration." *Religious Studies* 30 (1994) 1–16.

———. "Incarnation." In *The Cambridge Companion to Christian Philosophical Theology*, edited by Charles Taliaferro and Chad Meister, 95–107. New York: Cambridge University Press, 2010.

———. "The Necessity of the Present and Anselm's Eternalist Response to the Problem of Theological Fatalism." *Religious Studies* 43 (2007) 25–47.

———. "Omniscience, Eternity, and Freedom." *International Philosophical Quarterly* 36 (1996) 399–412.

———. *Perfect Being Theology*. Reason and Religion. Edinburgh: Edinburgh University Press, 2000.

———. "St. Augustine on Time and Eternity." *American Catholic Philosophical Quarterly* 70 (1996) 207–23.

Rolnick, Philip A. "Realist Reference to God: Analogy or Univocity?" In *Realism and Antirealism*, edited by William P. Alston, 211–37. Ithaca, NY: Cornell University Press, 2019.

Rosenkrantz, Gary and Joshua Hoffman. "What an Omnipotent Agent Can Do." *International Journal for Philosophy of Religion* 11 (1980) 1–19.

Rota, Michael. "A Problem for Hasker: Freedom with Respect to the Present, Hard Facts, and Theological Incompatibilism." *Faith and Philosophy* 27 (2010) 287–305.

———. "The Eternity Solution to the Problem of Human Freedom and Divine Foreknowledge." *European Journal for Philosophy of Religion* 2 (2010) 165–86.

Rowe, William L. *Can God Be Free?* New York: Oxford University Press, 2006.

———. "Comments on Professor Davis' 'Does the Ontological Argument Beg the Question?'" *International Journal for Philosophy of Religion* 7 (1976) 443–47.

———. "The Ontological Argument and Question-Begging." *International Journal for Philosophy of Religion* 7 (1976) 425–32.

Roy, Steven C. *How Much Does God Foreknow? A Comprehensive Biblical Study*. Downers Grove, IL: InterVarsity Academic, 2006.

Runzo, Joseph. "Omniscience and Freedom for Evil." *International Journal for Philosophy of Religion* 12 (1981) 132.

Sanders, E. P. "Historical Considerations." In *The Search for Jesus: Historical Methods and Modern Challenges*, edited by David M. Gribben, 60–91. New York: Oxford University Press, 2005.

Sanders, John. "Be Wary of Ware: A Reply to Bruce Ware." *Journal of the Evangelical Theological Society* 45 (2002) 221–31.

———. *The God Who Risks: A Theology of Divine Providence*. 2nd ed. Downers Grove, IL: InterVarsity Academic, 2007.

———. "On Heffalumps and Heresies: Responses to Accusations Against Open Theism." *Journal of Biblical Studies* 2 (2002) 1–44.

Saunders, J. T. "Of God and Freedom." *Philosophical Review* 75 (1966) 219–25.

Savage, C. Wade. "The Paradox of the Stone." In *Philosophy of Religion: The Big Questions*, edited by Eleonore Stump and Michael J. Murray, 9–12. Oxford: Blackwell, 1999.

Schrader, David. "The Anatomy of Divine Necessity." *International Journal for Philosophy of Religion* 30 (1991) 45–59.

Schreiner, Thomas R., and Bruce A. Ware, eds. *The Grace of God and The Bondage of the Will*. Grand Rapids: Baker, 1995.

———, eds. *Still Sovereign: Contemporary Perspectives on Election, Foreknowledge, and Grace*. Grand Rapids: Baker Academic, 2000.

Sennett, James F., ed. *The Analytic Theist: An Alvin Plantinga Reader*. Grand Rapids: Eerdmans, 1998.

Senor, Thomas. "The Compositional Account of the Incarnation." *Faith and Philosophy* 24 (2007) 52–71.

Seymour, Amy. "The Advantages of All-Falsism." Unpublished paper presented at the Society of Christian Philosophers' Pacific Regional Meeting, Westmont University, Santa Barbara, CA, Jan. 14, 2012.

Shaffer, Jerome. "Existence, Predication, and the Ontological Argument." *Mind* 71 (1962) 307–25.

Sider, Theodore. "Four-Dimensionalism." *Philosophical Review* 106 (1997) 197–231.

———. *Four-Dimensionalism: An Ontology of Persistence and Time*. Oxford: Clarendon, 2001.

———. "Presentism and Ontological Commitment." *Journal of Philosophy* 96 (1999) 325–47.

———. *Writing the Book of the World*. Oxford: Clarendon, 2011.

Simmons, Keith. "On an Argument Against Omniscience." *Noûs* 27 (1993) 22–33.

Skow, Bradford. *Objective Becoming*. New York: Oxford University Press, 2015.

Smith, Q. "Causation and the Logical Impossibility of a Divine Cause." *Philosophical Topics* 24 (1996) 169–91.

Soames, Scott. *Beyond Rigidity: The Unfinished Semantic Agenda of Naming Necessity*. Oxford: Oxford University Press, 2002.

Sobel, Jordan Howard. *Logic and Theism: Arguments For and Against Beliefs in God*. New York: Cambridge University Press, 2004.

Sorabji, Richard. *Time, Creation, and the Continuum: Theories in Antiquity and the Early Middle Ages*. Chicago: University of Chicago Press, 2006.

Sosa, Ernest, and Michael Tooley, eds. *Causation*. Oxford Readings in Philosophy. New York: Oxford University Press, 1993.

Spiegel, James S. *The Benefits of Providence: A New Look at Divine Sovereignty*. Wheaton, IL: Crossway, 2005.

Spinoza, Benedict. *Theologico-Political Treatise*. Translated by Martin D. Yaffe. Newburyport, MD: Focus, 2004.

Spitzer, Robert J. *New Proofs for the Existence of God: Contributions of Contemporary Physics and Philosophy*. Grand Rapids: Eerdmans, 2010.

Stackhouse, John G., Jr. "Jesus Christ." In *The Oxford Handbook of Evangelical Theology*, edited by Gerald R. McDermott, 146–58. New York: Oxford University Press, 2010.

Stalnaker, Robert. "Conditional Propositions and Conditional Assertions." In *Epistemic Modality*, edited by Andy Egan and Brian Weatherson, 227–47. Oxford: Oxford University Press, 2011.

Stein, Howard. "On Relativity Theory and Openness of the Future." *Philosophy of Science* 58 (1991) 147–67.

Stenner, Alfred J. "A Paradox of Omniscience and Some Attempts at a Solution." *Faith and Philosophy* 6 (1989) 303–19.

Stump, Eleonore. *Aquinas*. Arguments of the Philosophers. New York: Routledge, 2005.

Stump, Eleonore, and Brian Davies, eds. *The Oxford Handbook of Aquinas*. New York: Oxford University Press, 2014.

Stump, Eleonore, and Norman Kretzmann. "Atemporal Duration: A Reply to Fitzgerald." *Journal of Philosophy* 84 (1987) 214–19.

———. "Atonement and Justification." In *Trinity, Incarnation, and Atonement*, edited by Ronald Feenstra and Cornelius Plantinga, 178–209. Notre Dame: University of Notre Dame Press, 1989.

———. "Eternity." *Journal of Philosophy* 78 (1981) 429–58.

———. "Eternity, Awareness, and Action." *Faith and Philosophy* 9 (1992) 463–82.

Suarez, Francisco. *On Efficient Causality: Metaphysical Disputations 17, 18, and 19*. Translated by A. J. Freddoso. New Haven: Yale University Press, 1994.

Sullivan, Thomas D. "Omniscience, Immutability, and the Divine Mode of Knowing." *Faith and Philosophy* 8 (1991) 21–35.

Swinburne, Richard. *The Christian God*. Oxford: Oxford University Press, 1994.

———. *The Coherence of Theism*. 2nd ed. Oxford: Oxford University Press, 1993.

———. *Epistemic Justification*. Oxford: Oxford University Press, 2001.

———. *The Evolution of the Soul*. Rev. ed. Oxford: Oxford University Press, 1997.

———. *The Existence of God*. 2nd ed. Oxford: Oxford University Press, 2004.

———. "Omnipotence." *American Philosophical Quarterly* 10 (1973) 231–37.

———. *Providence and the Problem of Evil*. Oxford: Oxford University Press, 1998.

———. *Responsibility and Atonement*. Oxford: Oxford University Press, 1989.

———. "Tensed Facts." *American Philosophical Quarterly* 27 (1990) 117–30.

Talbott, Thomas B. "On Divine Foreknowledge and Bringing About the Past." *Philosophy and Phenomenological Research* 46 (1986) 455–69.

———. "On the Divine Nature and the Nature of Divine Freedom." *Faith and Philosophy* 5 (1988) 3–24.

Taliaferro, Charles. "The Coherence of Divine Power." In *Debating Christian Theism*, edited by Chad Meister et al., 158–68. Oxford: Oxford University Press, 2013.

———. "Divine Cognitive Power." *International Journal for Philosophy of Religion* 18 (1985) 133–40.

———. "The Magnitude of Omnipotence." *International Journal for Philosophy of Religion* 14 (1983) 99–106.

Taliaferro, Charles, and Chad Meister, eds. *The Cambridge Companion to Christian Philosophical Theology*. New York: Cambridge University Press, 2010.

Tallant, Jonathan. "Presentism and Truth-Making." *Erkenntnis* 71 (2009) 407–16.

———. "Time for Presence?" *Philosophia* 38 (2010) 271–80.

Thiselton, Anthony C. *The Hermeneutics of Doctrine*. Grand Rapids: Eerdmans, 2007.

Thomas, Robert. "The Hermeneutics of 'Open Theism.'" *Master's Seminary Journal* 12 (2001) 179–202.

Thomason, Richmond H. "Indeterminist Time and Truth-Value Gaps." *Theoria* 36 (1970) 264–81.

Thomason, Richmond H., and Anil Gupta. "A Theory of Conditionals in the Context of Branching Time." *Philosophical Review* 89 (1980) 65–90.

Timpe, Kevin. "Introduction to Neo-Classical Theism." In *Models of God and Alternative Ultimate Realities*, edited by Jeanine Diller and Asa Kasher, 197–206. New York: Springer, 2013.

———. "Truth-Making and Divine Eternity." *Religious Studies* 43 (2007) 299–315.

Todd, Patrick. "Against Limited Foreknowledge." *Philosophia* 42 (2014) 523–38.

———. "Geachianism." *Oxford Studies in Philosophy of Religion* 3 (2011) 222–51.

———. "Prepunishment and Explanatory Dependence: A New Argument for Incompatibilism About Foreknowledge and Freedom." *Philosophical Review* 122 (2013) 619–39.

———. "Soft Facts and Ontological Dependence." *Philosophical Studies* 164 (2013) 829–44.

Tomaszewski, Robert. "The Principle of Sufficient Reason Defended." *Idealistic Studies* 40 (2010) 267–74.

Tomberlin, James E., and Peter van Inwagen. *Alvin Plantinga*. Profiles 5. Dordrecht: Reidel, 1985.

Tooley, Michael. *Causation: A Realist Approach*. New York: Oxford University Press, 1988.

———. "Freedom and Foreknowledge." *Faith and Philosophy* 17 (2000) 212–24.

———, ed. *Laws of Nature, Causation, and Supervenience*. Analytical Metaphysics 1. New York: Routledge, 1999.

———. "Plantinga's Defence of the Ontological Argument." *Mind* 90 (1981) 422–27.

———, ed. *Time and Causation*. Analytical Metaphysics 2. New York: Routledge, 1999.

———. *Time, Tense, Causation*. New York: Oxford University Press, 1997.

Torre, Stephan. "*De Se* Knowledge and the Possibility of an Omniscient Being." *Faith and Philosophy* 23 (2006) 191–200.

Tozer, A. W. *The Knowledge of the Holy*. New York: HarperCollins, 1961.

Tuggy, Dale. "Three Roads to Open Theism." *Faith and Philosophy* 24 (2007) 28–51.

Urban, Linwood, and Douglas Walton, eds. *The Power of God*. Oxford: Oxford University Press, 1978.

Vallicella, William F. "Has the Ontological Argument Been Refuted?" *Religious Studies* 29 (1993) 97–110.

Van Fraassen, Bas C. *The Empiricist Stance*. New Haven: Yale University Press, 2004.

———. *An Introduction to the Philosophy of Time and Space*. New York: Random House, 1970.

———. *Quantum Mechanics: An Empiricist View*. New York: Oxford University Press, 1991.

———. *The Scientific Image*. New York: Oxford University Press, 1980.

Van Inwagen, Peter. "Ability and Responsibility." *Philosophical Review* 87 (1978) 201–24.

———. "And Yet They Are Not Three Gods But One God." In *Philosophical and Theological Essays on the Trinity*, edited by Thomas McCall and Michael C. Rea, 216–48. Oxford: Oxford University Press, 2009.

———. "Changing the Past." *Oxford Studies in Metaphysics* 5 (2010) 3–28.

———. "Creatures of Fiction." *American Philosophical Quarterly* 14 (1977) 299–308.

———. *An Essay on Free Will*. New York: Oxford University Press, 1986.

———. "Four-Dimensional Objects." *Noûs* 24 (1990) 245–55.

———. "Free Will Remains a Mystery." In *The Oxford Handbook of Free Will*, edited by Robert Kane, 158–77. New York: Oxford University Press, 2002.

———. "If God Knows the Future, What Is Free Will?" *Closer to Truth*. https://closertotruth.com/video/if-god-knows-the-future-what-is-free-will/.

———. "The Incompatibility of Free Will and Determinism." *Philosophical Studies* 27 (1975) 185–99.

———. "Indexicality and Actuality." *Philosophical Review* 89 (1980) 403–26.

———. *Material Beings*. Ithaca, NY: Cornell University Press, 1990.

———. "Ontological Arguments." *Noûs* 11 (1977) 375–95.

———. *The Problem of Evil: The Gifford Lectures Delivered in the University of St. Andrews in 2003*. Oxford: Clarendon, 2006.

———. "A Promising Argument." In *The Oxford Handbook of Free Will*, edited by Robert Kane, 475–83. 2nd ed. New York: Oxford University Press, 2011.

———. "Quantification and Fictional Discourse." In *Empty Names, Fiction, and the Puzzles of Non-Existence*, edited by Antony Everett and Thomas Hofweber, 235–47. Stanford: CSLI, 2000.

———. "Three Persons in One Being: On Attempts to Show that the Doctrine of the Trinity is Self-Contradictory." In *The Holy Trinity: East/West Dialogue*, edited by Melville Y. Stewart, 83–97. Dordrecht: Kluwer Academic, 2003.

———. "Two Concepts of Possible Worlds." *Midwest Studies in Philosophy* 11 (1986) 185–213.

———. "What Does an Omniscient Being Know?" *Oxford Studies in Philosophy of Religion* 1 (2008) 216–30.

Vanhoozer, Kevin J., ed. *Dictionary for Theological Interpretation of the Bible*. Grand Rapids: Baker, 2005.

Visser, Sandra, and Thomas Williams. *Anselm*. Great Medieval Thinkers. New York: Oxford University Press, 2008.

Wainwright, William J. "Monotheism." In *Rationality, Religious Belief, and Moral Commitment*, edited by Robert Audi and William J. Wainright, 289–314. Ithaca, NY: Cornell University Press, 1986.

———. "Omnipotence, Omniscience, and Omnipresence." In *The Cambridge Companion to Christian Philosophical Theology*, edited by Charles Taliaferro and Chad Meister, 46–65. New York: Cambridge University Press, 2010.

———. "The Ontological Argument, Question-Begging, and Professor Rowe." *International Journal for Philosophy of Religion* 9 (1978) 254–57.

———, ed. *The Oxford Handbook of Philosophy of Religion*. New York: Oxford University Press, 2005.

Walton, Douglas. "Some Theorems of Fitch on Omnipotence." *Sophia* 15 (1976) 20–27.

Ware, Bruce A. "An Evangelical Reformulation of the Doctrine of the Immutability of God." *Journal for the Evangelical Theological Society* 29 (1986) 431–46.

———. *God's Greater Glory: The Exalted God of Scripture and the Christian Faith*. Wheaton, IL: Crossway, 2004.

———. *God's Lesser Glory: The Diminished God of Open Theism*. Wheaton, IL: Crossway, 2000.

Webster, John, Kathryn Tanner, and Iain Torrance, eds. *The Oxford Handbook of Systematic Theology*. New York, NY: Oxford University Press, 2007.

Welty, Greg. "Theistic Conceptual Realism: The Case for Interpreting Abstract Objects as Divine Ideas." DPhil thesis, University of Oxford, 2006.

Westphal, Jonathan. "The Compatibility of Divine Foreknowledge and Freewill." *Analysis* 71 (2011) 246–52.

Whitaker, C. W. A. *Aristotle's* De Interpretatione: *Contradiction and Dialectic*. New York: Oxford University Press, 2002.

Widerker, David. "Libertarian Freedom and the Avoidability of Decisions." *Faith and Philosophy* 12 (1995) 113–18.

———. "Two Forms of Fatalism." In *God, Foreknowledge, and Freedom*, edited by John Martin Fischer, 97–110. Stanford Series in Philosophy. Stanford: Stanford University Press, 1989.

Widerker, David, and E. M. Zemach. "Facts, Freedom, and Foreknowledge." *Religious Studies* 23 (1987) 19–28.

Wielenberg, Erik J. "The New Paradox of the Stone Revisited." *Faith and Philosophy* 18 (2001) 261–68.

———. "Omnipotence Again." *Faith and Philosophy* 17 (2000) 26–47.

Wierenga, Edward. "Augustinian Perfect Being Theology and the God of Abraham, Isaac, and Jacob." *International Journal for Philosophy of Religion* 69 (2011) 139–51.

———. *The Nature of God: An Inquiry into Divine Attributes*. Ithaca, NY: Cornell University Press, 1989.

———. "Omniscience and Time, One More Time." *Faith and Philosophy* 21 (2004) 90–97.

———. "Omnipotence Defined." *Philosophy and Phenomenological Research* 43 (1983) 363–75.

———. "Omniscience." In *The Oxford Handbook to Philosophical Theology*, edited by Thomas P. Flint and Michael C. Rea, 129–44. New York: Oxford University Press, 2009.

———. "Prophecy, Freedom, and the Necessity of the Past." In *Philosophical Perspectives*, edited by James E. Tomberlin, 5:425–45. Atascadero, CA: Ridgeway, 1991.

Willard, Dallas. *The Divine Conspiracy: Rediscovering Our Hidden Life in God*. San Francisco: HarperSanFrancisco, 1998.

Williams, A. N. "Tradition." In *The Oxford Handbook of Systematic Theology*, edited by John Webster et al., 362–77. New York: Oxford University Press, 2007.

Wilson, Douglas, ed. *Bound Only Once: The Failure of Open Theism*. Moscow, ID: Canon, 2001.

Wingard, John C., Jr. "On a Not Quite Yet 'Victorious' Modal Version of the Ontological Argument for the Existence of God." *International Journal for Philosophy of Religion* 33 (1993) 47–57.

Wittgenstein, Ludwig. *Philosophical Investigations*. Translated by G. E. M. Anscombe et al. 4th ed. Malden, MA: Wiley-Blackwell, 2009.

Wood, Charles M. "Providence." In *The Oxford Handbook of Systematic Theology*, edited by John Webster et al., 91–104. New York: Oxford University Press, 2007.

Wyckoff, Jason. "On the Incompatibility of Divine Foreknowledge and Human Freedom." *Sophia* 49 (2010) 333–41.

Yates, John C. *The Timelessness of God*. Lantham, MD: University Press of America, 1990.

Yourgrau, Palle. "On Time and Actuality: The Dilemma of Privileged Position." *British Journal for the Philosophy of Science* 37 (1986) 405–17.

Zagzebski, Linda Trinkaus. *The Dilemma of Freedom and Foreknowledge*. New York: Oxford University Press, 1991.

———. "Does Libertarian Freedom Require Alternative Possibilities?" *Noûs* 34 (2000) 231–48.

———. "Foreknowledge and Free Will." In *Stanford Encyclopedia of Philosophy*, edited by Edward N. Zalta and Uri Nodelman, Aug. 25, 2011. https://plato.stanford.edu/archives/fall2011/entries/free-will-foreknowledge/.

———. "Omniscience." In *The Routledge Companion to Philosophy of Religion*, edited by Chad Meister and Paul Copan, 309–18. New York: Routledge, 2007.

———. "Omniscience and the Arrow of Time." *Faith and Philosophy* 19 (2002) 503–19.

———. "Omniscience, Time, and Freedom." In *The Blackwell Companion to the Philosophy of Religion*, edited by William Mann, 3–25. Cambridge: Blackwell, 2004.

———. "Omnisubjectivity." *Oxford Studies in Philosophy of Religion* 1 (2008) 231–47.

———. "Recent Work on Divine Foreknowledge and Free Will." In *The Oxford Handbook of Free Will*, edited by Robert Kane, 46–64. New York: Oxford University Press, 2002.

Zimmerman, Dean W. "The A-Theory of Time, Presentism, and Open Theism." In *Science and Religion in Dialogue*, edited by Melville Stewart, 791–809. Malden, MA: Blackwell, 2010.

———. "The A-Theory of Time, the B-Theory of Time, and 'Taking Tense Seriously.'" *Dialectica* 59 (2005) 401–57.

———. "Chisholm and the Essences of Events." In *The Philosophy of Roderick M. Chisholm*, edited by Lewis Hahn, 73–100. Peru, IL: Open Court, 1997.

———. "Immanent Causation." *Philosophical Perspectives* 11 (1997) 422–71.

———. "One Really Big Liquid Sphere: Reply to Lewis." *Australian Journal of Philosophy* 77 (1999) 213–15.

———. "Persistence and Presentism." *Philosophical Papers* 25 (1996) 115–26.

———. "Presentism and the Space-Time Manifold." In *The Oxford Handbook of Philosophy of Time*, edited by Craig Callender, 163–244. New York: Oxford University Press, 2011.

———. "The Privileged Present: Defending an 'A-Theory' of Time." In *Contemporary Debates in Metaphysics*, edited by Theodore Sider et al., 211–25. Oxford: Wiley-Blackwell, 2007.

———. "Temporary Intrinsics and Presentism." In *Metaphysics: The Big Questions*, edited by Peter van Inwagen and Dean W. Zimmerman, 206–19. Malden, MA: Basil Blackwell.